A history of humanitarianism, 1755–1989

MANCHESTER
1824

Manchester University Press

HUMANITARIANISM

SERIES EDITOR: BERTRAND TAITHE

This series offers a new interdisciplinary reflection on one of the most important and yet understudied areas in history, politics and cultural practices: humanitarian aid and its responses to crises and conflicts. The series seeks to define afresh the boundaries and methodologies applied to the study of humanitarian relief and so-called 'humanitarian events'. The series includes monographs and carefully selected thematic edited collections which cross disciplinary boundaries and bring fresh perspectives to the historical, political and cultural understanding of the rationale and impact of humanitarian relief work.

Islamic charities and Islamic humanism in troubled times
    Jonathan Benthall

Humanitarian aid, genocide and mass killings: Médecins Sans Frontières, the Rwandan experience, 1982–97
    Jean-Hervé Bradol and Marc Le Pape

Calculating compassion: Humanity and relief in war, Britain 1870–1914
    Rebecca Gill

Humanitarian intervention in the long nineteenth century
    Alexis Heraclides and Ada Dialla

The military–humanitarian complex in Afghanistan
    Eric James and Tim Jacoby

Global humanitarianism and media culture
    Michael Lawrence and Rachel Tavernor (eds)

Donors, technical assistance and public administration in Kosovo
    Mary Venner

The NGO CARE and food aid from America 1945–80: 'Showered with kindness'?
    Heike Wieters

A history of humanitarianism, 1755–1989

In the name of others

Silvia Salvatici

Translated by Philip Sanders

Manchester University Press

First published as *Nel nome degli altri. Storia dell'umanitarismo internazionale* in 2015, by Società editrice il Mulino

First English-language edition published in 2019 by Manchester University Press
Altrincham Street, Manchester M1 7JA

www.manchesteruniversitypress.co.uk

ISBN 978 1 5261 2014 4   hardback

ISBN 978 1 5261 2016 8   paperback

Typeset in Arno and Univers by R. J. Footring Ltd, Derby
Printed in Great Britain
by TJ International Ltd, Padstow

A history of humanitarianism, 1755–1989: In the name of others is an extended and updated edition of *Nel nome degli altri. Storia dell'umanitarismo internazionale*, published in 2015 by Società editrice il Mulino and translated into English by Philip Sanders.

Contents

Preface to the English edition	ix
List of abbreviations	xi
Introduction	1
Part I: Archaeology of international humanitarianism	15
1 Saving humanity, abolishing slavery	20
2 Colonial humanitarianism	35
Part II: Humanitarianism in wartime	49
3 *La guerre et la charité*	53
4 'Chaotic years of peace'	80
5 Aftermath of the Second World War: humanitarianism at a crossroads?	116
Part III: From Europe to the Third World	141
6 Fighting poverty and hunger	146
7 Humanitarian emergencies	181
Epilogue: a 'new humanitarianism'?	217
Bibliography	223
Index	243

Preface to the English edition

I had the idea of trying to reconstruct a long-term history of humanitarianism several years ago, more precisely in 2010, the year of the devastating earthquake in Haiti. The news of the dramatic event that had struck the Caribbean island was accompanied by reports on the international relief operation. An extraordinary humanitarian response matched the enormity of the catastrophe. There were some critical voices though: they noted the lack of coordination between the different humanitarian agencies; they stressed that the rapidity of the interventions undermined the process of obtaining the information necessary to administer the aid effectively; and they highlighted the role the relief could play in strengthening the interests of certain countries – such as the United States and France – on Haitian territory.

In 2010 I had just started my research on the United Nations Relief and Rehabilitation Administration (UNRRA), the UN agency tasked originally with getting aid to the populations severely affected by the Second World War. Some of the same questions (coordination problems, the connections between relief and reconstruction, the criteria for optimising resources) fuelling the public debate over the Haitian relief effort also appeared in my work, even though the historical conditions and contexts were different. I was prompted to reflect on the similarities and differences between what had happened in the past and what was happening in the present. I felt I had to answer a twofold need: to interpret the contemporary debate in the light of a long history of the international aid system, and to put UNRRA into a broader picture. I therefore began to work on an overview of the path followed by humanitarianism over a period of more than two centuries. I did so thinking I would have to engage in dialogue with the scholars who had covered this field of enquiry but that I would also have to address a wider public, which was often interested in the subject because of its relevance to current affairs.

The undertaking soon turned out to be more demanding than I had anticipated. The historiography on humanitarianism – fairly limited until a few years earlier – was growing with a speed that forced me into an ongoing revision and reorganisation of the work. At the same time, the literature concentrated on certain aspects while leaving others uncovered, and this made the reconstruction of the overall picture more difficult. So I enthusiastically greeted the publication of Michael Barnett's *Empire of Humanity: A History of Humanitarianism* (2011), since it gave me the chance to compare my work with the first attempt to offer a critical analysis of the international relief system that held the past and the present together. A further challenge came with the need for my book to mediate between international historiography and the potential Italian readership, given that the studies on humanitarianism had (and still have) had a limited development in Italy.

Nel nome degli altri (*In the Name of Others*) was published by Società editrice il Mulino in 2015, after extensive work in gathering material, reprocessing information and interpretations, and joining up the various historiographical paths. The English edition could not be the mere translation of the Italian text. The revision has been thorough and has primarily followed the invaluable suggestions of the referees who reviewed first my proposal for a publication by Manchester University Press and then the manuscript. It is them I would first like to thank. I then sought to incorporate essays and monographs published after 2015. I have not been able to take every last thing into consideration, and not only because of the increasing pace at which new studies on the history of humanitarianism are appearing. On the basis of the contents of the most recent publications I have gone into more depth on certain aspects and thematically organised some questions in a different way; I have modified the arrangement of the volume without overturning its structure. The English edition, then, is, to a large extent, different from the Italian, but it retains the same twofold aim: to engage in the scholarly debate, and to address non-specialist readers who are interested in the subject.

My work on the English edition received decisive impetus from the conventions and seminars that I have been privileged to attend. It would be impossible to mention all the colleagues who have contributed to the discussion at individual meetings but I would like at least to mention those who promoted the various initiatives and those with whom I have had the most intense exchange of ideas. Thanks, then, to Eleonor Davey, Heide Fehrenbach, Peter Gatrell, Fabian Klose, Daniel M. Maul, Johannes Paulmann, Kevin O'Sullivan, Caroline Reeves, Katharina Stornig, Corinna Unger, Birte Vogel, Jennifer Welsh and Davide Rodogno, to whom I am particularly grateful for the bibliographical information which he generously shared with me. A special thanks goes to Bertrand Taithe, a brilliant conversational partner and a constant source of ideas who supported the project for an English edition of my work from the very start. Finally, I would like to point out that the translation of the Italian text was made possible by Transition Grant 2015/2017 Horizon 2020, which was awarded to me by the University of Milan.

Abbreviations

AFSC	American Friends' Service Committee
ARA	American Relief Administration
ARC	American Red Cross
CARE	Cooperative American Remittances to Europe (later, Cooperative American Relief Everywhere)
COS	Charity Organisation Society
CRS	Catholic Relief Services
DDT	dichlorodiphenyltrichloroethane
FAO	Food and Agriculture Organization
FAU	Friends' Ambulance Units
FFC	Fight the Famine Council
FWVRC	Friends' War Victims Relief Committee
HCR	High Commissioner for Refugees
ICEF	International Children's Emergency Fund
ICRC	International Committee of the Red Cross
ILO	International Labour Organization
IRO	International Refugee Organization
JCA	Joint Church Aid
MSF	Médecins Sans Frontières
NATO	North Atlantic Treaty Organization
NGO	non-governmental organisation
OCHA	Office for the Coordination of Humanitarian Affairs
R2P	Responsibility to Protect
RCSJ	Red Cross Society of Japan
SCF	Save the Children Fund
SCIU	Save the Children International Union
UN	United Nations
UNBRO	United Nations Border Relief Operation
UNESCO	UN Educational, Scientific and Cultural Organization

UNHCR	United Nations High Commissioner for Refugees
UNICEF	United Nations International Children's Emergency Fund (now United Nations Children's Fund but retaining the acronym)
UNKRA	United Nations Korean Reconstruction Agency
UNRRA	United Nations Relief and Rehabilitation Administration
UNRWA	United Nations Relief and Works Agency for Palestine Refugees
USAID	US Agency for International Development
WFP	World Food Programme
WHO	World Health Organization
WILPF	Women's International League for Peace and Freedom
YMCA	Young Men's Christian Association

Introduction

Q: Are you in favour [of the intervention of troops on the ground in Kosovo]?
A: I'm in favour of ending the massacres and the forced population movements and I'm in favour of the protection of minors. If this makes the presence on the field necessary, then yes, I'm in favour, under the UN flag, like the HCR [High Commissioner for Refugees] did for Kurdistan, in Iraq, under our impetus. It isn't my decision but the allied countries' governments.[1]

This was one of the crucial passages in the interview given by Bernard Kouchner to the daily newspaper *Libération* on 15 April 1999, when he was French secretary of state for health and a few months before he became the UN representative in Kosovo. The armed intervention undertaken by a coalition of NATO states against the Belgrade government, in the name of the fundamental rights of the Albanian population of Kosovo, had been underway for over three weeks. Contrary to expectations, the Serbs had not capitulated a few days after the start of the bombing. Hundreds of thousands of refugees had fled to neighbouring countries and the possible use of troops on the ground to bring the operation to an end had become the subject of tense debate between the Western allies. Kouchner's words attracted immediate public attention not only because intervention on the ground was a controversial question but also because the then French health secretary had been one of the best-known (and most controversial) figures in international humanitarianism since he had taken part, in the early 1970s, in the foundation of Médecins Sans Frontières. So his statements in favour of an intensification of the military commitment in Kosovo immediately became an arrow in the bow of those who were defending the 'humanitarian value' of the NATO intervention and a controversial target for those who were against it.

Kouchner's position could be shared or criticised but it certainly came as no surprise. Even in the late 1980s, the 'French doctor' had been one of the most convinced advocates of the *droit d'ingérence humanitaire*, theorised by the expert in international law Mario Bettati and understood as 'the right to intervene despite borders and states, if suffering human beings ask for help'.[2] Kouchner's declarations in the spring of 1999 carried a particular weight though, since the war in Kosovo had marked a difference from previous military interventions undertaken by a coalition of states against another state in response to a persistent and systematic violation of fundamental rights.[3] In fact, in the case of the intervention in Iraq to defend the Iraqi Kurds (1991) and that in Bosnia-Herzegovina (1994–95) the United Nations Security Council had ratified the military operations, but the NATO bombing of the Federal Republic of Yugoslavia had started without this ratification.

I didn't hear clearly the echo of Kouchner's statements published in *Libération* – and of the criticisms they inevitably provoked – because I was too close to the events. When the decision to intervene in Kosovo was taken, I was in the north of Albania, employed on a socio-economic development project, and in April 1999 I was taking part in relief work for the Kosovar refugees, not unlike the other aid workers in the region. We were all of course fully aware of the international dynamics that had led to the NATO decision and the meaning of the opening of a new intervention front by sending in troops on the ground. Perhaps paradoxically, being in the midst of that desperate humanity fleeing the war made the politicians' decisions – as much as they influenced the conflict's progress – seem more distant. And so we ended up questioning ourselves especially on the immediate problems, instead of reflecting on the debate that was taking place elsewhere, on the nature and development of that 'humanitarian war'.

Only later, after years spent as an aid worker in the Balkans, did I start to carefully follow the debate of legal scholars, political commentators and international relations experts on so-called humanitarian interventions. This debate progressively extended and, as we know, concerned in particular the legitimacy of military actions defending human rights. It is a question that became crucial once again during later analogous armed interventions, such as that in Libya in 2011, ratified by the United Nations Security Council and once again conducted by a coalition of NATO countries. The use of armed humanitarian intervention was accompanied by the formulation of the UN doctrine of the Responsibility to Protect (R2P), which reiterated the obligations of the international community in cases of mass violations of human rights within individual states,[4] causing mixed reactions.

What further attracted my attention from the beginning in this discussion led by scholars and journalists was the reflection on the consequences that the establishment of humanitarian interventions, after the end of the Cold War, had had on the way of operating international aid. The most critical commentators have underlined how some humanitarian organisations have directly or indirectly supported the use of armed force to oppose human rights violations in a given country. The promotion of the 'right of intervention' by Bernard Kouchner, therefore, was only the more complete expression of an approval by part of the humanitarian world of Western governments' 'interventionism'.[5] What was also seen in the wartime and post-war situations was that the distribution of aid and assistance for people took place thanks to the protection provided by military forces, which allowed the humanitarian agencies to extend their field of action, to increase the volume of their work and to acquire greater visibility on the international scene.[6] In other words, the various players in relief for war victims acquired increasing weight, but this coincided with the progressive strengthening of the crossover between humanitarianism and warfare.

Many observers hold that all these changes were the expression of a deep crisis in humanitarianism.[7] Among the critics who have had particular influence it is worth recalling the American journalist David Rieff, who in 2002 published the book *A Bed for the Night: Humanitarianism in Crisis*, which was translated into several languages on the wave of its success and then republished as an e-book. In Rieff's opinion, in cases like the war in Bosnia Herzegovina or the intervention in Kosovo, the humanitarian agencies largely espoused the strategic and political aims of one of the sides in the field, namely the 'defenders of human rights', and because of this there was a failure of 'the notion that aid should be fundamentally apolitical and should have no other agenda than service and solidarity'.[8] In this type of analysis, subordination to the foreign policy of the Western powers (as advocates of humanitarian interventions) is the most serious symptom of the crisis in international humanitarianism.

Humanitarianism versus politics?

In the debate around the transformations that took place from the 1990s on, the link between humanitarianism and politics has emerged as a crucial issue; this is not only because the aid operations lost their non-political nature but also because the language of politics adopted the rhetoric of humanitarianism. This point of view is summarised effectively in statements by Régis Debray, the philosopher and writer, a prominent exponent of the French *tiers mondisme* in the late 1960s, and later a foreign affairs adviser to French president François Mitterrand. In a long article in *Le Monde diplomatique* in March 2013, Debray observed that public debate was now characterised by 'the substitution of the military with the humanitarian, of the hero with the victim, of conviction with compassion, of the social surgeon ['chirurgien social'] with the nurse, of cure with care [...]. Goodbye hammer and sickle, hello tweezers and bandages.'[9] In this passage, Debray was arguing, ironically, with the French left, since his intervention principally concerned the confirmation by the Hollande presidency of France's return into NATO's military command, decided by Nicolas Sarkozy in 2009. At the same time, Debray was underlining that the call to humanitarianism, as well as forming a justification for war, took the place of ideological motivations in the rhetoric used by the representatives of institutions in order to justify their decisions.

Debray's blunt observation was of interest as much to journalists as to scholars, which underlined the trend for contemporary institutions to justify the choices of international politics by appealing to the idea that the suffering of other human beings is intolerable, so putting it right is a moral duty. This in turn established that it was a political argument, focused on the values and feelings connected to the notion of humanitarianism. In this connection, we might note the works of the French sociologist and anthropologist Didier Fassin, who said the new political register of Western governments would be set 'today as the most likely to generate support among listeners or readers, and to explain why people often prefer to speak about suffering and compassion than about interests or justice, legitimizing actions by declaring them to be humanitarian'.[10] The reasons for the changes identified by Fassin might be sought in many of the phenomena usually used to characterise the contemporary situation: the end of the great ideologies; the crisis of the traditional political parties; the increasing distrust of the people in democratic institutions. Certainly coming into play is the need for government bodies to reformulate their role in protecting the common good within a context that now goes beyond the borders of the nation state in order to extend themselves in the globalised world and take on all of humanity as a basis for political legitimacy.[11] This very need has led, for example, to the creation of ministerial positions for international aid: the French case is the most significant since in certain legislatures between 1988 and 1997 there were government posts of this sort, for example those of the Ministre de la santé et de l'action humanitaire (1992–93) and the Ministre déléguée auprès du ministre des affaires étrangères, chargée de l'action humanitaire et des droits de l'homme (1993–95).[12]

The access to institutional roles by people from the world of international humanitarianism witnessed in recent years may be considered as one of the more immediately visible effects of these changes taking place in the political sphere. France again provides the best example from this point of view, in the shape of Bernard Kouchner. We have seen that in 1999 Kouchner was secretary of state for health at the Ministry of Social Affairs and Work, a role that he had previously covered for a short time in 1988, in the government of Michel Rocard, and in that same year he was nominated secretary of state for humanitarian action, a cabinet post. Kouchner was a minister four times after that, during the presidencies of François Mitterrand, Jacques Chirac and Nicolas Sarkozy. We might also remember an example concerning Italy: in 2013 Laura Boldrini entered parliament and was later elected president of the Chamber of Deputies. Boldrini worked for various UN agencies and from 1998 to 2012 was the Italian spokesperson for the UNHCR. Boldrini therefore boasts a major career as an official within the intergovernmental agency in which 193 members recognise its essentially political function of 'maintain[ing] international peace and security', as established by article 1 of the UN's founding charter. It is a striking fact, though, that the Italian media have always presented Boldrini's professional path in terms of a vague commitment to suffering humanity: her work for the UNHCR has even been described as a 'struggle waged against politics in all the world in order to voice the humanitarian dramas of our time'.[13] It seems to me that the tendency to represent a figure like Boldrini in these terms is indicative of the fact that belonging to the humanitarian world has ended up being considered, in itself, a guarantee of the moral qualities needed to represent citizens in an international institution. In the face of the growing loss of trust in 'professional politicians', the 'compassion professionals' seem able to provide a disinterested dedication in pursuing the common good and a greater sensitivity towards those who find themselves in a state of suffering. In this case, too, the use of the values and feelings connected to the notion of humanitarianism is able – in the words of Didier Fassin, 'to generate support among listeners or readers' – but it ends up strengthening the widespread tendency to pit political against humanitarian action, as if they were two different realities and 'good humanitarianism' could be the antidote to 'bad politics'.

A long history

In what context have the transformations that have led to the establishment of armed interventions in the name of defending human rights taken place? What was the path completed by humanitarianism before the end of the Cold War? My volume takes its cue from these questions. It places at its centre international aid as such, distinguishing it from armed humanitarian interventions, and reconstructs its history in the Western world before 1989. The purpose is not to draw up a list of 'traditional humanitarian principles', which should, according to the journalist and activist Fiona Fox, be put back into operation to overcome the alleged crisis in the international aid system.[14] My historic reconstruction above all intends to contribute to the critical reading of the present without falling into the false myths of the past.

The public interest in international relief has emerged in close connection with the establishment of humanitarian interventions and this has had a twofold effect. Firstly, the two issues have often been overlaid, even though the military actions defending human rights and the development of an international relief system are two connected but separate aspects of the history of contemporary societies. In addition, the research output has for a long time concentrated on the years following the end of the Cold War, and has paid little attention to earlier periods. Some years ago, Michael Barnett – a political scientist who is well known among experts in humanitarianism – observed that this imbalance in studies has ended up spreading a 'conventional version of events' in which 1989 is not a turning point but an out and out fracturing. From this moment of fracturing onwards, relief operations were subjugated to the dynamics of conflict, and humanitarianism was irredeemably mixed with politics. Barnett says that this 'conventional version of events' has had 'disorientating effects', which have hindered making the connections between the post-Cold War period and previous eras.[15] Further developing this reflection, we may add that the insistence on the recent crisis has encouraged the emergence – especially in journalism – of an image of the past in which humanitarianism was still 'healthy', in other words apolitical, disinterested and independent, the simple expression of the compassionate and altruistic spirit of virtuous men and women.[16]

In recent years the orientation of studies has significantly changed. Michael Barnett has wanted to remove himself from the 'conventional version of events', adding a historical overview to his analysis of today's humanitarian system.[17] Additionally, the historical research on this subject has multiplied, as can be seen just by running through the titles in the bibliography at the end of this book. The growing interest of historians has been translated into monographs and essays on specific periods and arguments – the colonial age and the expanding philanthropic networks, the assistance to victims in the two World Wars, the wars in the postcolonial world. They often attempt to retrace the origins of modern Western humanitarianism or, rather, identify the moment when the aspects emerged that still today characterise the international relief system. My book naturally fits into this new strand of studies, but the aim I have set myself is above all to reconstruct a wide-ranging narrative. The shift determined in 1989 can be understood only in the light of long-term processes, through which aid and relief have come to be part of government and supranational institutions' political agenda, becoming the subject of the relations between Western powers and the rest of the world.

To better understand how this volume is structured, it is worth clarifying what is meant by 'humanitarianism', for the further reason that the term is nowadays frequently used evocatively but ambiguously – describing situations and phenomena that are very different to one another. Even though there is no precise definition,[18] when we talk about 'international humanitarianism' we are referring to the organised help for individuals who are victims of war, natural disasters or disadvantaged economic circumstances in the countries in which they live. The overall deployment of the help is promoted by specific institutions and organisations, is regulated by *ad hoc* legislation and nowadays uses operating standards recognised at a supranational level. To reconstruct the past of all of this, I have tried to keep together – by crossing them over – different levels of enquiry, which refer back as much to the social and cultural transformations as to the changes in political and institutional processes that have marked the contemporary age. The analysis develops through a transnational approach but principally uses sources and literature relating to Europe and the United States; for this reason, too, what is described in the following pages remains above all a history of 'the supply-side of humanitarian actions'.[19]

The volume is divided into three parts. The first opens with the Lisbon earthquake of 1755 and it analyses a long time frame – up to the end of the nineteenth century. The two chapters reconstruct the emergence of a new 'culture of sensibility', the establishment of the anti-slavery movement and the development of a whole set of relief activities in the colonial territories, at the will as much of the missionaries as of the administrators sent from the metropolises. These events and processes generated the practices, knowledge and experience in Western societies that later encouraged the setting up of the contemporary humanitarian system. Thus, Part I of the volume examines the 'archaeological' phase.

Part II highlights the central role assigned by humanitarianism to the victims of the armed conflicts and begins with the foundation of the International Committee of the Red Cross (ICRC) in 1864. Coming into being from Genevan philanthropy, the ICRC aimed to reduce the cruelty in war through aid to the soldiers struck by enemy arms or by illness; the success of its programme was partly a result of the wide and rapid accreditation the new body managed to obtain from European governments. In the First World War, civilians became the primary recipients of its assistance but, above all, its primary aim was now not only to provide immediate relief to war victims. The condition of need of the European populations, in fact, did not end with the ceasefire: many of them continued to be afflicted by hunger, epidemics and forced migration. In the long post-war years, international aid was planned to combat the effects of all of this and it acquired a new meaning in the overall transition of the European countries from wartime to peacetime. The same function was relaunched and strengthened in the post-Second World War period, when the humanitarian programmes became the symbol of the victorious powers' will to write a new start for the history of humanity. At the same time, the planning of the aid laid the foundations for the reconstruction of societies overwhelmed by the conflict.

The two World Wars saw the expansion and transformation of the humanitarian mission, within which new private associations were set up, often tied to the religious philanthropic tradition but of different sizes and structures, each with specific fields of competence: a varied group which today we call 'non-governmental organisations' (NGOs). While it was establishing itself as one of the fundamental points on the agenda of liberal internationalism, the assistance of suffering humanity also became part of the mandate entrusted, first, to the League of Nations and later to the United Nations (UN), the two supranational bodies called upon to guarantee world peace and security.

When the long-term consequences of the Second World War seemed to have been overcome, humanitarianism's aims started to shift in a different direction. Part III of the volume opens on this new setting and concentrates on the development programmes that for almost twenty years made up the main activity of international aid, now fully deployed on a global horizon. The aim of these programmes was the economic and social advancement of Third World countries and flanked interventions for the industrialisation and mechanisation of agriculture, the projects for sanitation, education and professional training. The areas of activity in which international humanitarianism grew over time became an integral part of development politics.[20] The humanitarian projects were an essential component of the redetermination of relationships – economic, political, cultural – between the global North and South after the end of the colonial empires. In the late 1960s, in this deeply changed context, the armed conflicts that shook the fragile and still fluid postcolonial set-up brought humanitarian action for the victims of war back to the centre. The conflict immediately following the secession of Biafra from Nigeria (1967–69) was just the first in a series of dramatic events that captured public attention and were from time to time new emergencies within which the by now complicated reality of international aid was mobilised. The secession of Bangladesh and the war between India and Pakistan (1971), the fall of the Pol Pot regime and the Vietnamese occupation of Cambodia (1979), the famine following the dictatorship and the internal conflicts in Ethiopia (1984–85): these were the most significant cases through which humanitarianism took on or displayed some of the distinctive aspects that still characterise it today.

Humanitarianism and human rights

To what extent does the long history of international aid, the subject of this volume, refer to that of human rights, around which a wide debate has recently developed?[21] The paths of humanitarianism and human rights are of course intertwined. The period in which a new 'culture of sensibility' emerged, which encouraged the later development of international humanitarianism, was also the one in which the idea was established that all individuals enjoy natural rights. Liberal philosophical thinking contributed as much to the identification of those rights as to the spread of the conviction that no human being could tolerate the suffering of their fellow creatures.[22] But humanitarian action and recognition of fundamental rights have not followed the same path. To understand why, it is first worth recalling that there is a substantial difference between the way we today think of human rights and the way they were understood in past eras. The immortal human rights recognised in the late eighteenth century were part of a political project based on the construction of the state and the nation. In the 'Déclaration des droit de l'homme et du citoyen' of 1789 it was stated that, yes, the rights were due to human being as such, but it was the French nation that had to create them and defend them concretely. Throughout the nineteenth century, the fundamental rights were not in any way guaranteed at an international level but lived under the shadow of the state. Instead, the humanitarian movement developed by looking beyond the nation's borders, made an appeal above all to the dimension of feelings (rather than the recognition of the rights of every human being) and found in compassion its driving force.[23] In other words, motivating the actions aimed at providing relief for the suffering of others was not the intention of protecting the fundamental rights of all the members of the human community but an obedience to the moral values that should be the distinctive feature of civilised societies.

In the setting of humanitarianism, the argument on rights emerged in the post-First World War period,[24] when the determination of the international programmes for those considered most in need of care contributed to the identification of a right, still not clearly defined, of those receiving assistance. The most significant example is the approval by the LoN of the Declaration of the Rights of the Child (1924), in which it was established that children should be the first to receive help 'in times of distress' and that every hungry and sick minor should be fed and cared for. The ratification of that Declaration by the LoN did not envisage any obligation to adjust the national legislation of the member countries to the principles sanctioned in it, which contributed, though, to bringing on to the agenda of cooperation between states the duty to protect children, 'internationalising' their identification as a social group bearing specific needs and rights.[25]

It was in the forum of the United Nations, with the post-Second World War period, that the assistance to suffering humanity was connected to the recognition of the rights enjoyed by each individual, universally valid and equal for all, as sanctioned by the 1948 Declaration. The founding charter of the World Health Organization (WHO), for example, states: 'the enjoyment of the highest attainable standard of health is one of the fundamental rights of every human being without distinction of race, religion, political belief, economic or social condition'.[26] Nevertheless, in the following years the recognition of health as a fundamental right of every human being was not the linchpin on which the international aid projects promoted by the WHO developed. These, in fact, focused above all on the global distribution of knowledge and standardised techniques for the prevention and cure of illnesses; they did not deal with questions such as the relationship between health and inequality (racial, social, gender).[27] In the forum of the United Nations, then, the recognition of human rights was connected conceptually to the international community's duty to take care of its most needy members but did not translate into a real reformulation of the policies and practices of aid.

In this respect there were major developments in the early 1970s and they came from the world of non-governmental bodies, above all thanks to the birth of Médecins Sans Frontières in 1971. In fact, the French organisation based its own humanitarian mission on a twofold moral duty: caring for suffering humanity and offering direct testimony (*temoignage*) of abuses. Humanitarianism could not be split from speaking out against the violation of individuals' fundamental rights. The position of Médecins Sans Frontières was defined at the very moment when the international movement for human rights developed greatly and gained wide visibility.[28] We only need to think about the success of Amnesty International, the association founded in London in 1961 to protect political prisoners, which in little over a decade had multiplied its offices and become the quintessential champion of fundamental rights.[29] Nevertheless, humanitarian activism and that for the defence of human rights did not merge but kept different set-ups, one still centred on the provision of assistance and the other on the condemnation of the violation of fundamental rights.

The blurring of the distinctions between the two approaches and the overlap of the two operational settings took place only after 1989, following in particular the establishment of humanitarian interventions. In fact, the governments which led this type of military operation supported their decision by citing their duty both to defend the fundamental rights of other human beings, and to bring aid to the civil population of other countries when in serious conditions of need. The coalition of NATO member states that in 1991 undertook the Provide Comfort operation in Iraq, for example, did so in the name of the defence of human rights against the violations perpetrated by Saddam Hussein, but also of the need to distribute food and medicines to the persecuted Kurds, who were fleeing *en masse* to the mountains on the border between Turkey and Iraq.

In the 1990s, defending human rights and relief became part of the same agenda,[30] and this coincided with an expansion in the mandate of the humanitarian agencies, many of which are now active on several fronts: defending human rights; peace-keeping; the provision of aid following natural catastrophes; and social and economic development programmes. In the meantime, the most relevant NGOs have increased in size and are equipped with more complex structures, while humanitarian affairs has acquired growing weight within the United Nations.[31] But all this makes up the beginning of another chapter – still being developed – in the history of international aid, since the end of the opposition between the two blocs after almost half a century of Cold War has led to the rapid expansion of the areas of aid deployment, and the restructuring of humanitarianism's governance is considered by many the expression of its effective globalisation.[32]

Notes

1   Eric Favereau and Pierre Haski, 'Kouchner réclame des troupes au sol pour arrêter les massacres. Le secrétaire d'Etat à la Santé va plus loin que la position officielle', *Libération*, 15 April 1999. Kouchner refers to the operation Provide Comfort, which aimed to create a 'security area' in northern Iraq where the Kurds persecuted by Saddam Hussein's government could receive aid; the implementation of the humanitarian programme was led by the United Nations High Commissioner for Refugees (UNHCR).

2   Abbé Pierre and Bernard Kouchner, *Dieu et les hommes: Dialogues et propos recueillis par Michel-Antoine Burnier* (Paris: Robert Laffont, 1993), p. 123. For the theory of the right of intervention, see Bernard Kouchner and Mario Bettati, *Le devoir d'ingérence* (Paris: Denoël, 1987); and Mario Bettati, *Le droit d'ingérence: mutation de l'ordre international* (Paris: Éditions Odile Jacob, 1996).

3   On the difficult definition of 'humanitarian intervention' see the corresponding
    entry by Vaughan Lowe and Antonios Tzanakopoulos in the online *Max Planck En-*
    cyclopedia of Public International Law, at http://opil.ouplaw.com/abstract/10.1093/
    law:epil/9780199231690/law-9780199231690-e306?rskey=QiTdtA&result=1&prd=EPIL
    (accessed November 2018). Historians have called into question the idea that military
    initiatives in the name of the defence of fundamental human rights constituted a novel
    element that emerged in the 1990s, and they have retraced the origins of humanitarian
    interventions – both conceptually and from an international perspective – to the Europe
    of the nineteenth century. See for instance Gary J. Bass, *Freedom's Battle: The Origins of*
    Humanitarian Intervention (New York: Alfred A. Knopf, 2008); Fabian Klose (ed.), *The*
    Emergence of Humanitarian Intervention: Ideas and Practice from Nineteenth Century to
    the Present (Cambridge: Cambridge University Press, 2015); Davide Rodogno, *Against*
    Massacre: Humanitarian Interventions in the Ottoman Empire, 1815–1914 (Princeton, NJ:
    Princeton University Press, 2012); Brendan Simms and D. J. B. Trim (eds), *Humanitarian*
    Intervention: A History (Cambridge: Cambridge University Press, 2011).
4   International Commission on Intervention and State Sovereignty, *The Responsibility*
    to Protect: Report of the International Commission on Intervention and State Sovereignty
    (Ottawa: International Development Research Centre, 2001).
5   For a reflection on this, see Didier Fassin and Mariella Pandolfi (eds), *Contemporary*
    States of Emergency: The Politics of Military and Humanitarian Interventions (New York:
    Zone Books, 2010), in particular the introductory essay by the editors, 'Military and
    Humanitarian Government in the Age of Intervention', pp. 9–28.
6   Nils Gilman, 'Preface: Militarism and Humanitarianism', *Humanity: An International*
    Journal of Human Rights, Humanitarianism, and Development, 3:2 (2012), pp. 173–178.
7   See Johannes Paulmann, 'The Dilemmas of Humanitarian Aid: Historical Perspectives',
    in J. Paulmann (ed.), *Dilemmas of Humanitarian Aid in the Twentieth Century* (Oxford:
    Oxford University Press, 2016), pp. 1–31.
8   David Rieff, *A Bed for the Night: Humanitarianism in Crisis* (New York: Simon & Shuster,
    2002), p. 24.
9   Régis Debray, 'La France doit quitter l'OTAN', *Le Monde diplomatique*, March 2013, p. 7.
    The English word 'care' is used in the original French text.
10 Didier Fassin, *Humanitarian Reason: A Moral History of the Present* (Berkeley, CA:
    University of California Press, 2012), p. 3. In the original edition in French, the first
    sentence is slightly different from that in the US edition because Fassin talks about
    'adhésion des auditeurs ou des électeurs' instead of 'support among listeners or readers'
    (*La raison humanitaire: une histoire morale du temps présent*, Paris: Seuil/Gallimard, 2010,
    p. 10).
11 Ilana Feldman and Miriam Ticktin, 'Government and Humanity', in I. Feldman and M.
    Ticktin (eds), *In the Name of Humanity: The Government of Threat and Care* (Durham,
    NC: Duke University Press, 2010), p. 1.
12 See the list of members of the government who have held positions relating to 'action
    humanitaire' at http://archives.assemblee-nationale.fr/gouv_parl (accessed November
    2018).
13 Carlo Ciavoni, 'Boldrini, la lotta senza quartiere di Laura dalla parte dei senza diritti',
    Repubblica.it, 13 March 2013, at http://www.repubblica.it/politica/2013/03/16/news/
    racconto_boldrini-54693851 (accessed November 2018).
14 Fiona Fox, 'New Humanitarianism: Does It Provide a Moral Banner for the 21st
    Century?', *Disasters*, 25:4 (2001), p. 288.

15 Michael Barnett, *Empire of Humanity: A History of Humanitarianism* (Ithaca, NY: Cornell University Press, 2011), p. 5. For an analysis of the debate on the effects the end of the Cold War had on humanitarianism see Michael Schloms, 'Le dilemme inévitable de l'action humanitaire', *Cultures et Conflits*, 60 (2005), pp. 85–102.

16 This is the image that emerges, for example, from the report on Italian non-governmental organisations by the journalist Valentina Furlanetto, *L'industria della carità: Da storie e testimonianze inedite il volto nascosto della beneficienza* (Milan: Chiarelettere, 2013).

17 Barnett, *Empire of Humanity*. A long history – a concise one – is also offered by Jonathan Benthall, 'Relief', in Akira Iriye and Pierre-Yves Saunier (eds), *The Palgrave Dictionary of Transnational History* (New York: Palgrave Macmillan, 2009), pp. 887–893.

18 Johannes Paulmann, 'Conjunctures in the History of International Humanitarian Aid During the Twentieth Century', *Humanity: An International Journal of Human Rights, Humanitarianism, and Development*, 4:2 (2013), pp. 215–238; Matthew Hilton, Emily Baughan, Eleonor Davey, Bronwen Everill, Kevin O'Sullivan and Tehila Sasson, 'History and Humanitarianism: A Conversation', *Past and Present*, 241:1 (2018), pp. e1–e38.

19 I owe this expression to Davide Rodogno, whom I thank for having shared with me the synopsis of his forthcoming volume *Night on Earth: Interwar Humanitarian Programs in the Faultlines of Western Civilization*. As Emily Baughan pointed out, 'the ways the work of aid organizations has been shaped, altered and, at times, resisted by its "beneficiaries"' are 'the most difficult histories to get at' – in Hilton et al., 'History and Humanitarianism', p. e26. However, several attempts have been made in this direction; see for example Pierre Fuller, 'North China Famine Revisited: Unsung Native Relief in the Warlord Era, 1920–1921', *Modern Asian Studies*, 47:3 (2013), pp. 820–850; Mark R. Frost, 'Humanitarianism and the Overseas Aid Craze in Britain's Colonial Straits Settlements, 1879–1920', *Past and Present*, 236:1 (2017), pp. 169–205.

20 On the separation between relief and development introduced in studies from the 1940s onwards, see Paulmann, 'The Dilemmas of Humanitarian Aid', pp. 6–10.

21 See for example the debate put forward in the journal *Past and Present*: Stefan-Ludwig Hoffmann, 'Human Rights and History', *Past and Present*, 232:1 (2016), pp. 279–310; Lynn Hunt, 'The Long and the Short of the History of Human Rights' and Samuel Moyn, 'The End of Human Rights History', *Past and Present*, 233:1 (2016), pp. 323–331 and pp. 307–322.

22 Norman S. Fiering, 'Irresistible Compassion: An Aspect of Eighteenth-Century Sympathy and Humanitarianism', *Journal of the History of Ideas*, 37:2 (1976), pp. 195–218; Lynn Hunt, *Inventing Human Rights: A History* (New York: W. W. Norton, 2007).

23 This would be at the origin of the antipathy of the human rights activists to the language of humanitarianisms, 'a language often perceived as laden with outmoded notions of charity, protection, sentiment', according to Richard Ashby Wilson and Richard D. Brown, *Humanitarianism and Suffering: The Mobilization of Empathy* (Cambridge: Cambridge University Press, 2009), p. 8. On the complex relationship between humanitarianism and human rights see also Bruce Mazlish, *The Idea of Humanity in a Global Era* (New York: Palgrave Macmillan, 2009), pp. 1–16.

24 Bruno Cabanes, *The Great War and the Origins of Humanitarianism (1914–1918)* (New York: Oxford University Press, 2014).

25 Emily Baughan, *Saving the Children: British Humanitarianism in Europe and Africa, 1914-1945*, thesis submitted to the University of Bristol for the degree of Doctor of Philosophy, 2014; Joëlle Droux, 'L'internationalisation de la protection de l'enfance: acteurs, concurrences et projets transnationaux (1900–1925)', *Critique internationale*, 3

(2011), pp. 17–33; Dominique Marshall, 'Humanitarian Sympathy for Children in Times of War and the History of Children's Rights, 1919–1959', in J. A. Marten (ed.), *Children and War: A Historical Anthology* (New York: New York University Press, 2002), pp. 184–199.

26 Constitution of the World Health Organization, p. 2, at http://whqlibdoc.who.int/hist/official_records/constitution.pdf (accessed November 2018).

27 Sunil Amrith, *Decolonizing International Health: India and Southeast Asia, 1930–65* (London: Palgrave Macmillan, 2006), pp. 72–98.

28 On human rights in the 1970s, see Jan Eckel and Samuel Moyn (eds), *The Breakthrough: Human Rights in the 1970s* (Philadelphia, PA: University of Pennsylvania Press, 2014).

29 Jan Eckel, 'The International League for the Rights of Man, Amnesty International, and the Changing Fate of Human Rights: Activism from the 1940s through the 1970s', *Humanity: An International Journal of Human Rights, Humanitarianism, and Development*, 4:2 (2013), pp. 183–214.

30 Hoffmann, 'Human Rights and History'.

31 Barnett, *Empire of Humanity*, pp. 161–179.

32 Peter Walker and Daniel Maxwell, *Shaping the Humanitarian World* (London: Routledge 2009), pp. 60–78.

Part I

Archaeology of international humanitarianism

> UNHAPPY mortals! Dark and mourning earth!
> Affrighted gathering of human kind!
> Eternal lingering of useless pain!
> Come, ye philosophers, who cry, 'All's well,'
> And contemplate this ruin of a world.
> Behold these shreds and cinders of your race,
> This child and mother heaped in common wreck,
> These scattered limbs beneath the marble shafts –
> A hundred thousand whom the earth devours,
> Who, torn and bloody, palpitating yet,
> Entombed beneath their hospitable roofs,
> In racking torment end their stricken lives.[1]

In these lines, Voltaire was describing the death and destruction brought by the earthquake that devastated Lisbon in 1755. This dramatic episode was defined as the first modern natural disaster and is often cited as *l'événement inaugural*[2] of contemporary humanitarianism.[3] The reasons for the modernity of this event can be traced back to the reaction of the Portuguese monarchy, which considered the response to the emergency to be its own responsibility. This was the first occasion on which there had been an attempt at a centralised intervention for relief and reconstruction. At the same time, there was a sort of international mobilisation to send aid to the Portuguese capital, where three-quarters of the homes had been destroyed and the victims numbered in the tens of thousands. In his *Memoirs of the Reign of King George the Second*, Horace Walpole recalled for example the decision of the British parliament to accept the crown's request and send the Portuguese earthquake victims and the British residents of Lisbon £100,000, partly in cash and partly in 'provisions and utensils'.[4] The aid sent to Portugal from other countries was an indication of the emergence of a new sensibility to others' suffering, of which Voltaire's lines were evidence. In the *Poem on the Lisbon Disaster* the French philosopher questioned himself on the human condition, on divine justice, on the presence of good and evil in the world. Voltaire was distraught at the victims' pain and identified with those men and women 'whom the earth devours'.

The recognition of the suffering of fellow human beings and the display of sympathy were recurring elements in the arguments of the *philosophes*. The Enlightenment and natural law philosophers placed an emphasis on establishing an ethos dictated by those feelings – such as pity and understanding – that every human being could not but experience, and they contributed to forging the idea of a community compassionate towards its more needy members.[5] This idea spread through western Europe not only based on philosophical reflection but also on a varied literary production. The circulation of plays, poems and, above all, novels with dramatic plots that stressed the description of feelings and appealed to the readers' emotional involvement contributed to spreading a new 'culture of sensibility', according to which human beings were naturally inclined to share in the pain of the others and to judge it to be unacceptable.[6] The philosophical and literary works highlighted how, over the course of the eighteenth century, the rejection of suffering became part of modern culture. The idea that the pain of others was intolerable contributed to spreading the conviction that actions aimed at giving comfort and relief corresponded to a moral duty.

This duty was also advocated by the renewed religious spirit that pervaded the Christian world in the eighteenth century, pushing its believers to action. The Evangelical Great Awakening played a very important role. This involved a whole array of diverse movements that intended to 'wake up' from their 'spiritual sleep' the churches that had come out of the Reformation. It underlined the need for a living faith, appealed to the emotions and feelings of the believers, and placed religious experience at its centre. Each member of the community of the faithful was, in other words, called upon to consecrate their life to the service of God through evangelical work and behaviour that complied with the moral principles of the Bible, which imposed forms of authentic piety. These predicaments were what led the followers of the Great Awakening – which in the nineteenth century became one of the most important phenomena of Protestantism – to take an active role in the face of the recognition and emotional sharing of others' pain.[7]

The initiatives through which the need to offer relief to, or to bring to an end, others' sufferings was followed up had a twofold intent. On the one hand, they sought to guarantee help and assistance to the needy, who included the new poor living in the emerging industrial cities. On the other hand, they demanded reforms capable of changing the order of reality behind so much human pain: the abolition of torture, for example, or the regulation of working conditions in factories. Furthermore – and this is the most important aspect from our point of view – the questions placed at the centre of the collective actions generated by a 'humanitarian' impulse did not remain confined to individual national communities but went beyond their borders. Emotional engagement and range of action were extended to foreign men and women, to distant populations. The sense of responsibility towards individuals suffering in unknown, distant places came into being at the moment when western Europe (including Britain) and North America were becoming the hubs of a global network within which goods, capital and labour circulated. It was this network that charted the new, extended 'geography of sensibility'. The most significant examples of the mobilisation that crossed national boundaries were the anti-slavery movement and the philanthropic work of missionaries all over the world, both appearing at the same time as the construction of the colonial empires.[8]

The movement that advocated the abolition of slavery came out of the recognition of the suffering of other individuals, different in their condition of slavery and their race but nevertheless part of the great human family. The slave system, accused of being inhuman and barbaric, was fought through an intense public opinion campaign and by using 'modern' forms of mobilisation, such as petitions or boycotts of products from the plantations. The religious movements played a crucial role in motivating and promoting the struggle against slavery. Far from their native countries, the missionaries joined the battle against the slave system with proselytism, which was, for them, their main aim, and with a combination of work in the fields of education, medical treatment and sanitary care. The intention was to respond to the moral duty to provide relief to others' suffering not just by standing up against slavery but also by offering indigenous populations the necessary aid to get out of the material and moral misery that oppressed them. The colonial administrations themselves – whose foundations rested on the strength of arms through which the empires were built – considered they had to demonstrate at least some goodwill, and included among their objectives the improvement in the living conditions of the colonised populations and, more generally, their acquisition of the qualities which, at that time, were the sole prerogative of Western societies.

The emergence of a new 'culture of sensibility', the abolitionist movement and missionary philanthropy are usually placed at the origins of contemporary humanitarianism, commonly understood as the organised aid intended for individual victims of war, natural disasters and disadvantaged economic circumstances in their own countries. It was an organised aid that, over time, was equipped with specific institutions, *ad hoc* legislation and internationally recognised operating standards. However, everything came into being in the period between the eighteenth and nineteenth centuries with the confirmation of a new spirit of participation in the suffering of others, among whom the colonies' slaves and subjects were of major importance. Outlining a similar genealogy means a certain degree of arbitrariness, increased by a possible linguistic misunderstanding, which it is best to clarify straight away. Today, talking about 'humanitarianism' means referring, as we have just said, to a humanitarian regime that is made up of laws, practices and institutions. In the common understanding of the term, the dimension of the action – by now complex – to provide aid to other human beings prevailed over the feeling from which it had drawn its stimulus. But in the early decades of the nineteenth century – when we have the first recognised usages of the words 'humanitarianism', in English, and '*humanitarisme*', in French – the predominant reference was to the emotions felt in the face of the suffering of fellow human beings and to the spontaneous participation in the pain of others. Not only this but in Britain 'humanitarianism' and 'humanitarian' were mainly used in a negative sense, to mean an excess of pointless sentimentalism, and this was also true of their equivalents in France.[9] The gap between the daily acceptance of these terms and the assumed age of the origins of humanitarianism therefore invites us to greater caution, encouraging us not to place past and present on too black and white a line.

This is how we can sum up the reasons why in this introduction to Part I we do not talk about humanitarianism's 'age of origins' but about its archaeology. The intention is to understand which of international humanitarianism's premises, seen in the light of their later developments, were already present in the historic period characterised by a new 'culture of sensibility', by the abolitionist movement's battles and by the activities of colonial philanthropy. The analysis of these premises is not aimed at drawing an evolutionary path destined to take us seamlessly to the present state of humanitarianism. Above all, it is an attempt to better understand the specific context in which a cultural sensibility took shape and new behaviours appeared – which, in one way or another, we are still heirs of – without forgetting that the later historical path could have taken other directions.

Another consideration is the use of the terms 'humanitarian' and 'humanitarianism' in the following pages to ensure that the reader is not led to project onto this era the meaning they have in the present. Referring to the 'archaeological' period, both terms will be used in the sense that refers to the feelings of human solidarity, to the moral duty of providing aid and relief from which it drew its origin.

Notes

1   Voltaire, *Poem on the Lisbon Disaster; or an Examination of the Axiom, 'All is Well'*, in *Toleration and Other Essays*, translation and introduction by Joseph McCabe (New York: G. P. Putnam's Sons, 1912), p. 255.

2   I am repeating the definition suggested by Paul Ricoeur in his essay 'Remarques d'un philosophe', in Institut d'Histoire du Temps Present, *Ecrire l'histoire du temps présent: En hommage à François Bédarida* (Paris: CNRS Editions, 1992), pp. 35–41.

3   Russell R. Dynes, 'The Lisbon Earthquake of 1755: The First Modern Disaster', in Th. E. D. Braun and J. B. Radner (eds), *The Lisbon Earthquake of 1755: Representations and Reactions* (Oxford: Voltaire Foundation Publications, 2005), pp. 34–46; Jean-Paul Poirier, *Le tremblement de terre de Lisbonne: 1755* (Paris: Odile Jacob, 2005); John F. Hutchinson, 'Disasters and the International Order: Earthquakes, Humanitarians, and the Ciraolo Project', *International History Review*, 1 (2000), pp. 1–36.

4 Horace Walpole, *Memoirs of the Reign of King George the Second* (London: Henry Colburn Publisher, 1846), vol. II, pp. 77–78.

5 Norman S. Fiering, 'Irresistible Compassion: An Aspect of Eighteenth-Century Sympathy and Humanitarianism', *Journal of the History of Ideas*, 37:2 (1976), pp. 195–218.

6 Thomas Laqueur, 'Bodies, Details and the Humanitarian Narrative', in Lynn Hunt (ed.), *The New Cultural History* (Berkeley, CA: University of California Press, 1989); Thomas Laqueur, 'Mourning, Pity and the Work of Narrative in the Making of Humanity', in R. Ashby Wilson and R. D. Brown (eds), *Humanitarianism and Suffering: The Mobilization of Empathy* (Cambridge: Cambridge University Press, 2009); Karen Halttunen, 'Humanitarianism and the Pornography of Pain in Anglo-American Culture', *American Historical Review*, 100:2 (1995), pp. 303–334; Lynn Hunt, *Inventing Human Rights: A History* (New York: W. W. Norton, 2007); Thomas Haskell, 'Capitalism and the Origins of the Humanitarian Sensibility', *American Historical Review*, 90:2–3 (1985), pp. 339–361 and 457–566 (in two parts), later republished in Thomas Bender (ed.), *The Antislavery Debate: Capitalism and Abolitionism as a Problem in Historical Interpretation* (Berkeley, CA: University of California Press, 1992).

7 Fiering, 'Irresistible Compassion'; M. J. D. Roberts, *Making English Morals. Voluntary Association and Moral Reform in England, 1787–1886* (Cambridge: Cambridge University Press, 2004).

8 The periodisation that identifies in abolitionism and colonialism the origins of international humanitarianism is widespread; for example, it is put forward by Michael Barnett in *Empire of Humanity: A History of Humanitarianism* (Ithaca, NY: Cornell University Press, 2011).

9 On the importance of the etymology of the term 'humanitarianism', see Maurice Tournier, 'Humanitaire est-il apolitique de naissance?', *Mots. Les languages du politique*, 65 (2001), pp. 135–145.

1

Saving humanity, abolishing slavery

> And further, consider with your self, if you were in the same Condition as the Blacks are ... who came as Strangers to you, and were sold to you as Slaves; now, I say, if this should be the Condition of you or yours, you would think it hard Measure; yes, and very great Bondage and Cruelty.[1]

George Fox said this in a sermon that later became a famous text published in 1676. The son of a Puritan weaver from Leicester, Fox is considered one of the founding fathers of the Religious Society of Friends, whose members became known as Quakers. Fox undertook long journeys motivated by his evangelical work and desire to extend his own knowledge of human society in the conviction that the 'light of the soul' should be pursued with Bible reading but also through experience. During the months he spent in Barbados in 1671, the English preacher 'discovered' the cruelty of slavery, which he witnessed directly. The experience he had in the Caribbean islands was translated into the recommendations – quoted in the epigraph to this chapter – that Fox addressed to his followers, exhorting them to imagine themselves slaves in order to understand the harshness of the servile condition. The believers were invited to teach the word of God to the black people in their ownership, who would then be able to become part of the great Christian family. In another passage in his sermon, Fox hoped for the liberation of the slaves who had faithfully served their masters for a long period of time. 'This I say', stated Fox, 'will be very acceptable to the Lord, whose Servants we are'.[2]

In most historical reconstructions, the Quaker preacher's declarations are marked as the cornerstone of anti-slavery. It is necessary, however, to remember that it was not until a century later that the condemnation of slavery became a priority for the Quakers and the Society of Friends played an important role in promoting a public campaign on the subject. The initial stage of the anti-slavery movement is placed therefore in the final decades of the eighteenth century and it is commonly believed that from that moment on, abolitionism began its inexorable march towards the triumph of the right cause. The main steps on this march were taken in Britain and comprised the first petition against the slave trade, delivered to the British parliament in 1783, the passing of the Act for the Abolition in the Slave Trade in 1807, and finally of the abolition of slavery in all the territories of the British empire, enshrined in law in an Act of 1834. Furthermore, this is the version that the central figures in the abolitionist battle themselves – primarily the British ones – gave, influencing the later historical reconstructions for a long time.[3]

From the Second World War on, however, intense historiographical work has questioned the entirely positive image of the struggles against slavery, underlining its setbacks and contradictions, analysing its socio-economic as well as religious motivations, and extending the enquiry beyond Britain alone. The most recent studies have dealt with the question from a transnational perspective. The development of abolitionism continued between Europe and the Americas until 1888, when Brazil, too, abolished slavery, which then became illegal in the whole of Latin America.[4] But the path has been reconstructed also of the international mobilisation that during the twentieth century attempted to oppose the persistence of more or less hidden forms of forced labour.[5] This is not the place either to go over again the global history of the struggle against slavery, or to analyse in detail the rich collection of studies carried out up to today, but thanks to these we can at any rate try to answer a crucial question for the purposes of our argument: why is the anti-slavery movement considered an important component in the archaeology of humanitarianism?

The main reasons can be summarised in the following terms. In the first place, the battle against slavery was intimately connected with the recognition of the suffering of other human beings, different because of their servile condition, from another race and often from geographically distant populations. This recognition was considered in itself a demonstration of humanity, Christianity and civilisation. In the second place, the abolitionist cause was associated with 'modern' forms of mobilisation, which, in Britain particularly, channelled a broad popular involvement and aimed to pressurise the relevant institutions. The creation of associations, information campaigns, popular petitions and widespread boycotting of products from the plantations were significant expressions of the new development of collective action against the slave trade and slavery. Finally, it is the global dimension that places anti-slavery in the pre-history of international humanitarianism: the commitment to the abolition of slavery and the trade in human beings connected different countries and continents, charting a vast field of action and promoting a close network for exchanging information, experience and knowledge. This global expansion, however, cannot be considered regardless of the different national and imperial contexts, which influenced the motivations behind and tendencies in abolitionism.

All of these aspects will be examined in the following sections, without any claim to being exhaustive or even any intention of reporting paradigmatic cases or of reconstructing a family tree for the contemporary humanitarian system. Instead, the aim will be to provide some examples that can show certain behaviours, mentalities and practices introduced by the anti-slavery movement that subsequently came to be used in the development of a system for international relief.

The cruelty of the whites and the suffering of the blacks

As we have seen, George Fox identified in slavery a form of cruelty the intensity of which could be understood by putting oneself in the place of men and women in chains, imagining their suffering. Similar arguments were brought up again in the mid-eighteenth century, when anti-slavery became a position broadly shared within the North American Society of Friends. This was the result of a new reformist drive that looked with concern at the well-being of the religious community's members, considering it an indicator of an excessive attachment to worldly goods. In the setting of the more general appeal to spirituality that ran through Quaker society, the ownership of slaves was reproachful for two reasons: on the one hand, it was considered the expression of a material wealth that was to the detriment of caring for the spirit; on the other hand, it was judged as a cruel practice that violated the principles of Christianity. The brutality of slavery caused the suffering of people of colour who had been reduced to a servile condition, as stated in a document approved at the Friends' annual meeting in Philadelphia in 1754.[6] In this text, though, the argument's axis was shifted to the 'Violence and Cruelty' intrinsic to the very act of buying and owning other human beings and to the fact of enjoying the fruits of their labour. Presented in these terms, slavery became a synonym for immorality; its expansion 'harden[ed] the Heart' and transformed Christians into individuals who were worse than the pagans.[7]

Immorality remained one of the main arguments anti-slavery made use of in the following decades too, when, no longer just the ethos of a single religious community, it became the object of a vast public campaign. This was the moment when the condemnation of slavery shifted to the demand for its abolition: compassion transformed into collective action to remove the origin of others' suffering. After 1776 this collective action followed distinct, though intertwined, roads in the now independent United States of America and Britain, the former home country. In any case, the unacceptability of slavery remained connected to the idea that it derived from a brutal and therefore abhorrent behaviour.

This conviction rested primarily on religious motives. In the evangelical world crossed by the Great Awakening, the inhumanity shown by those who traded or owned slaves was interpreted as a violation of Christian principles. For example, Granville Sharp, a leading figure among the promoters of the abolitionist battle in Britain, in one of his many essays repeated an argument already presented in the Philadelphia document when he wrote: 'Slavery is absolutely inconsistent with Christianity, because we cannot say of any Slaveholder, that he doth not to another, what he would not have done to himself!'[8] The consequences of a similar 'inconsistency' went beyond the guilt of individuals. Indeed, the slave owners who ignored the teachings of the Gospel were putting the integrity of the entire Christian community at risk since individual degeneration was an element of moral breakdown and could encourage the spread of corruption.[9]

The condemnation of the practice of slavery as a demonstration of inhumanity appeared in philosophical argument too. Philosophical works – most of all *The Theory of Moral Sentiments* by Adam Smith (1759) – significantly contributed to the spread of a new 'culture of sensibility', according to which no member of the human community worthy of being considered such could remain indifferent to the pain of others and its causes.[10] On this basis, the abolitionists were able to present the practice of slavery as a proof of the progressive barbarisation of the white man's world, which was inflicting terrible sufferings on its fellows or, at any rate, felt no compassion towards them. The chains around the ankles and wrists of the black people reduced to slavery broke the tie of sympathy that should have united all members of the human family and indicated the immorality of the white slave owners. The arguments of those who condemned the immorality of the slave system drew widely on Enlightenment philosophical works.[11] For example, in the essays, articles and public speeches of the British abolitionists the criticisms of slavery expressed frequently by Montesquieu in his monumental work *The Spirit of the Laws* (1748) were frequently referred to. The use of the distinguished Enlightenment philosopher's statements was usually selective, in that what counted for the abolitionist cause was being able to benefit from his authority in order to support the moral condemnation of slavery. Use was made, then, of some of his most effective passages, such as the one in which he declared that the right of ownership of one man over another 'is, in its own nature, bad. It is neither useful to the master nor to the slave' (XV, 1).

So the arguments that supported the emergence and development of the mobilisation against slavery were motivated by the recognition of the suffering of black people but they focused on worries about white society. Ignoring the suffering of men and women in chains proved a deep moral degradation. By extension, fighting slavery meant the demonstration of humanity and Christianity.

According to many of its opponents, slavery had effects on its victims that went far beyond suffering. They considered that complete submission and oppression had deprived the slaves of awareness and maturity, reducing them to a similar condition as that of children, who needed a guide to reach adulthood. Their humanity still had to grow and be fully developed.[12] This argument provided one of the justifications for the demand for the gradual emancipation of the slaves. Nicolas de Condorcet's well known work *Réflexions sur l'esclavage des nègres* perhaps offers the most effective possible example of this way of reasoning, which remained broadly held until the early decades of the nineteenth century. The French philosopher, a leading early exponent of the French anti-slavery movement, held that the condition of oppression had deprived black people of 'man's natural feelings'. They needed a long period of tutoring before being able to exercise all the responsibilities that the status of free individuals implied. In Condorcet's opinion this was why the question of emancipation had to be tackled with great care and freedom could be returned only gradually to the slaves.[13]

What is relevant to our archaeology of humanitarianism is the crossover between the paternalistic approach implicit in the references to the slaves' un-awareness and ineptitude, and the greater attention paid to the pains suffered by men and women in a servile condition. Compassion was merged with the idea that those giving aid were informed guides, capable of leading the by now emanci-pated black people to the acquisition of complete humanity. For the abolitionists, the recognition of the suffering of the 'brothers and sisters from Africa' was motivated by the conviction that freemen and slaves belonged to the same human community but at the same time it was expressed through a protective attitude that was, in fact, paternalistic. The difference in the levels of capability of those who enjoyed freedom and those who were subjugated by a bond of servility was, however, considered only transitory, as it was bound to disappear thanks to the benevolent action of those who helped to emancipate the slaves.

According to the supporters of the slave system, though, the low level of capability of the people of colour was indelible, since it was inherent – part of their very nature. The arguments used by the American pro-slavery public bodies are significant in this regard. The defenders of slavery usually described the insti-tution as benevolent[14] but their position on this point became clearer and more complex around the 1830s. In this period there was a shift in the discussion of slavery, for several reasons. The abolition of the slave trade (in 1807 in Britain and the year after in the United States) had not led to the result the abolitionists were hoping for – namely, the extinction of slavery as a 'natural effect' of the prohibition of the trade in African men and women. The anti-slavery movement had identified a new aim in emancipation, while the debate had been extended and radicalised, especially in the United States. Here, the pro-slavery front demonstrated a renewed strength and in its confrontation with its opponents two contradictory positions became established that were both, however, centred on the unacceptability of cruelty.[15]

The abolitionists described systematically and at length the horrendous tortures the slaves were submitted to. The supporters of the slave system coun-tered that the black people were not in fact forced into a condition of suffering but, on the contrary, enjoyed their masters' protection. Men and women of colour were not equipped with the same capabilities as white people, so granting them their freedom meant depriving them of the indispensable protection of their owners and breaking a tie that was useful to both sides. The defence of this deduction's goodness ended up making use of the same arguments and the same conceptual tools used by the abolitionists. For the supporters of slavery, the insistence on this institution's benevolent nature became central. From their point of view, the good owner displayed sympathy towards his slaves by satisfying their material needs but also by educating them, wisely mixing tolerance and punishment. The benevolent masters – observed the anti-abolitionists – prevented the black people in their service from falling into the miserable condition they would inevitably have attained without the help of white people.[16] With these arguments it was emancipation that ended up being presented as cruel. In other words, the abolitionists were condemning the inhumanity of slavery and the slavery supporters were condemning the inhumanity of the emancipationists. For example, the slave trader and owner Zephaniah Kingsley, from Georgia, wrote in a short pamphlet published in 1828: 'the idea of slavery, when associated with cruelty and injustice, is revolting to every philanthropic mind; but when the idea is associated with justice and benevolence, slavery, so called, easily amalgamates with the ordinary conditions of life'.[17] By using this type of argument the pro-slavery apologists showed that they, too, had their own language of compassion, which showed itself to be fluid and malleable, useful in justifying different, opposing aims.

Acting and convincing

An unmissable date in the usual timelines of abolitionism is 1787, the year in which the Society for Effecting the Abolition of the Slave Trade, better known as the Abolition Society, came into being. Nine of its twelve founders were Quakers who had been committed to the anti-slavery cause for some time; the others were evangelical Anglicans, including the previously mentioned Granville Sharp, who had made himself known through his essays against slavery. The London organisation rapidly acquired international fame, became a reference point for abolitionists in other countries and a model for the similar associations that were founded later, beginning with the Société des Amis des Noirs, which was founded in 1788 by some of the best-known intellectuals opposed to slavery: Condorcet, Abbot Grégoire, Lafayette, Mirabeau and Sieyès.[18]

With the establishment of the Abolition Society, the rejection of slavery's cruelty and the attempt to put an end to the suffering of those who underwent it became the main policy issues of a formalised association. This organisation thereby became a fully-fledged part of humanitarianism's archaeology. From this point of view, the identification of two closely connected fronts of action is particularly important. In fact, the Abolition Society suggested promoting information and mobilisation campaigns against slavery and the slave trade but it soon found itself set up as an influential lobby, aiming to win the approval of politicians in the abolitionist battle.

William Wilberforce, one of the most celebrated figures in the British anti-slavery movement, had a very important role in this sense. An evangelical Christian, well known for his philanthropic commitment, and a powerful member of the British parliament, Wilberforce was 'converted' to the anti-slavery cause by members of the newly formed Abolition Society and immediately became one of the leading actors in the transformation of the Society's aims into political action. The Slave Trade Act of 1807, which abolished the slave trade, is usually associated with its name.[19] The lobbying work – carried out with greater or lesser degrees of success – remained fundamental to the life of the Abolition Society, even when, in 1823, it was refounded and took the name of the Anti-Slavery Society.

The political pressure that first the Abolition Society and then the Anti-Slavery Society were able to apply, on the one hand, lay in the fact that their most powerful members exercised considerable influence within the institutions themselves and, on the other hand, derived from the awareness-raising work and a vast, well structured social mobilisation largely arranged by local anti-slavery organisations. This strong, compact, popular involvement was one of the elements that marked out the British movement[20] and which contributed to an emphasis on its study by those who have sought to determine the links between the history of abolitionism and the emergence of contemporary humanitarianism.

In Britain, the achievement of a broad consensus was pursued by circulating as widely as possible any information that could make known the cruelty of slavery and the slave trade, and leverage the idea that no human being could tolerate the suffering of which they were the cause. Tales from those colonies whose economies were based on the slave system were given a primary role in the work of persuasion carried out through public conferences but also through pamphlets, illustrations and newspaper articles. The news about slaves arriving from the colonial possessions and reaching the national press remained, however, on the pages of specialist publications, such as *The Anti-Slavery Reporter*, which from the year of its foundation in 1825 was one of the best-known public voices against slavery.[21]

We will come back to the question of the statements originating in the various imperial territories because it deals with a significant aspect of the global dimension of the abolitionist argument. For the moment what interests us is to observe how that argument developed in close connection with the growing weight exercised, in that historical phase, by public opinion on the political sphere. The impact on society of the anti-slavery campaigns clearly showed the role that the media were beginning to play in placing the promoters of a battle fought in the name of humanity alongside an increasingly wide number of supporters, with a different degree of conviction and involvement. The powerful entry of the press in the raising of awareness of the suffering of other human beings was a further, important element in the archaeology of international humanitarianism.

Popular petitions were also a vital tool in the mobilisation against slavery. They were used both to pressurise institutions and to offer individuals the chance of concrete action, spreading the anti-slavery commitment at the grassroots level. At the end of 1787 the first major petition for the abolition of slavery gathered almost 11,000 signatures from the 50,000 inhabitants of Manchester, one of the industrial cities that were going through a new phase of development and growth in well-being.[22] The gathering of signatures, locally and nationally, was scattered throughout the movement's later history and intensified around the mid-1830s, when the goal became the immediate emancipation of the slaves. The Slavery Abolition Act of 1834 did not mark the end of the activism because the British parliament had accepted the hypothesis of gradualism and therefore introduced a mechanism for progressively freeing the slaves in the empire's territories. Men and women, but not children, were forced to remain dependent on their masters for between four and six years. This period – in line with the paternalistic approach already mentioned – was called 'apprenticeship'. This form of enforced labour, which ended up being no different from slavery, was the subject of a new battle until – in 1838 – all the 'apprentices' were declared free.

The new phase of the anti-slavery movement, focused on the campaign against apprenticeship, saw a succession of petitions promoted by women's organisations, which thus acquired a central role of sorts. Their initiatives signalled a difference from the previous decades when the signing of petitions was considered the exclusive prerogative of men, in line with the separation between the public and private spheres. This change took place on the wave of the increasingly persistent condemnation of the victims' – missionaries and converted slaves – persecution in the colonies. The outrage caused by this type of violence played an important role in raising public awareness. Conditions like this meant the participation of women in petitions could be seen as a shoring up of their support for the missions. It was the religious aspect, in other words, that allowed the female anti-slavery associations to expand their activities. This was how the commitment to defending other human beings who were suffering enabled women to break through the boundaries of gender between public and private spheres and to win new spaces in which to be central players. However, this did not subvert the gendered hierarchies because the involvement of the abolitionist women remained confined to certain specific areas and did not put under discussion their exclusion from being represented. In fact, the leadership of the Anti-Slavery Society remained solidly male and it was not until around the middle of the century that women won greater space and independence in the leadership, and by that time, in the British context, the anti-slavery cause had lost some of its political value.[23] So the organised mobilisation around a humanitarian cause took shape also through the allocation of specific gender roles, reflecting and reinforcing the male and female social constructs.

Women were also the central figures in another form of mobilisation that flanked the information campaigns and petitions: the boycott of products from the colonies, and sugar in particular. The first call to abstain from the consumption of sugar was launched in 1791 and had between 300,000 and 400,000 supporters. The initiative's success was the expression both of the huge numbers of anti-slavery supporters and of the expansion of consumption: sugar had become the necessary ingredient for afternoon tea and puddings, one of British cooking's most famous desserts. From the start the boycott campaign addressed men and women, leveraging the role of women in the management of family spending. Above all, it was female resourcefulness to argue that giving up the purchase of certain products meant refusing to contribute to the exploitation of slaves, and therefore to transform the use of sugar within the home into a moral and political question. The wives and mothers thereby brought into the daily routine of private life the public cause of emancipation. The emergence of an 'anti-slavery domestic culture' can be seen in these sales boycotts but was also determined by the selection of the products that were bought, which acquired a clear ethical value. Sugar bowls were sold with the phrase 'East India sugar not made by slaves' on them, while the famous image of the black slave on his knees with his ankles and wrists in chains was put on bracelets and hairpins.[24] The boycott failed to affect the financial success of slaveholders but it contributed to the widening of the abolitionist struggle,[25] bringing it into the houses of sympathisers and activists. The 'domestication' of anti-slavery humanitarianism closely tied the mother country's daily life to the reality in the colonies. At the same time, it transformed compassion for those who were suffering into a symbolic gesture, including it in the 'normality' of everyday life.

Global networks and national anti-slavery

In introducing the figure of George Fox, we recalled his trip to Barbados as a necessary background for the position he later took against slavery. This was simply one of the earliest and most famous biographical examples where the anti-slavery choice was motivated by personal discovery of the brutal treatment to which the men and women working in the plantations were subjected. The vision and emotional sharing of the slaves' sufferings formed the cornerstone on which was founded the later commitment of certain free men against a similar cruelty. Their experience was transformed into crucial evidence at the time when other people, who had never seen with their own eyes what was going on in the colonies, had to be convinced of the virtuousness of the anti-slavery battle. For example – but very many similar stories could be recalled – the Baptist minister William Knibb returned in 1832 from Jamaica to contribute to the abolitionist campaign being led at home. At a conference held in London before a large audience of philanthropists Knibb explained that he had crossed the Atlantic to recount the realities of the Jamaican plantations, or in other words to make public 'scenes and incidents, most of which have fallen under my own observation'.[26] The vivid story of someone who had personally observed the inhumanity of the treatment of black people became the most effective tool to get white people in the home country to identify with their sufferings.

Slavery's cruelty was recounted through the evidence of the many missionaries, who, just like William Knibb, had moved to the Western powers' colonial possessions. The British case is once again particularly relevant because of the phenomenon's size and characteristics. Indeed, since the 1770s information circulating between the Caribbean and Britain had been supporting the anti-slavery movement, but from the beginning of the following century this circulation increased enormously in geographical extent as the colonial possessions progressively came to include new regions in Asia, Australasia, North America and South Africa. In the context of this process of expanding imperial borders, missionary action took on an increasingly important role in connecting the home country and the colonies on the anti-slavery question. The organisations in the metropolises – such as the Nonconformist Baptist Missionary Society, London Missionary Society and Church Missionary Society, all founded in the 1790s – gathered information from different continents and became locations for the promotion of a more general debate on the suffering of others and on the moral duty to put the situation right. In turn, this debate was disseminated in the opposite direction, from the metropolis to the colonies, contributing a global dimension to the mobilisation against slavery.[27]

The routes between the imperial colonies determined the global geographies of anti-slavery, as we have just seen in the British case. At the same time, the connections between the movements started in the individual countries lent a transnational character to the condemnation of the cruelty of slavery in the name of humanity. Some scholars hold that this character can already be identified in the first phase of anti-slavery's development, looking at the intense circulation of ideas and the close network of contacts that joined the British and American Quakers.[28] This was why people talked about a transatlantic abolitionism, which, after the end of slavery in the British empire, took on different traits but did not disappear.[29] In fact, many of the leading figures in Afro-American abolitionism – including Frederick Douglass, William Wells Brown and Henry Highland Garnet – stayed in England between the 1830s and 1860s, where they held public conferences, printed their works and worked alongside local organisations.[30] Through their journeys, the Anglo-American tie within the anti-slavery mobilisation stayed alive until the American Civil War, after which slavery was abolished across the whole of the United States.

The international dimension comes into play in the first period of the anti-slavery movement even when looking only at the two sides of the English Channel. As we have already observed, the conceptual contribution of the French Enlightenment was of great importance to British abolitionism, especially on the level of the arguments against the slave system. At the same time, the British abolitionists promoted the translation into French of the most famous pamphlets published in English; they travelled between different cities in France to spread information about slaves' living conditions and encouraged the birth of the

Société des Amis des Noirs. The relationship with the British context is also significant for understanding the second stage of French abolitionism. We should remember that in revolutionary France slavery was abolished in 1793, following the slaves' revolt in Saint-Domingue, but it was a short-lived victory since the slave system was reintroduced in 1802 by Napoleon Bonaparte. A new mobilisation developed in the following decades and the battle for emancipation carried on until slavery was once again abolished by the French in 1848. The network of relationships established across the Channel was also important in this period: the new anti-slavery organisation set up in France in 1834 – called the Société Française pour l'Abolition de l'Esclavage – took as its model the Anti-Slavery Society and its newspaper – L'Abolitioniste – received financing from Britain.[31]

With the establishment of the British and Foreign Anti-Slavery Society – founded in London in 1839, after the abolition of the 'apprenticeship' – the international horizon of British abolitionism became explicit, since the new organisation's aim was 'to aid in the universal abolition of slavery'.[32] The British and Foreign Anti-Slavery Society very rapidly became a centre of world importance for providing information about slavery and it developed a vast network of international relations. Furthermore, its activists pressurised the British authorities, which during the nineteenth century promoted a series of treaties with which the international legislation on the slave trade was extended.

Fifty years from the foundation of the British and Foreign Anti-Slavery Society, slavery was also abolished in the last territories of the American continent, in Cuba in 1886 and in Brazil in 1888. At the same time, though, the struggle against slavery was a motive for a renewed international mobilisation that extended into the early years of the following century. The new aim was now the eradication of the trade in human beings, as well as of the forms of enforced labour that still persisted on the African continent. Highlighting this were statements and reports from missionaries and military expeditions in Africa, which tended to downplay the recent role of Western countries and which described slavery and the slave trade as local phenomena.[33]

The almost centuries-old path that anti-slavery had so far followed had developed within the evangelical world but the revival in these years was characterised by the commitment of the Catholic Church, which led to the birth of new organisations in Europe. Examples of Catholic-inspired bodies were the Société Antiesclavagiste de France, the Société Antiesclavagiste de Belgique and the Società Antischiavista d'Italia, which all began work in the 1880s. The European organisations regarded the eradication of slavery from regions of Africa as a shared aim, which had to be pursued by all those who had 'a true understanding of human dignity and solidarity'.[34] There was active cooperation, then, between the different societies, including the British ones, on the level of the circulation of information, reciprocal publicity of initiatives through press bodies and exchange of material.[35] The collaboration between the activists built itself up on a common argument, which condemned the barbarism of the African populations and often described slavery and the slave trade as phenomena directly linked to the practice of the Islamic religion. The transnationalism of the anti-slavery mobilisation found one of its strong points in the promotion of Christian values and in the proclamation of the moral superiority of the Western populations.[36]

European diplomacy legitimised this reasoning and placed anti-slavery on the international political agenda. The so-called Berlin African Conference of 1884–85 was crucial in this respect. The conference was called by Chancellor Otto von Bismarck in order to resolve the question of the Congo – over which Britain, Belgium and Portugal had claims – and more generally to regulate the expansion of the major powers in West and Central Africa. Ample space was given over to the debate on the transformations on the African continent to which the European interventions had provided impetus and to the advancement of the civilising process. In this regard, a primary role was attributed to the eradication of the slave trade and every form of slavery in the African regions. Sovereignty over Congo was conferred to Leopold II of Belgium in the name of the protection of the local population and the struggle against slavery. It was, most of all, through Britain's will that the so-called Berlin Act of 1885 established that the colonial powers should guarantee the abolition of the slave trade and slavery in their respective spheres of influence. The decisions taken in Berlin and the consequent actions taken by the participating countries were relaunched years later by the Brussels Anti-Slavery Conference (1889–90).[37] With the Berlin and Brussels initiatives, the appeal to demonstrating humanity implicit in the struggle against slavery became an integral part of the imperial rhetoric of civilisation.[38]

First the Berlin African Conference and then the Brussels Conference were reference points for the non-governmental mobilisation against slavery and contributed to providing it with impetus. The different national societies shared the broad objectives established in the two meetings and stood alongside the authorities in their own countries in pursuing them, strengthening the association between anti-slavery, civilising mission and colonialism at exactly the moment when the European powers were extending or rapidly building their empires. The Société Antiesclavagiste de Belgique celebrated the colonial wars of Leopold II and when the order imposed in Congo by the Belgian sovereign turned out to be inhuman and repressive and itself to be founded on the exploitation of enforced labour, the Société rejected every accusation and spoke only about individual cases of violence.[39] In Belgium, France and Germany, anti-slavery activists contributed to gathering funds for military excursions in Africa.[40] This did not happen in Britain, but nonetheless the activists invoked the abolition of slavery as a justification for colonial intervention.[41]

The transnational dimension of the late-nineteenth-century anti-slavery revival should not let us forget that it also developed thanks to the relationship with the national authorities through sharing their imperial policies' programmes and aims.[42] So it is not only global expansion that determined the importance of the campaigns against slavery for the archaeological stage of international humanitarianism. Another important aspect comes into play with anti-slavery: the connection between the mobilisation against the suffering of others and national politics.

Notes

1   George Fox, *Gospel family-order, being a short discourse concerning the ordering of families, both of whites, blacks, and Indians / by G.F. (1676)* (London?, s.n., 1676), p. 18.

2   *Ibid.*, p. 16.

3   Christopher Leslie Brown, *Moral Capital: Foundations of British Abolitionism* (Chapel Hill, NC: University of North Carolina Press, 2006), pp. 8–22.

4   See, among others, Robin Blackburn, *The American Crucible: Slavery, Emancipation and Human Rights* (London: Verso, 2011); Seymour Drescher, *Abolition: A History of Slavery and Antislavery* (Cambridge: Cambridge University Press, 2009); Olivier Pétré-Grenouilleau, *Les traites négrières: Essai d'histoire globale* (Paris: Éditions Gallimard, 2004).

5   See, for example, W. Caleb McDaniel, 'Abolitionism', in A. Iriye and Pierre-Yves Saunier (eds), *The Palgrave Dictionary of Transnational History* (London: Palgrave Macmillan, 2009), pp. 6–8.

6   *An Epistle of Caution and Advice, Concerning the Buying and Keeping of Slaves*, p. 2, at http://triptych.brynmawr.edu/cdm4/document.php?CISOROOT=/HC_QuakSlav&CISOPTR=1547&CISOSHOW=1544 (accessed 29 November 2017).

7   *Ibid.*, pp. 1, 2.

8   Granville Sharp, *The Law of Liberty, or the Royal Law* (London, 1776), p. 33, cited in Christopher L. Brown, *Moral Capital: Foundations of British Abolitionism* (Chapel Hill, NC: University of North Carolina Press, 2006), p. 180.

9   Brown, *Moral Capital*.

10 Norman S. Fiering, 'Irresistible Compassion: An Aspect of Eighteenth-Century Sympathy and Humanitarianism', *Journal of the History of Ideas*, 37:2 (1976), pp. 195–218; Lynn Hunt, *Inventing Human Rights: A History* (New York: W. W. Norton, 2007).

11 David Brion Davis, *The Problem of Slavery in Western Culture* (Ithaca, NY: Cornell University Press, 1966), pp. 422–445.

12 Catherine Hall, *Civilizing Subjects: Metropole and Colony in the Imagination 1830–1867* (Chicago, IL: University of Chicago Press, 2002), pp. 107–109.

13 Robin Blackburn, *The Overthrow of Colonial Slavery 1776–1848* (London: Verso, 1988), p. 171.

14 Joyce E. Chaplin, 'Slavery and the Principle of Humanity: A Modern Idea in the Early Lower South', *Journal of Social History*, 24:2 (1990), pp. 299–315.

15 Margaret Abruzzo, *Polemical Pain: Slavery, Cruelty, and the Rise of Humanitarianism* (Baltimore, MD: Johns Hopkins University Press, 2011), pp. 120–158.

16 *Ibid.*

17 Zephaniah Kingsley, *Balancing Evils Judiciously: The Proslavery Writings of Zephaniah Kingsley*, edited by D. Stowell (Gainesville, FL: University Press of Florida, 2000), p. 4, cited *ibid.*, p. 145.

18 On the relationships between the French and British anti-slavery movements see Lawrence C. Jennings, *French Anti-Slavery: The Movement for the Abolition of Slavery in France, 1802–1848* (Cambridge: Cambridge University Press, 2000).

19 Blackburn, *The Overthrow of Colonial Slavery*, pp. 136–158.

20 Seymour Drescher, *Capitalism and Antislavery: British Mobilization in Comparative Perspective* (London: Macmillan, 1986).

21 Catherine Hall, *Macaulay and Son: Architects of Imperial Britain* (New Haven, CT: Yale University Press, 2012), pp. 84–86.

22 Drescher, *Capitalism and Antislavery*, pp. 70–71.

23 Clare Midgley, *Women Against Slavery: The British Campaigns 1780–1870* (London: Routledge, 1992).

24 Clare Midgley, 'Slave Sugar Boycotts, Female Activism and the Domestic Base of British Anti-slavery Culture', *Slavery and Abolition: A Journal of Slave and Post-Slave Studies*, 17:3 (1996), pp. 137–162; Charlotte Sussman, *Consuming Anxieties: Consumer Protest, Gender and British Slavery, 1713–1833* (Stanford, CA: Stanford University Press, 2000).

25 Stacey M. Robertson, 'Marketing Social Justice: Lessons from Our Abolitionist Predecessors', *Moving the Social: Journal of Social History and the History of Social Movements*, 57 (2017), pp. 21–36.

26 James Losh and William Knibb, *Speeches of James Losh, Esq., and the Rev. William Knibb, on the Immediate Abolition of British Colonial Slavery* (Newcastle: J. Blackwell & Co., 1833), pp. 12–13. On William Knibb's participation in the British anti-slavery movement, see Hall, *Civilizing Subjects*.

27 Alan Lester, 'Thomas Fowell Buxton and the Networks of British Humanitarianism', in H. Gilbert and C. Tiffin (eds), *Burden or Benefit? Imperial Benevolence and Its Legacies* (Bloomington, IN: Indiana University Press, 2008), pp. 31–48; Alan Lester and David Lambert, 'Geographies of Colonial Philanthropy', *Progress in Human Geography*, 28:3 (2004), pp. 320–341.

28 Huw T. David, 'Transnational Advocacy in the Eighteenth Century: Transatlantic Activism and the Antislavery Movement', *Global Networks: A Journal of Transnational Affairs*, 7:3 (2007), pp. 367–382.

29 Amanda B. Moriz, *The Empire of Humanity: The American Revolution and the Origins of Humanitarianism* (New York: Oxford University Press, 2016), pp. 79–102.

30 Richard J. M. Blackett, *Building an Antislavery Wall: Black Americans in the Atlantic Abolitionist Movement 1830–1860* (Baton Rouge, LA: Louisiana State University Press, 1983); Kathryn Kish Sklar and James Brewer Stewart (eds), *Women's Rights and Transatlantic Antislavery in the Era of Emancipation* (New Haven, CT: Yale University Press, 2007).

31 Jennings, *French Anti-Slavery*; Pétré-Grenouilleau, *Les traites négrières*, pp. 227–234; Seymour Drescher, 'British Way, French Way: Opinion Building and Revolution in the Second French Slave Emancipation', *American Historical Review*, 96:3 (1991), pp. 709–734.

32 Drescher, *Abolition*, p. 267. Thomas Davies considers the British and Foreign Anti-Slavery Society an example of the expansion of international non-governmental organisations (INGOs) in the early decades of the nineteenth century, see Thomas Davies, *NGOs: A New History of Transnational Civil Society* (London: Hurst, 2013), pp. 32–33.

33 Daniel Laqua, 'The Tensions of Internationalism: Transnational Anti-Slavery in the 1880s and 1890s', *International History Review*, 33:4 (2011), pp. 705–726.

34 From the letter of the Archbishop of Tolouse to the Société Antiesclavagiste de France, cited *ibid.*, p. 709.

35 *Ibid.*; see also Amalia Ribi Forclaz, *Humanitarian Imperialism: The Politics of Anti-Slavery Activism, 1880–1940* (Oxford: Oxford University Press, 2015), pp. 14–29.

36 Forclaz, *Humanitarian Imperialism*, pp. 30–36.

37 Suzanne Miers, *Britain and the Ending of the Slave Trade* (London: Longman, 1975), pp. 236–291.

38 Suzanne Miers, 'Humanitarianism at Berlin: Myth or Reality?', in S. Förster, W. J. Mommsen and R. Robinson (eds), *Bismarck, Europe and Africa: The Berlin Conference 1884–1885 and the Onset of Partition* (Oxford: Oxford University Press, 1988), pp. 333–346.

39 Laqua, 'The Tensions of Internationalism', p. 714.

40 *Ibid.*, p. 713.

41 Kevin Grant, *A Civilised Savagery: Britain and the New Slaveries in Africa, 1884–1926* (New York: Routledge, 2005), pp. 24–31.

42 Ribi Forclaz, *Humanitarian Imperialism*.

2

Colonial humanitarianism

'Jane, come with me to India: come as my help meet and fellow-labourer' .... 'Oh St. John!', I cried, 'have some mercy!'

I appealed to one who, in the discharge of what he believed his duty, knew neither mercy nor remorse. He continued: – 'God and nature intended you for a missionary's wife. It is not personal, but mental endowments they have given you: you are formed for labour, not for love. A missionary's wife you must – shall be. You shall be mine: I claim you – not for my pleasure, but for my Sovereign's service'.[1]

This is a crucial passage of dialogue between St John Rivers and Jane Eyre, heroine of the book of the same name (1847). The novel with which Charlotte Brontë won fame reworked many elements of the culture of the British empire, and the stories of the central characters referred back to events in the Caribbean plantations or the evangelisation of the Indian population. This episode was bringing out one of the most frequent themes in female literature set in the colonies, namely the participation of women in missionary work. St John River, a man driven by deep devotion, saw in marriage to Jane the perfect complement of his own future in India for his 'Sovereign's service'. The young English church-man's project reflected the specific role that Victorian society assigned to the female population in the expanding empire. Women were required to make a sacrifice to spread among the population a model of Christian life together with Western society's values.[2]

The character of St John River, and the peculiar marriage proposal he made to Jane, are literary inventions indicative of the crossover between life in the metropolis and in the colonies, also from the point of view of the questions dealt with in this volume. They remind us firstly that the choice to set off on the missions – taken largely in Nonconformist religious environments – was part of the possible future English men and women imagined for themselves. In other words, the material and spiritual care of suffering individuals who lived in faraway worlds in the first decades of the nineteenth century had come onto the cultural horizon of Western societies. In the second section of this chapter we will see how the decision of men and women to join the missions spread over other continents corresponded to the emergence of a transnational network of philanthropic activity which developed in close interaction with the relief work carried out at home. This interaction is clear both if we look at the type of initiatives (and the ways in which they were carried out) 'in the field' and if we take into consideration the origins and set-up of the associations that were being founded to support the missionaries' work. In the archaeology of international humanitarianism we therefore also have to include its symbiotic relationship with 'domestic philanthropy', which we will analyse through examples relating to the British, American and French contexts.

If interpreted in a more general sense, the dialogue and characters invented by Charlotte Brontë remind us also of the fact that the simple subjects of the English crown felt themselves to be an integral part of a great domain that included different and very distant peoples. For this very reason – we may add, going beyond what Brontë writes – they felt called upon in the debate on the fates of the colonised subjects. The interests of the home country's inhabitants in the populations of the East or West Indies, Sierra Leone or Australia derived most of all from the conviction that acquiring new colonies meant taking on, as civilised countries, certain responsibilities. The concrete content of these responsibilities was discussed, starting with the value the now moral public recognised in compassion and benevolence. The prevailing idea was that the imperial government had an obligation to deal with the colonised subjects' living conditions, of understanding the reasons for their suffering and of finding a solution to end it or at least to relieve it. The crossover between responsibility, compassion and benevolence permeated the whole European colonial experience. Further on we will analyse two examples: the public debate in Britain during the first phase of the new British expansionism, and the project of the *mission civilisatrice* carried out in republican France. We will also see – again using examples concerning the British and French empires – how this crossover contributed to shaping the colonies' administration. The officials sent by the home country translated into concrete measures the directives defined in London or Paris and in this way contributed to the inclusion in national policies of relief for distant and different peoples.

Benevolent administrations

In Britain the question of the roles the imperial power was called upon to take on had already emerged in the 1780s, especially in relation to India, which was the main British possession. It was in this phase that the theory was established of trusteeship, which held that the administration of India was to be understood as a transitory arrangement tacitly entrusted to the British by the local population in their own interests. That is, according to this theory it was the local population who themselves granted the exercise of power to a European people, who were duty bound to protect that population while they were waiting to be able to acquire their own national sovereignty. The idea of trusteeship took shape within the political debate on the limitation of powers of the East India Company and on the strengthening of the crown's direct control over the colonised regions. The question provoked a wider discussion, however, both about the ways in which Britain's trusteeship in India would have to be practised and about the objectives it should have. And, of course, in its later development the debate was not only about the Indian subcontinent but about all the territories acquired in the expansion of the empire.[3]

The conviction became widespread that the administration of the colonies implied a demonstration of benevolence, the improvement of the colonised peoples' living conditions and an assumption of responsibility for their future, understood also as guiding them along the path of acquiring the qualities that, at the time, only Western societies had. On the one hand, these ideas were circulating among the political and administrative élite and, even if they found different degrees of acceptance, they significantly influenced the policies applied in the colonies. Between the late eighteenth century and the early decades of the nineteenth century, these policies were, above all, aimed at securing a more heavily centralised system of government in the vast territories over which the British flag flew. On the other hand, the conviction that the imperial mandate implied benevolence and assumption of responsibility dominated public opinion, which became part of the judgement of the colonising authorities' response to their obligations. The clearest example of this is the abolitionist campaigns, which we have already discussed in Chapter 1. With their condemnation of the barbarities of the slavery system and the pressure put on the institutions, they translated a somewhat vague appeal to compassion and responsibility into a precise demand for all the empire's territories: the abolition of slavery.[4] The dismantling of the slave system was specified as one of the tasks of the imperial authorities. On this subject it is important to remember that the suffering of the slaves was considered unacceptable because it was thought they were also part of the great human family, but this family was imagined as a hierarchy determined by the Western people's higher degree of civilisation.

Between the late eighteenth century and the first decades of the following century the appeal for the demonstration of humanity promoted by the public debate and reinterpreted by British officials became a vital component of the Britain's new imperial identity. At the same time, the reality of the empire shaped the argument around the suffering of others and the need to put an end to it, an argument that would probably have taken on different forms and content if it had not arisen from the imperial experience.[5] Benevolence and paternalism, universality of the human condition and hierarchy among peoples, sympathy and dominion: all these elements not only coexisted but were in fact the indivisible features of the face of British colonial humanitarianism.

Let us try to examine more closely certain characteristics of this colonial humanitarianism through a specific example, the famine that in 1837–38 severely hit the Daob area in northern India (present-day Uttar Pradesh). The dramatic situation in the Daob profoundly struck Emily Eden, writer and sister of the governor general in India, George Eden. In some letters written while she was travelling back from visiting her brother, Emily gave an account of the macabre spectacle that met her eyes in January 1838 and described the bodies of women and children transformed by hunger: 'You cannot conceive the horrible sights we see', she wrote, 'particularly children; perfect skeletons in many cases, their bones through their skin, without a rag of clothing, and utterly unlike human creatures'; 'the women look as if they had been buried, their *skulls* look so dreadful'.[6]

The hunger that afflicted distant populations became a cause of concern and collective mobilisation only in end-of-the-century Britain.[7] However, in the face of the dramatic of the famines that by the start of the nineteenth century had already claimed large numbers of victims, the colonisers thought that it lay with government to provide aid and lend relief. Such emergencies were a significant testing ground for the British administration. The priority for the colonies' administrators was to guarantee the population the minimum necessary for survival until the famine had been overcome. The search for an adequate solution was influenced by the debate on pauperism and on the undesirable consequences of charity that in the home country had accompanied the approval of the Poor Law Amendment Act of 1834. The fear of making the beneficiaries dependent on relief spurred the authorities to identify the correct response to a lack of food. So the recruitment was arranged of the needy within a plan of public works, dedicated mainly to road construction. Drawing up the plan was not simple though. On what criteria should the men and women to be employed be selected? What was right level of pay that they should receive? How could the colonisers' benevolence be prevented from driving the Indians to parasitism?[8]

The criteria for employment in public works were inspired by the approach adopted in Britain with the Poor Law Amendment Act. In this way the British authorities put the Indian peasants decimated by famine on the same level as the new poor classes generated by industrialisation. The two fundamental principles used were 'hardship' and 'eligibility', in other words, the condition of need – not otherwise specified – and physical capabilities – in spite of the general malnutrition – necessary for carrying out the work in question. It was established as well that the rates of pay for these labourers would be kept as low as possible to 'stimulate' the workers to seek better-paid work elsewhere, thus keeping labour in circulation. Naturally, this fitted with the intention to keep down the costs of the entire programme. The English administrators widely discussed the minimum quantity of food necessary to ensure the survival of the Indians in order to establish a minimum rate of pay for people employed in these public works. Because this employment was presented as a form of relief for the indigenous population, non-homogenous criteria were adopted and the pay varied from one district to another. A survey carried out in 1938 showed that many people became ill because of malnutrition and a lack of clothing, and were thus unable to work any more.[9]

In terms of its benefits for the local population, the plan to respond to the famine appeared less consequential, but this plan did mark a turning point in the conception and administration of aid.[10] In fact, the solution of sanctioning the colonial government to provide relief to the suffering of indigenous subjects implied an institutionalisation of benevolence that ended up opposing any local philanthropic tradition. The relief work traditionally carried out by the Indian population was tied, on the one hand, to the preservation of the élite's powers (in that they could maintain their prestige through the demonstration of benevolence) and, on the other hand, to the reception of the needy in the places of worship of the various religions practised in the region. This widespread, grassroots philanthropic work was now considered by the colonial powers to be the expression of superstition and exotic rituals.[11] This dismissive attitude on the part of the British authorities did not of course erase the indigenous customs of charity, which remained in place, but it certainly excluded them from the construction of a humanitarian action that Western society recognised as such.

The solutions adopted in northern India arose from the immediate necessity of responding to an emergency, but in these same years programmes also took shape that were specifically planned 'to render further colonization humane and controlled from the very start'.[12] After the abolition of slavery in all the territories of the empire, the protection of the indigenous peoples was identified as a crucial point in the demonstration of humanity that the British administration had to offer. The problem arose from the growing presence of settlers in South Africa, Australia, New Zealand and North America who were taking land at the expense of the local population, who were subjected to an often violent dispossession. The issue was raised, both in public debate and in institutional settings, by the exponents of the abolitionist movement, which was now reformulating the contents of its commitment to 'distant sufferers'. In 1837 the Aborigines' Protection Society was set up in London, many of whose founding members had distinguished themselves in the struggle against slavery.[13] Among these was Thomas Fowell Buxton, William Wilberforce's successor as leader of the anti-slavery campaign in the House of Commons. Buxton himself had asked for and obtained in 1835 the opening of a parliamentary inquiry to investigate the consequences of the substantial emigration of settlers on the indigenous populations in Canada, Newfoundland, New South Wales and Van Diemen's Land.[14]

The *Report of the Select Committee on Aborigines (British Settlements)*, published two years later, was based on the gathering of numerous testimonies from British colonial possessions. It not only sketched the abuses suffered by the indigenous peoples but was also intended to provide the authorities with the recommendations to rethink the empire's administration in line with the principles of responsibility and benevolence towards the colonised peoples. The writers of the report and their supporters thought the stakes were very high. The example of humanity that the British had given with the abolition of slavery, a cause of national pride, would have been compromised had the misappropriation of the indigenous peoples' lands and the requisition of their goods been pursued across the increasingly vast territories of the empire. To deal with all this the report did not envisage a limitation on the colonisers' intervention but a strengthening of it. It lay with the British authorities, at home and overseas, to adopt the measures necessary to protect the indigenous populations and maintain control over the settlers' interests.[15]

The Select Committee's work opened the road to the institution of the Protectorates of Aborigines in Australia and in New Zealand, between 1838 and 1840. More generally, the Select Committee's report was a reference point for those administrators of the colonies convinced that the empire's territories should be governed in such a way as to demonstrate compassion and sympathy for its new subjects. The programmes through which the crown's representatives tried to put into practice their idea of humanitarian governance took on various forms, according to the choices of individual officials and the specific contexts. Overall, though, the policies for the protection of indigenous populations proved to be unsuccessful. On the one hand, this was because of the pressure and hostility of the settlers and on the other because those policies were not sufficiently focused on the priority of those they intended to protect: access to the land. In the space of little more than a decade, the step was made from the intention of protecting the indigenous peoples to that of integrating them within the settlers' communities, which had by now grown and stabilised. The words used to describe this project by George Grey, governor in Cape Colony between 1854 and 1861, are significant. Speaking about the region of British Kaffraria, Grey imagined that it would be transformed into a province populated in part by Europeans, in part by the local natives – the Xhosa. The latter, said the governor, would have to be 'won by our exertions to Christianity, trained by us in agriculture and simple arts', and to be made 'accustomed to our ways and aware of their advantages, attached to us from a sense of benefits received'.[16] The colonial administration had to arrange the instruction, relief and training of the indigenous people, winning over their gratitude and transforming them into civilised subjects and good Christians. The pursuit of this transformation was the linchpin of the humanitarian governance that was tried out in the territories of the British empire.

Colonialism, civilisation and the demonstration of humanity did not cross over only in Britain's imperial politics. This crossover marked the entire history of imperialism, albeit in different formats. For example, in the France of the Third Republic, the twin call to the *mission civilisatrice* and the moral duty of liberating the non-European peoples oppressed by ignorance and illnesses took on specific characteristics. The conviction that France had the task of bringing civilisation to the populations of its colonies did not arise of course in this phase, characterised by a renewed expansionist impulse, but acquired a particular resonance with the return of the democratic institutions. The new government dealt with the need to reconcile aggressive imperialism with the republican ideals that inspired it, and the notion of *mission civilisatrice* was a cornerstone in this regard. It was rooted in the certainty of French society's moral and material superiority but also in the perfectibility of human nature. It was thought that the Asian and African peoples could follow a path of growth and learning that would enable them to capitalise on the potential they had been gifted with as human beings.[17]

The emancipatory impulse and the trust in both its rationality and its scientific understanding guided the policies of the metropolis and the choices of the colonial officials, who had as their objective the liberation of the colonies' subjects from everything that determined their state of prostration and suffering: ignorance, illnesses, the threats of a naturally savage environment, the dangers of unhealthy living conditions. Let us try to see, through an example, how these assumptions were translated in projects and works carried out in the colonies. A significant case study is the work by the governor general of West French Africa, founded in 1895. Ernest Roume, the governor sent a few years after to Dakar, dedicated himself to the systematic exploitation of local resources but at the same time he intended to raise the material conditions in which the indigenous populations were living. His view was that measures aimed at improving the state of health of the colony's subjects were of particular importance. Roume therefore started a sanitation programme, and this became the preferred way of deploying relief to distant peoples for the colonial administrations.

The programme's main aim was to tackle smallpox, malaria and yellow fever, through the recruitment of doctors and paramedical staff, the disinfection of stagnant waters and the use of smallpox vaccine. Apart from the individual measures, it aimed above all at a radical change in Africans' way of living. The medical staff had to work in close contact with the local administrators to teach the villagers the basic rules of sanitation, which included instructions for both digging wells and collecting rubbish, as well as guidelines for looking after the home and the person. The intention was to replace what the French administration considered to be unhealthy ancestral habits with modern hygienic precautions.[18]

Although it followed specific directions, the programme promoted in West Africa was in line with the medical and scientific culture that marked the public debate and the sanitation policies in the metropolis. In republican France, the 'bacteriological revolution' – developed from the 1860s and 1870s, thanks to the theories of scientists like Koch and Pasteur – had changed public health policies. In the years before Roume's arrival in Dakar, a movement of French professionals had promoted a campaign for the centralisation, standardisation and modernisation of national sanitary policies. The arguments used and the demands made by this campaign were a reference point, culturally and politically, for colonial administrators such as Ernest Roume.[19] Their measures revealed not only the interaction between the metropolis and the imperial territories, but also the role played by Western science in determining the criteria and practices through which the aid and relief operations looked to bring assistance to other peoples.

The results of the programme developed in West Africa did not repay the trust placed by Roume in science as the driver of civilisation. The impossibility of operating effectively over all the territory under the administration's jurisdiction forced it to choose specific areas in which to concentrate its interventions. The cities, where most of the French people lived, were given preference while the vast rural areas, where most of the local population was to be found, were ignored. Moreover, the improvements in hygiene conditions in the cities were actually very modest, as a result both of the lack of resources and specialist staff and of the difficulty of introducing Western convictions about public and personal hygiene to the African populations.[20] At the end of Roume's mandate, however, sanitation remained an important sector in the administration of French western Africa and, more generally, a crucial question in the interpretation of the *mission civilisatrice* as a demonstration of responsibility for and sensitivity to the condition of the peoples in the colonies.

Philanthropists around the world

The improvement of the conditions, both material and moral, of non-European people did not come into play only in the politics supported by the metropolises in the colonies or in their interpretation by the empire's officials. The issue was also central to the missionary movement. From the late eighteenth century, and for over a century after that, many men and women, driven by strong religious faith, left their home countries for far and unknown places, following or anticipating the way colonial empires were built. The evangelisation of 'pagan' people was their main concern but the common objective was to facilitate a process of transformation that would guarantee a higher quality of earthly living conditions as well as salvation in the afterlife. The religious and secular agendas were inevitably intertwined in the projects developed by missionary-philanthropists: the redemption of the souls of African and Asian people and the improvement of their material living conditions were two effects of the same goal.

The intersection of the two agendas is also clear when we look at associations started to support – financially, morally and logistically – missionary programmes. For example, in Britain, eighteenth-century evangelical revivalism was the impulse that founded the Baptist Missionary Society (1792), the London Missionary Society (1795) and the Church Missionary Society (1799). These organisations were formed in relation with the abolitionist movement and followed the example of the Abolition Society: some of their founders were well known anti-slavery advocates and they tried to pressure institutions to gain their support. At the same time, the new societies were closely connected to the pre-existing religious philanthropic associations, and they extended their voluntary work beyond national borders. British missionary societies combined evangelisation with the condemnation of slavery and with a commitment to care and aid efforts. This commitment grew stronger as the empire expanded and the number of missions increased.[21]

The relationship between philanthropy exercised in Britain and missionary activities carried out in the colonies is also described in the biographies of many who were dedicated to charity and aid in their home countries before they left for other continents. The connection between the two choices – to take care of the poor in their home countries and of indigenous people in Africa and Asia – is not important only because they were both motivated by the moral duty to alleviate the suffering of other human beings by taking care of them. The crossover of home and overseas philanthropy is important because it meant, as we previously highlighted in relation to anti-slavery, that a transcontinental circulation was under way of beliefs and practices regarding the acknowledgement of people in need and the taking of action.[22] This intertwining was so common that it became the subject of literary fiction. An enlightening example is Charlotte Yonge's novel *The Daisy Chain* (1856), which was a bestseller in England in the nineteenth century, although it was later largely forgotten. The protagonist, Ethel, was driven by a profoundly altruistic spirit. She first dedicated herself to the impoverished community of Cocksmoor, the fictional town where she lived, and then to the people of the Loyalty Islands in the South Pacific. The young woman, in fact, had decided to stand beside her brother when he chose to become a missionary. Yonge based Ethel's character on the stories told by prominent people she knew in the missionary environment. When she described the poverty of Cocksmoor and the underdevelopment of the Loyalty Islands, she wanted to highlight the link between charity work at home and a growing global movement in aid for the indigenous people of the colonies.[23]

Another particularly important characteristic of British colonial philanthropy must be mentioned. The empire's officials, merchants and other money-makers were all males, while the representatives of missionary societies were men and women. As we previously observed, Charlotte Brontë's Jane Eyre refused St John's marriage proposal while *The Daisy Chain* heroine joined her brother in the Pacific. In reality, Ethel's choice was more common: many Protestant women left their homes alongside their husbands or brothers. During the initial decades of activity in the empire's territories the missions themselves encouraged couples and families to travel to the colonies so that they could be a concrete example of the Christian meaning of family.[24] In this way, women reached the territories of the empire, where they took on personal responsibilities teaching Christianity to indigenous people, mostly through catechism and the education of girls.

The impact made by women in missions was recognised in the 1830s, with the creation of the Society for the Promotion of Female Education in the East (1834), the first organisation to authorise women to leave for the colonies on their own.[25] This choice was in line with the organisation's educational activities, carried out until then by the wives and sisters of missionaries. It was born out of the intention to focus on the 'hapless daughters of the East' the 'deepest simpathies' (sic) for underdeveloped people.[26] In the preface to Society's own book about its first twelve years, its most authoritative source, the Reverend Noel, observed that the work of young women volunteers in Cairo, in Borneo and on the Malaysian peninsula could only 'excite the interest and command the cooperation of every person who has either zeal for religion or compassion for human sorrow'.[27] With these words Noel legitimised the work of women missionaries, who contributed to the evangelisation supported by every good Christian and who followed the moral duty – shared by every human being – to alleviate others' sufferings.

Looking at women's work in British missions allows us to highlight an important element of the archaeology of humanitarianism that we are tracing. Women gradually earned a key role in anti-slavery initiatives in their home countries – as we have seen – as well as in colonial philanthropy. Being involved in these activities meant women could access unexplored areas and could have a stronger presence in the public sphere. At the same time, their work was limited to the fields considered to be feminine: childcare, assistance to mothers and education of young girls. This range of activities carried out on various continents helped to reshape the definitions of the gender roles that defined Western societies. The task assigned to women was to ensure that the women of Cairo, Borneo and Malaysia achieved the same moral virtues that their teachers, tutors and healthcare assistants possessed. In fact, a crucial part of the project to improve the living conditions of colonised people was teaching them to be loving mothers, capable wives and good Christians, by reinterpreting and renegotiating models of motherhood, family and faith based on the culture that the educators came from. An important aspect of the history of international humanitarianism thus emerged: gender difference contributes to determining the roles of those providing aid and of the activities they organise.

Of course, the evangelical missionary movement was not limited to Britain but was widespread in countries with a significant Protestant presence. Among these, the United States is an example of how the geography of philanthropic activities did not necessarily develop hand in hand with the growth of a colonial empire, as was the case with Britain. In the case of the United States, the efforts of evangelical churches to Christianise 'pagan' people surged at the end of the nineteenth century. Missions were seen as the outposts of a growing American culture, which was able to show compassion in the face of the suffering of far-away people and at the same time export its high level of civilisation abroad.[28] For example, US missionary initiatives in the Philippines were in line with the agenda of the

American colonial administration and in countries such as China and Japan they developed alongside the political and economic interests of the US government. Overall, the actions of the missionary movement reached a very broad horizon and created a network of global action that connected projects developed in Asia and the Middle East with the Christianisation and the aid work carried out in the home countries.[29] For example, a small organisation such as the Women's Missionary Federation – founded in 1865 and an expression of the Norwegian Lutheran Church of America – was active in China, South Africa and Madagascar, but also in Alaska and on Native American reservations.[30] Evangelisation, relief and civilisation evolved together and constituted the key points of a new transnational moral order, represented by the American missionary movement.[31]

The US schools, hospitals, clinics and orphanages built all over the world depended on missionaries working there but also on the support they received from the home country. The men and women – by the end of the nineteenth century, two-thirds of the population of missions were women – who worked in the field were also the correspondents on the bulletins and publications of various missionary societies. The goal of these publications was to keep sympathisers interested, calling upon not only their faith but also their feelings. For example, in 1874 *Woman's Work for Woman*, published by American Presbyterian women missionaries, asked its readers for prayers but also for 'sympathy' and 'interest',[32] necessary to actively engage and bring concrete change. Lotteries, markets and 'missionary teas' organised in the home countries were opportunities to raise funds for the evangelisation of and aid to 'pagan people' but also to spread among compatriots 'missionary intelligence', which was the ability to empathise with others' sufferings and the will to sacrifice oneself to end them.[33]

The twin appeal, to faith and to the sense of belonging to the one big family that is humanity, was a central element of the promotional narratives associated with Catholic efforts in aid of 'distant sufferers'. A significant example is the mobilisation campaign launched by child protection organisations in the mid-nineteenth century, when Catholic missions gained renewed momentum. The most notable was the Holy Childhood Association, founded in 1843 by the Bishop of Nancy, which soon reached all of Catholic Europe and North America. It was started following the reports of missionaries who denounced infanticide and the abandonment of children as common practices in China. On the one hand, the Holy Childhood Association supported Catholic missions in China so that they welcomed abandoned and unwanted children and babies in dedicated residences and raised them in a Christian fashion; on the other, it promoted the fundraising necessary to sustain local initiatives. It used the publication of appeals, leaflets, handbooks, brochures and reports to sensitise and inform Western Catholics and to encourage their donations.[34]

The texts they circulated – in line with philanthropic beliefs of the nineteenth century – insisted upon the innocence and helplessness of children, who were presented as the human beings who most needed protection and guidance. In turn, the children of China needed protection and guidance the most, because of the level of their suffering. In the history of humanity, the Christian world had stood out for the importance it attached to protecting childhood: this is the message that the Holy Childhood Association reiterated when encouraging its followers to contribute to the cause. Doing so would be proof that they were good Christians and would fulfil a moral duty. On the other hand, the Chinese 'pagans' showed inhumanity by letting innocent creatures suffer. The juxtaposition of their behaviour and the Christian effort 'contributed to a discourse that took the treatment of childhood and the status of child welfare as yardsticks of civilization'.[35] The moral condemnation of the Chinese became an integral part of the narratives used to present, support and legitimise the work of Catholic missionaries with abandoned children. The extensive and lively Chinese philanthropic activities, which boasted a long tradition, remained in the shadows.[36]

It is difficult to summarise these disparate elements of the complex history of the missionary movement. They can only show some of the ways in which the missionary experience contributed to the archaeology of international humanitarianism. Firstly, we highlighted the link between faith and compassion, understood as a moral duty no human being can avoid. This link was the basis for the intertwining of the religious and the secular agenda, the double objective being to secure for far-away people salvation in the afterlife and an improvement of their material living conditions. We must not forget that this intertwining generated the motivations and practices that during the nineteenth century made Western people familiar with relief for children, women and men in distant and unknown territories.

The other key aspect is the tendency of aid programmes in the colonies to use a prescriptive approach: the 'benefactors' made themselves interpreters of the needs of indigenous people, assigned them a hierarchy of priority and arbitrarily decided what the solutions should be. This certainly does not mean they were not able to recognise the differences in the social and cultural contexts in which they were working: often missionaries lived among the locals – they knew their traditions and they made them known in the West through networks in which missionaries shared information and experience. Furthermore, the aid programmes were always the outcome of redefinition, adapting and negotiation between Western philanthropists and local populations. However, missionaries did not recognise the partiality of their projects and their principles. In the context of philanthropic activities carried out in the overseas territories of European empires for over a century, the will and the ability to provide relief were constantly associated with the conviction of Europeans that they were informed guides, able to show others the solution to their condition of suffering. As we previously observed regarding the anti-slavery movement, this paternalistic approach is a key to interpretation of the entire history of international humanitarianism.[37]

Notes

1   Charlotte Brönte, *Jane Eyre* (Oxford: Oxford University Press, 1993 [first edition 1847]), pp. 423–424.
2   Cora Kaplan, 'Imagining Empire: History, Fantasy and Literature', in C. Hall and Sonya O. Rose (eds), *At Home with the Empire: Metropolitan Culture and the Imperial World* (Cambridge: Cambridge University Press, 2006), pp. 191–211; David Deirdre, *Rule Britannia: Women, Empire and Victorian Writing* (Ithaca, NY: Cornell University Press, 1995), pp. 5–7.
3   Andrew Porter, 'Trusteeship, Anti-slavery, and Humanitarianism', in A. Porter (ed.), *The Oxford History of British Empire, Vol. III: The Nineteenth Century* (New York: Oxford University Press, 2001), pp. 198–221; on the origins and developments of political trustee-ship in England see Kevin Grant, 'Trust and Self-determination: Anglo-American Ethics of Empire and International Government', in Mark Bevir and Frank Trentmann (eds), *Critiques of Capital in Modern Britain and America: Transatlantic Exchanges 1800 to the Present Day* (London: Palgrave, 2002), pp. 150–173.
4   Porter, 'Trusteeship, Anti-Slavery, and Humanitarianism'.
5   *Ibid.*
6   Emily Eden, *Up the Country: Letters from India* (London: Virago, 1983), pp. 64, 65.
7   James Vernon, *Hunger: A Modern History* (Cambridge, MA: Harvard University Press, 2007), pp. 17–40.
8   Sanjay Sharma, *Famine, Philanthropy and the Colonial State: North India in the Early Nineteenth Century* (New York: Oxford University Press, 2001).
9   *Ibid.*
10 Peter Walker and Daniel Maxwell, *Shaping the Humanitarian World* (London: Routledge, 2009), p. 18.
11 Sharma, *Famine, Philanthropy and the Colonial State*.
12 Alan Lester and Fae Dussart, *Colonization and the Origins of Humanitarian Govern-ance: Protecting Aborigines across the Nineteenth-Century British Empire* (Cambridge: Cambridge University Press, 2014), p. 23.
13 Porter, 'Trusteeship, Anti-Slavery, and Humanitarianism', pp. 209–210.
14 Lester and Dussart, *Colonization and the Origins of Humanitarian Governance*, pp. 86–89.
15 *Ibid.*, pp. 86–104.
16 *Ibid.*, p. 252.
17 Alice L. Conklin, 'Colonialism and Human Rights, a Contradiction in Terms? The Case of France and West Africa, 1895–1914', *American Historical Review*, 103:2 (1998), pp. 419–442; see also Adam J. Davis and Bertrand Taithe, 'From the Purse and the Heart: Exploring Charity, Humanitarianism, and Human Rights in France', *French Historical Studies*, 34:3 (2011), pp. 413–432.
18 Alice L. Conklin, *A Mission to Civilize: The Republican Idea of Empire in France and West Africa, 1895–1930* (Stanford, CA: Stanford University Press, 1997), pp. 40–72.
19 *Ibid.*
20 *Ibid.*
21 Andrew Porter, *Religion Versus Empire? British Protestant Missionaries and Overseas Expansion, 1700–1914* (Manchester: Manchester University Press, 2004), pp. 39–63.
22 Alan Lester and David Lambert, 'Geographies of Colonial Philanthropy', *Progress in Human Geography*, 28:3 (2004), pp. 320–341.

23   Talia Sheffer, 'Taming the Tropics: Charlotte Yonge Takes on Melanesia', *Victorian Studies*, 47:2 (2005), pp. 204–214.

24   On the exemplary value given to the family in missionary discourse see Esme Cleall, *Missionary Discourses of Difference: Negotiating Otherness in the British Empire, 1840–1900* (London: Palgrave Macmillan, 2012), pp. 29–47.

25   Patricia Grimshaw and Peter Sherlock, 'Women and Cultural Exchanges', in N. Etherington (ed.), *Missions and Empire* (Oxford: Oxford University Press, 2005), pp. 173–192; Jane Haggis, 'White Women and Colonialism: Towards a Non-recuperative History', in C. Midgley (ed.), *Gender and Imperialism* (Manchester: Manchester University Press, 2003), pp. 45–75.

26   Society for the Promotion of Female Education in the East, *History of the Society for the Promotion of Female Education in the East* (London: Edward Suter, 1847), p. 5.

27   *Ibid.*, p. viii.

28   Ian Tyrrel, *Reforming the World: The Creation of America's Moral Empire* (Princeton, NJ: Princeton University Press, 2010), pp. 49–73.

29   Merle E. Curti, *American Philanthropy Abroad: A History* (New Brunswick: Rutgers University Press, 1963), pp. 99–137; Emily Rosenberg, 'Missions to the World: Philanthropy Abroad', in L. J. Friedman and M. D. McGarvie (eds), *Charity, Philanthropy, and Civility in American History* (Cambridge: Cambridge University Press, 2003), pp. 241–258.

30   Betty Ann Bergland, 'Settler Colonists, "Christian Citizenship" and the Women's Missionary Federation at the Bethany Indian Mission in Wittenberg, Wisconsin, 1884–1934', in B. Reeves-Ellington, K. K. Sklar and C. A. Shemo (eds), *Competing Kingdoms: Women, Mission, Nation, and the American Protestant Empire, 1812–1960* (Durham, NC: Duke University Press, 2010), pp. 167–197.

31   Tyrrel, *Reforming the World*, pp. 49–73.

32   'A Little Hard', *Woman's Work for Woman*, 4 (September 1874), p. 170, cited in Patricia R. Hill, *The World Their Household: The American Woman's Foreign Mission Movement and Cultural Transformation, 1870–1920* (Ann Arbor, MI: University of Michigan Press, 1985), p. 105.

33   *Ibid.*, p. 108.

34   Katharina Stornig, 'Between Christian Solidarity and Human Solidarity: Humanity and the Mobilisation of Aid for Distant Children in Catholic Europe in the Long Nineteenth Century', in F. Klose and M. Thulin (eds), *Humanity: A History of European Concepts in Practice from the Sixteenth Century to the Present* (Göttingen: Vandenhoeck & Ruprecht, 2016), pp. 249–266.

35   *Ibid.*, p. 262.

36   Caroline Reeves, 'Developing the Humanitarian Image in Late Nineteenth- and Early Twentieth- Century China', in H. Fehrenbach and D. Rodogno (eds), *Humanitarian Photography: A History* (New York: Cambridge University Press, 2015), pp. 115–139.

37   Michael Barnett thinks paternalism is part 'of the very nature of humanitarianism' (Barnett, *Empire of Humanity*, p. 12).

Part II

Humanitarianism in wartime

The spectacle, which was visible everywhere at daybreak on 25 June, was a fearful one. The dead were so thick that we had to shift them away to set up the tents: half-dressed, bloated and blackened, they were lying in every position. Wounded horses dragged themselves forward, neighing; others, disembowelled, threw themselves down. Overturned carriages, shattered gun carriages, broken weapons, equipment, blood-covered rags covered the countryside [...].

That immense desolation remained for days and days until teams of farm-workers, lined out in rows, had finished gathering the corpses up into the huge holes dug for the purpose.

We became so accustomed to this pitiful work that we were no longer even aware of it. We gave commiserations to the wounded that were found still alive after many hours, after whole days of abandonment on the field.[1]

These are the words Giulio Adamoli, a volunteer in the army of the Kingdom of Sardinia, used in his memoirs to describe the battlefield of Solferino, the day after the victory won by the Franco-Piemontese forces over the Austrian army on 24 June 1859. It had been a particularly bloody battle, in which around 40,000 men were killed or seriously wounded; many of the latter died because of a lack of treatment. The evocative power of the blood spilled near the little northern Italian town is commonly associated with the birth of the Red Cross, and Solferino has become the symbolic place of the origins of international humanitarianism. It was here – after witnessing the harrowing spectacle of the wounded abandoned on the field – that Henry Dunant, from Geneva, had the idea of an organisation for aid to soldiers and he followed up on his plan immediately afterwards. Humanitarianism – in the version that became accepted over time, and which has influenced one part of its studies – ended up being represented simply as the 'good creature' that came to life out of the horrors of war.

Historiography has now effectively called into question the trend of overlapping the foundation of the Red Cross and the origins of humanitarianism,[2] but the birth in Geneva of the International Committee of the Red Cross (ICRC) definitely marked a turning point. It led to the completion of acts that were already in progress, it catalysed the different forces in action and it intercepted shared opinions and feelings. In the first instance, the new organisation directed aid and treatment work towards war victims, marking the boundaries for action that were to retain a central role for a long time. As well as this, the initiatives promoted by the Genevan committee as early as the beginning of the 1860s for soldiers struck by enemy fire or illness encouraged the process of interpenetration between humanitarianism and warfare. This took a leap forward in the Franco-Prussian War and then again in the First World War. At the same time, Europe took centre stage for humanitarian operations. This principally Eurocentric perspective lasted for around a century, intertwining itself with the redefinition of both the geopolitical map of Europe and the international balance of power.

We can identify in the path of action followed by the Genevan committee certain elements that, in the ensuing decades, characterised the development of the international aid system. One element was the emergence of groups with a specific humanitarian vocation – caring for war victims. These new entities often drew their impulse from religious philanthropy but they were also connected to the different expressions of the growing international activism. An important example is the Save the Children Fund, which, founded in 1919, had a threefold origin: the British philanthropic tradition; the spirit of internationalism that condemned the punitive Treaty of Versailles; and the network of supranational cooperation that intertwined itself with feminist associations. This humanitarian organisation dedicated to aid for children was only one of the ever more numerous bodies on the wartime and post-war scenes, each with its own distinctive symbol, like the ICRC's red cross on a white background – the star of the Friends, or the Young Men's Christian Association's triangle with its apex pointing downwards.

These new groups expressed their private commitment in a context in which humanitarian issues were the subject of increasing public, governmental and inter-governmental interest. This attention had already been captured and put to use by the far-sighted ICRC but it was now developing more clearly. Its initial stages are seen in programmes in the League of Nations' social affairs section, then the creation of *ad hoc* government agencies – like the American Relief Administration set up by the US government in 1919 – and finally the mandate given to some UN agencies. By referencing these major steps we can state that the institutionalisation process was one of the cornerstones of the definition of the modern humanitarian system, since national governments and supranational bodies over time acquired greater responsibilities in the context of relief for suffering humanity.

We must not, however, consider that the increasingly significant role taken on by these governmental and intergovernmental institutions was an inevitable or inescapable process of humanitarianism's modernisation, or that this development was opposed to the development of the non-governmental organisations (or indeed opposed by them). Vice versa, the expansion of the skills and interests of states or intergovernmental agencies went side by side with that of association building. The interaction between the different groups was decisive in the development of humanitarian practices and policies. To mention just one example that we will come back to in more depth, the associations' activism – which applied different forms of pressure but also made their expertise available – was decisive in the launch of the League of Nations' humanitarian initiatives. Reconstructing the path of humanitarianism through the programmes of the governmental agencies and the intergovernmental bodies by following the dynamics through which aid policies became part of international relations is therefore necessary but not sufficient. We must broaden the picture to include the non-governmental organisations and understand how far their actions also answered forms of collective mobilisation or public opinion campaigns; above all, we must follow the relationships of collaboration, comparison and mutual conditioning between the various players who were central to the deployment of international aid. It is only in this way that we can describe – together with the history of the organisations – how, historically, humanitarianism's fields of intervention were defined, how the recipients were identified and how the relief practices were shaped.

This is what is attempted in the following pages, starting from the first phase of development of the Red Cross and the establishment of a war humanitarianism planned for soldiers. However, the fact that certain smaller-scale aid operations – such as the Quakers' – were directed exclusively at civilians from the time of the Franco-Prussian War is not forgotten. With the First World War and its dramatic impact on European societies, the experience gained over the previous decades was forced to progress far beyond aid to the wounded. It had to deal with a situation marked by the impoverishment and hunger of civilian populations who were exhausted by the long years of war, by epidemics, and by the enforced movements of men and women as a result of wartime events and also the redefinition of state borders set out in peace treaties. The programmes with an international scope, as they developed within the fragile European order, had a fundamental role in identifying the specific subjects to direct aid to. In line with the debate and actions of the philanthropic tradition, the care of infants, for example, was established as having a leading role as a form of humanitarian relief, a prominent position that had been strengthened by the figure of the child as the perfect example of an innocent war victim. The emergence of refugee populations as recipients of aid was significant. So too was the consequent introduction of the criteria and procedures to establish which fleeing civilians could be placed in the category of 'recipients' of what the international community was prepared to make available. These two great areas of intervention (children and refugees) remained the primary concerns while the world of humanitarianism began to be populated by professionals. These professionals, male and female, tended to move between the different centres of what we would call today 'humanitarian crises', and to serve different organisations at different times, passing from religious associations to intergovernmental agencies and thereby circulating particular sets of relief practices through a variety of contexts.

The violence and destruction of the Second World War brought an unimaginable degree of civilian suffering and need, which in turn gave humanitarianism a specific meaning. For the victorious powers, and the United States in particular, the display of empathy towards the war's victims amounted to a test of civilisation against the enemy's barbarities. The aid to the populations who had been the object of Nazi-Fascist aggression made up an integral part of the reconstruction plan and became the symbol of a new beginning in the history of humanitarianism. Feeding and clothing civilians – children in particular – giving out basic medical care, stopping the spread of epidemics: these remained the main activities of the international programmes, whose intentions, though, were reformulated in the light of humanitarianism's new aspirations. For example, the conviction – already widely held in the philanthropic tradition – was emphasised that aid and care should go beyond immediate relief and bring a genuine 'rehabilitation', physical and moral, to the recipients.

The interpretations of this 'rehabilitative' process remained varied, ambiguous and at times contradictory. They partly recalled the welfare policies launched by the New Deal and this was also the reason why many American social workers entered the ranks of the first UN agency – the United Nations Relief and Rehabilitation Administration (UNRRA). At the same time, the creation of the aid programmes was inspired by the previous experiences of post-war relief, thanks also to the staff who had acquired their own skills immediately after the First World War in the setting of the League of Nations or non-governmental organisations. Undoubtedly, the post-Second World War era was a great laboratory for humanitarianism. Within it, old and new convictions, practices and skills interwove themselves and were reformulated, standardised and ratified. In this sense, the UN agencies, with their mandate for leadership and coordination, had a major role, progressively conditioned by the dynamics of the emerging Cold War.

Notes

1   Giulio Adamoli, *Da San Martino a Mentana: Ricordi di un volontario* (Milan: Fratelli Treves, 1892), p. 76, cited in Nina Quarenghi, *Solferino e San Martino tra realtà e memoria* (Verona: Cierre, 1999), p. 54.
2   Bertrand Taithe, 'The "Making" of the Origins of Humanitarianism?', *Contemporanea: Rivista di storia dell'800 e del '900*, 18:3 (2015), pp. 489–496.

3

La guerre et la charité

The Crimean War in 1854 brought to light a heroine who has become one of the great figures of our times because of her altruism and courage: Florence Nightingale. [...] Her self-sacrifice at the bedside [of the wounded] echoed throughout the world and made the souls ready to understand the humanitarian message. Dunant, the 'man in white', who with his own hands took care of over a thousand wounded at Solferino and gained the fraternal collaboration of the Piedmontese farmworkers in this assistance, was able to count straightaway on the support of public opinion, which recalled Florence Nightingale, *the lady with the lamp*, who at Scutari toured silently between the wounded soldiers' beds.[1]

This is how Henri Coursier introduced the figure of Henry Dunant, the Swiss businessman, linking him to the equally famous Florence Nightingale, the British nurse. It is one of the most important passages in a volume that recalled, on the centenary of the battle of Solferino, the crucial events in the foundation of the Red Cross and the emergence of the revolutionary mission that characterised it. Coursier, who worked for the International Committee of the Red Cross (ICRC), was attempting to provide a well structured framework of the political and social reasons that a century before had led to the foundation of a new organisation dedicated to the care of soldiers wounded in combat. But even his narrative ended up highlighting the brave deeds of individual people. This emphasis recurs frequently in the celebratory historical reconstructions underlining the Red Cross's pioneering role in organised humanitarian action.

In this respect, the portrayal of Henry Dunant is instructive. On the bloody battlefield of Solferino the thirty-year-old from Geneva earned the label of 'hero' not for being distinguished in combat but for saving the wounded. He was deeply moved by the suffering of the injured soldiers and devoted himself to their care; he involved local people in his aid work by appealing to the pity every human being should feel for fellow beings in distress. It was the strength of this appeal that stirred the spirits of many other men and women when *A Memory of Solferino* was published in 1862. This pamphlet described with great intensity and in detail his experience in Piemonte. 'The man in white' – as he was later to be called, in reference to his colonial clothing style but also to the purity of his moral values – concluded his account of the events at Solferino with a call to set up 'societies for the relief of the wounded in the different European countries' that would place on the battlefield 'voluntary orderlies and voluntary nurses, zealous, trained and experienced'.[2] His pamphlet had enormous success, and Dunant himself personally made every possible effort to ensure that his proposal to create 'societies for the relief of the wounded' did not fall on deaf ears. And so he passed into history as the father of the Red Cross, founded in 1863.

Dunant's character is usually juxtaposed with that of Gustave Moynier, another prominent figure on the 'Committee of Five', out of which the ICRC later came into being. A lawyer and a distinguished member of Geneva's various charities, his realism and rationalism were a counterpoint to Dunant's idealism and passion. The accounts that for decades dominated the subject of the origins of the Red Cross always tended to stress individual volunteer work and the sensibility and courage of individual men and women. It is a type of narrative that was certainly useful in bringing the history of a complex organisation closer to the wider public. At the same time, it created certain exemplary figures and strengthened the idea that the whole meaning of humanitarian actions is enclosed within the goodwill of the person performing them and in the strength of self-sacrifice.

The history of the beginnings of the Red Cross and the role it has had in the overall path of humanitarianism is quite complex. Following the biographies of its most prominent central characters, particularly Dunant and Moynier, is a useful way of sketching all the aspects of the picture. Some of these lead us back to the transformations we saw underway in previous decades, such as the development of a new 'culture of sensibility' or the extension of Western charity's range of action. The emergence of a *philanthropie militaire* – as defined by Gustave Moynier and Luis Appia, the Swiss military doctor and another member of the 'Committee of Five'[3] – was then tied to a whole set of factors, including the modernisation of warfare and the spread of war correspondence. The latter led to public opinion receiving more detailed information on the brutality of the combat and on the suffering of the soldiers, who, with the introduction of military conscription, were no longer a handful of professionals but the 'Sons of the Nation'.

Solferino and beyond

Portraying Florence Nightingale on the same pages as the description of Henry Dunant's work was not, of course, an original idea by Coursier. The Crimean War (1853–56) and Nightingale's aid work were unavoidable precedents for the 'hero of Solferino', and they formed part of the major transformations in the conduct and perception of war. The story is well known how Florence Nightingale – a devout Christian actively involved in relief to the sick and poor, and a supporter of the

British movement for social reform – organised and personally trained a team of thirty-four volunteer nurses, who set off in 1854. The operation had already received the authorisation of the British government, which had been fighting against the Russian army for almost a year within an alliance involving France, the Ottoman empire and the Kingdom of Sardinia. The nurses led by Florence disembarked at Scutari (now a district of Istanbul), which was the headquarters of the British expedition to the Crimea. They did not restrict themselves to looking after the wounded soldiers but tried to encourage the complete reorganisation of the military hospitals. The very high mortality rates at these hospitals were due to infectious illnesses and a lack of treatment rather than the seriousness of the wounds received on the battlefield.

All of this became sadly well known to the British public, who were struck by the state of the soldiers' abandonment but also by the figure of Florence Nightingale, and she was soon known as 'the lady with the lamp'. The unmistakable reference to the British nurse came from an article in *The Times* celebrating the self-sacrifice of the woman dedicated to taking care of the wounded in the hospitals of Scutari, which were totally inadequate to the size of the emergency:

> She is a 'ministering angel' without any exaggeration in those hospitals, and as her slender form glides quietly along each corridor, every poor fellow's face softens with gratitude at the sight of her. When all the medical officers have retired for the night and silence and darkness have settled down upon those miles of prostrate sick, she may be observed alone, with a little lamp in her hand, making her solitary rounds.[4]

The reference to the lamp naturally invoked the image of the light it gave off and accentuated the angelic portrayal of Nightingale. In its turn, this portrayal was a counterpoint to the description of the overcrowded wards and the unhygienic conditions in which the hospitalised soldiers had been abandoned. The 'ministering angel' had to fight against the military authorities' indifference to the soldiers who were now unfit for duty. It was no coincidence that it was a *Times* journalist who penned the classic description of Florence Nightingale. The famous English newspaper's correspondents played a leading role in reporting the Crimean War, 'the first subject of modern reportage',[5] followed soon after by the Italian Wars of Independence. In fact, around the middle of the nineteenth century, the 'communication revolution' – attributable primarily to the use of the telegraph, the development of the railway network and the spread of the popular press – significantly changed information about war. The news arrived more quickly from the battlefields, reached more people, provided better details and allowed the conflict's progress to be followed more closely. All of this enabled those who were far from the scenes of battle to have a much greater sense of involvement.

Naturally, the more detailed and comprehensive circulation of war news interacted with the 'culture of sensibility'. As we have seen, it had begun to spread from the middle of the previous century and had permeated far-reaching initiatives aimed at relieving, or putting an end to, others' suffering. A humanitarian impulse contributed to the new pity for those mangled on the battlefield. It was the same impulse that had equally driven – and was still driving – the voluntary societies looking after the needy at home, the anti-slavery movement and the philanthropists operating overseas in the colonial territories. It is no surprise, then, that the nickname of the 'lady with the lamp' for Florence Nightingale was given by Henry Wadsworth Longfellow, the American poet. Longfellow was a public supporter of anti-slavery who, in his poem *Santa Filomena* (1857), looked at the example of the British nurse and celebrated her assistance of the soldiers as one of the noblest acts of human compassion.[6]

The Crimean War, the example of the 'lady with the lamp' and her energetic campaign to improve the hospitals and military medical services were important reference points for Henry Dunant. In fact, in *A Memory of Solferino* he mentioned as being 'well-known' what Florence Nightingale had 'accomplished [...] through her passionate devotion to suffering humanity'.[7] And why did his pamphlet and initiative have such great success?

Dunant came from the world of Genevan philanthropy, which had a long tradition of activism and was particularly dynamic. In the mid-nineteenth century it was at the centre of a dense network of contacts and projects with other European countries. Henry grew up in a family that followed Calvinist revivalism, which had found many followers in the Swiss city after the end of the Napoleonic wars. He was fervently religious and since he was a boy had been a member of one of the many associations dedicated to assisting the poor. He had later been one of the founders of the local section of the Union Chrétienne de Jeunes Gens, the Christian youth association founded in Paris in 1852 on the model of the Young Men's Christian Association (YMCA – an acronym we will come across again), which had come into being in London some years before. Apart from being a philanthropist he was a young businessman and it seems that his journey to Piedmont was to meet Napoleon III in order to obtain some trade licences in Algeria.[8] But certainly his long experience in religious charity work influenced both his reaction to the mangled bodies on the battlefield and the words and the tone he later chose to relate his own experience. The brief 'memory' was intended to be a book that 'no one could read without feeling a deep emotion'; 'the subject matter was so pitiful and the descriptions so frightening that no person of good will would have been able to reject the formula proposed in conclusion',[9] that of setting up, in peace time, associations of volunteers for relief to the soldiers.

It was this proposal that struck Gustave Moynier, one of the selected readers to whom Dunant sent his pamphlet. It is interesting to reflect on the reasons for this interest in the idea launched by the 'hero of Solferino'. A lawyer and part of an upper-middle-class Genevan family, Moynier was the typical mid-nineteenth century utilitarian philanthropist dedicated to the material and spiritual assistance of the new working classes. He was a devout Christian but did not share Dunant's passionate evangelism. He had already given many years of his life to the harsh promotion of initiatives such as the battle against alcoholism and child mortality, or the care of orphans. In 1859 he had become president of the Geneva Society for Public Utility, an association of philanthropists started thirty years before through the goodwill of the more enlightened citizens. On the one hand, the idea of creating organisations dedicated to the care of soldiers responded to the moral duty of the practising Christian to follow the parable of the Good Samaritan in the face of the horrors of contemporary warfare and to defend the value of human life. On the other hand, that very idea was in line with the aims and plans of the charitable world familiar to Moynier. It therefore seemed appropriate to him to discuss the proposal launched by Dunant within the Society for Public Utility.[10]

From the discussion it emerged that the importance the president had recognised in the questions brought up in *A Memory of Solferino* were largely shared in the Society. It gave the task of following up the initiative to a small group made up of Moynier himself, Henry Dunant and three other influential members of the Society and this was the beginning of the 'Committee of Five'. Who were the 'expert philanthropists' summoned to flank the more well known figures of Moynier and Dunant? Théodore Maunoir and Luis Appia were both physicians and surgeons with a great deal of experience behind them in medical charity and military medicine. The final member of the committee was General Guillaume Henri Dufour, who was famous for having led the confederate army against the 'rebel cantons' in the Sonderbund War (1847). The members who remained less well known brought to the committee – the driving force behind the Red Cross coming into existence – the skills, the convictions and a network of contacts from medical charity and military medicine, but also from the military world.

The coexistence of such diverse experiences and approaches was enabled by a background assumption: the intention of the new organisation and the plan behind it was not to put an end to all war but to 'humanise' it. Dunant had brought a dramatic image back from the Battle of Solferino and launched an appeal for wounded soldiers to be cared for independently of their uniforms; his pamphlet had at its core the neutrality of relief but it did not contain any references to pacifism. In their *La guerre e la charité* – published in 1867 with the idea of giving a theoretical and programmed vision to the emerging Red Cross movement – Gustave Moynier and Luis Appia argued for the need to oppose the cruelty of war but did not explicitly condemn it. The two authors believed that the atrocities committed during military interventions were the disproof that European society had reached the highest level of civilisation and put ever getting there at risk. Guaranteeing the relief of sick and wounded soldiers meant reducing the degree of cruelty of war and therefore contributing to the advance of Western civilisation. The two most intellectually distinguished members of the

'Committee of Five' reinterpreted in the context of war relief the convictions and reflections of the charity culture of the time. They also restated the idea, which we saw put forward in previous decades, that the humanitarian impulse was a symbol of civilisation. So humanitarianism in war did not come into being as an equal and opposite reaction to warmongering in the same way that the pacifist movement had developed in the mid-nineteenth century. It began instead as a way of easing the wounds resulting from armed conflicts.

The small group set up by the Society for Public Utility soon transformed itself into an independent body. It took the name of International Committee to Assist the War Wounded, which was later changed to International Committee of the Red Cross. In 1863 the Committee organised a major international conference to promote its plan. The event was held in Geneva and involved the main figures of European charity, doctors and various other professionals, and also government representatives. The influential network of the Committee members' contacts and the diplomatic missions led by Dunant on the back of his success played a fundamental role in convincing the authorities in various countries (including Prussia, Britain and France)[11] to take part in this non-official event organised by a private body. This was one of the initiative's most important aspects – its development outside of the already established alliances between the European powers, involving small and large states at the same time.[12]

The final resolution approved at the end of the conference was substantially loyal to what Moynier and the other organisers had set out. The document called for the constitution in every country of voluntary associations that in wartime would be asked to cooperate with army medical services to arrange adequate aid for the wounded. The associations had to coordinate with the military authorities and prepare the staff, who would have to operate on the battlefield and behind the lines. It was also planned that the individual organisations would remain in constant contact with each other to share their experiences and maintain a joint course of action. The Genevan committee was given a lead role in this. The concluding recommendations concerned, firstly, the relationship between national states and the future associations: the latter would have to be sponsored by their own country's government and encouraged as much as possible in the achievement of their aims. As well as this there was a request for the recognition of the neutrality of the medical staff, volunteers from the relief societies, ambulances, military hospitals and also, of course, the wounded soldiers. Finally, it was hoped the adoption of an internationally accepted emblem would guarantee the recognisability of the people and places that were to be considered neutral.

These directives had to be approved by individual governments in the setting of an international assembly in order not to remain simply recommendations. After the conference, the International Committee strove to call a congress that would bring together the state representatives and that would be able to ratify a binding agreement for the signatories. The organisation of the congress took place with the agreement of the Swiss federal government, with which Moynier and the others had initiated a close working relationship from the very beginning. The term 'international' in the official name referred to the aims but not the nature of the committee, which had its roots in the Swiss context. The official meeting of the representatives of sixteen governments – including France, Prussia, Russia, Britain and, naturally, Switzerland – took place in August 1864. The convention ratified at the end of the discussions was signed by twelve of these countries. It presented the obligation to care for wounded soldiers whatever their nationality and to recognise the neutrality of doctors, volunteer assistants, ambulances and hospitals. Finally, the First Geneva Convention recommended a red cross with a white background as a distinctive emblem for the staff and the aid vehicles. This design – destined for great success – echoed the Swiss flag, switching its colours round, and at the same time referenced a powerful Christian symbol.[13]

The 1864 convention is usually seen as the founding act of the regulatory whole that was later called 'international humanitarian law'. It is worth recalling, though, that it was giving new life to proposals put forward by philosophers and lawyers at the end of the eighteenth century and to solutions that had been previously experimented with. During the eighteenth century it was not uncommon for there to be agreements between enemy armies under which hospital staff were treated as non-combatants, and sick and wounded soldiers received sufficient care to be sent back to their side rather than being made prisoners. The idea of a permanent arrangement, to be respected in all future conflicts, came out of these strictly *ad hoc* agreements. It was supported not only by legal experts but also by doctors and philanthropists from various countries. It even reached the stage of looking at the establishment of specific hospital staff for the care combatants.[14] This, though, was never put into action, which was the opposite of what happened with the proposal launched by Dunant after the Battle of Solferino: that proposal was taken up by the 'Committee of Five' and supported by most of the European powers.

In the 1860s the time was ripe for such a change thanks to the coming together of all the factors we have so far highlighted. Firstly, there was the widespread conviction that identifying with others' suffering was an expression of profound humanity. Next was the international impulse that crossed over different charity settings. Then there was the different level of collective involvement with the combatants' fates, partly due to war journalism but also partly because some military service was becoming non-voluntary. Most European countries had introduced military conscription and so the suffering experienced by the soldiers was now associated with the faces of men from home. The unknown men who received public sympathy could have been – at that very moment or in the near future – that public's very own sons. The movement for 'humanising the war' was therefore connected to a radical change in the relationship between the state, the people and the army.

The Geneva Convention and the simultaneous initiation of the first national associations for the relief to soldiers – what would go on to become the Italian, French and British Red Cross Societies – undoubtedly signalled a crucial step on the path to humanitarianism. The care of the war wounded was becoming one of its particular areas of interest, through the assistance for armed men struck down by enemy fire or illnesses. These men were granted exclusion from combatant status and the right to specific treatment. New bodies were also set up – on a national basis but connected internationally – that were dedicated to this same operational area. It is important to underline the nature of these bodies, since they were private associations that sanctioned the leading role given to the governing authorities for voluntary assistance on battlefields.

The collaboration between public authorities and private associations on assistance to war victims, sanctioned by the 1863 Geneva Convention and that of the following year, was not a completely new development. The American Civil War had provided an important precedent. In 1861 the US federal government had set up the Sanitary Commission. The Commission's members included several leading figures from the most relevant medical and charitable associations that had been active from the start of the Civil War in assisting wounded soldiers. In close collaboration with the Army Medical Bureau, the Commission had continued to supply staff for the hospitals, to look after medical supplies and to carry out work to prevent the spread of epidemics. All of this was carried out through volunteers, mostly women, and was financed through donations.[15] Despite its recognition from the government, the Sanitary Commission had kept its status as a private organisation and – as the author engaged a few years after the end of the conflict to write the Commission's history stated – counted on the 'intelligence, humanity and patriotism of the American people'.[16]

The course of action, the volunteer system and the operational methods used by the Sanitary Commission were all fairly similar to the plan of the Genevan committee, which had some material at its disposal on the relief given to troops during the American Civil War.[17] There is an interesting observation to make on how the appeal for adequate medical care for soldiers was made in a short number of years on both sides of the Atlantic. The campaign launched by Florence Nightingale – who had become a very popular figure in the United States – contributed to making it known, but it was really achieved through charitable work and it brought about a particular type of public–private interaction within a field of action that rapidly became known as 'humanitarianism'.

We should make one final observation regarding the 1864 Convention. One of the recommendations approved by the conference was not taken up. There was no mention of the commitments the governments had to take on in promoting the individual relief societies, although the ratification of the agreement certainly gave a major push to their development in the different national contexts. In certain countries – including France, Belgium, Prussia and Italy – the new bodies for relief to soldiers had been set up in 1864, grafting themselves onto existing local charities or getting medical professionals involved. In Italy, the national society for aid to the sick and wounded in war (Associazione di Soccorso ai militari feriti e malati in tempo di guerra) was established through the efforts of some members of the Italian medical society.[18] Prominent military people also took part in this founding stage: the case of the British National Society for Aid to the Sick and Wounded in War – whose first president, Colonel Robert Loyd Lindsay, was a veteran of the Crimean War[19] – is instructive. Different countries' societies came into being from particular routes and had different set-ups, primarily concerning the (formal and informal) ties that bound them to their national governments. In this first phase, the humanitarian societies that were set up within individual states were still disparate and jumbled, and it took several decades for all the societies to take the name of the Red Cross.

A few years after the first international conference in Geneva and with the growing number of signatories to the 1864 Treaty, the present and future role of the ICRC seemed less than clear in comparison with the flourishing of the national societies for the aid to soldiers. The Convention's success resulted in the emergence of an important area of activity, the regulation of armed conflicts through international laws. The International Committee immediately put itself forward as the key organisation for this issue: it did everything it could to ensure that an ever greater number governments ratified the Geneva agreements, and attempted to monitor the extent of the application of its directives. At the same time, the ICRC was acting to promote the advance of legislation for the 'humanisation' of war. One goal was reached in 1906, when the obligation to take care of soldiers irrespective of their nationality and the recognition of their rescuers' neutrality were extended from land battles to sea conflicts too.

In addition, the Genevan committee – whose president was Gustave Moynier from 1864 to 1910, Dunant having disappeared from the scene because of his involvement in a financial scandal – was attempting to coordinate the national relief societies and set out guidelines for the entire Red Cross movement. This was a difficult aim to achieve though, as the individual associations were independent and many of them had developed a direct relationship with their own governments and were taking totally separate 'national roads' to war humanitarianism.

The Franco-Prussian War (1870–71) was the first major testing ground for the Red Cross. This war tested different templates and approaches and at the same time started up a new phase in the history of relief for the victims of armed conflicts.

Battlefield testing: 1870–1914

And here we are at the Franco-Prussian War. It was here that the societies used all their active resources and struggled with exemplary energy. In 1870 they were able,

to a greater extent than in the past, to oppose the weapons of charity and those
of violence, and fight a hard war against war itself. After a useful apprenticeship
period, they took advantage of their past experiences.[20]

This is how Gustave Moynier, in his book on the history and the possible future of
the Red Cross, recalled the experience of the Franco-Prussian War. In his opinion
it had marked a leap in quality for the organisational machine that was the Red
Cross, although it had been fine-tuned up to that point. That war was the largest
armed conflict in the period between the Napoleonic Wars and 1914, and was
considered one of the first examples of modern warfare. The bloody conflict of
1870–71 certainly marked a development in the history of relief operations, which
had already been planned and also experimented with on a small scale. On this
occasion, though, they were deployed on the battlefield and emerged as specific
components of warfare.

As we have seen, during the Crimean War journalism had already played
a major role in arousing public interest in the plight of the wounded or sick
soldiers. In the Franco-Prussian War this role was greater still. The mobilisation
of the international press and the coverage of events were more wide-ranging.
For example, members of the British press competed against each other to offer
the most news items and aimed to conduct successful investigations such as
the one more than twenty years before that had denounced the British military
authorities' lack of concern for their wounded soldiers. The accounts coming
from the French territories gave such a vivid picture of the battles that an English
journalist, commenting on the 'mass of picturesque and minute detail' sent by
his colleagues, said: 'our sympathies have been brought forth almost as if our
own flesh and blood had been sufferers'.[21] So the descriptions of the war that
circulated in the daily papers fuelled the emotional involvement of a huge public.
This contributed to the legitimisation of the relief work, which, in its turn, was to
become the subject of the newspapers' attention.

The connection that was established between information and war humanitarianism was, however, even closer. As the British case showed,[22] the press
representatives and the Red Cross societies' volunteers in the battle areas
exchanged updates on the progress of the conflicts, the besieged cities and the
situations that most urgently required the arrival of aid. The description of the
war that emerged between 1870 and 1871, emphasising the suffering and the need
to provide relief, was also the result of this sharing of news, forecasts and evalua-
tions between news professionals and the new players from voluntary relief.

But who more exactly were these new players? The national societies that
had been set up at the behest of the Geneva Committee undoubtedly took on
the main role. In Moynier's history, only three of the fifteen affiliated European
societies did not mobilise to aid the wounded in the Franco-Prussian War. The
others offered their help 'in a variety of ways: financial contributions, material
goods, sending medicines and medical staff, and mobile field hospitals'.[23] The

mobilisation, then, took place firstly within the individual states through the collection of offerings of various types. The ICRC set up an office specifically designed to coordinate the aid and distribute the resources from the non-warring countries. They did so using the increasingly sophisticated international financial tools that allowed enormous sums of money to be transferred across Europe. At the same time, various national societies – including those of Britain, Switzerland and the Netherlands – sent their own volunteers and aid vehicles to the conflict zones. Naturally, the greater deployment of forces concerned the warring countries. The experiences of the Prussian Red Cross (Centralkomitee des Preußischen Vereins zur Pflege im Felde verwundeter und erkrankter Krieger) and the French society (Société de Secours aux Blessés Militaires des Armées de Terre et de Mer) turned out to be particularly important.

In the Kingdom of Prussia the question of assistance for sick or wounded soldiers had from the very beginning received careful consideration from the government and especially from the royal family. As well as this, the war with Austria in 1866 had been an important testing ground for the volunteers wearing the emblem of the Red Cross and the experience prompted the Prussian authorities to pursue a twofold policy for the organisation of relief services. On the one hand, the army's medical skills were improved, focusing on the professionalisation of the staff, a more effective allocation of resources and a hierarchical organisation of responsibilities and skills. On the other hand, the reorganisation of the voluntary body for wartime relief was planned as a mirror image of the army reorganisation. This took place through the widespread creation of training courses, the advance preparation of the necessary materials – from bandages to vehicles for transporting the wounded – and the strengthening of the central committee, which was to carry out coordination and supervision. In 1870–71 this sort of set-up showed its effectiveness even within the limits allowed by wartime emergency and the Prussian relief society worked strictly under the military authorities' control, as did all those from countries in the German confederation.[24]

At the eve of the war, however, La Société de Secours aux Blessés Militaires des Armées de Terre et de Mer was still a club for aristocrats and prestigious doctors with some experience in war aid. Although the organisation had relations with the imperial government, its structure was still weak, it had few resources and it was not well known to the French people. In fact, the campaign of voluntary donations it ran for funding at the beginning of fighting had very poor results. Then, in the midst of the conflict, a voluntary movement of aid donors developed who were supported by religious orders, charitable associations, individual municipalities and private donors. These groups of volunteers, who went around displaying the symbol of the red cross on a white background, acted independently of the civil and military authorities. It was only later that the government tried to take control of the situation by exclusively granting the Société de Secours all the aid operations, health inspections and the fundraising.[25]

The French and German cases illustrated the different paths followed by the national societies in their first years of life, but at the same time the Franco-Prussian War confirmed the deep crossover between wartime force and aid mobilisation. The impact of the Prussian Red Cross's effectiveness in significantly reducing the mortality rate became well known and, alongside the experience of the French-German conflict, the relief action in the theatre of war received wide approval. At the same time, voluntary assistance to the combatants took on the connotation of a test of national loyalty and a display of national spirit, not just in the German world. During the war, the Société de Secours had presented its work assisting the wounded as the expression of the values of the republican government, French civilisation and its respect for humanity, in contrast to the German barbarities.[26]

The experience of the French–German war had other implications too. Rationalisation, centralisation and professionalisation now became indispensable to the smooth running of the aid machine. There had to be a reconciliation between two sides: one was the appeal to compassion, emotional participation and that impulse which seemed to have pushed Henry Dunant to aid the wounded at Solferino; the other was the demand for rationality, order and competence. This drift in the argument on humanitarian action, and the principles on which it should have been inspired, did not just concern the Prussian context but seemed to be more widely shared. For example, in a long report published at the end of the war by the British aid society, this was the praise for the work of a team of volunteers that had acted behind the lines, directing help to crucial places and receiving the ambulances loaded with the wounded:

> It is impossible not to be struck with the business-like character of their work. This appears to me to be its teaching, and it shows that, under the conditions at least in which this branch was placed, it is impossible to be as precise in the administration of relief to wounded and sick men in war as it is to be in ordinary mercantile transactions.[27]

Rationality and self-discipline were therefore considered basic requirements for the successful outcome of aid operations as much as for economic operations, and the abilities required from the volunteers were identified as a result.[28] The 'hero of Solferino' had shown courage and sensibility but his followers also had to be competent, efficient and, to a certain extent, equipped with entrepreneurial spirit. The emphasis placed on reason and that placed on passion did not seem immediately reconcilable and already at this embryonic stage there was a certain ambiguity in the selection of staff dedicated to relieving the suffering of others. On the one hand, there was an appeal to an internal vocation and the compassionate impulse of sensitive souls; on the other, rationality was looked upon as an essential gift which had to support precise skills. The tension between assumed – mutually exclusive – natural inclinations and the acquisition of newly introduced qualifications became clearer later on, when professionalisation was considered one of the cornerstones of the modernisation of humanitarianism, but it already suggested the uncertain ideal profile of aid workers.

The emblem of the red cross on the white background was not the only one to appear in the areas of conflict between the French and Germans. Although it was less visible, the black and red star of the recently formed Friends' War Victims Relief Committee (FWVRC) was also present. We have already seen the prominent role played by the Quakers in the emergence of the anti-slavery movement and more generally in the vast mobilisation to bring relief to the suffering of others. From the beginning of the nineteenth century, this mobilisation among the Quakers in Britain had taken the form of action planned to respond to specific emergencies: the Greek War of Independence; the famine in Ireland; the Crimean War; and, in particular, the devastation of the coasts of Finland following British naval bombardments. That mobilisation thus comprised impromptu projects, and involved few volunteers and used limited resources. In 1870, though, the British Quakers started a specific body, which had its own symbol, and they made one of its fields of action intervention in war and post-war situations.[29]

The number of men and women wearing the black and red star on their arm in the Franco-Prussian War was naturally quite a lot lower than that of those displaying the red cross. There were around 100 of the latter from Britain, while there were around half the number of Quakers. Despite their lower numbers the Quakers were an important element. That is, in the first phase of the humanitarianism of war the Red Cross was the main player but not the only one. In addition, the work carried out by the FWVRC presents us with a different concept of assistance to war victims from the one promoted by the ICRC. In fact, the Quakers did not provide care for the soldiers – sick or wounded – but for the civilians who had been forced to evacuate, who were impoverished by the war effort or deprived of their sources of support. Robert Spence Watson – a British politician and lawyer – was one of the first volunteers to leave for France. In his diary he described his team's arrival in the small town of Woippy in Lorena and explained how they decided to distribute the Friends' aid to the local people:

> The place is well within the French lines, and we did not expect to find any distress there. The curé was absent, but we talked with many of the villagers, and with the Maire and we found that this town of 1,260 people was nearly at starvation point. The inhabitants are fruit and vegetables growers, but all their vegetables have been eaten by the French. They are living on horse flesh, and have been for two months. Many children, but no cows – no milk. [...] Thus we find that this must be one of our relief places at once.[30]

It was the condemnation of war, leaving aside the reasons for which it was being fought, which drove the Friends' relief work. Assisting the soldiers would have meant supporting, albeit indirectly, the armies' logic. Indeed, the more radical members of the Quaker movement even opposed acting on behalf of civilians, since they considered that this sort of initiative would end up supporting the war machine. This remained a minority position but it gathered up one of the dilemmas of aid work in wartime – it could be developed only by being fully set up as an essential component of warfare.

In the French territories devastated by the armed conflict with the Germans, the volunteers marked out by the red and black star carried out their work with different methods from those of their Red Cross colleagues. The distribution of aid was not done directly by the staff from Britain but was entrusted to local committees. Their conviction was that only local people could understand the real needs of the population and check the level of urgency. The key figures in setting up these committees were the priest, mayor and teacher of every village. The Quaker representatives were convinced that this was the best system for distributing aid.[31] What emerged, even though it was on the basis of a small-scale experience, was twofold: the problem of defining a hierarchy of needs in view of a limited availability of resources; and the intuition that this difficulty could be overcome only through a form of collaboration between aid workers and those they were helping.

But who were the men and women that, in the theatre of the Franco-Prussian War, took care of wounded soldiers and starving farm workers, in the name of different organisations? The medical staff was usually made up of professionals paid according to their qualifications, while the constitution of the volunteer teams was quite varied. Among the British Quakers, prominent figures like Robert Spence Watson were not uncommon. Many of the volunteers who set off for the Continent were intellectuals who knew the language and culture of the warring countries and some were from important families in the Society of Friends. This was the case, for example, with Augusta Fry and Richenda Reynolds, the granddaughters of the Quaker Elizabeth Fry, who was well known in Britain for her charity work and her battles to reform the prison system.

The staff of the British Red Cross also included people from a vast network of activists, academics and journalists driven by their commitment to the cause of war relief. Then there were men and, above all, women who had previously been involved in charity work at home or could boast some nursing experience. But there was no shortage of people without experience in aid and in the following decades the British Relief Society was still continually referred to through the image – entirely female – of an 'amateur lady'. At the start of the new century, though, this was much less the case, because of the systematic staff training and the laws regulating the presence of volunteers in war situations.[32] The Prussian Red Cross, however, was already able in 1870 to deploy its volunteers, who had been trained in the previous years. This was particularly the case of the nurses: by the will of Queen Augusta they had been trained at the local centres of the National Women's Association, which the queen herself had founded.[33]

In 1870–71, the first large-scale deployment of relief operations for war victims undoubtedly brought a significant female presence onto the warfare stage – but only behind the lines. This presence was not something to be taken for granted, despite what their continuing care work – considered mothers' and wives' jobs – might lead us to think. The involvement of women had been widely debated in previous years and at the congresses held by the ICRC conflicting positions had been held. On one side, there were those who imagined female participation in-volving only collecting donations or preparing bandages and clothing, counting on the traditional dedication of women to traditional charity work; on the other side, though, there were those who saw a possible future female commitment on the battlefield.[34] This sort of opening up in the British and Prussian relief societies happened exactly in 1870. Then the field of action by women wearing the red cross expanded from initiatives carried out at home to the theatre of battle. Naturally, the allocation of specific tasks 'normalised' the female presence, bringing it back within the borders of a hierarchy of skills determined by gender. Women had to take on the role of assistants to male staff, carrying out jobs like giving out food and drinks, and being employed only in the hospitals far from the battle lines.

Female participation in aid operations in the ranks of the Red Cross, on the one hand, opened up to women new spheres of competence. It encouraged their distancing from the domestic setting and brought them into a context – armed conflicts – that had an exclusively masculine arrangement. On the other hand, the allocation of different types and levels of jobs reinforced gender inequalities, since it confirmed the feminine connotation of care work, which was given a lower status. These were similar dynamics to those we have seen crossing over the 'colonial philanthropy' experience. In this case they were translated into a structured division of roles, which was one of the pivots on which the process of the professionalisation of humanitarianism was developing.

The decades following the end of the Franco-Prussian War were marked by the growth and strengthening of Red Cross national societies. The relief organisa-tion had demonstrated its importance not only in how war events developed but also in its ability to channel collective participation both by appealing for action against to the unbearable suffering of other human beings and by ap-pealing to the national spirit. This demonstration, which was also the subject of stories distributed by the press and of public debate among experts, promoted the full development of the national societies, under government aegis. As Gustave Moynier observed in *La Croix-Rouge, son passé et son avenir*, the states now looked at the Red Cross as 'not an ephemeral, temporary institution but capable of meet-ing the long-term needs of war wherever it was waged'.[35]

To give one major example, in Italy in 1875 King Vittorio Emanuele II became high protector of the national Red Cross while Princess Margherita was named patron of the female section. Between 1882 and 1884 the Croce Rossa Italiana (CRI) became a charitable trust through some specifically created legal measures. This distinguished it from other charity organisations since it was under the supervision of the Ministries of War and the Navy, and was authorised – during wartime emergency – to use the state railway and telegraph services as a part of the army.[36] This type of set-up was not an Italian peculiarity but was characteristic of most of the national societies. This saw their exclusive use of the red cross on a white background recognised as a sort of 'special status' that established their tie to the governing authorities and regulated their relationship with the military authorities.

In his pamphlet Dunant had expressed the hope that national societies for the relief of wounded soldiers would come into being in all of the countries of Europe, but the movement that led to the constitution of those societies took place outside Western and European borders. The Ottoman empire had already announced its adoption of the Geneva Convention in 1865. This choice was tied above all to its intention to keep an open front in its relations with European countries. Indirectly, though, it opened the way for the plan to set up a national society for the relief to soldiers that had been promoted by some European doctors living in Constantinople and local staff who had specialised abroad. A promoting committee was established that maintained relations with the Genevan Committee and started negotiations with the imperial government's representatives in order to found an Ottoman relief society. This did not, however, reach the stage of creating a permanent organisation. It was only during wartime that a committee was set up for the relief of wounded soldiers. This functioned as a support body to the army medical units and was wound down once the war had finished. The first time was the Russo-Turkish War (1877–78), when the Ottoman organisation for assistance to soldiers appeared on the field with the name of the Red Crescent Society and its corresponding emblem.[37] The red cross on a white background, a Christian symbol, was alien to the Ottoman world and evoked the banners of the Crusades. For this reason, the authorities of the Sublime Porte had negotiated with the ICRC for the possibility of using a different image but keeping the same colours.

The appearance of the new organisation, and the new emblem, was particularly significant in the context of a war concluded with violent disturbances that shook the Balkan region and roused great interest among European powers, above all Britain. In 1875 a revolt had broken out in Bosnia Herzegovina against the imperial authorities and the following year in the Ottoman province of Rumelia insurgents had killed Ottoman officials and Muslim civilians. According to the official statistics from the government in London, the repression of the revolts in Rumelia by the imperial Ottoman forces led to the destruction of some sixty villages and the killing of around 12,000 people. The British press devoted ample space to the very hard reaction of the Sublime Porte, giving a detailed description the violence of the Muslim forces and underlining the unacceptability of similar 'atrocities'. Almost at the same time, a huge, multifaceted protest movement had developed in Britain. On the one hand, it denounced the oppression of Orthodox Christians and the minorities within the Ottoman empire's borders. On the other hand, it harshly criticised the British Conservative government for its inaction in the face of what was happening.[38] Numerous committees that had organised aid programmes for the Balkans, financed through public donations, came into being out of the protest movement. The action on the ground (rebuilding destroyed villages, distribution of basic necessities, hospital management) had favoured the Christian populations, even though formal impartiality was maintained. This opened the way to the organisation of aid for the civilian population that took place in the 1877–78 war.[39]

The mobilisation of the *ad hoc* committees countered the inaction of the British National Society for Aid to the Sick and Wounded in War, which, in the face of the violence in the Balkans, had chosen to follow the London government's line of non-intervention and had not started relief programmes. After the explosion of conflict, this position could no longer be maintained and the British Red Cross Society committed itself to taking part in the assistance for soldiers, on both sides of the conflict, as required by the Geneva Convention, although the British National Society for Aid was accused, especially by those who had protested against the Ottoman 'atrocities', of favouring the Turkish army, given the British government's fears of possible Russian expansion in the Balkans. The different political plans for the future of the Balkans influenced the organisation of war aid. This influence was also tested by the establishment of the Red Cross societies – officially recognised by the Geneva Committee – that represented the different national communities in the region. In 1876 the Montenegrin and Serbian Red Crosses came into being and while the Russo-Turkish War was underway, in 1878, the Bulgarian Red Cross also appeared, led by one of the prominent members of the Bulgarian independence movement. Not unlike the Red Crescent Society for the Ottoman empire, the Bulgarian Red Cross intended to show the level of civilisation and modernity the Bulgarian population had achieved, at the same time bringing forward its request for independence.[40]

At the very same moment the Red Crescent Society and the 'national' Red Cross societies of the different Balkan peoples appeared on the battlefield of the Russo-Turkish War, a first society for soldiers' relief was also set up in Japan. During the 1877 civil war (the Seinan War) the association called Haku-Ai (All-Embracing Love) came into being, with the aim of assisting wounded combatants from both sides. The name of the new organisation was chosen with a great deal of care. In the Meiji era (1868–1912) the term *haku-ai* was widely used to mean relief work and institutions. The origins of this term were much older though, since they went back to the Buddhist value of 'all-embracing love', which was equivalent to the Confucian virtue of 'shared humanity'. The twofold reference to Buddhist and Confucian values corresponded to the intention of making the mission of Haku-Ai-Sha more easily acceptable to Japanese society.

According to what was set out in the society's founding document, this mission was also inspired by the initiatives that had already been undertaken by Western countries to take care of soldiers on their battlefields. So in Japan the emergence of war humanitarianism came from a meeting of stimuli from overseas – which could bring the country closer to the Western world – and the call to return to values that were deeply rooted in local culture. The establishment of a genuine national society for the relief of soldiers took place only later, however, following interests developed in that area within the imperial setting. The Japanese government saw in the mobilisation dictated by humanitarian issues on the one hand the strengthening of the national spirit and on the other an element that would improve the country's standing in the world. In 1886 Japan signed the Geneva Convention and the following year Haku-Ai-Sha was transformed into the Red Cross Society of Japan.[41]

In the United States, too, the foundation of the national Red Cross Society happened only in the 1880s, and 1881 to be more precise. The American Red Cross (ARC) came into being after lengthy negotiations led principally by Clara Barton, who became its first president. She was a teacher who had been born into a strongly anti-slavery family, was close to the women's suffrage movement and had been a volunteer for assistance to Unionist soldiers in the Civil War. Barton has often been described as the heroic mother of the ARC, the female version of Henry Dunant. Apart from any myth-making, the figure of Clara Barton is important because she takes us back to the complex origins of the ARC. The US Sanitary Commission, which we have already referred to, and more generally the aid work for those wounded in the Civil War that was carried out by medical and charity associations, were their inescapable background. The United States' isolationist tendencies had prevailed in its rejection of the 1864 Convention, despite the close relations the Sanitary Commission's representatives had maintained with the ICRC. In the early 1870s, Barton spent a lot of time in Europe. She met Gustave Moynier and Luis Appia and was one of the volunteers deployed by the Geneva Committee during the Franco-Prussian War. She developed the conviction that the United States should become part of the international movement that was assembled around the red cross on a white background. On her return home she therefore promoted a huge mobilisation intended to achieve this aim. She understood that to gain greater consensus between her fellow Americans the programme for a possible American section of the Red Cross had to be formulated in a way that took account of the country's specific situation. The United States was still engaged in the difficult reconstruction process following the end of the Civil War and was therefore not very interested in international questions. For this reason she underlined the opportunity to create an organisation capable of also operating in peacetime:

> Although we in the United States may fondly hope to be seldom visited by the calamities of war [...] – wrote Barton in her popular pamphlet *The Red Cross of the*

Geneva Convention: What It Is – our southern coasts are periodically visited by the scourge of yellow fever; the valleys of Mississippi are subject to destructive inundations; the plains of the West are devastated by insects and drought, and out cities and country are swept by consuming fires. In all such cases, to gather and dispense the profuse liberality of our people, without waste of time or material, requires the wisdom that comes of experience and permanent organization.[42]

Putting forward the hypothesis that the US section of the Red Cross, once it was officially set up, could also deal with the victims of natural disasters enabled her to focus attention on the national situation, softening the suspicion of an international project whose centre was in Europe. At the same time, this kind of approach drew from the now broadly based conviction that the suffering of others could not leave us indifferent and required instead a planned course of action that was rational and not extemporised. The plan was successful, even in the political environment of the time: in 1882 the Senate ratified the Geneva Convention and named the American Red Cross as its official aid agency in armed conflicts. The combination of action on two fronts – in war and in peace – emerged as a characteristic trait of the Red Cross on that side of the Atlantic and the 'American amendment' was referred to in order to emphasise the specific situation of the US compared with the European model.[43]

In the following twenty years, however, the American government saw the ARC as just one of the many associations making up the varied charity world. Things began to change with the Hispano-American War (1898), even if the US military authorities – fearing that combat operations might be held up – reduced the tasks of the Red Cross staff to a minimum. The personnel therefore directed most of their treatments and care to Cuban civilians. At the end of the conflict the ARC had notably strengthened its credibility on a national level, most of all because – as the US president stated to Congress – the American administration had been able to count on its work in order to 'pursue noble aims' and demonstrate its own concern for the conditions of other people's suffering.[44] Congress soon ratified the new statutes of the ARC, which set up a type of partnership with the federal government that no private society could ever have enjoyed.

The definitive turning point happened later though, at the end of Clara Barton's long presidency of the ARC. This coincided with a new revision of the statutes that placed the management of the ARC in the hands of a central committee which was one-third made up of government nominees, including a representative of the Department of State and another from the Department of War. The ARC was converted into a semi-government body and the new course undertaken in the following years was strictly tied to the reform programme of the Progressive Era. The local offices multiplied and the ARC attained a truly national coverage. Its internal structure was rationalised and efforts were intensified to professionalise relief work. It was in this new form that the ARC arrived at the eve of the First World War.[45]

In the Great War

The First World War, with its disruptive effects, profoundly marked the path of war humanitarianism. The vast movement that developed under the symbol of the red cross on a white background took on a new central role that affected the arrangement of various players (the Geneva Committee, the national societies) in terms of their aims and their ways of working.

The years between 1914 and 1918 significantly changed the ICRC's profile and field of action. In the decades following its foundation, the ICRC tried above all to play a role coordinating the different national societies, encouraging their formation and development, and supplying them with specific support during war situations. The direct involvement of the ICRC on the field had remained marginal though and the Geneva Committee had leveraged its moral influence in order to bring the national states back to respecting the principles established in 1864 and extended in 1906. During the First World War, however, the ICRC found itself an active role as a neutral intermediary between the warring countries and carried it out by starting in particular with two specific tasks: the reporting of violations of the Geneva Convention and the protection of prisoners of war. The latter was a largely new area of intervention. The ICRC fully developed a practice already started in the Balkan Wars – visits to soldiers' prison camps to check their condition. This type of intervention had not been set out in the Geneva Convention and the legislative reference for ICRC was instead the 1907 Hague Convention on Laws and Customs of War, which had established the rules for the treatment of prisoners of war. The camp visits were organised on the basis of specific agreements stipulated by the Geneva Committee with the individual warring countries. The aim was to trace the soldiers captured by the enemy army and put them in touch with their families, so that they could receive letters and packages. In addition, the ICRC representatives drew up reports on the conditions of the prisoners' detention, which were initially made public but which were later delivered exclusively to the countries involved.[46] Through this practice the ICRC had introduced a further field of action for war humanitarianism, and at the same time had put into practical effect its will to act as a neutral party. It was exactly for this that in 1917 it was awarded the Nobel Prize for Peace.

For the Red Cross societies of the warring countries, the Great War was a phase of intense mobilisation that strengthened some of the processes that had already been begun in the previous years: the patriotic interpretation of aid work; the close relationships with their governments; the close ties to the military authorities, which controlled the medical assistance given to the combatants. The feminisation of the staff also accelerated: since the male population was enrolled *en masse*, the initiatives for helping the wounded or sick largely involved women. Voluntary service for the Red Cross was an integral part of the mobilisation of women for the homeland and ended up being assimilated into men's military commitments. It is significant that the women in the Italian Red Cross were described – because of their uniforms – as the 'white army' and that the qualities of discipline, bravery and intrepid self-sacrifice were increasingly considered indispensable for them.[47] So the growing number of women who were choosing the symbol of the red cross were being offered a militarised and male model of humanitarianism despite the maternal figure used to embody the organisation's mission, a figure which continued to appear on postcards and posters until the end of the conflict.[48]

The national societies' close relationship with their governments and the interpretation of aid work in the light of the dynamics of war did not just concern mobilisation at home. The intervention of the Red Cross societies in the warring countries was another tool through which states pursued their international policy aims. The ARC was a significant example of this. Its activities found their place in the internationalist design of President Woodrow Wilson and this marked a change in the role played by the organisation on the level of foreign policy. The assistance – already deployed in the period of neutrality – given to civilians of European countries firstly respected the conviction that promoting the development of modern democratic societies was an antidote to the destructive power of war, and a necessary premise for re-establishing a lasting peace.

In Italy, for example, before the United States had entered the war the ARC had taken part in the management of schools, orphanages and canteens for refugees and military families. Thanks to the autobiographical novels of Ernest Hemingway and John Dos Passos,[49] the work of the US Ambulance Service work is still alive in the collective memory. It dedicated itself to the care of wounded soldiers from 1917 but the ARC undertaking had a broader reach and included welfare and public health programmes. Towards the end of the war, specific initiatives were started in the fight against malaria, the training of healthcare staff and child health protection, and these were continued in following years. The ARC and the US government intended not only to support the Italian war effort by first getting ahead of and then going alongside the military alliance, but also to strengthen the ties – political, diplomatic and cultural – between the two countries.[50] So the Italian case clearly highlights how the humanitarianism represented by the Red Cross took on a specific meaning in the context of US foreign policy and the internationalist project that inspired it.

For the Red Cross Society of Japan (RCSJ), the undertaking on the European theatre of war had a different value. The RCSJ, which had gone through a major development after the Russian–Japanese conflict (1904–05), was naturally used for aid to the national army deployed against the German forces in Asia. However, between 1914 and 1916 the RCSJ regularly sent medical units to Europe, to the allied countries' military hospitals. The staff of the team sent to Britain in January 1915 recalled their sense of displacement and inadequacy due to their lack of understanding of the English language and the local customs and habits, but despite these obvious difficulties the organisation's judgement on the work under-taken in the European theatre was mostly positive. In fact, the main intention was to demonstrate that they completely shared the principles sanctioned by the 1864 Convention, showing a positive image of Japan and therefore easing their diplomatic relations with Western countries. Its active participation in the 'humanisation of war' project – launched by the Geneva Committee – was intended as tangible proof of the Japanese empire's civilisation.[51]

The First World War was undoubtedly a crucial phase in the history of the Red Cross movement. The ICRC and the national societies saw their legitimisa-tion and approval increase and the flags with the white and red symbol gained a permanent place in the representations of the 1914–18 theatre of war. However, the Red Cross's acknowledged central role contributed to eclipsing – at least in the collective memory – the other groups that took part in assisting the victims of war, such as the Quakers. Their intervention was more extensive and diversified than it had been in the past and this time took their cues not only from Britain but also from the United States.

The British Quakers gave their assistance to civilians alongside aid to military personnel struck by enemy fire or illness. This aid was entrusted to the Friends' Ambulance Units (FAU), which worked behind the lines in France and Belgium. The Friends' War Victims Relief Committee (FWVRC), though, brought aid to over 4,000 civilians and covered a geographical area stretching over the opposing fronts, also reaching Poland, Russia, Germany and Austria. This division into two distinct organisations, with different aims, reflected above all the internal tensions within the British Quakers on the position to take on the war in progress and what the acceptable level of involvement was. The FWVRC held the official pacifist line of the Society of Friends, which the FAU was less strongly attached to. Nevertheless, in both cases the young men who left as volunteers for continental Europe were mainly conscientious objectors who, in the name of the rejection of war that was part of their faith, had not been willing to take up arms.[52]

In 1917, with the entry of the United States into the conflict, the American Friends' Service Committee (AFSC) was added to the British organisations. The new body, set up by the American Quakers for the very purpose of taking part in aid operations in the theatre of war, worked in close collaboration with the ARC, which President Wilson had granted exclusive responsibility for all the medical services connected to the wartime situation and the general coordination of the relief programmes. The Friends had already worked with the ARC nationally, in interventions following natural calamities. This had enabled it to obtain the authorisation from Congress and the military authorities to access the combat zones. This authorisation was by no means to be taken for granted, since the institutions had a certain diffidence towards the Quakers because of their con-demnation of war and their practice of conscientious objection. It was to tackle this diffidence that the AFSC, on the one hand, emphasised the patriotic spirit shown in the organisation, stressing the service provided to the country through its aid work. On the other hand, the AFSC gave importance to the professional dimension of its work and tried to recruit qualified staff and prove its organisational efficiency, leaving in the background the ethical and religious motivations for its dedication to caring for suffering humanity. [53] During the conflict, the AFSC experienced rapid growth in terms of both fundraising capacity and field operations. While it kept important points of contact and shared the background motivations, the Quakers' humanitarian commitment on both sides of the Atlantic therefore followed distinct paths, largely determined by the national settings they were tied to.

The Great War's dramatic impact on Western societies also led to the emergence of new bodies committed to international aid. The humanitarian response to the conflict's destructive force rested largely on previous, religion-based, philanthropic experiences that were reworked with a different aim and with a range of action that extended beyond national borders. This was the case with the American Jewish Joint Distribution Committee, which was founded in 1914 to answer the specific need for help of the Jewish population struck by the wartime events in central and western Europe and the Middle East. The new association, which became known by the diminutive 'Joint', was set up by certain notable members of the New York bourgeoisie. Many of them were politically active and supporters of the Democratic president Woodrow Wilson, and they had already connected the name to philanthropic initiatives. This enabled Joint's representatives to establish a special relationship with the US authorities, which became progressively closer and was aimed especially at the use of governmental diplomatic channels for sending aid to the countries it was intended for. Its financing and functional structure remained exclusively private, mainly due to the way the organisation took advantage of the networks of associations that already existed. On the one hand, Joint involved most of the American Jewish associations in fundraising, which therefore covered all of the United States and had great success. On the other hand, it turned to collaboration with societies that were already active inside the countries the aid was intended for, so that it could be more easily distributed to the recipients. It was this reorganisation of the Jewish philanthropic tradition in a new framework that allowed Joint to rapidly acquire an operational dimension and to establish itself as the most important body for international aid to Jews during the First World War.[54]

Another important body contributed to the deployment of US humanitarian action during the Great War: the Young Men's Christian Association. The YMCA – also simply called the 'Y' – was founded in 1844 as a philanthropic association aimed at saving young men who arrived in the cities of the industrial revolution from moral corruption by offering them suitable forms of entertainment. In the various Western countries, national sections of the organisation rapidly developed and progressively extended their range of activities, including for example the education of the working classes and professional training. In 1914, various national societies mobilised – primarily the British – but by far the most significant participation was that of the US YMCA. In the early years of the twentieth century it went through a profound reorganisation – in terms of a rationalisation and professionalisation of its services – expanding its roots within society and strengthening its ties with various institutions. In April 1917, the start-up of a massive intervention programme in the theatre of war took place in close coordination with the federal government and was presented as a resolution dictated by patriotism and the spirit of communion with the soldiers' fates. A volume published a few years later by the association itself underlined that 'through the [YMCA] the American people endeavored to discharge its obligation to the American soldier and sailor and to honor their preferred claim on the material and spiritual resources of the nation'.[55] Actively intervening to alleviate the suffering produced by the war therefore meant showing themselves to be faithful to the values the American population recognised.

The volunteers from the 'Y' carried out their work in collaboration with the ARC but at the same time they were staking their claim on the specific nature of their own skills and concentrating on relief for soldiers that was material (such as the distribution of supplementary rations) and spiritual (for example collective Bible reading). The Christian association, whose own symbol was a red triangle with its apex pointing downwards, next to a red cross on a white background, was not new to aid activities of this type, already having had experience both in the Civil War and in the armed conflict between the United States and Spain (1898). But the First World War marked a change in the way it carried out a humanitarian programme designed for the war context. The YMCA's work, then, acquired particular importance in a specific context, that of assistance to prisoners of war on both sides. The distribution of staple goods and 'comfort work' by the 'Y' staff were planned and performed – before the entry of the United States into the war – in close collaboration with US government representatives and were in line with the new intervention front started up by the ICRC.[56]

In autumn 1918, when hostilities came to an end, Henry Dunant and Gustave Moynier had been dead for almost a decade. The number of dead and the degree of violence reached in the years of conflict seemed to contradict any possibility of fulfilling the project for the 'humanisation of war' fought for by the organisation that both the Genevan philanthropists had contributed to founding. The Geneva Convention had been repeatedly violated despite the ICRC's attempts to keep some form of check on the armies' actions in order to impede and report the contraventions of the rules established in 1864 and renewed in 1906.[57] And yet Dunant's and Moynier's project could not be declared a failure because the humanitarianism of war had now been established. In achieving this result, the main role had been played by the Red Cross, through its national societies and their special relationship with governments, the deployment on the field of thousands of men and women dedicated to caring for the wounded, and the official mediation function carried out by the Geneva Committee.

Even in this phase, however, non-governmental organisations had also come on the scene, many of which were religiously inspired, and which had brought different symbols, motivations and approaches to the humanitarian context. This joint presence of different actors – inter-governmental, semi-public and private – marked war aid and took on an even greater weight in the following years, when the aid programmes became one of the tools through which the international community sought to tackle the complex transition towards peace.

Notes

1 Henri Coursier, *La Croix-Rouge Internationale* (Paris: Press Universitaires de France, 1959), pp. 14–15.

2 Henry Dunant, *A Memory of Solferino* (Geneva: ICRC, 2013 [reprint of the 1939 edition by the American Red Cross]), p. 124.

3 Gustave Moynier and Luis Appia, *La guerre et la charité: traité théorétique et pratique de philanthropie appliquées aux armées en campagne* (Geneva: Cherbuliez, 1867), p. 117.

4 Edward Tyas Cook, *The Life of Florence Nightingale* (London: Macmillan, 1913), vol. I, pp. 236–237.

5 Coursier, *La Croix-Rouge Internationale*, p. 14.

6 Particularly relevant are the fifth and the sixth stanzas of the poem *Santa Filomena*: 'The wounded from the battle-plain, / In dreary hospitals of pain, / The cheerless corridors, / The cold and stony floors. / Lo! in that house of misery / A lady with a lamp I see / Pass through the glimmering gloom, / And flit from room to room.' In the penultimate stanza Henry Wadsworth Longfellow repeats the image of the 'lady with a lamp': 'A Lady with a Lamp shall stand / In the great history of the land, / A noble type of good, / Heroic womanhood.'

7 Dunant, *A Memory of Solferino*, p. 120.

8 Pierre Boissier, 'Henry Dunant', *International Review of the Red Cross*, 14:161 (1974), pp. 395–419.

9 Coursier, *La Croix-Rouge Internationale*, p. 16.

10 John F. Hutchinson, *Champions of Charity: War and the Rise of the Red Cross* (Boulder, CO: Westview Press, 1996), pp. 11–30.

11 Matthias Schulz, 'Dilemmas of "Geneva" Humanitarian Internationalism: The International Committee of Red Cross and the Red Cross Movement, 1863–1918', in J. Paulmann (ed.), *Dilemmas of Humanitarian Aid in the Twentieth Century* (Oxford: Oxford University Press, 2016), pp. 35–62.

12 Mark Mazower, *Governing the World: The History of an Idea, 1815 to Present* (London: Allen Lane, 2012), pp. 68–69.

13 Hutchinson, *Champions of Charity*, pp. 31–52.

14 *Ibid.*, pp. 24–25.

15 John Duffy, *The Sanitarians: A History of American Public Health* (Urbana, IL: University of Illinois Press, 1990), pp. 110–125; Judith Ann Giesberg, *Civil War Sisterhood: The US Sanitary Commission and Women's Politics in Transition* (Boston, MA: Northeastern University Press, 2000).

16 Charles J. Stillé, *History of the Sanitary Commission Being the General Report of Its Work During the War of the Rebellion* (Philadelphia, PA: J. B. Lippincott., 1866), p. 19.

17 Schulz, 'Dilemmas of "Geneva" International Humanitarianism', pp. 40–41.

18 Chiara Staderini, *La Croce Rossa Italiana fra dimensione associativa e riconoscimento istituzionale* (Firenze: Noccioli Editore, 1995).

19 Rebecca Gill, *Calculating Compassion: Humanity and Relief in War, Britain 1870–1914* (Manchester: Manchester University Press, 2013), p. 25.

20 Gustave Moynier, *La Croix-Rouge, son passé et son avenir* (Paris: Sandoz & Thuillier, 1882), p. 103.

21 Cited in Rebecca Gill, '"The Rational Administration of Compassion": The Origins of British Relief in War', *Le Mouvement Social*, 227:2 (2009), pp. 9–26, at p. 11.

22 *Ibid.*, pp. 11–12.

23 Moynier, *La Croix-Rouge*, p. 124.

24 Hutchinson, *Champions of Charity*, pp. 105–149; David P. Forsythe, *The Humanitarians: The International Committee of the Red Cross* (Cambridge: Cambridge University Press, 2005), pp. 23–33.

25 Bertrand Taithe, *Defeated Flesh: Welfare, Warfare and the Makings of Modern France* (Manchester: Manchester University Press, 1999), pp. 164–174.

26 Bertrand Taithe, 'The Red Cross Flag in the Franco-Prussian War: Civilians, Humanitarians, and War in the "Modern" Age', in R. Cooter et al. (eds), *War, Medicine and Modernity* (Stroud: Sutton, 1998), pp. 22–47.

27 National Society for Aid, *Report of the Operations of the British National Society for Aid to the Sick and Wounded in War During the Franco-Prussian War 1870–1871* (London: Harrison & Sons, 1871), p. 151.

28 Gill, '"The Rational Administration of Compassion"'.

29 John Ormerod Greenwood, *Quaker Encounters: Friends and Relief* (York: William Sessions, 1975), vol. I, pp. 41–79.

30 Robert Spence Watson, *The Villages Around Metz* (Newcastle upon Tyne: J. M. Carr, 1870), p. 20.

31 Greenwood, *Quaker Encounters*, pp. 52–54.

32 Gill, '"The Rational Administration of Compassion"', p. 17.

33 Hutchinson, *Champions of Charity*, pp. 119–121.

34 *Ibid.*, pp. 80–82, 127–128.

35 Moynier, *La Croix-Rouge*, p. 149.

36 Staderini, *La Croce Rossa Italiana*.

37 Nadir Özbeck, 'Defining the Public Sphere During the Late Ottoman Empire: War, Mass Mobilization and the Young Turk Regime (1908–1918)', *Middle Eastern Studies*, 43:5 (2007), pp. 802–803.

38 Davide Rodogno, *Against Massacre: Humanitarian Interventions in the Ottoman Empire, 1815–1914* (Princeton, NJ: Princeton University press, 2011), pp. 142–160.

39 Dorothy Anderson, *The Balkan Volunteers* (London: Hutchinson, 1968), pp. 3–74.

40 Gill, *Calculating Compassion*, pp. 96–123.

41 Frank Käser, 'A Civilized Nation: Japan and the Red Cross, 1877–1900', *European Review of History: Revue européenne d'histoire*, 23:1–2 (2016), pp. 16–32.

42 Foster Rhea Dulles, *The American Red Cross. A History* (New York: Harper & Brothers, 1950), p. 13, citing Clara Barton, *The Red Cross of the Geneva Convention: What It Is* (Washington, DC: Rufus H. Darby, Steam Power Book and Job Printer, 1878).

43 Julia F. Irwin, *Making the World Safe: The American Red Cross and a Nation's Humanitarian*

Awakening (New York: Oxford University Press, 2013), pp. 13–34; Marian Moser Jones, *The American Red Cross from Clara Barton to the New Deal* (Baltimore, MD: Johns Hopkins University Press, 2013), pp. 3–115.

44 William McKinley, *Message of the President to Congress*, Papers Relating to the Foreign Relations of the United States, 1898, LXIII, cited in Irwin, *Making the World Safe*, p. 27.

45 Irwin, *Making the World Safe*, pp. 35–66; Jones, *The American Red Cross*, pp. 115–166.

46 Forsythe, *The Humanitarians*, p. 31; Annette Becker, *Oubliés de la Grande Guerre: Humanitaire et culture de guerre 1914–1918. Populations occupées, déportés civils, prisonniers de guerre* (Paris: Éditions Noêsis, 1998), pp. 180–228; François Bugnion, *Le Comité International de la Croix-Rouge et la protection des victimes de la guerre* (Geneva: CICR, 1994), pp. 90–95.

47 See Stefania Bartoloni, *Italiane alla Guerra: L'assistenza ai feriti 1915–1918* (Venice: Marsilio, 2003).

48 See the pictorial essay in Hutchinson, *Champions of Charity*, in particular picture 11.

49 Of course I refer to Ernest Hemingway, *A Farewell to Arms* (New York: Charles Scribner's Sons, 1929) and to John Dos Passos, *1919* (New York: Library of America, 1932).

50 Julia F. Irwin, 'Nation Building and Rebuilding: The American Red Cross in Italy During the Great War', *Journal of the Gilded Age and Progressive Era*, 8:3 (2009), pp. 407–439.

51 Yoshiya Makita, 'The Alchemy of Humanitarianism: the First World War, the Japanese Red Cross and the Creation of an International Public Health Order', *First World War Studies*, 5:1 (2014), pp. 117–129.

52 Greenwood, *Quaker Encounters*, pp. 165–218; Daniel R. Maul, 'American Quakers, the Emergence of International Humanitarianism, and the Foundation of the American Friends Service Committee, 1890–1920', in J. Paulmann (ed.), *Dilemmas of Humanitarian Aid in the Twentieth Century* (Oxford: Oxford University Press, 2016), pp. 63–90.

53 *Ibid.*

54 Jaclyn Granick, 'Waging Relief: The Politics and Logistics of American Jewish War Relief in Europe and the Near East (1914–1918)', *First World War Studies*, 5:1 (2014), pp. 55–68.

55 William H. Taft and Frederick Morgan Harris, *Service with Fighting Men: An Account of the Work of the American Young Men's Christian Association in the World War* (New York: Association Press, 1922), p. xxi.

56 Kenneth Steuer, *Pursuit of an 'Unparalleled Opportunity': The American YMCA and Prisoner-of-War Diplomacy Among the Central Power Nations During World War I, 1914–1923*, Gutenberg-e Series (New York: Columbia University Press, 2009).

57 Geoffrey Best, *Humanity in Warfare: The Modern History of the International Law of Armed Conflict* (London: Methuen, 1983), pp. 217–224.

4

'Chaotic years of peace'

> Early last year, when visiting my home, I found in the top nursery a box full of my
> letters and diaries, carefully preserved by my sisters. As I re-read them, the past
> came vividly before my eyes. Most of them were written during the last war and the
> chaotic years of peace that followed. They told of the relief work in which I had been
> engaged in many different countries – in Holland, France, Corsica, North Africa,
> Serbia, Austria and Russia.[1]

With these words Francesca Mary Wilson began her introduction to her autobiographical volume *In the Margins of Chaos: Recollections of Relief Work in
and Between Three Wars*, published in London in 1944. Francesca was born in
Newcastle upon Tyne in 1881, a Quaker, and became a teacher after completing
her studies at Newnham College, Cambridge. In 1916 she followed in the footsteps
of her brother and two cousins and joined the Friends assisting refugees in France.
The following year she left France for Corsica, where she again worked in caring
for refugees, this time Serbs, on behalf of the Serbian Relief Fund, a private
association of famous British philanthropists with the patronage of the Queen.
The aid to the Serbian civilians in turn led her first to the coasts of the present
Tunisia and then, after the end of the war, to the recently constituted Kingdom of
Jugoslavia. Subsequently, Francesca Wilson was transferred to Vienna, which had
been devastated by the destruction of the war, to work firstly with the Friends and
then the recently founded Save the Children Fund.

The year 1920 took her to a new destination – Russia, which was struck
by famine. There she took aid to the population – decimated by hunger and
disease – under the programme promoted by a US agency, the American Relief
Administration (ARA). She was still with the Quakers in Spain when it was
devastated by the Civil War and she assisted the Polish refugees in Hungary in
1939–40.[2] While she was writing *In the Margins of Chaos*, Francesca continued
to work with the Friends in England, still with the refugee population. The now
professional expert in international relief knew very well that after the end of the
war extraordinary aid operations would be required:

> Hordes of disabled men, displaced populations struggling to get home, prisoners dying of typhus and starvation, hunger diseases in cities, famine and epidemic in country areas – all these situations will have to be faced again, on a much vaster scale, at the outbreak of peace, as they were last time.[3]

The literary device of recounting rediscovered letters and diaries written twenty years earlier concealed her desire to make the best use of the humanitarian work she had carried out in the past in order to give useful hints in the present. This is evident in the fact that Wilson concluded her volume with an appendix entitled 'Some Lessons from Personal Experience of Relief Work'. Indeed, a year later she was once again operating in the field, at the service of the United Nations Relief and Rehabilitation Administration (UNRRA): we will return to this in the next chapter. The figure of Francesca M. Wilson interests us here for other reasons, too. Her biography offers some significant points for reflection on the history of humanitarianism in the years between the wars.

It is often emphasised that this period saw a sort of parting of the waters in that international humanitarian action was forced to measure itself against Second World War's dramatic consequences; it became the prerogative of specific institutions, which defined certain of its basic areas of competence. Naturally, these new elements are undeniable and one just has to think of the importance of the League of Nations to realise it. The new arrangement was the incarnation of the internationalism of the victorious powers emerging from the war – and the United States and Britain in the first place – and had a crucial role in promoting humanitarianism as a matter of cooperation between different countries.

Assistance to refugees, public health and child protection were among the sectors in which this cooperation showed itself to be most profitable, and it formed an important legacy for the intergovernmental agencies after the Second World War. The initiative of individual governments also contributed to include humanitarianism within the sphere of relations between states. The most relevant example is certainly that of the ARA, led by Herbert Hoover. It was the future president of the United States – who was already known for having directed the aid operations for civilians in Belgium during the German occupation in 1914–17 – who put into action the vast post-war plan intended to feed the children of central and eastern Europe and the Near East. And it was Hoover who organised the massive despatch of aid to Bolshevik Russia in the most dramatic years of the famine (1921–23). The ARA contributed to determining the pre-eminence of the United States on the scene of humanitarianism after the First World War, and in their turn, the aid programmes were an important part of US international policy.

But why does the figure of Francesca Wilson encourage us to complicate this picture, and to look at it from a different perspective? Her biography connects the aid work for civilians performed during the First World War with the work carried out in the years between the two World Wars – and then with that in the Second

World War. But it also adds something to the very long tradition of Quaker intervention on battle scenes.[4] The career path of this professional in relief for victims of armed conflicts reminds us that the new intergovernmental and governmental organisations after the First World War aspired to give humanitarianism a new aspect but were also fed by past experiences. The emergence of a transnational humanitarian regime that was not occasional and entrusted to governmental and international institutions led to a turning point which rested on the well tested ideas and practices developed previously. The new organisations made use of the expertise of men and women who had been carrying out relief work in distant countries for some time: Francesca Wilson is just one example.

It is an example that allows us to highlight another aspect: the joint presence – in the setting of international humanitarian programmes – of bodies of different natures, such as those for which Wilson worked in the different regions of Europe. The years between the two wars were marked by the operations of the League of Nations and governmental agencies such as the ARA, but the private associations also had an important role. As a whole, they made up a varied, fluid picture. The Friends' committees and programmes, the expression of activism over a long period, were flanked by temporary bodies founded in response to individual emergencies. These bodies brought together representatives from the world of philanthropy and politics, counted on the involvement of public opinion, and collaborated with governmental and international institutions on well defined programmes. In this respect, the experience of the American association Near East Relief is significant. It had a top position in relief for refugees in Asia Minor and was also a witness, together with the ARA, to the importance taken on by humanitarianism in the internationalist policies of the United States in the 1920s.

Some of the organisations founded for specific circumstances, though, did not remain temporary. This was the case with the Save the Children Fund, which was founded in London in 1919 in the context of a campaign to assist children in all of Europe, even the countries of former enemies. The organisation soon reformulated its mission, setting itself long-term aims, and it played an important role – well beyond just the British context – in the definition of childhood as the specific recipient of humanitarian actions.

Most of the associations, even though they were of different natures and inspirations, collaborated with the governmental bodies and especially with the League of Nations, which represented an essential reference point for them, a place for coordination but also for playing a central role. This leads us to another observation. The years between the two World Wars undoubtedly made up a crucial phase in the process of humanitarianism's institutionalisation, which, in the contemporary era, has progressively reduced the role played by private, confessional, voluntary initiative. It is equally true, though, that this process was neither unavoidable nor linear: we have to read it in the context of joint presence, negotiation and collaboration between the different bodies – institutional and private – that showed themselves open to the flow of skills and intervention models developed in the various programmes.

Finally, the profile of Francesca Wilson is also illuminating in relation to the establishment – within the framework of the emerging humanitarian system – of a female professional figure who was given specific skill areas to work in. We have already seen the widespread presence of women in the 'archaeology' of humanitarianism – the anti-slavery movement, colonial philanthropy – as much as in aid work on the European battlefields performed by the Red Cross and the Friends. After the First World War, for certain key figures the female tendency towards humanitarian work, encouraged by the crossover between it and care work, took on the traits of a new profession. It was marked out by mobility on the international scene, by the building of wide reporting networks, by the close relationship with national and international institutions and their representatives. One impulse in this direction came from the building of international women's associations, which rested on a very long tradition but was now looking confidently to the League of Nations, sharing the internationalist spirit on which it was founded and offering to contribute actively to its programmes.

Internationalism and humanitarianism

> Red Cross effort is thus far flung. It will continue to be so. But the movement represented by this work has likewise assumed an intimate place in the daily life of our people at home. The army of workers which has been recruited and trained during the war must not be demobilized. All our experience in the war shows clearly that there is an unlimited field for service of the kind which can be performed with peculiar effectiveness by the Red Cross.[5]

This is what Henry P. Davison, president of the American Red Cross War Council – which was by then being dismantled – stated in March 1919. He had just returned home after visiting some of his organisation's European missions and put out in the open what was obvious to sector experts (but not just to them): the ceasefire had not put an end to the serious needs of the civilian population. Beyond the specific crisis areas – such as the Balkans and the Middle East – in most European countries malnutrition and epidemics continued to keep the death rate at dramatically high levels. In the immediate post-war period the continued provision of relief was certainly not considered indispensable only by the ARC official: the British and American Friends – to give just one significant example – jointly promoted a food programme for German children, and in 1920s Germany the *Quäkerspeisung* (Quaker food) became a synonym for international aid.[6] Davison's considerations, though, looked well beyond the hypothesis of not 'demobilising' the people who were now expert in aid for suffering populations.

The project supported by the president of the ARC War Council was more ambitious and referred to the entire Red Cross movement. In fact, the intention was to unify the individual national societies in a single, supranational body that not only would enter in action in wartime emergencies but would also promote *ad hoc* projects in peacetime, encouraging welfare development. This hypothesis naturally did not come from the convictions of a single individual: on the one hand, it was in line with the operations of the ARC in previous years; on the other, it had found itself a place in the internationalist vision of US President Woodrow Wilson. In Henry Davison's project, which enjoyed Wilson's support, the new international body founded under the red cross emblem would fight epidemics and relieve the consequences of natural disasters; above all, it would drive on welfare policies in different countries and encourage cooperation between states. Essentially, Davison and his supporters saw in the future International Red Cross a body that complemented the League of Nations: both the institutions guaranteed peace and stability in the world by acting, respectively, on the humanitarian front and the political and diplomatic front. The United States was planning a federal body, made up of the individual national societies, that would in this way develop common aims and identify tools and methods to achieve them.[7]

In Geneva this vision did not receive much agreement. The members of the ICRC, including its president, Gustave Ador, certainly thought a revision of the initial project, which was totally focused on wartime emergency, was necessary. For this reason it was decided not to limit relief to wounded soldiers and prisoners of war but to include the civilians struck by famines and epidemics. It was not intended, however, to overturn the organisation's system, putting up for discussion its approach to humanitarian aid. If we remember that the ICRC, despite having gained great international recognition, was rooted in the Swiss context and was used to dealing with individual governments according to traditional diplomatic methods, then we can see that the idea of transforming the Red Cross into a supranational body was alien to its way of reasoning and acting. The ICRC's resistance to the US project therefore expressed the tension between two different interpretations of the role the Red Cross would have to take on in post-war society, and – in a wider sense – between two different conceptions of international humanitarianism.

From the formal point of view, the project advanced by the ARC became reality. At the congress of national societies held at Cannes in 1919, Davison's proposal was approved, and next came the League of Red Cross Societies,[8] the federal body planned to make humanitarianism one of the linchpins of the new cooperation between states. As it turned out, though, the League remained for all the inter-war years a rather marginal body in the context of the Red Cross's great family. At its constitution only the five national societies of the victorious countries – Britain, France, Italy, Japan and the United States – joined and when the number of members increased the problem arose of overcoming the internal differences in creating shared policies. Additionally, the ICRC used its authority and diplomatic strength to reduce the League's mandate as much as possible – it was in fact limited to coordinating aid for victims of natural disasters – while all the operations for 'humanitarian protection' in conflict situations remained the prerogative of the ICRC.

The project of creating the 'humanitarian counterpart' of the League of Nations did not manage to take off, then, but it was the League of Nations itself that took on an unforeseen major role in the field of international aid. Relaunched by Woodrow Wilson at the end of the war as the expression of liberal inter-nationalism, that first universal organisation of cooperation had to guarantee its member states peace and security. Its main functions were preventing recourse to arms, standing up against secret diplomacy and ensuring respect for international treaties, and so its main work was political and diplomatic. The League of Nations' founding contract (the Covenant) referred to work in a broad 'humanitarian' sense only in terms of trafficking women and children, and slave trading. In both cases, the League of Nations' task was to encourage collaboration between states to fight against these two phenomena. The measures in the organisation's founding charter were tied to the past mobilisation against the trade in human beings. This had been a fundamental component in the battle against slavery, and after the abolition of slave trading in most Western countries it had led – mainly at the will of Britain – to some attempts at intergovernmental cooperation to suspend the market in men and women, which had by now become illegal.

The League of Nations' founding fathers had imagined its commitment in the humanitarian context would be supplementary and of little account. But the initial scenario they imagined changed for two reasons. The first was the fact of the grave post-war emergencies. Then there was the fact that the Genevan organisation was a reference point not only for political internationalism but also for associations, philanthropists, scientists and intellectuals. Private organisations looking for an institution to refer to; the great powers intending to avoid their excessively direct involvement; the small states unable to manage emergencies on their own: all these bodies called on the League of Nations. They did so in the face of the waves of refugees caused by the redefinition of borders imposed by the peace treaties, in the face of the explosion of epidemics and in the face of the consequences of the economic crisis. The League of Nations' social affairs section grew beyond every prediction. The degree of cooperation between the different countries was far greater than that obtained on the political and diplomatic fronts. The work of the social affairs section – such as the health and social programmes or those for child protection – were transformed into a great laboratory that enhanced and grew the internationalism that had technical, intellectual and scientific specialisa-tions.[9] But what does all this mean from the point of view of cooperation for humanitarian projects? How did the League of Nations contribute to imprinting a specific character on the emerging system of international aid?

The first aspect to highlight is the boost the organisation gave to the global net-work of collaborations. Let us take as an example the public health programmes with which the League of Nations became a sector of work and international intervention. Germany and the Soviet Union took part in the League of Nations' health and social programmes before even becoming member states, as did the United States, which never became a member. The training of medical and para-medical staff, the reporting of statistical data on diseases, the development of the measures necessary to tackle the spread of epidemics (for example through vaccinations) – all these initiatives triggered a wide network of collaborations. Their centre for propulsion and coordination was the Health Organization, set up as an internal League of Nations section and directed by the Polish epidemi-ologist Ludwik Rajchman. The Organization contributed to transmitting the shared notions of preventive medicine and public health, which were developed in the Western world but which subsequently spread and were applied far beyond its borders. In 1925 an epidemiology statistical centre was set up in Singapore from where research programmes were carried out in most of South East Asia and on the coasts of southern Africa.[10] Furthermore, Rajchman was also the head of a team of experts who supplied 'technical assistance' to Nationalist China between the end of the 1920s and the start of the following decade.[11]

Through the creation of these sorts of projects the League of Nations im-printed a global dimension not only on the network of collaborations but also on the areas of intervention, which included different continents and connected Western countries and colonial territories. In this sense, the role the Genevan organisation took in lending impetus and resonance to the new international debate on slavery was of great significance. In the decades before the Great War, the persistence of various forms of slavery outside Europe had been the subject of a vast mobilisation involving countries such as Britain, France and Italy, a mobilisation that had taken on a transnational character.[12] The discussion re-emerged in the 1920s and one of its fundamental points was the condemnation of the plight of the indigenous peoples, exploited as a workforce and deprived of their freedom even though the system of slavery had been formally banned for a long time. It was the British activists in particular, represented by the Anti-slavery and Aborigines Protection Society,[13] who identified the League of Nations as an indispensable contact point to carry forward their battle.

The League of Nations was the ideal centre for the circulation of information and reflection on the suffering generated by the persistence of different forms of slavery in some regions of Africa. In addition, the anti-slavery movement created pressure for the problem to find a response on an international level through the new intergovernmental body. The campaign condemning the slave trade still practised in Ethiopia influenced the decision within the League of Nations to set up a commission on slavery; more generally, the masses of documents sent to Geneva on the working conditions of the indigenous populations in non-European territories encouraged the ratification of the Slavery Convention in 1926.[14] With the Convention, slavery and the slave trade were finally banned, not just by individual measures on a national level but also by an intergovernmental agreement signed by many countries. Although there was universal convergence on the topic of slavery, the document did not include *ad hoc* measures against the different forms of enforced labour, which had also been broadly condemned in previous years.

The problem of forced labour was kept apart from that of slavery and was considered to be under the competence of the International Labour Organization (ILO). The ILO had been set up during the Paris Peace Conference and was conceived as a tool for overcoming social conflicts and economic interests through dialogue and cooperation, with the purpose of promoting peace and stability. Although the core of its mandate concerned the effects of industrialisation, the ILO became the most important centre for documentation on living conditions in the colonial empires, since its own officials recognised that the topic of forced labour could not be tackled without considering the situation in the colonies. The result of the work carried out by the ILO on this front was undoubtedly disappointing if we look at the Convention Concerning Forced or Compulsory Labour, ratified in 1930. In this document the signatory countries undertook 'to suppress the use of forced or compulsory labour in all its forms within the shortest possible period' but the document did not mention in any way the specific situation of the colonies.[15] However, at the same time, the ILO did gather evidence on different forms of 'new slavery' and spread this information through publications and conferences; and it encouraged the widening of the debate on the inhuman treatment of colonised peoples.[16]

In the years between the two World Wars, therefore, the condemnation of the ill-treatment of the populations in the colonies, which was supported by humanitarian motivations, took on as reference points the League of Nations and the ILO. And yet the ILO and the League had been planned from their inceptions as institutions to give stability to the international order within which the colonial system existed, and had been inspired by the very ideologies on which the empires rested.[17] Furthermore, these same bodies were not limited to being simple passive receptors of reports and documents on the different forms of slavery but encouraged the circulation of information and critical reflections. They contributed to putting into contact the different organisations in the 'new abolitionism' and encouraged the standardisation of the methods of enquiry into the living conditions of non-European peoples. So from the point of view that interests us here, the work of the League and the ILO was far from irrelevant, since both organisations strengthened the placing of humanitarian questions in the sphere of international action and promoted their institutionalisation.

The League of Nations marked an important step in the history of humanitarianism because it permanently included it among the fields of intergovernmental competence. However, this step should not be understood as an exclusion of the non-state organisations that were already active in the sector. On the other hand, the League of Nations collaborated intensively with the major associations that had gained international relevance and recognition, gathering and reprocessing their demands, working in partnership on individual projects and using their financing in the face of the lack of funds from governments. For example, the Rockefeller Foundation, the influential American philanthropic society founded in 1913, financed most of the League of Nations' health programmes for over a decade.[18] Geneva, additionally, was at the centre of wide cooperation networks that included groups that were different in their ends and their motivations. An important example concerns the major collaboration between the Social Section of the League and a vast transnational network of associations on the subject of the treatment of women and children. The positions of the various groups formally or informally included in this network could differ on crucial questions, such as the role of states in the fight against trafficking women. But it was through their conciliations and reprocessing that both the Convention for the Suppression of the Traffic in Women and Children (ratified in 1921) and the procedures introduced by the League of Nations to monitor its application took shape. So the non-governmental organisations, missionary societies and philanthropic associations that had long been busy on the ground all helped to shape an institutional framework for the international response to the problem of trafficking.[19]

On the political and diplomatic front, the League of Nations was a terrible failure because aggressive Nazi-Fascist nationalism got the better of liberal internationalism and the world plummeted towards a new war. But the programmes promoted by the Social Section broadened the organisation's operational horizon well beyond its original mandate and were an important stage on the road taken by humanitarianism. In the years between the two World Wars, humanitarian activities took on specific characteristics: they became part of intergovernmental politics and of the relationship between states; they embraced a global horizon from the point of view of the countries called to cooperate and of the intervention areas; and they were the outcome of intense collaboration between private and institutional bodies. As well as this, the League of Nations promoted the training of officials, technicians and experts – the new professionals of international co-operation – who, in many cases, later placed themselves in the service of the United Nations. All of this accompanied the determination (or re-determination) of the areas of competence for humanitarianism: we have already referred to public health, working conditions in non-European regions and the trafficking of human beings. Over the next paragraphs we will examine two further areas of intervention that were particularly relevant: relief to children and refugees.

On the children's side

One morning in May 1919 two women began distributing leaflets to passersby in Trafalgar Square. They were Barbara Ayrton Gould, a representative of the

British section of the Women's International League for Peace and Freedom, and Eglantyne Jebb, a well known figure in the world of London philanthropy. On the leaflet there was a photograph of a little boy, portrayed completely naked to highlight the disproportion of his limbs and the frailty of his small body. Prominently above the image, in capitals, was the headline *A STARVING BABY*, while the short text below explained that the boy in the photograph was only one of millions of malnourished European children and that there was only one way to help them – 'to restore free intercourse between the nations and allow the starving countries to feed themselves'.[20]

The leaflet intended to condemn the deprivation experienced by children in the countries that had lost the war – such as Austria, where the photograph had been taken – and which had now been hit by the heavy British sanctions. Barbara and Eglantyne were arrested for distributing unpatriotic propaganda but the uproar provoked by the event was worth a few nights in prison. The news of their arrest spread quickly and the image of the malnourished Austrian child ended up on in the newspapers. The attention of the press contributed to a shift of opinion on the problem of economic sanctions and the urgency of mobilisation to help their most innocent victims, the children. This mobilisation was the main aim of the newly created Save the Children Fund (SCF), in whose name the two women arrested for unpatriotic propaganda were handing out leaflets.

The episode of the leafleting in Trafalgar Square is well known and is often presented as the event that gave birth to the organisation Save the Children, of which Eglantyne Jebb has long been considered the founding mother. The new body soon became one of the main players in humanitarian activism in the post-First World War period and contributed to the establishment of the protection of childhood as a priority for intervention and to the figure of the child as the best representative of an aid recipient. The foundation of the association dedicated to 'saving the children' was therefore important but it certainly cannot be attributed simply to either the single demonstration against British sanctions or the will of Eglantyne Jebb. Rather, the creation of the SCF was brought about by the convergence of several factors. A major one of these was the liveliness of British philanthropy, which was certainly not new to making childhood the focus of its work; another was post-war internationalism, understood in its different expressions. The conviction that, in a context of strong economic and political interdependence, cooperation between states encouraged peace and prosperity not only guided the Anglo-American diplomatic action that led to the creation of the League of Nations: that same conviction was widely spread among the citizens of Western countries and contributed to animating the activities of groups and movements that acted on a local basis but were connected to broad international networks, such as those that joined the pacifist or feminist associations.

Save the Children, therefore, was not in fact the creation of Eglantyne Jebb. It is useful, though, to recall some aspects of her biography since they provide a key for the reading of the history of the organisation associated with her name.[21] Eglantyne was from a well-off English family and was one of the first women to be educated at Oxford. After her degree, she taught for a short period at a school in a working-class district of Marlborough in Wiltshire, developing a marked interest in the social problems she had come into contact with via her pupils. She pursued this interest by dedicating herself to voluntary work at the Charity Organisation Society (COS), which was the most important philanthropic association in late-Victorian England. On behalf of the COS, Jebb published the report of an inquiry in 1906 into the social problems of the city of Cambridge that faithfully reflected the principles of scientific philanthropy. The author analysed the living conditions of the working classes in detail and suggested the adoption of relief policies that would quantify the amounts of aid appropriate to different degrees of need, promoting the moral advance of the poor and preventing their dependence on charity becoming chronic. One part of the inquiry was dedicated to children, based on the conviction that childhood and adolescence were the stages of life when vices and virtues are acquired and during which it is therefore necessary to intervene to forge the morally irreproachable adults of the future.[22]

In 1913, after the conclusion of the Second Balkan War, Eglantyne made a journey to Macedonia on behalf of the Macedonian Relief Fund, founded ten years before following nationalist revolts that broke out in the Balkan region. The foundation of the Macedonian Relief Fund had been the outcome of the political and public mobilisation that in England had condemned the harsh repression by the Ottoman authorities, referring back to motivations and issues from the protests that exploded against the 'atrocities' of the Sublime Porte in the 1870s.[23] Charles and Dorothy Buxton, Eglantyne Jebb's brother-in-law and sister – both liberals – were among the leading figures in the Macedonian Relief Fund and they were the ones to ask Eglantyne to leave for the Balkans.

It was Charles and Dorothy Buxton again who involved Eglantyne Jebb in the activities of the Fight the Famine Council (FFC), the association founded in 1919 with the purpose of condemning the armistice's 'punitive' clauses, which had already become well known. The FFC brought together a group of activists from the philanthropist, socialist, feminist and pacifist movements. Its goal was to bring to public attention the consequences of the conditions imposed by the victors on the civilian populations of the defeated countries, and at the same time to pressurise the institutions to revoke the measures considered unjust. The Women's International League for Peace and Freedom (WILPF) – which Dorothy Buxton also belonged to – took part in the FFC's initiatives too. The WILPF had been founded in 1915 when Europe was in total conflict, setting itself the aim of the production by women of the tools necessary to abolish war from the face of the earth. Internationalism, pacifism and feminism were inseparable components of the WILPF's agenda and the claim to women's rights was closely connected to the commitment to improving the living conditions of all of humanity.[24]

The FFC's initiatives therefore joined together different groupings and the reconciliation of their demands was not obvious. The idea of creating a section for fundraising to offer immediate aid (food, medicine, clothing) to all the children in Europe, regardless of their nationality, also came from the intention of finding that reconciliation. The Save the Children Fund – as the new section was called – was a meeting point for the different souls of the association. This was, on the one hand, because the response to primary needs (hunger, disease, cold) could easily be pointed out as the quintessence of humanitarian action, free from any political implication,[25] and, on the other hand, because philanthropic rhetoric – even in the Victorian age – had heavily stressed the innocence of childhood, and now children could be pointed out as the perfect examples of victims of the states' international policies. The recall to 'pure' humanitarianism and the concentration on the assistance of children made it easier for the SCF to win consensus in public opinion, as the outrage aroused by the Trafalgar Square episode and the solidarity displayed towards the main characters in the leafleting showed.

But it was not her arrest for distributing unpatriotic propaganda that led to Eglantyne Jebb heading what would in the space of a few months become an independent organisation. Rather, Eglantyne became the president of the SCF for three reasons: she was able to take advantage of a vast network of relations; she enjoyed great authority in the philanthropy world; and she was not politically engaged. Her figure was very acceptable to the members of the organisation who feared the emergence of more radical positions – represented, for example, by the WILPF – who they thought would compromise the widening of the consensus on the SCF. Eglantyne Jebb seemed to be the best person to govern that jumble of heterogeneous charitable, intellectual and political impulses that had led to the formation of the new body.[26] Her appointment signalled the will to construct a depoliticised image of humanitarian action embodied by the SCF.[27]

Under Jebb's management, the organisation grew rapidly, both in terms of its visibility and the support it gained at home, and in terms of its international plan. The sum of £1,300,000 obtained in the fundraising campaign of 1921 was considered an authentic record of the voluntary donations and a few years later the SCF was able to boast that it was operational in twenty-four countries between Europe and the Near East. This expansion of the British organisation's activities coincided with the establishment of a vision of humanitarianism. On the one hand, it was dictated by the profound consequences of the First World War; on the other, it incorporated the new spirit of international cooperation, taking the League of Nations as an institutional reference point.[28] The network of international collaborations that the SCF wove together in its very first years is significant in this regard.

The aim of the SCF was to go beyond occasional collaborations tied to individual projects in order to firm up longer-lasting alliances that would contribute to ensuring the organisation's presence on the post-war aid scene. It was not a coincidence that Jebb asked for and obtained the sponsorship of the ICRC. In this way the SCF established an important tie with Geneva, where it was necessary to be present if the intention was to enter the arena where humanitarianism was becoming a crucial element of the relationship between states. The decisive step for the SCF's entry into this arena was achieved through the constitution in 1920 of the Save the Children International Union (SCIU), a sort of umbrella organisation that aimed to bring together all the groups operating in the field of assistance to children. The SCF played an important role in promoting the formation of the SCIU, which chose Geneva as its base and aimed to become the main reference for the League of Nations on the subject of aid for children.

The SCIU was set up as a federation of independent national committees (made up of lawyers, teachers, doctors and social workers) and was one of the first bodies in the post-war period to recognise equal representation for the defeated and victorious countries. It was this choice that guaranteed it wide accreditation among the internationalists of Europe and a wide development: two years after its set-up the organisation had brought together seventeen different committees scattered over all of Europe.

In its first years of work it dealt with the distribution of aid to needy children, particularly in central and eastern Europe. When the emergency had passed, the SCIU sought, however, to redefine its mandate and to be classified as an international agency for the spread of 'good practice' in child protection on the subjects of health, education and child labour. Starting off from this arrangement, the main aim of the SCIU became that of helping the smaller states – created in the geopolitical redefinition of Europe contained in the peace treaties – to reach the standard of Western civilisation on the protection of children. The many countries represented within the organisation therefore adopted different, asymmetrical profiles because some were classified as bearers of a positive child relief model and others remained as recipients of the aid necessary in achieving that model.[29]

Under the new mandate that it had been given, the SCIU turned to drawing up the Declaration of the Rights of the Child, which was then approved by the League of Nations in 1924. The Declaration's ratification came at the end of lengthy diplomatic work, conducted personally by Eglantyne Jebb as the SCIU's representative. In its five concise articles, that document established that children 'must be the first to receive relief in times of distress', that every hungry and sick child had to be nourished and cared for, and that childhood should be protected 'against every form of exploitation'.[30] The text avoided all the questions that in previous years had proved to be controversial, for example regarding the primacy of the state or of the family in child care, or recourse to public assistance rather than to aid provided by private associations. The Declaration sanctioned the right of minors to relief but at the same time it strategically limited itself to very general proclamations that could readily gather wide consensus.[31]

The Declaration of the Rights of the Child became the policy document for the Child Welfare Committee, set up by the League of Nations as an internal body within the secretariat. The Assembly of the League of Nations established that the new body had to simply record and debate the experience of different countries on certain issues: under-age marriage, child health and labour, economic support for families, the repatriation of refugee children. In the years afterwards, the Child Welfare Committee – within which the British representatives exercised significant influence – dealt mainly with eastern countries, such as Czechoslovakia and Hungary, still based on the belief that they should reach full development as societies and national communities. Reformulating in an international context the convictions that she had developed with the Charity Organisation Society, Eglantyne Jebb – a leading figure on the Committee – stated that supporting childhood was crucial for contributing to the route of these countries 'on the path of progression' because today's children were tomorrow's citizens.[32]

The collection of documentation and the discussions had little follow-up and the concrete results of the Committee's work were modest, just as the impact of the Declaration of the Rights of the Child remained weak. However, the founding stage of the international mobilisation for children is often dated to the 1920s and the Child Welfare Committee is normally pointed out as the ancestor of the International Children's Emergency Fund (UNICEF), even if that UN agency's origins are not directly connected to the Committee. But while it is not accurate to say that the Committee was the parent of UNICEF, it certainly was the base where the League of Nations and humanitarian associations 'internationalised' the problem of assistance to children, including it on the agenda of aid and co-operation between states.

A 'new' humanitarian emergency: refugees

After the First World War, the president of the ARC and many other insiders underlined the protracted emergency situation, which was also due to consistent flows of refugees resulting from wartime events and the redefinition of borders after the peace treaties. In the period between the two World Wars, and particularly in the 1920s, special relief programmes, international agreements and policies determined the emergence of refugees as specific subjects of humanitarianism. The central figures in these were individual states and the League of Nations but also the associations that collaborated with them, not limiting themselves to representing the operational arm but contributing to defining the interventions' methods and contents.[33]

The first massive wave of fleeing men and women that contributed to making assistance to refugees the preeminent 'humanitarian question' was that of the Russians. The civil war and famine forced more than a million people to leave Bolshevik Russia. Many reached the bordering countries and some carried on westwards: according to an ARC estimate in November 1920, Poland, Germany and France received the greatest number of Russian refugees.[34] The following year, the Moscow government revoked citizenship from all those fleeing, who thus were reduced to the condition of stateless persons.

The phenomenon of civilians fleeing beyond the borders of their own countries was of course not new. It had already taken on worrying proportions during the Balkan Wars (1912–13) when the withdrawal of the Ottoman empire from continental Europe and the definition of a system of nation states in the Balkan region had entailed the forced movement of hundreds of thousands of people. The problem then exploded with the First World War because the land conquests of the armies and the shifting of the fronts caused the violent uprooting of millions of civilians.[35] However, in the post-war period the question arose in different terms. The new flux of refugees from Russia, which disturbed the fragile international order established with the peace treaties, on the one hand was a reason for worrying about humanitarian associations, now significantly developed and working on an international level. On the other hand, it was a problem of the competence of the new intergovernmental body, the League of Nations, since the refugees – in that they were individuals far from their own countries and therefore no longer able to enjoy the protection of a nation state – were an international problem *par excellence*.

It was this combination of reasons that led to a figure within the League of Nations being appointed to deal with the problem of the Russians fleeing west. The creation of the High Commissioner for Refugees is usually identified as the starting point of the institutional commitment to refugees on an international level. Certainly it was something new from this point of view but it is worth remembering that it was also the outcome of concerted pressure applied by the representatives of a group of associations of various nationalities, led by the president of the ICRC, Gustave Ador. It was Ador who, in February 1921, composed an appeal in which he referred to approximately 800,000 refugees spread throughout Europe in absolute poverty and without legal protection. In the document, the League of Nations was asked to intervene since it was 'the only supernational political authority capable of solving a problem which is beyond the power of exclusively humanitarian organizations' and the appointment was suggested 'of a General Commissioner for the Russian Refugees'.[36] This proposal became a concrete resolution a few months later, after an intergovernmental congress entirely dedicated to the topic. The nomination of Fridtjof Nansen as High Commissioner for Refugees was a measure taken by the Council of the League of Nations but it did so in the light of opinions expressed both by a vast network of humanitarian societies and by individual states. The convergence of the different players in the decision to create a specific office to resolve the problem of the Russian refugees was determined as much by the incapacity of the national authorities to tackle a migratory flux considered potentially destabilising as by the significance questions of a humanitarian nature had by then attained in international public debate.

It is worth recalling the profile of Fridtjof Nansen in order to understand the reasons for his nomination and the significance attributed to his appointment. A scientist and explorer and diplomatic envoy of the Oslo government during the war, Nansen entered the Assembly of the League of Nations as a member of the Norwegian delegation and it was in this role that he received the appointment before conducting an inquiry into the repatriation of prisoners of war. Through this, Nansen strengthened his skills as a diplomat, having acquired specific knowledge about aid and built a wide network of relations with the associations in the sector. All these circumstances – along with the fact that he spoke on behalf of a neutral country – made him the ideal candidate for the position of High Commissioner for Refugees. He was expected to define the legal status of the Russian refugees and arrange either for their repatriation or for their 'integration' in other countries.[37]

The High Commissioner's first measure concerned the issuance of a personal document for the men and women fleeing Russia that guaranteed them recognition of their refugee status. The certificate issued by the League of Nations to these refugees allowed the authorities of the 'welcoming' countries to identify the many people who were passing over their borders, in line with the regulation of frontier crossings that had recently been established through the generalised adoption and recognition of the passport. It was on the basis of these needs that an intergovernmental congress specifically arranged for the purpose in 1922 approved the so-called 'Nansen passport', in other words, an identity certificate with which the refugees could travel. More precisely, the ex-citizens of the newly formed Soviet Union could legally enter the states that had ratified the use of the League of Nations' document.

The 'Nansen passport' is often regarded as the first basic step on the road that led to the later legal definition of the refugee. Of course, the innovation sanctioned by this measure is undeniable but it must not be equated with the legislation that is currently in force, forgetting that the condition of being a refugee certified by the League of Nations' 'passport' did not have a universal value. In other words, it was not given to a single individual on the basis of having been forced to leave the home country. Instead, that condition was recognised to a set of people identified on the basis of their nationality and a specific event; or, rather, the certificate was issued to Russian men and women because of the revolution and the civil war. The logic of how the 'Nansen passport' worked is easily understood if we look at the later cases in which it was used. In fact, having introduced it for the Russian refugees, the High Commissioner planned to release the document bearing his name to those Armenians who had survived the genocide and were now refugees outside the new borders of the Turkish state. The release of the 'passport' could not be extended to the Armenians, however, without the consent of individual countries, which were called on to express themselves on the validity of the League of Nations' 'guest pass' within their borders. The same thing happened with the later widening of the system to the Assyrians and other Christian minorities from territories that had previously belonged to the Ottoman empire.

In conclusion, then, the first form of recognition of the condition of being a refugee was planned as a temporary measure to be applied only in certain cases. It remained tied to precise 'stopgap emergency measures',[38] identified as such by the states joined together in the League of Nations' Assembly. Furthermore, the refugee status planned by Fridtjof Nansen did not concern the individual but a set of people, in line with the predominance – in the culture and politics of the post-war years – of collective rights and the protection of national communities instead of individual freedoms. Finally, it must be kept clearly in mind that the release of the 'Nansen passport' enabled the identification of the refugees on the borders or in the countries in which they had found refuge but it left open the problem of their destiny and the solutions to be adopted on that question.

From the moment he was called on to take measures for the men and women fleeing post-revolutionary Russia, Fridtjof Nansen acted in the conviction that the refugees' arrival should be considered a temporary emergency, to be resolved through repatriation. The great powers, France and Britain in particular, were pushing in the same direction. Negotiating the return of the refugees with the Soviet authorities would have solved *a priori* the problem of the resources necessary for making arrangements for them in the countries affected by the migratory flux but the question was not just a financial one. The establishment of homogeneous national communities was considered a fundamental requisite for the consolidation of the European democracies and therefore for the entire post-war reconstruction project. From this point of view, reunification with the society from which the refugee population had come – was the ideal solution on the political and ideological level, as otherwise that population would be a 'foreign body'. The High Commissioner's consultancy committee associations – some of which were the direct expression of the refugee communities, such as the Comité des Zemstvos et Villes russes – were opposed to the repatriation programme since those who had escaped would have been persecuted once they re-entered the Soviet Union. The re-entry programme was started all the same following the necessary dealings with the Moscow authorities. The first repatriations were organised from Bulgaria but operations were very soon interrupted because of the difficult diplomatic relations between the Soviet government and the countries affected by the Russian migration.[39]

Nansen also attempted the policy of repatriation in the case of the Armenian refugees. The High Commissioner forcefully supported the proposal to encourage the emigration of the genocide survivors to the Transcaucasian Republic of the Soviet Union, which had annexed the territories of Armenia in 1922, marking the end of the latter's attempt to set itself up as an independent state. The programme started by the High Commissioner in collaboration with the authorities in Yerevan did not achieve significant results and the people affected were a negligible minority. It is important to recall it, however, because it was a further step in the political formulation of the idea that refugees should be relocated within the borders of a real or presumed home country, among people of the same nationality, religion and language. This idea, then, was guiding the first steps in the creation of the international system for refugees and profoundly influenced its later advances too.[40]

The conviction that questions related to refugees were intimately connected to the protection of the integrity of national communities led the League of Nations to tackle in addition the problem of the population exchange between Greece and Turkey. This was a further important case in which the High Commissioner was called to intervene. The exchange between the Muslims resident in Greece and the Greeks living in Turkey was set out in the Treaty of Lausanne, signed in 1923. This agreement was reached after a decade of exiles and forced migrations that had dramatically accelerated during the Greco-Turkish War (1919–23) and were being retrospectively legitimised. Nansen publicly took on the responsibility for this measure, which was very controversial but hoped for by most parties, and reflected the conviction that the homogeneity of nations should be guaranteed, even through drastic resolutions such as the enforced movement of populations. As well as this, the League of Nations provided logistical support during the operations to move hundreds of thousands of people and in Greece it attempted to facilitate the difficult accommodation arrangements for the refugees from the Anatolian peninsula within the borders of their 'motherland'.[41]

The case of the Armenian genocide survivors and that of the Russians fleeing after the Bolshevik revolution showed, however, that repatriation, albeit significant in determining institutional measures, did not offer an effective solution to the 'refugee problem'. The League of Nations' High Commissioner therefore also started a programme that had to facilitate the integration of the refugee population within the countries ready to welcome them. The linchpin of this programme was a professional training path, entrusted to the International Labour Organization (ILO). The ILO itself was to connect the training pathway with the availability of posts, the notification of which was made by the individual governments. They presided over a selection process in which possible employers and representatives of the refugees' associations also took part. With this system, the Russians fleeing the civil war and the Armenians who had escaped the genocide became emigrants capable of filling the specific labour requirements of certain countries. It is no coincidence that the League of Nations and the ILO considered what was put into practice with the holders of the 'Nansen passport' as a pilot project, to be extended later on to respond to growing European unemployment.

The programme never reached this second stage and the pursuit of the initial aim met several hurdles. In the post-war years, many European countries placed harsher restrictions on immigration and strengthened their borders, and in the end only France welcomed a significant number of migrants/refugees. The difficulties encountered in Europe pushed the ILO into starting up the placement of some of the refugees in Latin America, in the countries where there were greater possibilities of work. In order to have a significant impact, the plan for emigration to South America had to be accompanied by setting up an *ad hoc* fund able to guarantee financial coverage and provide the operations with more breathing space. This funding proposal for the initiative, however, was scuppered, but the League of Nations and the ILO stated they had at any rate achieved some success in providing stable accommodation for the Russians and Armenians in the countries that had offered them work.[42] Certainly, the two organisations began a policy of resettlement through work that met with fairly widespread application after the Second World War.[43]

The problem of ensuring adequate financing did not only concern the programme of placement in Latin America but was, to an extent, structural. The League of Nations guaranteed the High Commissioner for Refugees coverage of the costs only for administrative management, while the individual interventions had to be approved and financed each time. Setting up a new office, therefore, sanctioned the fact that protection and relief for refugees were an area of intergovernmental competence. At the same time, though, Fridjof Nansen's degree of autonomy was severely limited by the need to negotiate every project with individual governments in order to get ratification and money. It is worth recalling that despite the important functions taken on by the League of Nations, the states remained the major players in the management of the refugee problem and more generally of 'humanitarian questions', which had by now become part of the agenda of international relations. In some cases it was the national governments themselves that took on the responsibility for immediate aid for refugee populations, which is what happened in Yugoslavia, Bulgaria and Czechoslovakia with the Russian migrants. And in the Near East the mandatory powers – France and Britain – took part directly in the evacuation, the temporary care and the territorial redistribution of the Russian, Armenian, Greek and Assyrian refugees. The emergency represented by the refugees then became part of the public debate in which the Western powers justified the mandate system itself, ratified by the League of Nations.[44]

Among the various players who contributed to the emergence of the current international system for refugees there was also a part for private initiative, from the point of view both of the relationship established with the League of Nations and from the direct work in creating relief programmes. As we have already recalled, it was the humanitarian associations – led by the ICRC – that put pressure on the League of Nations to create the figure of the High Commissioner, who was assigned a crucial role in formulating and putting into practice the institutional response to the refugee problem.[45] Nansen knew perfectly well, though, that the institutional response could not ignore the collaboration with the big organisations that were already working in the field, and who therefore had indispensable connections, resources and qualifications. The setting up of a consultative committee made up of representatives of different associations (including the ICRC, the YMCA and Save the Children[46]) came out of this awareness, as did the decision to select the High Commissioner's delegates in the countries affected by the Russian immigration from the staff who were already in the service of the Red Cross. So the professional experience developed within one of the most significant non-governmental organisations ended up directly serving the League of Nations.

The humanitarian associations were also significant in directly managing the assistance given to the refugee population. John Hope Simpson, a well known exponent of British liberalism, in his thorough study of the refugee population in the years between the World Wars – still considered today an indispensable reference point in the history of refugee studies – wrote: 'It is fair to say that the greater part of material assistance has been provided by private organisations, some of them set up *ad hoc*, but some with more general functions of which refugee work is only one'.[47] Among the organisations 'with more general functions', which were already known in the field of international aid and were dedicated to the refugee population, we must of course remember the ICRC, but also the Friends, the SCF and the ARC. The last, for example, had a pre-eminent role in the assistance of the Russian refugees[48] due to its greater resources; in the setting of the projects for western Europe and the Balkans, the ARC provided basic necessities and medical care to hundreds of thousands of refugees who had arrived in Greece after the Greco-Turkish war.[49]

The relief work undertaken by the private associations took on even greater importance when the question of refugees acquired different meanings and the League of Nations entered a phase of substantial deadlock. In the Europe of the 1930s, the phenomenon of flight especially concerned those persecuted for political and racial reasons: at least 400,000 people – mostly Jews – escaped from Nazi Germany, and the number was more or less the same of the Republicans who abandoned Spain after the victory of the Francoists. The latter were welcomed for the most part in France, whereas the impasse in the international system for refugees hinging on the League of Nations was laid bare, as is well known, by the refugees who started to leave the Third Reich from 1933 onwards. For them there was neither a 'Nansen passport' nor a specific relief plan: the question was discussed by the League of Nations but the member countries failed to reach agreement.

What had changed compared to ten years earlier when a shared programme had been agreed to respond to the Russian refugee emergency? The economic crisis of 1929 and the start of the Great Depression had led in all countries to a harsh tightening of the immigration laws, which in the past had already been a hurdle to the welcoming of refugees and were now an insurmountable barrier. On top of this, Germany had re-acquired a position as a 'great power' and was making its weight felt in the forum of the League of Nations too: the ratification of measures to protect those persecuted politically and racially by National Socialism was held back by the fear of diplomatic tensions with the Hitler government. The economic crisis and the new set-up of European politics closed the spaces from which humanitarianism had emerged as common ground in cooperation between states. The next proof of this closure came with the resignation, in 1935, of the High Commissioner for Refugees Coming from Germany, the American James G. McDonald. He had been nominated two years previously by the Council of the League of Nations, which had wanted to entrust the question to an external expert. McDonald led long and not very profitable negotiations to offer reception to Jews and non-Jews fleeing National Socialism. After the issue of the Nuremberg laws in 1935, he stated that the League of Nations should have tackled the reasons behind that increasingly massive flight by standing up to the German government; he resigned to strengthen his position.[50]

The question of the refugees once again became the subject of an intergovernmental policy with the setting up, in 1938, of the Intergovernmental Committee on Refugees (IGCR), the only concrete result – as has often been noted – of the Evian Conference, called by Franklin Delano Roosevelt to discuss the problem of refugees from Germany. The new body, wished for in the first place by the US president, was not very effective in accomplishing its twofold mission: negotiating with the National Socialist government the conditions for the emigration of Jews; negotiating with other countries the possibility of offering men and women escaping from persecution a permanent home.

The creation of the Intergovernmental Committee on Refugees is nonetheless significant because it made clear the loss of trust in the League of Nations and the decline of the international system for refugees that had emerged around it in the 1920s.[51] Only one component of that system had shown itself able to respond to the dramatic flight of the Jews from the Third Reich: the private agencies, and particularly those from the Jewish world. 'The resources and machinery of the world organizations of Jewry were placed at the service of emigration',[52] wrote John Hope Simpson, and underlined their 'extreme efficiency' in providing tens of thousands of people with the logistical support in order to leave Germany, assistance during the difficult journey and the possibility of settling elsewhere. This 'extreme efficiency' frequently had to face up to the rigidity of governments of countries where the organisations operated: the associations of the English Jews, for example, had to ensure the British authorities that no Jewish refugee admitted would become a public expense, in other words, that no one would be a burden on public welfare.[53] Only at the end of 1938 did Britain, and other Western countries, start to change its policies towards the population fleeing National Socialism: but this by now was the prelude to the humanitarianism of war.

The US programmes in the Middle East and eastern Europe

> We, the remaining of the deportees, women and children, were forced to walk without being allowed even to buy some bread to eat. Frequently we were robbed by Turks and the gendarmes, as if they would carry us safely to our destiny which was entirely unknown to us. So for thirty two days we were obliged to wander through mountains and valleys. Fatigue and hunger enforced by the whip of the cruel gendarmes, diminished the number of the deportees. After many dangers whose description would take much time, a few women and children, included I myself, arrived at Aleppo, Syria, in the beginning of September 1915. Since then I am supported by the Hon. Consulate of U.S.A. in Aleppo, Syria.[54]

In January 1920 Nafina Hagop Chilinguirian filled in the form necessary to ensure the support of the US authorities in her request for the return of her goods held in a foreign country: with these words the young woman tried to summarise the tragic events that had struck her family, and her people, in the restricted space of the questionnaire. In her brief tale Nafina recalled the dramatic events of the deportation that was an integral part of the genocide of the Armenians at the hands of the Turkish authorities. The adult men were killed *en masse* and then the women and children were led to the desert regions of Mesopotamia. All those who managed to get to the destination, surviving the forced march and escaping the abductions, were massed together in concentration camps.

At the end of the First World War, the fate of Nafina was different from that of the other survivors because she had obtained US citizenship through her marriage to Hagop Chilinguirian, who had emigrated to the United States following the massacres of the Armenians carried out in the 1890s and had later returned to his homeland. Because she was a US citizen, Nafina received protection and financial support from the US consulate in Aleppo; the same consulate had been a point of arrival and redistribution of aid for the Armenian survivors, at least until Washington entered the war and its diplomatic relations with the Ottoman empire were broken off. Finally, Nafina and her two children emigrated across the Atlantic.[55]

Nafina Hagop Chilinguirian's testimony sheds light on an unusual path because most of the survivors of the genocide did not have a second homeland to welcome them and they could only invoke their condition as refugees using the 'Nansen passport'. Nevertheless, Nafina's story is significant because it reflects the importance of the mobilisation for Armenians in the Ottoman empire in the context of American humanitarianism, first with the massacres at the end of the nineteenth century and then with the 1915 genocide. In particular, the work in the Middle East for the genocide survivors was an expression of the United States' new central role on the international aid stage, which in the post-First World War period was profoundly marked by the projects and the individuals coming from across the Atlantic. Some scholars maintain that the pre-eminent role of the

United States was fundamental in signalling a change in direction and in determining the establishment in those years of a new humanitarianism, one that we can define as modern.[56] The US programmes undoubtedly mobilised enormous resources and were an important component in the international policy of the Washington government. The examples we are talking about in this section – the intervention in the Middle East for the Armenian genocide survivors and the one in Bolshevik Russia against the famine – are certainly important. But other case studies could be added, such as the Chinese famine of 1920–21, the consequences of which were dealt with jointly by international and local relief societies.[57] At any rate, it is appropriate to interpret the initiatives of the US organisations within the larger humanitarian mobilisation of the post-First World War period and the meaning it took on in the international policies of the period. In addition, we must not forget that the idea of a modern humanitarianism – professional and secular – had been circulating in other countries before it did so in the United States, and its materialisation through specific programmes still rested on the reprocessing of longer-term experiences and skills.

It was Near East Relief that had a major role in the creation of the American aid for the Armenians. According to its first president, James L. Barton, the organisation's origins lay in a telegram sent in September 1915 to the American secretary of state by the US ambassador to Constantinople, Henry Morgenthau. In the short text Morgenthau stated with lucid awareness that 'the destruction of the Armenian race in Turkey [was] rapidly progressing' and he hoped for a body to be set up that could raise funds and provide help to the survivors.[58] The appeal was immediately accepted by the representatives of certain philanthropic societies and the committee that they started – which then took the name of Near East Relief – was immediately occupied both in an enormous information campaign about the violence perpetrated against the Armenians and in a hugely successful fundraising campaign.

The story of James L. Barton and the origins of Near East Relief – retold in many later publications – is illustrative for several reasons. In the first place, it allows the connection to emerge between the mobilisation of private citizens and the impulse of governmental institutions, which later maintained a special relationship with the new association. This was always of a private nature but the relationship with the governmental contacts and the US diplomats was crucial for the expansion of its network of activities.[59] Secondly, the tale about its origins indirectly allows the profile to be highlighted of the people who promoted the initiative to provide humanitarian aid for the Armenians. We can begin with Barton himself, who was one of the founders of the new organisation as secretary of the American Board of Commissioners for Foreign Missions, one of the most important Christian missionary societies, which was founded in 1810 as an expression of evangelical revivalism. Cleveland H. Dodge was also a leading figure among those who actively put into action Morgenthau's appeal. He was the owner of a large brass company, a Presbyterian, and one of the best-known New York philanthropists. Setting up Near East Relief and its later work in aid to refugees from Armenia – but also Greece, Assyria and those belonging to other Christian minorities – had its roots therefore in scientific American philanthropy and at the same time maintained a tie with the missionary work carried out in previous decades. Finally, the reference in Barton's report to the immediate and fortunate response obtained by the founders of Near East Relief means giving proper consideration to a further aspect: the attention paid by public opinion to the 'Armenian question', related by the most important press organisations and the subject of numerous conferences and informative pamphlets. The inception of Near East Relief was located therefore at a meeting point of the state, the associations' activism and popular interests, under an interweaving that – as we have seen – is a constant in the history of humanitarianism.

Between 1915 and 1916 Near East Relief worked mainly on private fundraising, seeking to keep close attention on the Armenian situation. As had already happened in response to the massacres of the 1890s,[60] the mobilisation for the Armenians was accompanied by an information and awareness-raising campaign that stressed the intolerability of the violence suffered by other human beings. But while in the past the call to solidarity with individuals far away had been motivated on a religious basis – and, moreover, in this case the recipients were Christians slaughtered by Muslims – now the idea that had precedence was that undertaking a humanitarian mission meant opposing 'barbarity' (that of the Turks) and stating the values of (Western) civilisation. The fundraising was aimed at the local purchase of foodstuffs, to be distributed through the network of missions already present in the area. Fundraising was always a strong point of Near East Relief: in the course of its existence it collected $110 million and at its peak it was feeding 300,000 people a day.[61]

After the end of the war, and the occupation by the victors of the Middle Eastern territories of the Ottoman empire, Near East Relief decided on a new set-up for its work and in the first place entrusted it to a greater extent to American relief workers sent to the field. Rather than further involving the staff of the missions, it preferred to rely on women and men with a professional role. Their task was not simply to distribute essential goods, give basic medical assistance and manage orphanages and welcome centres. The programmes for the new refugee settlements, and in particular for the orphans, included the construction and management of schools, starting up professional training courses, beginning small manufacturing work, and the management of initiatives for leisure.[62] The American organisation did not intend to limit itself to offering immediate aid: it also aimed to start rehabilitation schemes that would allow the aid recipients to gain the tools and capabilities to be able to provide for themselves afterwards. Only in this way was it felt that humanitarian action would be really effective, showing that it was something other than a mere act of charity.

The hoped-for rehabilitation of the recipients was in its turn planned as the tool through which to pursue a profound social and cultural transformation, which would start with the Armenian communities and then cover the whole region. The aid had to combat the backwardness of the Middle Eastern peoples and open the road to modernity and progress, of which American society was the most perfect representation. For the missionary societies, relief work was tightly entwined with proselytising, as we saw in Part I of this volume. Especially in the first period of its activity, Near East Relief took as an important reference point the missionary network in the Middle East. Its approach was of a different sort, though, because it was based broadly on the principles and aims of scientific philanthropy. For the American organisation, humanitarian aid was the vehicle for the achievement of an advanced, modern civilisation and its mission was exclusively secular, even though it was pervaded by Christian principles and values.[63]

The leaders of Near East Relief were convinced that their humanitarian programmes were intimately connected to international peacemaking and shared the idea of collective security promoted by the League of Nations.[64] At the same time, the Middle East appeared to the League of Nations to be a crucial area of intervention in which to carry out its function of ensuring the international community a lasting peace and stability. This conviction also influenced the initiatives undertaken to soothe the wounds inflicted by the war on certain groups of people, and humanitarian aid could strengthen the role of 'agent of geopolitical transformation' that the League of Nations had taken on through the system of mandates.[65] Particularly important was the programme for the Armenian women and children who had been kidnapped during the massacres and deportations and then remained in Muslim society. The first measure on the subject was taken in 1920 with the constitution of the Commission of Inquiry for the Protection of Women and Children in the Near East, which had the task of gathering information about the disappeared people and developing possible lines of action for the League. Setting up this type of commission was part of the Treaty of Sèvres, signed that same year, which obliged the Turkish authorities to collaborate with the League of Nations' representatives for the achievement of their mandate. The Commission's activity was based mainly on the work carried out in the field by relief officers from the League, which had opened two 'rescue homes' – one in Constantinople and the other in Aleppo – for women and children who had fled their captors.[66]

The Aleppo rescue home was open from 1921 to 1926. A Dane, Karen Jeppe, was called to be in charge of it. Jeppe had spent fifteen years in the Ottoman empire with the Deutsche Orient Mission, founded in 1895 by the evangelical pastor Johannes Lepsius in order to give assistance to the survivors of the Armenian massacre. During her long stay in western Anatolia Jeppe was predominantly concerned with education and health programmes. Her nomination by the League of Nations was above all due to pressure from the Scandinavian delegates, who included Henni Forchhammer, the vice-president of the International Council of Women, the historic organisation in which women of different nationalities were gathered.[67] The Council was closely tied to the philanthropic and relief dimension and in the period after the First World War identified in the struggle against the trafficking of women and children one of its main fields of action. Jeppe became a professional relief worker serving the international community thanks to the skills she had acquired through her missionary experience and the lobbying capabilities of one of the most highly accredited women's organisations in the League of Nations' Assembly.

The Aleppo rescue home, which hosted around 300 people between 1922 and 1923, was intended to be not only a refuge for those who had fled their captors. The intent was, rather, to unite reception and rehabilitation. During their stay, women and children followed professional training courses that were to provide them with the necessary tools to fend for themselves in the immediate future and on those courses they learned to cultivate the land, make rugs and shoes, work leather or to embroider.[68] The acquisition of new professional skills, which would benefit the entire Syrian economy, was to be part of a deeper process of moral regeneration. The aim was to enable individuals who had been long-term prisoners in the Muslim community to return to being – in the words of Jeppe herself – 'human beings'.[69] In its turn, the rescue of Armenian women and children was to encourage all of Middle Eastern society to reach a degree of civilisation and a superior moral order, of which Christianity remained a fundamental component. As in the case of Near East Relief, humanitarian aid was planned as the keystone to triggering very deep social and cultural transformations that would accompany the definitive overcoming of post-war instability in the Middle East and elsewhere.

The worry about the precariousness of the situation that had arisen at the end of the Great War and the intention to build a new order that was as consistent as possible with the values and interests of the United States were also behind the American programme in Russia. On 13 July 1921, the appeal made by great Russian intellectual Maxim Gorky for aid on behalf of the millions of Russians who risked starvation because of a terrible famine was made public in Moscow. In his aid request, Gorky described the effects of a terrible drought but the causes of the disaster that was claiming a shocking number of victims were not only natural. The lack of rain and the early summer heat had arrived at the end of a long period of contraction in agricultural production, aggravated by the war and the revolution, and then the civil war and the requisitions of wartime communism. In the face of the tragedy that had struck the Russian people, claimed Gorky, no individual of any sensitivity would be able to remain indifferent. His appeal was to a Western public made up of men and women who, on the basis of a shared 'humanitarian morality', would seize the occasion of the famine in Russia to demonstrate the unacceptability of the suffering of their fellows, translating their empathy into immediate action.

Gorky's message was published in the papers of various European countries and in the *New York Times* and was read by millions of people. Among these was Herbert Hoover, known both at home and abroad in those years as 'the Great Humanitarian'. What was the source of this appreciative appellation for the future US president, whose name ended up being associated above all with the Great Depression? Hoover, the successful manager of a big mining company and deemed in government circles to be a man of demonstrated competence, on account of his entrepreneurial skills and his vast network of international contacts – was asked, immediately after the start of the First World War, to organise the aid operations for the civilian Belgian population, reduced to starvation under the German occupation. Hoover had founded the Commission for Relief in Belgium, a private society through which he showed his great diplomatic abilities, since he managed to get the arrival of food aid in Belgium accepted not just by the German occupying forces but also by the English authorities, the embargo's proponents. The Commission organised the arrival of aid in the country while its distribution was delegated entirely to the Belgian authorities; the US organisation's representatives checked that the supply of the foodstuffs took place according to the rules, handled the accounts and planned the operation's development. This management of the programme applied entrepreneurial criteria and working methods, and most of the staff who worked for Hoover came from the business world. The resources arrived from the governments of the United States, France and Britain, from private donations and – in a fairly modest amount – from trading activities, such as the sale of the food products brought into Belgium. In the four and a half years it remained active, the Commission for Relief in Belgium fed around eight million people.[70]

When the United States entered the war, Hoover returned home and was welcomed as the 'saviour of Belgium'. President Wilson put him in charge of the Food Administration and at the end of the conflict he accompanied the US delegation to Paris for the signature of the peace treaties as the future head of aid operations for Europe. So the skills he had acquired in the humanitarian-inspired food programmes led Hoover into the group of statesmen called to redefine the international post-war order. The American Relief Administration (ARA), a governmental agency, was set up in February 1919 with the purpose of using the funds allocated by the American Congress; under the leadership of the 'saviour of Belgium' it distributed four million tonnes of food and other basic necessities in all of Europe. In this way Washington's direct intervention wrote an important page in post-war humanitarianism in Europe.

Once the programme launched by Congress had been concluded, the government agency was closed and Hoover founded a private society named the American Relief Administration European Children's Fund (ARAECF), which was anyway commonly called ARA: the full name remained only on paper. So the new organisation ended up having a name the same as the government body that had preceded it, just as it kept very close relationships with the authorities in Washington. It was this second ARA that arranged the feeding of around a million and a half children between central western Europe and the Near East, where the intervention was nonetheless more limited and much smaller than that of Near East Relief. And it was two years from the setting up of this second ARA that Herbert Hoover thought of accepting Gorky's appeal.

What were the reasons that led Hoover to plan a humanitarian intervention in Russia and the government authorities to support it? The programme was established in the context of a decisive internationalist policy put forward by the United States, which, from the economic point of view, was in the first place intended to speed up European reconstruction. The accomplishment of a new stability in Europe was, in fact, a necessary premise for the reactivation of the positive forms of financial and commercial interdependence between the two sides of the Atlantic, ensuring the payment of the war credits by the European countries and guaranteeing North American exports. In the decision to aid Russia under Lenin's leadership, what also counted, albeit to a lesser extent, was the need to dispose of the US surplus of cereal crops. Connecting the different motivations was the will – to use the words of Hoover himself – to 'stem the tide of bolshevism'.[71] Indeed, according to a simplified vision of the dynamics that led to the October revolution, it was thought that misery and starvation had opened the door to the Bolsheviks achieving power. The same concentration of food aid in western European countries between 1919 and 1921 had been dictated by the conviction that responding to the population's primary needs meant reducing the risk of a revolutionary wind spreading west beyond the borders of Soviet Russia. Aiding the Russian citizens who had been so dramatically hit by the famine would be weaken the internal consensus for Bolshevism and, hopefully, lead to the fall of the regime. Starting off from this assumption, Hoover conceived the food programme for Russia and obtained the necessary support from the government authorities.

We must not think, however, that the humanitarian question – in other words, the declared intent to save millions of human lives – was merely instrumental to the achievement of a political objective of a different nature. For the Great Humanitarian, standing up against the force of the Soviet revolution was in itself a humanitarian project because Bolshevism, for him, was synonymous with material and moral misery, and restoring a democratic society to individuals meant giving them back their full human dignity. Humanitarianism's agenda and the political one converged within a precise vision of the world.[72]

Naturally, it was not just the ARA that mobilised for Russia while it was in the grip of famine. In August 1921, the ICRC and the League of Red Cross Societies jointly called a conference in Geneva in which the representatives of twenty-two states and thirty humanitarian organisations of different nationalities took part. Following the meeting, a committee was set up for aid to the Russian population, which named as its High Commissioner Fridjtof Nansen (who also served as the High Commissioner for Refugees, as noted above). What was soon called the 'Nansen mission' operated in different ways to the ARA. While the American organisation wanted its own staff to maintain control over the distribution of aid, Nansen agreed that most of the foodstuffs intended for the population would be delivered directly to the Soviet authorities. This type of solution caused many disputes and the Norwegian commissioner was accused of being a Bolshevik sympathiser. Beyond the immediate criticisms, it is important to observe what waiving intervention meant in the definition of the criteria for distribution of basic necessities or in the selection of the 'beneficiaries'. Nansen in fact waived the right to control – in joint partnership or not with the local authorities – the effects of aid on the society it was intended for. The choice of this solution was probably due to the weakness of the European coalition's representative during the nego-tiation with the Soviets: the governments that had just promoted the initiative did not guarantee Nansen *ad hoc* financing and the supplies he managed to make available were, overall, rather more modest than the aid ensured by the ARA.[73]

The 'Nansen mission', administered from an office in Moscow, was anyway a reference point for the few humanitarian organisations operating autonomously in Russia, particularly the British Friends and the SCF. The Friends had already arrived by the time the famine exploded, since intervention in the Bolshevik-led country came within the area of the numerous relief programmes planned by the Society of Friends for post-war Europe. Nor did the Quakers leave – as the ARA did – once the peak of the crisis had passed. The British Friends followed an established model, in line with their vision of humanitarianism. To respond to the emergency exposed by Gorky they organised some broad-based fundraising and their activity in the Soviet territories was based exclusively on private donations, small and large. The Quaker staff – who included Francesca Wilson, whom we have already mentioned – above all distributed food rations, at one stage exclu-sively to children. This was a choice in line with many post-war humanitarian programmes but, according to some observers, it had dramatic consequences because it contributed to 'adding to the number of orphans; parents left children at their doors [the doors of relief officers] and walked away to die'.[74] The aims of the Quakers' programme were redefined and subsequently centred on aid to families, while childhood remained the exclusive area of intervention for the SCF, which in 1922 managed more than 1,000 canteens for children in the province of Saratov, a major urban centre in the Volga valley, the region worst hit by the famine. In the SCF newspaper, *The Record*, the choice of limiting its intervention to childhood was underlined to counter any suspicion that the Bolsheviks might gain some advantage from the aid. In fact, the non-involvement in politics of children was emphasised: they should not have to pay for the choices of adults.[75] It is no coinci-dence that *The Record* often quoted a statement by George Bernard Shaw that was so dear to Eglantyne Jebb: 'I have no enemies under the age of seven'.[76]

The American missionary societies did not produce autonomous programmes for Russia but worked on behalf of the ARA. The American Friends Service Committee followed a different road to the British Quakers and took part in the Soviet undertaking under the Hoover organisation. Indeed, the latter determinedly followed the aim of centralising and taking under his control all the aid operations conducted on Soviet territory by American bodies. To this end, the Great Humanitarian summoned the organisations that had already contributed – under his coordination – to aiding post-war Europe and obtained their affiliation to the ARA, which absorbed all the programmes for the starving Russian population. This also contributed to making the ARA the central figure in the mobilisation against the famine in Russia.[77]

The ARA intervention was certainly impressive. Initially, it was planned only for children, with the intent of feeding a million of them. But when the heads of the organisation arrived in the country they realised the dimensions of the tragedy were much greater than they had realised. Herbert Hoover understood that feeding a million children would not really change the state of things and that it was necessary to extend the programme to adults too, with the particip-ation of the US government. In December 1921 – when, as the newspapers wrote, the recently arrived winter threatened to leave sixteen million people dead – Congress approved the requested financing and boosted the intervention force that Hoover had already started up in Russia. The country was divided up into ten districts, to each of which an American head and team were sent. The selection of staff was considered a crucial step in starting the ARA's activities. Sometimes the choice was made in line with the previous aid programme: those who had served in Poland, Austria or in another European country were the ones who left for Russia. Moreover, it was mainly ex-soldiers from the US army, especially younger soldiers with a certain level of education. Some could count on the experience they had already gained with the ARA, but many others had no experience of humanitarian activities; what pushed them to the Soviet regions in the grip of famine was a spirit of adventure, attraction to the unknown and the desire to challenge fate on an arduous and dangerous mission. The ARA representatives were commonly called Hoover's Boys, a name which reflected as much the personal involvement of the Great Humanitarian in the organisation's management as the entirely male character of the staff. Russia was not considered a country for women and the humanitarian work managed mainly by ex-soldiers in a territory considered hostile ended up taking on as characteristic qualities courage and strength rather than a capacity for care and compassion. No recogni-tion was given to the training and experience that many women by now possessed and their candidature for the ARA's selection of staff was not considered.[78] In talking about figures such as Francesca Wilson we have highlighted the estab-lishment of a female professionalism in the years between the wars but this was certainly not a generalised phenomenon and we have to take into account the widespread resistance and counter-thrust that hindered the emergence of women in the environment of humanitarianism.

The American mission in Russia was not completely 'masculinised' though. The disincentive to female participation could not affect the organisations whose staff had converged in the columns of the ARA as a result of the plan for the centralisation of aid wanted by Hoover. Women were especially well represented in the Quakers – who maintained their own operational unit under the ARA banner – and usually they could boast specific training and were experts passionately dedicated to humanitarian activities. This was the case, for example, with Anna J. Haines, a qualified nurse employed for several years by Philadelphia's social service, who had already arrived in Russia in 1917 in the service of the American Friends Society Committee and remained long-term in the country even after the period she spent with the ARA, intending to create a nursing school.[79] It was Anna Haines who sent Hoover a letter that voiced the recurrent criticisms among the Quakers that the ARA put US economic interests – for example, getting more corn to arrive than wheat – ahead of the philanthropic purposes of the mission in the Soviet regions. More generally, the criticisms revealed two contrasting visions of humanitarianism, as Hoover himself underlined in his letter replying to Haines:

> If I were to make a summary as to my judgement of your state of mind, I should say it is due to visualization of relief problems in terms of individual givers and of individual sufferers instead of in terms of our political institutions, our public sentiment, and the needs and means of saving the lives of millions.[80]

Hoover's comment referred to the changes that had already transformed the world of American philanthropy in the final decades of the nineteenth century, when charitable organisations replaced individual charity, promoting a scientific approach to the analysis of needs and becoming the contacts of the institutions for public relief policies. According to Hoover, the Friends' approach was the expression of a charitable tradition that had now been overtaken, while 'modern' philanthropy should be taken as a model for an international humanitarianism centred on institutions, and expression of the United States' entire society.

That national community, which demonstrated its humanitarian spirit through the powerful ARA, needed to have an explanation and narrative of the aid programme carried out – with the donations of many private citizens and the financing of the state – in a country governed by Bolsheviks and therefore considered an opponent of liberal democracies. The aid could have been interpreted as incomprehensible support to an enemy regime. The press played an important role in opposing this interpretation and the ARA was worried about maintaining a close relationship with the newspapers in such a way as to 'regulate' shadows and light in the news of aid operations to Soviet Russia.[81] Immediately after the start-up of the aid programme, the organisation's line was of limiting as much as possible fearful stories and gruesome details in order to highlight the capacity of the relief activities and their efficiency and effectiveness. The organisation's official photographer and film maker, Floyd Traynham, dedicated some of his photos to the bodies of children disfigured by famine but most of all he portrayed the crowded feeding centres for children, the unloading of hundreds of sacks of corn, the food supplies ready for distribution, and the clinics and hospitals where the malnourished and sick could receive appropriate treatment.[82] What was strongest in the images Traynham produced for the ARA was therefore a grammar of the humanitarian tale that referred back to the efficiency and power of the benefactors. This same narrative triumphed twenty years later with the US programme for the relief of Europe liberated from Nazi-Fascism.

Notes

1   Francesca M. Wilson, *In the Margins of Chaos: Recollections of Relief Work in and Between Three Wars* (London: John Murray, 1944), p. vii.
2   Siân Roberts, *Place, Life Histories and the Politics of Relief: Episodes in the Life of Francesca Wilson, Humanitarian Educator Activist*, thesis submitted to the University of Birmingham for the degree of Doctor of Philosophy, 2010.
3   Wilson, *In the Margins of Chaos*, p. vii.
4   See Chapter 3.
5   American Red Cross War Council, *Statement of Henry P. Davison, Chairman, on Behalf of the American Red Cross War Council* (Washington, DC: American Red Cross, 1919), p. 7.
6   Johannes-Dieter Steinert, 'Food and the Food Crisis in Post-War Germany, 1945–1948: British Policy and the Role of British NGOs', in F. Just and F. Trentmann (eds), *Food and Conflict in Europe in the Age of the Two World Wars* (Basingstoke: Palgrave Macmillan, 2006), pp. 266–288; Elisabeth Piller, 'German Child Distress, US Humanitarian Aid and Revisionist Politics, 1918–24', *Journal of Contemporary History*, 51:3 (2016), pp. 453–486.
7   Irwin, *Making the World Safe*, pp. 141–184; John F. Hutchinson, '"Custodian of the sacred fire": The ICRC and the Postwar Reorganisation of the Red Cross', in Paul Weindling (ed.), *International Health Organisations and Movements, 1918–1939* (Cambridge: Cambridge University Press, 1995), pp. 17–35; Bridget Towers, 'Red Cross Organisational Politics 1922: Relations of Dominance and the Influence of the United States', in Weindling (ed.), *International Health Organisations*, pp. 36–55.
8   In 1983 the League of Red Cross Societies was renamed the League of Red Cross and Red Crescent Societies, and eight years later the International Federation of Red Cross and Red Crescent Societies.
9   Susan Pedersen, 'Back to the League of Nations', *American Historical Review*, 112:4 (2007), pp. 1091–1117; Zara Steiner, *The Lights That Failed: European International History, 1919–1933* (Oxford: Oxford University Press, 2005), pp. 359–371; Mazower, *Governing the World*, pp. 141–153.
10 See Weindling (ed.), *International Health Organizations*, in particular the chapter by: Martin David Dubin, 'The League of Nations Health Organisation', pp. 56–80; Marta Aleksandra Balínska, 'Assistance and Not Mere Relief: The Epidemic Commission of the League of Nations, 1920–1923', pp. 81–108; Lenore Manderson, 'Wireless Wars in the

Eastern Arena: Epidemiological Surveillance, Disease Prevention and the Work of the Eastern Bureau of the League of Nations Health Organisation, 1925–1942', pp. 109–133.

11   Marta Aleksandra Balińska, *Une vie pour l'humanitaire: Ludwik Rajchman, 1881–1965* (Paris: La Découverte, 1995), pp. 81–167.

12   See pp. 30–32.

13   Kevin Grant, *A Civilised Savagery: Britain and the New Slaveries in Africa* (New York: Routledge, 2005), pp. 159–164. The Anti-slavery and Aborigines Protection Society came into being in 1909 through the merger of the Anti-Slavery Society with the Aborigines' Protection Society; we have spoken about both of these bodies in Chapter 1.

14   See Amalia Ribi Forclaz, *Humanitarian Imperialism: The Politics of Anti-Slavery Activism, 1880–1940* (Oxford: Oxford University Press, 2015), pp. 69–76, and pp. 117–136 on the Italian anti-slavery movement that in the 1920s and the 1930s prepared the ground for more decisive intervention of the Fascist government in the Horn of Africa.

15   Frederick Cooper, *Decolonization and African Society: The Labor Question in French and British Africa* (Cambridge: Cambridge University Press, 1996), pp. 55–56.

16   James P. Daughton, 'Behind the Imperial Curtain: International Humanitarian Efforts and the Critique of French Colonialism in the Interwar Years', *French Historical Studies*, 34:3 (2011), pp. 503–528; James P. Daughton, 'ILO Expertise and Colonial Violence in Interwar Years', in Sandrine Kott and Joëlle Droux (eds), *Globalizing Social Rights: The International Labour Organization and Beyond* (Basingstoke: Palgrave Macmillan, 2013), pp. 85–97; Daniel R. Maul, *Human Rights, Development and Decolonization: The International Labour Organization, 1940–70* (Basingstoke: Palgrave Macmillan, 2012 [first edition Essen, 2007]), pp. 17–30.

17   Mazower, *Governing the World*, pp. 154–187; Grant, *A Civilised Savagery*, pp. 135–166.

18   Ludovic Tournès, 'La philanthropie américaine, la société des nations et la coproduction d'un ordre international (1919–1946)', *Relations Internationales*, 151 (2012/13), pp. 25–36.

19   Daniel Gorman, *The Emergence of International Society in the 1920s* (Cambridge: Cambridge University Press, 2012), pp. 52–108; Barbara Metzger, 'Towards an International Human Rights Regime During the Inter-War Years: The League of Nations' Combat of Traffic in Women and Children', in K. Grant, Ph. Levine and F. Trentmann (eds), *Beyond Sovereignty: Britain, Empire and Transnationalism, c. 1880–1950* (Basingstoke: Palgrave Macmillan, 2007), pp. 54–79.

20   The leaflet is reproduced in Clare Mulley, *The Woman Who Saved the Children: A Biography of Eglantyne Jebb Founder of Save the Children* (Oxford: Oneworld Publications, 2009).

21   On Eglantyne Jebb see Linda Mahood, *Feminism and Voluntary Action: Eglantyne Jebb and Save the Children, 1876–1928* (London: Palgrave Macmillan, 2009); and Linda Mahood, 'Eglantyne Jebb: Remembering, Representing and Writing a Rebel Daughter', *Women's History Review*, 17:1 (2008), pp. 1–20.

22   In the words of Eglantyne Jebb: 'For better or for worse, what women and men are at twenty, that they generally are for life. If up to that age they have been suffered to live self-indulgently, it is only the rare exceptions who will be capable of great self-denial.' *Cambridge: A Brief Study in Social Questions* (Cambridge: Macmillan & Bowes, 1908), p. 156.

23   See pp. 68–69.

24   Leila J. Rupp, *Worlds of Women: The Making of an International Women's Movement* (Princeton, NJ: Princeton University Press, 1997), pp. 3–12; Jo Vellacot, 'A Place for Feminism and Transnationalism in Feminist Theory: The Early Work of the Women's International League for Peace and Freedom', *Women's History Review*, 2:1 (1993), pp. 23–56.

25 Emily Baughan and Juliano Fiori, 'Save the Children, the Humanitarian Project and the Politics of Solidarity: Reviving Dorothy Buxton's vision', *Disasters*, 39:2 (2015), pp. 129–145.

26 Mahood, 'Eglantyne Jebb', pp. 14–15.

27 Baughan and Fiori, 'Save the Children'.

28 Emily Baughan, '"Every Citizen of Empire Implored to Save the Children!" Empire, Internationalism and the Save the Children Fund in Inter-war Britain', *Historical Research*, 86:231 (2013), pp. 116–137.

29 Joëlle Droux, 'L'internationalisation de la protection de l'enfance: acteurs, concurrences et projectes transnationaux (1900–1925)', *Critique internationale*, 3 (2011), pp. 17–33; Joëlle Droux, 'Life During Wartime: The Save the Children International Union and the Dilemmas of Warfare Relief, 1919–1947', in J. Paulmann (ed.), *Dilemmas of Humanitarian Aid in the Twentieth Century* (Oxford: Oxford University Press, 2016), pp. 185–206.

30 Dominique Marshall, 'Humanitarian Sympathy for Children in Times of War and the History of Children's Rights, 1919–1959', in J. A. Marten (ed.), *Children and War: A Historical Anthology* (New York: New York University Press, 2002), pp. 184–199.

31 Emily Baughan, *Saving the Children: British Humanitarianism in Europe and Africa, 1914-1945*, thesis submitted to the University of Bristol for the degree of Doctor of Philosophy, 2014.

32 *Ibid.*

33 By way of example, the organisations working with Russian refugees are discussed by Dzovinar Kévonian, 'L'organisation non gouvernementale. Nouvel acteur du champ humanitaire. Le Zemgor et la Société des Nations dans les années 1920', *Cahiers du monde russe*, 46:4 (2005), pp. 739–756.

34 John Hope Simpson, *The Refugee Problem: Report of a Survey* (London: Oxford University Press, 1939), p. 82.

35 Peter Gatrell, *The Making of the Modern Refugee* (Oxford: Oxford University Press, 2013), pp. 21–51.

36 Claudena M. Skran, *Refugees in Inter-war Europe: The Emergence of a Regime* (Oxford: Oxford University Press, 1995), p. 84; see also Gatrell, *The Making of the Modern Refugee*, pp. 55–58.

37 Claudena M. Skran, 'Profile of the First Two High Commissioners', *Journal of Refugee Studies*, 1:3–4 (1988), pp. 277–296.

38 John G. Stoessinger, *The Refugee and the World Community* (Minneapolis, MN: University of Minneapolis Press, 1956), p. 33.

39 Skran, *Refugees in Inter-war Europe*, pp. 149–157.

40 *Ibid.*, pp. 170–177.

41 *Ibid.*, pp. 157–167; Bruce Clark, *Twice a Stranger: How Mass Expulsion Forged Modern Greece and Turkey* (Cambridge, MA: Harvard University Press, 2006).

42 Skran, *Refugees in Inter-war Europe*, pp. 189–193.

43 See pp. 134–135.

44 Susan Pedersen has highlighted that the League obliged the mandatory powers 'to *say* that they were governing [mandatory territories] differently', in response to the pressure applied by journalists, petitioners and humanitarian lobbies; Susan Pedersen, *The Guardians: The League of Nations and the Crisis of Empire* (Oxford: Oxford University Press, 2015), p. 4.

45 On the collaboration between ICRC and the League of Nations see Francesca Piana, 'L'humanitaire d'après-guerre: prisonniers de guerre et réfugiés russes dans la politique

du Comité international de la Croix-Rouge et de la Société des Nations', *Relations Internationales*, 151 (2012/13), pp. 63–75.

46   Dzovinar Kévonian, *Réfugiés et diplomatie humanitaire: Les acteurs européens et la scène proche-orientale pendant l'entre-deux-guerres* (Paris: Publications de la Sorbonne, 2004), pp. 343–353.

47   Simpson, *The Refugee Problem*, p. 172.

48   *Ibid.*, p. 174.

49   Mark Mazower, *Salonica, City of Ghosts: Christians, Muslims and Jews 1430–1950* (London: Harper Perennial, 2005), pp. 358–359.

50   Skran, *Refugees in Inter-war Europe*, pp. 194–202.

51   Tommie Sjöberg, *The Powers and the Persecuted: The Refugee Problem and the Intergovernmental Committee on Refugees (IGCR), 1938–1947* (Lund: Lund University Press, 1991).

52   Simpson, *The Refugee Problem*, p. 186.

53   *Ibid.*, p. 341.

54   Typewritten document (quoted verbatim here) reproduced in Peter Balakian, *Black Dog of Fate: A Memoir* (New York: Basic Books, 2009 [1st edition 1997]), p. 203.

55   *Ibid.*

56   Branden Little, 'An Explosion of New Endeavours: Global Humanitarian Responses to Industrialized Warfare in the First World War Era', *First World War Studies*, 5:1 (2014), pp. 1–16, at p. 2; Keith David Watenpaugh, *Bread from Stones: The Middle East and the Making of Modern Humanitarianism* (Oakland, CA: University of California Press, 2015).

57   Pierre Fuller, 'North China Famine Revisited: Unsung Native Relief in the Warlord Era, 1920–1921', *Modern Asian Studies*, 47:3 (2013), pp. 820–850; on the American Red Cross in China in the same period, see Caroline Reeves, 'Red Cross, Blue Express: Chinese Local Relief in an Age of Humanitarian Imperialism, Shandong 1923', in J. Paulman (ed.), *Dilemmas of Humanitarian Aid in the Twentieth Century* (Oxford: Oxford University Press, 2016).

58   James L. Barton, *Story of the Near East Relief (1915–1930)* (New York: Macmillan, 1930), p. 4.

59   Davide Rodogno, 'Non-state Actors' Humanitarian Operations in the Aftermath of the First World War: The Case of the Near East Relief', in F. Klose (ed.), *The Emergence of Humanitarian Intervention: Ideas and Practice from the Nineteenth Century to the Present* (Cambridge: Cambridge University Press, 2015), pp. 185–207, at p. 191.

60   Ann Marie Wilson, 'In the Name of God, Civilization, and Humanity: The United States and the Armenian Massacres of the 1890s', *Le Mouvement Social*, 2 (2009), pp. 27–44.

61   Watenpaugh, *Bread from Stones*, p. 86.

62   *Ibid.*, pp. 92–93.

63   *Ibid.*, pp. 84–85.

64   Rodogno, 'Non-state Actors' Humanitarian Operations', p. 191.

65   Pedersen, *The Guardians*, p. 5.

66   Vahram L. Shemmassian, 'The League of Nations and the Reclamation of Armenian Genocide Survivors', in R. G. Hovannisian (ed.), *Looking Backward, Moving Forward: Confronting the Armenian Genocide* (New Brunswick: Transaction, 2003), pp. 81–111.

67   Keith David Watenpaugh, 'League of Nations' Rescue of Armenian Genocide Survivors and the Making of Modern Humanitarianism, 1920–27', *American Historical Review*, 115:5 (2010), pp. 1315–1339.

68   Shemmassian, 'The League of Nations and the Reclamation of Armenian Genocide Survivors'; Kévonian, *Réfugiés et diplomatie humanitaire*, pp. 151–157.

69 Watenpaugh, *Bread from Stones*, p. 138.

70 George H. Nash, *The Life of Herbert Hoover, Vol. II: The Humanitarian 1914–1917* (New York: W. W. Norton, 1988); Thomas D. Westerman, 'Touring Occupied Belgium: American Humanitarians at "Work" and "Leisure" (1914–1917)', *First World War Studies*, 5:1 (2014), pp. 43–53.

71 Quoted in Bertrand M. Patenaude, *The Big Show in Bololand: The American Relief Expedition to Soviet Russia in the Famine of 1921* (Stanford, CA: Stanford University Press, 2015), p. 32.

72 *Ibid.*, pp. 28–34.

73 Skran, 'Profile of the First Two High Commissioners'; Marin Coudreau, 'Le Comité International de Secours à la Russie, l'action Nansen e le Bolcheviks (1921–1924)', *Relations Internationales*, 151 (2012/13), pp. 49–61.

74 John Ormerod Greenwood, *Friends and Relief* (York: William Sessions, 1975), p. 245.

75 Linda Mahood and Vic Satzewich, 'The Save the Children Fund and the Russian Famine of 1921–23: Claims and Counter-Claims about Feeding "Bolshevik" Children', *Journal of Historical Sociology*, 22:1 (2009), pp. 55–83; Baughan and Fiori, 'Save the Children, the Humanitarian Project and the Politics of Solidarity', pp. 133–134.

76 Dorothy F. Buxton and Edward Fuller, *The White Flame: The Story of the Save the Children Fund* (London: Longmans, Green and Co., 1931), p. 83.

77 Patenaude, *The Big Show in Bololand*, pp. 47–48. British aid to Russia was second to American efforts in terms of its size – see Tehila Sasson, 'From Empire to Humanity: The Russian Famine and the Imperial Origins of International Humanitarianism', *Journal of British Studies*, 55:3 (2016), p. 521.

78 *Ibid.*, pp. 49–51.

79 Anna J. Haines, *Health Work in Soviet Russia* (New York: Vanguard Press, 1928), p. vi.

80 Patenaude, *The Big Show in Bololand*, p. 604.

81 *Ibid.*, pp. 135–139.

82 See the collection of photographs among the ARA documents at the Hoover Institution Archives (Stanford University), *Register of the American Relief Administration. Russian Operations Records 1919–1925*, box 395–411. A small portion of the ARA photos are the work of Nellie Gardner, an American journalist who took part in the promotion of ARA's work, although she was not officially employed by the organisation. Save the Children sent to Russia the *Daily Mail* photographer George Mewes in order to record the reality of the famine and to mobilise support from the British public – see Sasson, 'From Empire to Humanity', p. 531.

5

Aftermath of the Second World War: humanitarianism at a crossroads?

My dear Governor Lehman:

On the first anniversary of the creation of UNRRA, I wish to send to you and to the members of your staff my warmest congratulations on the great progress which you have made during this last year […] and my renewed good wishes for the successful fulfillment of your noble undertaking […].

This Government has endeavored in every way to support you and your staff to the fullest limit of our ability. This has not always been an easy task in the face of the pressing and staggering demands which the fighting of a deadly war on many fronts has placed and will continue to place upon our resources of manpower, of supplies and transportation. But we are determined that the sacrifices of the liberated peoples shall be rewarded and that, to the extent we have it in our power to help, these people shall promptly receive the clothing, food, and the other supplies which they need to start life over.

I am confident that your inspiring leadership, together with the cooperation of the member governments, will result in making UNRRA an enduring example of international cooperation in action.[1]

This is how President Franklin Delano Roosevelt addressed the director general of the United Nations Relief and Rehabilitation Administration (UNRRA), Herbert H. Lehman, in November 1944. A leading figure in the Democrat Party and governor of the State of New York from 1933 to 1942, Lehman had been a strong supporter of the New Deal. However, he had not been given the office of director general of the intergovernmental organisation that had to take the necessary aid to the populations hit by the war 'to start a new life' just because of his career as a politician and public administrator. His intense and lengthy work in the religiously inspired philanthropic world contributed to providing him with the necessary skills for his new undertaking. In particular, Lehman had taken part in the activities of the American Jewish Joint Distribution Committee from its foundation. In the post-First World War period, 'the Joint', as it was known, had concentrated its work in eastern Europe[2] and since the mid-1930s it had played a leading role among the associations dedicated to relief to the Jews fleeing Nazi persecution: even more important was his work assisting the genocide survivors. We will return to this further on; what we are pointing out here is the relevance of the faith-based associations in the path Lehman took before taking on the leadership of UNRRA.

Roosevelt's letter to Lehman did not only emphasise the 'endeavor' given by the US government to support the aid work in the regions liberated by the Allies but offered further evidence of the central role taken on by the United States in the creation of the new intergovernmental body. UNRRA came into being in 1943 as a result of an agreement against Nazi-Fascism signed at the White House by the representatives of forty-four states belonging to the United Nations. Presenting it to the world as the 'humanitarian arm' of the Grand Alliance that would soon defeat the Axis powers, the US president underlined that UNRRA's task was basically to bring 'relief and help in the rehabilitation for the victims of German and Japanese barbarism'.[3] Roosevelt recalled the contrast between the barbarities of the perpetrators of violence and the demonstration of civilisation represented by feeling compassion for its victims, a contrast that was not, as we know, new in the question of humanitarianism.

The setting up of UNRRA had its roots in the specific historic moment. The plan for the new international body had taken shape since the American relaunch of an internationalist policy that intended to build a juster, safer world after the tragedy of war, taking inspiration in part from Woodrow Wilson's previous programme. In Roosevelt's plan, though, the United States' impetus for the definition of a new world order had also to include social security: his plan joined up on this point with the idea of welfare developed in the years of the New Deal and was now considered ready to be exported internationally.[4] The scheme aimed to relieve the suffering generated by the wartime events as the first step. It would therefore be reductive to consider UNRRA merely an example of the US domination of post-war humanitarianism, though it is undoubtedly crucial to highlight the relationship between international aid and the reconstruction projects.

According to its founding fathers, UNRRA had to mark a significant deviation from the experience of the post-First World War era. The overall balance of losses was now much more dramatic and the weight of the ruins recalled the unleashing of a destructive force that had undermined the very foundations of Western society. Looking after the wounded from a similar tragedy required extraordinary effort and commitment, based on planning the interventions, on rationalising the resources and on the coordination of the various players arriving on the scene.[5] Taking advantage of these arguments, the UNRRA planners stressed the idea that the international aid operations would take a new path.

It is worth remembering that, in the institutional debate on humanitarianism, the rhetoric of 'foundation' (or re-foundation) recurs frequently.[6] Starting from Henry Dunant and the beginnings of the ICRC, moving on to the reorganisation of the national societies of the Red Cross a few decades later or to Herbert Hoover's ARA in the post-First World War period, the new bodies that from time to time appeared on the international aid scene often presented themselves as renovators determined to make an impact on the mobilisation for suffering humanity. In the post-Second World War era, the emphasis placed on the 'new beginning' echoed and strengthened certain elements that had emerged in the past, first of all the appeal to modernisation. This term was understood as rationalisation, professionalisation, the use of science and technology as essential requisites for humanitarian work. In addition, the role given to the new intergovernmental bodies coincided with the insistence on the centrality of the institutions. Through their supervision and coordination functions they were to relegate to a secondary level the private, religion-based associations.[7] Finally, the rhetoric of the 'new beginning' took on a specific meaning precisely because humanitarianism was now connected to the relaunch of internationalism and multilateralism.[8]

After the Allies' victory over Nazi-Fascism, aid and relief policies had to be the outcome of authentic international cooperation: in 1944 President Roosevelt recalled writing as much to Herbert Hoover but similar convictions were widespread in the British Labour Party, which was soon to lead the country. On this subject, the words with which Philip Noel-Baker introduced his reflection on relief and reconstruction are significant. The convention in which he spoke was promoted by the Fabian Society to plot recovery after the end of hostilities. An international relations scholar, Noel-Baker was already a prominent politician and Labour MP and could also boast the valuable experience of having worked with the secretary-general of the League of Nations. He had also experienced the challenges and dilemmas of humanitarianism on the field: he was from a Quaker family and had served as a volunteer during the Great War for the Friends Ambulance Units. Setting the discussion on the topics of relief and reconstruction he asked, rhetorically:

> In the first years after the war, the United Nations will be organizing the greatest act of collective charity that history records. The vital issue about Relief is this: shall this charity remain an 'act of charity' alone, saving perhaps some lives, ending more quickly the hunger and the misery of the Nazis' victims, but leaving no permanent result, no lasting effect on the policies which Governments pursue? Or shall it be made the first experiment in practical economic co-operation? Shall it create a habit by which the nations will learn to work together for their common prosperity? Thus, to lay the foundations for lasting peace?[9]

The identification of the post-war years with the start of a 'New Deal', due to the unprecedented spirit of international cooperation embodied first by UNRRA and then the UN, spread widely from public debate at the time to the studies carried out afterwards. Naturally, the innovative elements and the instability brought by the post-Second World War era are undeniable, just as the role played by the intergovernmental organisations set up in the mid-1940s is undeniable.

This chapter looks at the long-term post-war programmes, and we will see how UNRRA and the UN implemented policies, practices and professionalism that had been defined in the previous experiences of humanitarianism and within the framework of the 'New Deal', and how longer-term approaches were reiterated. It is immediately worth highlighting an element of continuity with the post-First World War era: in the 1940s – as had happened in the 1920s – it was Europe that remained at the centre of the humanitarian programmes. Devastated by 'one of the grimmest ordeals of history', as Eisenhower wrote to Lehman in the winter of 1945,[10] the European continent had become the place and the symbol of the abyss which the war had caused Western civilisation to fall into. The post-war rebirth could not but start from Europe. Aid and relief were the essential preconditions to plan the reconstruction and then to re-establish an international order that still had one of its linchpins in Europe – even if its background details had been altered. In the second half of the 1940s, dealing with the topic of refugees, homeless people and malnourished children meant talking about the European population, but the Euro-centric set-up of the humanitarian programmes would prevail for almost a decade, due to the long post-war period but also because of the Cold War.

A final observation on the post-war programmes and their effects on the history of humanitarianism: UNRRA is usually thought of as the first UN agency. It is worth clarifying the meaning of this definition in order to avoid mistakes being made about the link between the two bodies. UNRRA was conceived of as a temporary organisation and when its offices closed permanently, in 1947, the path to the UN's constitution had already been completed. As is known, one of the fundamental stages on this journey had been marked by the meetings at Dumbarton Oaks: at this place in Washington the representatives of Britain, the United States, China and the Soviet Union began to draw up the architecture of the new international body and drafted its constitutional charter. This was ratified by the San Francisco conference in 1945, while in the following year the end of the League of Nations was decreed. In 1947 some of the UNRRA programmes, as well as some of its staff, were absorbed by the UN even though its aid and relief work became just a segment of the organisation's wider political agenda on international peace and security. From the institutional point of view there was no direct link between UNRRA and the UN but the former was certainly a major laboratory for that international cooperation project that the UN was called upon to permanently embody.

In the years of conflict

Even if it was the measures taken at the conclusion of the war that drew the attention of contemporaries as much as of historians, the dynamics of the armed conflicts had had a specific impact on the actors and the orientations of international humanitarianism. Before dealing with the long post-war era, let's take a step back, to the years of conflict.

The wartime events, in their extreme dramatic force, had put to the test the existing organisations. This was not only because of the enormous burden of suffering the organisations had to face but also, and above all, because the events had challenged them on the level of public recognition of their victims and the condemnation of their butchers, and they were called upon to face up to the very meaning of humanitarian action. The most symbolic example, as well as the most debated, concerned the ICRC.

It was in the Europe overwhelmed by total war – its engagement in Asia remained marginal – that the ICRC dedicated its activity in the areas defined by the conventions whose signing the Committee itself had promoted and which had set the foundations for international humanitarian law. As we have seen, the founding Convention, signed in 1864 and further extended in 1907, concerned the protection of soldiers wounded during combat, but a later agreement, concluded in 1929, regulated the treatment of prisoners of war and continued in line with the work the Committee had carried out since the Balkan Wars.[11] During the Second World War, as in the First, the relief to soldiers captured by enemy armies remained a priority for the ICRC, which also managed to obtain the equivalent status of military prisoners for foreign citizens of enemy nationality interned in special camps by the governments of most of the belligerent countries. In this way the Genevan Committee's direct intervention was extended to the civilian population too.[12] The negotiations for entry to the camps, the gathering of information, the transport of medicines and food rations were conducted not only with Britain and the United States but also with Germany, which had signed the Convention in 1929 and had not withdrawn after Hitler's accession. Through the mixed committee made up of the Swiss and Swedish Red Cross, the ICRC also took part in the relief operations for occupied Greece and this was one of most important initiatives for the civilian populations.[13] But the central chapter in the official history of the ICRC was written in the 11,000 visits to prisoners of war, the information provided to hundreds of thousands of families and the tons of packages distributed in the camps.[14] And it was all of this that supplied the main reasons for giving the Nobel Peace Prize to the ICRC. The award took place in 1945, although the Prize referred to the previous year; the red cross on a white field offered the Western world a symbol to appeal to in order to mark a contrast between the humanitarian commitment and the inhuman impetus to death and destruction the war had demonstrated. At the same time, the Nobel Prize reinforced the ICRC's accreditation in the international community and its perception as the perfect example of a body serving humanity. On the basis of this accreditation, the Committee promoted a revision of the Conventions signed in 1864, 1906 and 1929, whose credibility had been severely compromised by the unprecedented wartime violence. In 1949, new Conventions were signed and they also concerned the protection of civilians in wartime – as well as wounded soldiers and prisoners.[15]

During the Second World War the policies and the very principles of the Red Cross dramatically illustrated their limitations, faced with the extermination of the Jews. In all of its activities, the Committee in Geneva kept as a point of reference the German Red Cross, which had been Nazified after the rise of Hitler and was later led by Ernst Grawitz, an SS colonel and one of the best-known authors of pseudo-medical experiments on the deported Jews. The ICRC never had systematic access to the Nazi camps but already from the mid-1930s, as a result of the negotiations conducted with the German authorities, the organisation's representatives had begun their visits. It was not, however, considered appropriate to take specific measures or to make public declarations on the Nazi concentration camp system. Even though it is difficult to identify with certainty the moment when the ICRC realised that the anti-Jewish persecution would culminate in the 'Final Solution', in 1942 the mass of information received from delegates allowed a fairly clear picture to be put together of what was happening in the Europe Hitler dominated. In October of that same year, though, the approval of a condemnatory document that mentioned the racial persecution ferociously enacted by the Nazi regime was rejected by the majority of the members of the ICRC Assembly.[16] Later, however, a programme was developed to take relief supplies inside the concentration camps.[17]

The controversial debate that developed over the following decades[18] interpreted the behaviour of the ICRC in the light of two factors in particular: on the one hand, the influence of the policies adopted by the Swiss government – to which, as we have seen, the Genevan Committee was closely tied – in line with a declaration of neutrality that was never the same as an effective interruption in relations with Germany; on the other hand, the choice of the Committee to respect a legal and restrictive interpretation of its mandate, understood as the application of the principles sanctioned by the Conventions. The motivations the ICRC used to support its decisions partly went back to the need to keep diplomatic relations with Germany open, since this was the indispensable condition for continuing to assist prisoners of war and wounded soldiers, as set out in the Conventions. The ICRC's main arguments concerned the nature of the organisation and the meaning of its humanitarian mission. It made a particular appeal to the principles of impartiality and neutrality that the Committee had considered, at the time of its foundation, the linchpins of the aid programme to wounded soldiers from all the warring armies, without distinction between allies and enemies. Several decades later, impartiality and neutrality were again suggested as essential conditions for humanitarian action; there was a resolute distinction between care for the victims and taking a distance from the persecutors because the latter implied a recognition of right and wrong, a clear indication of responsibilities and a consequent lining up with one of the sides in the case.[19]

Most of the literature has focused on comparisons between the accusations made against the Red Cross and the reasons it gave in its defence. In this setting, it seems more useful to reflect on the ICRC issues by asking what their meaning was for the history of humanitarianism where the Committee was a major player not only for the actions it undertook but also on a symbolic level. A first, unavoidable, issue concerns the effectiveness of humanitarian law which in the Second World War ended up being thwarted since formal respect for the Conventions – witnessed for example by Red Cross delegates on visits to German prisoner-of-war camps – existed alongside genocide. Furthermore, the total war and the extermination meant that the principles of impartiality and neutrality were translated into dumb paralysis in the face of the elimination of a people. In 1943, loyalty to those principles was defended by the Genevan Committee as an example of coherence, but it contradicted the idea of the intolerability of the suffering of others, from which humanitarian action had originated: the choice of abstaining from the condemnation of the butchers coincided with the impossibility of protecting the victims. Apart from representing 'the greatest failure in the history of ICRC'[20] the Holocaust opened a deep wound in the very way in which humanitarianism had been thought of and enacted by one of its main interpreters. The significance of this wound reached far beyond the individual organisation's issues.

At any rate, the implications of the wartime experience were manifold and in certain ways changed the characteristics of the humanitarian operations and their main players. The war catalysed the circuits of transnational solidarity that already existed and gave an impulse to setting up new bodies dedicated to relief for the civilian populations overwhelmed by the total conflict. In spring 1942, a mobilisation of British citizens to help Greece, which had been reduced to starvation under German occupation, led to the creation of the Oxford Famine Relief Committee, a committee that soon changed into a real association. It became known as Oxfam and took on a high-level role among the non-governmental organisations, as it would be profiled in the following decades. Among Oxfam's founders and supporters there were many of the actors whom we have already met several times in the ranks of the promoters of new humanitarian initiatives: members of the evangelical churches; Quakers; representatives of the philanthropic world. In addition to these were many members of the League of Nations Union, the British association started to promote peace and the ideals embodied by the League of Nations. The specific campaign around which the Oxford Famine Relief Committee was set up was reminiscent in certain ways of the one that more than twenty years before had led to the creation of the Save the Children Fund, in that it disputed the British embargo on the territories occupied by the German army and promoted the creation of programmes to send food and medicine to the starving civilian population.[21]

A year after the beginnings of Oxfam, on the other side of the Atlantic, the association called Catholic Relief Services (CRS) – founded on the initiative of

Catholic bishops in America – started operations. Although decidedly smaller in number than those of the Protestants and Jews, the US Catholics already boasted an array of philanthropic initiatives carried out in other countries; the new element brought by the CRS related to the setting up of a centralised body that aimed to express the manifold local situations. This was how the Catholic associations responded to the requests made by the US government, which was advocating the merger of the smaller groups within bodies that could be recognised on a national level. The CRS, which became the most important US non-governmental organisation in the post-Second World War era, started its activities with the assistance of men and women from the Polish diaspora following the invasion of the Polish Republic by German troops (to the west) and Soviet troops (to the east).[22]

The formation of new organisations intensified in the immediate post-war period but while the conflict was still underway it contributed to extending and making more complex the panorama of international relief administered by private agencies. Naturally, within this setting there were once again the now established actors in relief for victims of armed conflicts, such as the Friends. The Quaker organisations also mobilised for the Polish diaspora and a team of humanitarian professionals – including the already mentioned Francesca Wilson – worked in the refugee camps in Hungary alongside the local Red Cross and the Polish YMCA.[23] Thereafter, 'Hitler's early success prevented work in Europe', and the Friends' activity 'became global' because some units were sent to North Africa, India and China.[24] The centre of the Quaker intervention was Europe once again as the Allied army advanced and the Friends were among the first voluntary societies to become operational in the liberated countries. In Italy, for example, at the beginning of 1944 Quaker organisations had already signed agreements with the military authorities for aid to foreign refugees together with the British Red Cross, the Joint and the American Red Cross.[25]

The Allies' successes and the progress of the liberation of Europe altered the potential framework of action for humanitarian aid and led to some important changes. The immediate needs of the populations that had lived through the occupation and the shift of front were immeasurable, and responding effectively to the emergency was essential for maintaining control over the regions removed from Nazi-Fascism and pursuing military operations. The military authorities were aware of this as much as the governments of the Allied countries were, which aimed at introducing bodies and mechanisms appointed to coordinate and supervise international aid initiatives. In Britain, the government impetus was decisive in setting up, in summer 1942, a body – the Council of British Societies for Relief Abroad – that brought together the biggest humanitarian societies on the international scene. It functioned as a reference for the authorities in London and had to harmonise the private agencies' initiatives with the needs of the Allied armies.[26] A similar body – the American Council of Voluntary Agencies – was set up in 1944 in the United States,[27] again in response to the demands for coordination made by government. Two years earlier, moreover, the US government had – under the supervision of the State Department – set up an agency for the accreditation of the organisations that were seeking to take on a role in the post-war relief context and obtain public funding for it. The agency – the War Relief Control Board – was called upon to optimise the use of US resources, at the same time checking the quality of the organisations and their purposes; naturally, it also worked as a filter and led to a drastic reduction in the overall number of associations with a humanitarian calling.[28]

The wartime experience coincided with a collective broadening of the non-governmental organisations, but it also generated the need to give them legitimisation and a space in the international set-up through specific representative and coordinating bodies. In addition, old and new private humanitarian entities consolidated their roles and were able to establish themselves by becoming the reference points for their national governments' relief policies. The central role of individual states in determining the set-up of the humanitarian regime during these years should, therefore, not be undervalued, even if the public debate and historiography have concentrated on the simultaneous emergence of the new intergovernmental bodies, UNRRA and the UN.

Rehabilitating Europe

> We make the rounds [of the camp for displaced persons] in the company of the director Tomasek, and an elderly British welfare officer and a nurse from Wisconsin. These volunteers no longer consider themselves as nationals of their homeland but as internationals responsible for the saving of the lost and abandoned.[29]

This is what Katie Louchheim said in her short tale, written years later, of her experience in the service of UNRRA. At just over twenty years of age, the wife of one of Roosevelt's staff on the New Deal, Katie had worked for the section of the State Department that had, under the leadership of Herbert Lehman, planned the future aid programmes in the countries liberated from Nazi-Fascism. With the setting up of UNRRA, Lehman's staff had nearly all moved to the new organisation; Louchheim had received a post in the press office and for this reason visited some refugee camps in Germany in the summer of 1945.

Her stay in Europe was only temporary, but several thousand men and women from the United States – including the nurse from Wisconsin – had been taken on by UNRRA to serve in delivering aid programmes and so they remained in Europe for months or even years. Neither was the elderly welfare officer Katie met in Mannheim an exception: the British were widely represented on the staff of the new international organisation, which comprised solely Anglo-Saxons for around two years.[30] Writing many years after the events, it was still important for Louchheim to emphasise the internationalist spirit that characterised the staff of the first UN agency. The press officer's memoirs re-echo the organisation's insistence on the fact that wearing the UNRRA uniform meant forgetting they were 'nationals of their homeland' and putting themselves at the service of the victims of Nazism and Fascism, regardless of their nationality.

The appeal to the internationalist spirit and the ambition to take care of all of suffering humanity were symbolised by the stylised globe that was UNRRA's logo, which was then taken up by the UN. The real world in which UNRRA brought relief and rehabilitation was actually rather more restricted than the logo showed. Outside the borders of Europe, the new intergovernmental agency started its programmes only in the Philippines (which had still not achieved complete independence from the United States), Korea (liberated from the Japanese and occupied by the Allied forces) and Cihang Kai-shek's China. UNRRA placed Europe firmly at the centre of its mission. It was operational – even though with programmes of different levels of commitment – in twelve countries: Greece; Yugoslavia; Albania; Czechoslovakia; Poland; Islands of the Dodecanese; Finland; Hungary; the Soviet Republics of Belarus and Ukraine; Germany (only for displaced persons); and Italy, even if its inclusion – as an ex-enemy country – in the UN aid programme had been the subject of severe tension. Supplies worth $2.5 billion were sent to Europe while the value of all the deliveries outside Europe was around a fifth of this figure.[31] In June 1946, the staff employed in the biggest Asian mission – that in China – numbered around 1,200, while the programme for displaced persons in Germany, which had the highest percentage of staff deployed in Europe, involved around 5,200 personnel.[32] In short, the allocation of resources – material and human – clearly reflected UNRRA's Euro-centric axis.

In the various countries they served, the men and women of the UNRRA distributed food parcels, shoes and blankets, sprayed dichlorodiphenyltrichloroethane (DDT) and administered basic medical treatment. All these emergency interventions, aimed simply at offering immediate relief, were not considered sufficient in themselves. The organisation's ambition was instead to create the necessary conditions for those men, women and children who were at that point in time fed and clothed by international relief to be able, in the immediate future, to look after themselves autonomously. 'Help the people to help themselves' was UNRRA's motto from its very beginning, and it was printed on hundreds of thousands of brochures, repeated in every public debate and used in reports. According to Paul Baerwald, honorary president of the American Jewish Joint Distribution Committee, this manifesto statement was already the property of the Jewish organisation he represented; Herbert Lehman had come across it in the years he spent with the Joint and then made it the cornerstone of UNRRA's activities.[33] The claim to the motto's paternity is not relevant in itself. However, the idea that it was not enough to relieve the suffering of others and that it was necessary to produce a transformation in the conditions of those suffering had been circulating throughout the history of humanitarianism. It began in the period of its 'archaeology' and had been re-established with the post-First World War programmes. It is important to attempt to understand how that idea was interpreted and what the exact content of the programmes was in the post-Second World War era, in the face of the enormity of the disaster but also the mass deployment of relief in the field.

In its very name the United Nations Relief and Rehabilitation Administration associated the appeal for relief with the idea of rehabilitation, in other words the more complete process of re-acquiring individual and collective strengths and capacities. The term 'rehabilitation' summed up the proposal to 'help the people to help themselves'; it alluded to reconstruction even while wishing to remain on a separate level and was therefore ambiguous. Overall, the idea of rehabilita-tion was translated into two lines of intervention, only on the surface separated one from the other. On the one hand, it concerned support for agricultural and manufacturing activities that had been reduced to the absolute minimum terms in regions occupied by Nazi-Fascism; on the other, it concerned collaboration with local institutions and the introduction of practices of social work in those countries where the organisation was operational.

When the fighting had really ceased in all of Europe, UNRRA supported the activities usually regarded as humanitarian (food, healthcare, etc.) with a plan for the recovery of agricultural and manufacturing production. This was conceived as the extension of immediate relief, inasmuch as only by reactivating agriculture and industry could the European population be guaranteed, in the near future, access to the basic necessities it lacked. In short, the logic was the same as that which had pushed the ARA into exporting to the famine-struck Russia not just food and medicines but also seeds and fertilisers, in order to give some impetus back to farming. The limitations placed by the UNRRA Council – made up of one representative of all the member countries – on the Administration's plan for the industrial sector exactly followed this line. In fact, it set out that there should be support (through sending raw materials, machinery, experts) only for the structures whose products (food, fuel, medicines) were necessary for the relief of civilians, or those that contributed to the provision of public services such as water, electricity, hygiene, transport and communication. However, even if the term 'reconstruction' was carefully avoided and the term 'rehabilitation' was used instead, the overall implications of the interventions in the productive sectors could not be denied. The official historian of UNRRA, George Woodbridge, in his pages on the 'rehabilitation' of agriculture was forced to acknowledge that this had not been anything other than 'reconstruction, if reconstruction can be defined as activities which tend to change the economy rather than to bring it to the level at which it formerly stood'.[34] Woodbridge quoted as examples the replacement of animals for haulage with tractors and the mass introduction of chemical fertilisers, but his considerations were of a more general kind than the specific questions mentioned.

Regardless of what anyone wanted to call them, the programmes for restarting production in Europe implied the employment of change processes of a broader nature. They were inspired by a specific model of economic development, and were the expression of that international political project launched by Roosevelt that was the fundamental impulse for the creation of the first UN agency. It is significant that in Italy (third, after Poland and Yugoslavia, in terms of investments in the 'rehabilitation' of productive activities) the UNRRA programme has simply been considered an early version of the Marshall Plan, in the collective memory as much as in historiography.[35] However, it would be misleading to think that the United States had conceived UNRRA and its humanitarian mission as merely a tool with which to establish its own political hegemony in Europe. It is true, instead, that the project of that humanitarian mission came to life together with a more complex plan for socio-economic transformation, of which the United States was to be the motor inside an Anglo-American axis. Even though all the states that were members of UNRRA took part in the financing of its activities, 94 per cent of the contributions came from the United States, Canada and Britain.[36]

A key to the interpretation of the 'rehabilitation' concerned the relationship with the governmental institutions of the recipient countries. In general, the UNRRA officials thought that collaboration with the local bodies was essential: they had to give them support and offer them consultancy, both to encourage their complete recovery and to transmit specific skills and working methods. In particular, UNRRA was focused on promoting the establishment of scientific methods, 'objective' criteria and standardised procedures for the identification of needs. The training of local welfare staff – primarily social workers – met this demand. It was considered an effective solution to go beyond the simple response to the immediate emergency and leave a long-term legacy in the places where the organisation was operational.[37] Overall, 'help the people to help themselves' meant promoting the establishment of practices and policies considered the expression of the modern concept of welfare, inspired as much by the New Deal as by the projects for the reform of the welfare state set up in Britain.

The 'rehabilitation' of the victims of war took on particular connotations in the context of the programme for the refugee population, which had the greatest visibility of the UNRRA initiatives.[38] As is well known, the Second World War and the immediate post-war period saw the largest and most dramatic population movement experienced in Europe, and within it the UN identified a distinct category of refugees whom it was ready to take care of. A specific definition was coined for them: displaced persons (DPs). This term referred to all those civilians who found themselves outside their own homeland for reasons connected to the war, but only those from countries aligned against the Axis powers had the right to protection and material assistance from the military authorities and UNRRA. So the choice made by their country of origin during the conflict played an important role in their being (or not being) recognised as refugees who could expect international protection: those belonging to the Allies' enemy nations, now defeated, did not have this right.

This way of identifying displaced persons was in line with the criteria adopted by the League of Nations. In this case, though, the principle of nationality was connected to the attribution of a collective responsibility, extended to all the members of the different countries, for the atrocities committed in wartime. The most important example of this way of proceeding concerned the exclusion from international relief of the *Volksdeutsche*, in other words the nearly twelve million people of German nationality who after the end of the war were expelled from central eastern Europe because it was the German population as a whole, regardless of individuals' stories, that was considered ultimately responsible for the tragedy that had just concluded with the defeat of Nazism. Naturally, the distinction between belonging to enemy or Allied countries was not of significance for those who had been persecuted by Nazi-Fascism for religious, political or racial reasons: the 'persecutees' – as they were called in the documents – were provided with protection and relief, regardless of their nationality.

Who were the displaced persons, most of whom were in the refugee camps of occupied Germany and also in Austria and Italy? They were largely those who had been deported as forced labourers, mostly from central eastern Europe and the Balkans (Soviets, Poles, Czechoslovaks, Yugoslavs) but also from the territories conquered by Nazism in the west (French, Belgian, Dutch). They were united with those deported for political or racial reasons, primarily the Jews: in the aftermath of the war they were in a minority because the Nazi death machine had not allowed many to survive. Finally, among the displaced persons there were also the civilians who had fled west with the advance of the Red Army: men and women of different nationalities – in particular from the Baltics, Poland and Ukraine – partly fleeing from the horrors of the war but above all hostile to the Soviet occupation forces.

Immediately after the liberation, the displaced persons were presented to the world as the perfect examples of victims of war. They were one of the favoured subjects of the photographers working for UNRRA on the organisation's information brochures and press releases, which were of great importance for its accreditation in international public opinion. In talking about the displaced persons there was particular reference to those deported for forced labour, in other words the 'slaves of the Nazi regime', as they were often called, implicitly underlining the role played by the Allies in breaking their chains. In this sense, humanitarian action really seemed like the completion of the tyrant's defeat at the hand of the army.[39] UNRRA was called upon to assist the refugee population according to the conditions set out in the signed agreements, in the different occupied zones, with the military forces; these kept for themselves the responsibility and control of all the operations that concerned displaced persons, as well as certain specific functions such as safeguarding public order. The agency dealing with aid and relief was instead given the management of the camps and the organisation of all the services (healthcare, education, leisure) that had to be carried out internally. The relationship with the military authorities remained a controversial issue for the representatives of UNRRA. On the one hand, UNRRA complained about a reduction in its autonomy and tried to increase its room for manoeuvre; on the other, it negotiated, reformulated and adapted its intervention on the basis of the occupying forces' priorities and objectives. What emerged overall, despite the ongoing tensions and opposing points of view, was an overall system of practices that arose from the interaction of humanitarian programmes with military ones, both sets heavily influenced by the dynamics that marked out the international context in the immediate post-war period.[40]

The refugee population, subdivided by nationality, was gathered together inside numerous camps: in 1946, UNRRA stated that it was running over 800 in the zones of Germany governed by the Anglo-Americans.[41] The basic criterion for the division of the displaced persons between the different assembly centres was nationality. The creation of entirely Polish or Ukrainian or Baltic (inside which there were separate zones for Estonians, Latvians and Lithuanians) camps was able to facilitate the resolution of organisational and logistical problems but it was planned above all as the essential precondition for the repatriation programme. In the post-Second World War era, the return to countries of origin was considered the fundamental tool for dealing with the refugee question, as had happened over twenty years previously with Nansen and the League of Nations. The return home of millions of displaced persons could only have happened gradually but it had to remain as the main aim; according to the agreements concluded with the military authorities, the management of all the repatriation operations remained firmly in those authorities, while UNRRA was to deal with relief for refugees in preparing for their departure and then during the long, rough journey. Things did not go according to plan. For instance, although the displaced persons who came from western countries did indeed soon return to their places of origin, many of those who should have left for eastern Europe refused to be repatriated. The new geo-political set-up was the primary reason for this refusal. For example, Estonians, Latvians and Lithuanians no longer had a homeland to return to, since the Baltic states had been annexed by the Soviet Union, while many of the displaced Poles did not intend to re-enter a country that did not correspond any more to its old borders and over which hung the threat of Soviet interference.[42]

Between 1945 and 1947 the overall number of displaced persons reduced notably but around a million people remained in the camps spread over Germany, Austria and Italy. UNRRA still had the task of seeing to their care but it was not the only organisation operating within the assembly centres. At the same time that the relief for displaced persons had emerged as a problem, with the advance of the Allied forces over Europe, the more distant or more recently formed voluntary associations had also mobilised to offer their contribution and had worked in close collaboration with the Allied military forces. As soon as the UN agency became operational, to all intents and purposes it took on a coordination function – as set out in its mandate – and attempted to regulate the non-governmental organisations' access to the camps. To be able to assist the displaced persons in occupied Europe, it was necessary to obtain a specific accreditation from the military authorities and come to an agreement with UNRRA. This type of procedure had been put in place to control, regulate and plan the humanitarian societies' interventions but also to contain their space for action and recognise UNRRA's central position as an intergovernmental agency, bringing an innovative approach to relief and rehabilitation. Private associations, however, could make available motivated, and in many cases qualified, staff as well as material resources to contribute to a significant extent to the assistance of displaced persons.

A very high-level role was played in this sense by the Joint, which, on the one hand, could count on its solid experience developed in the context of humanitarianism, and, on the other, became the centre for fundraising for the Jewish survivors of the extermination. In Germany, Austria and Italy the Joint provided basic necessities and medical staff and also organised schools, training courses, recreational activities, and religious events and functions.[43] The American Jewish Joint Distribution Committee was the humanitarian expression of the sentiment of 'dedication, loyalty and love for the remnants of the sword and the camps', a sentiment fed by the world Jewish population even in the awareness that separating it from the survivors was 'an electric wire', in other words, the immeasurable distance from the experience of the Holocaust.[44]

Besides the specific case of the Joint, UNRRA in general trusted the private agencies more for 'the restoration of mental health, morale, and the dignity of the individual achieved by recreational, spiritual, and vocational training programs'.[45] In the refugee camps – but also within the population of the different countries in which UNRRA was operational – the YMCA organised sports activities and entertainment for children, the British Friends Relief Service created educational programmes and professional training courses, and all the religious societies were involved in 'religious services'. The project, embodied by the United Nations' first agency, of a secular and institutionalised humanitarianism, coexisted with the delegation of important functions and responsibilities to the non-governmental organisations. At the same time, that project ended up endorsing an idea of 're-habilitation' in which religion took on a crucial role because it not only alleviated spiritual suffering but also contributed to the re-acquisition of behaviour that was considered healthy and morally correct. It is undoubtedly important that in 1945 the UNRRA worker Francesca Wilson, with whose testimony we opened Chapter 4, recognised as a distinctive characteristic of modern humanitarianism the 'non-proselytising impulse'.[46] But this must not allow us to forget that the humanitarianism Wilson was looking at as modern included in its vision and implementation of relief the practices of the religious tradition, for example legitimising their validity in 'the restoration of mental health, morale, and the dignity'.

UNRRA was not the only reference point for the voluntary associations. During the first stage of the liberation, when the UN agency was not yet operational, voluntary associations provided their relief work by collaborating directly with the military authorities but later on they maintained certain specific spheres of action. A striking example concerns the work carried out by the British societies through the mediation of the Council of British Societies for Relief Abroad (COBSRA) in support of the German population and more precisely the refugees expelled from central eastern Europe. These people – as we have already highlighted – were excluded from making use of international relief, as were all the national groups belonging to the enemy alignment against the Allies. However, the increasingly conspicuous arrival of men and women exhausted by their long journeys and their sufferings, without a place to be received and without any means of support, soon began to worry the British government and its authorities in occupied Germany from the point of view of maintaining public order, but even more because of the fear that the 'mass of dispossessed' could turn out to be an incubator for dangerous diseases.[47]

The question of assistance for Germans expelled from eastern Europe was presented to the London authorities in even more complex terms. With the appearance of the first reports in the major newspapers about the dramatic conditions of these German refugees from eastern Europe, a public opinion campaign developed that denounced these people's state of abandonment and called for immediate measures. The main promoter of this mobilisation was Victor Gollancz – publisher and businessman, but also politically involved in the Labour Party, independent activist and controversial public figure – who in August 1945 sent an open letter entitled 'In Germany Now' to the *News Chronicle*. In his text he exhorted the British authorities and his fellow citizens not to remain motionless, and in making the case for the German refugees he stated 'The only thing that matters [...], is that a man is a man first, and a German, a Czech or a Pole, a long way afterwards'.[48] Such a vision of humanitarianism, centred on the need to relieve to the suffering of others as fellow human beings regardless of their nationality, was certainly not new but at that moment it laid bare the contradictory internationalism of the aid policies supported by the UN. Naturally, this vision was not only Gollancz's: the appeal that followed his letter in the *News Chronicle*, entitled 'Save Europe Now', signed by intellectuals such as Gilbert Murray and Earl Russell, gained widespread credit among the general public and was also supported by certain British humanitarian societies, including Oxfam.

The solution finally adopted by the London government responded as much to the requests made by the 'Save Europe Now' campaign as to the concerns of the British military in Germany and led to an ever greater commitment by the associations present in the field to the relief of German refugees. Their reference point, also through the mediation of the Council of British Societies for Relief Abroad, was mainly the British government, whose policy choices influenced the humanitarian programmes.[49] As can be understood even from one such example, the undeniable importance of the new role played by UNRRA as an intergovernmental agency did not reduce the weight of the national players in determining the appearance of aid in post-war Europe. Nor can we think of the post-Second World War era as a phase of marginalisation for private associations, which were instead called upon to build closer relationships with national governments and develop their reporting to the new intergovernmental bodies: first UNRRA, and then the UN.

Building the United Nations

When we make a building for the UN, we must have in mind what is the UN? It is an organization set the nations of the world in a common direction and gives to the world security. I think it is difficult to get this into steel and stone. But if we make something representing the true spirit of our age, of comprehension and solidarity, it will by its own strength give the idea that that is the big political effort, too.[50]

With these considerations the well known Brazilian architect Oscar Niemeyer gave advance notice of the creation of the skyscraper that would become the headquarters, but also the symbol, of the UN. The task of designing the UN's base had been entrusted to Niemeyer and other famous professionals – including Le Corbusier – at the end of a long debate on the choice of the city that would host the building. The League of Nations had been headquartered in Geneva, and the European countries wanted to keep the seat of the body succeeding it in Europe, but since the League was no longer at the centre of international politics it was not even imaginable that their hopes would become reality. It would instead be the United States to host the new organisation because of the major role it played in promoting its formation. San Francisco was the location wanted by Washington's representatives and by the Latin American and Asian countries; the Soviet Union and the European countries in general pushed for the east coast, which was more easily reached crossing the Atlantic. The question was resolved thanks to the donation of John D. Rockefeller, who had acquired in Manhattan the land necessary for the buildings that would become the UN headquarters.[51] The various options for the location are just an example of the tensions in the UN's start-up phase, tensions that were progressively accentuated by the emergence of the Cold War. Nonetheless, in 1947, when he issued his statement, Niemeyer could still recall the image of the nations that, after the defeat of Nazi-Fascism, were set 'in a common direction', and reused the rhetoric of a new start in the history of peoples, based on the spirit of 'comprehension and solidarity' risen from the rubble of the war.

Despite the widespread insistence on the idea of a new foundation of international cooperation, the constitution of the UN was directly tied to the previous
experience of the League of Nations. Like the League, the new intergovernmental
body aimed to guarantee peace and collective security and many of those called
upon to design its structure and start its activities had already taken part in
the Genevan operation. At the wish of the United States, a further component
of the League of Nations was brought back and strengthened by the UN: the
implementation of economic and social programmes. Its commitment was more
limited to activities more closely definable as humanitarian, even though these
were explicitly mentioned in the areas of competence listed in article 1 of the UN
Charter. In short, it would be misleading to project our perception of the UN as
the pre-eminent party in the humanitarian context onto the organisation's first
phase of life. In the aftermath of its constitution, the aid and relief programmes
did not immediately become part of the organisation's permanent agenda but
were entrusted mainly to agencies conceived of as temporary, with the purpose
of bringing to an end the 'rehabilitation' work for the European population hit by
the war.

The International Children's Emergency Fund (ICEF) was set up in 1946 to
run the UNRRA programmes for children for a further three years. Naturally,
the direct inheritance of the activities of the previous UN agency, which was at
the winding-down stage, went back to the by now established recognition of children – and mothers – as the main focus of humanitarianism.[52] At the same time,
childcare took on great importance within the reconstruction project that was
to lead to the birth of new democratic societies in the shattered post-war world.[53]
ICEF, like UNRRA, concentrated its interventions in Europe: between 1947
and 1950 over 80 per cent of the budget was taken up by initiatives in European
countries. To a large extent the resources were used for the delivery in Poland,
Italy, Austria or Germany of basic necessities for children, and food in particular:
'milk, fats, and cod-liver oil, had almost become synonyms' for ICEF, wrote the
agency's departing director of programmes in Europe in 1950.[54] A further element
of continuity with the UNRRA set-up concerned the emphasis on collaboration
with national governments and local institutions of the individual countries. In
this case, too, the aim was to create the conditions for their future autonomy, at
the same time redefining the standards of relief and welfare organisation.[55] It is
significant that the food plans for children involved the distribution of added
rations through school canteens following the criteria set out by local authorities,
but they also included the creation of specific courses in technical training for
the pasteurisation of milk, its reduction to powder and later preservation. The
end was not only to feed the children from the countries hit by the war but also to
spread principles and standardised procedures based on what was set out by food
science experts and nutritionists, who were becoming established in those years
as important professional figures in planning reconstruction.[56]

In 1950, ICEF's mandate was renewed for a further three years, which began a phase of discussion on the organisation's future. At stake was no longer relief for European societies, which was already on the road to recovery, but the possible extension of the geographical area and fields of competence of the UN agency for childhood. The world beyond Europe, which was starting to be affected by the process of decolonisation, was ICEF's potential new field of action, since it was aiming to move on from completing the post-war relief work to socio-economic development in Asia, Africa and Latin America. In the three-year interlude ICEF had moved 'its main emphasis towards programmes of long-range benefit to children of developing countries' and the Assembly General decided to transform it into a permanent agency.[57] The redefinition of its mandate was translated into a name change for the UN body for childhood, which ultimately came to be known simply as the United Nations Children's Fund (though it has retained the acronym UNICEF). The disappearance of the term 'emergency' from the agency's official name was intended to register the end of the temporary commitment to post-war relief programmes. It was certainly through these programmes that the UN forged its expertise in support for children, which had drawn on the previous philanthropic tradition in producing its own practices and policies, and now it was projecting them beyond the boundaries of the Western world. We will return to this more extensively in Part III. The last aspect to be recalled here instead concerns UNICEF's balance sheet: during the 1950s there was a gradual reversal in the relation between investments for projects in non-European countries and those in Europe itself; it was only in the following decade, however, that the latter were squeezed so far as to make up only 2 per cent of the total expenditure.[58]

The United Nations High Commissioner for Refugees (UNHCR) was also conceived of as a temporary body to take on the role carried out until then by the International Refugee Organization (IRO), which in its turn had taken the place of UNRRA in 1947. The IRO's mandate lay essentially in the resolution of the post-war refugee problem – as set out above, this concerned those people who had refused repatriation and were still resident in the German camps – through resettlement in other countries where they had been offered a job.[59] The IRO programmes had transformed the displaced persons into miners for Belgium or France, manual workers for Britain, farm workers for the United States or Australia, and domestic workers for Canada.[60] In this way the *ad hoc* intergovernmental agency reformulated and developed the project started twenty years earlier – on a much smaller scale – by the League of Nations and the ILO. The IRO, too, considered that professional training was necessary the settlement of the refugees in the countries ready to give them work. Many of the camps were transformed into training centres and, more generally, involvement in specifically activated work programmes became one of the essential tools for the displaced population's rehabilitation (or its 'preparation for a new life'), as citizens of Western society.[61] Between 1947 and 1951, more than 700,000 men and women left the centres in Germany and their move elsewhere took place at an equal pace with consolidation of a new international order, which in Europe saw the Iron Curtain drawn across the border between the two German Republics, the Federal and the Democratic.

The departures of the refugees coincided with the start of a new flow of arrivals, made up of citizens of eastern Europe fleeing west. The question had emerged in 1948, though to a very limited extent, with the arrival in power of the communists in Czechoslovakia and the consequent exit from the country of thousands of supporters of the 'Third Republic'. When the IRO's mandate approached its conclusion, a small number of Second World War refugees were still awaiting placement, while the phenomenon of civilians arriving from eastern Europe was an unresolved issue. At the UN Assembly the creation of a new body was planned, whose possible areas of competence were discussed at length. This body was to be the Office of the High Commissioner for Refugees (UNHCR). Especially at the wish of the United States, the UNHCR saw its functions limited to just the legal protection of asylum seekers, who could obtain the ratification of their status through the organisation and possibly be on their way towards a welcoming country. The UNHCR had to set up a sort of 'legal bridge' which ran from the moment men and women in flight lost the protection of their own country of origin until their judicial recognition elsewhere. Unlike the organisations that had gone before it, the new UN agency was not called upon to see to the relief of refugees, and nor did it have the budget to do so. Its mission, therefore, waived the component of relief and care that had historically made up the core of international humanitarianism. The reasons for this gap were economic – the UNHCR was supposed to be a flexible and only temporary body – but the gap was also an expression of the desire to delegate to the nation states the refugee question, which was now particularly thorny because it was directly connected to the dynamics of the Cold War. The US government was the first to stand against the strengthening of the UN Commission, and to entrust the management of refugees from beyond the Iron Curtain to its own national agencies, supported by federal finances.[62] For certain vital areas from the point of view of international political stability, the UN set up specific agencies with a mandate tied to the relief of a distinct group of refugees: the case of the United Nations Relief and Works Agency for Palestine Refugees, set up in 1949, undoubtedly represents the most significant example.[63]

The policies of the individual states on asylum were at the time governed by the Geneva Convention, approved by the UN General Assembly in the same year, 1951, that the UNHCR became operational. The 1951 Convention Relating to the Status of Refugees followed the general principle set out in the Universal Declaration of Human Rights in which 'everyone has the right to seek and to enjoy in other countries asylum from persecution' (article 14). The Convention signed in Geneva was conceived of as the cornerstone of the international system of protection of civilians forced to leave their own countries, and established that the term 'refugee' was applicable to any person who:

> As a result of events occurring before 1 January 1951 and owing to well-founded fear of being persecuted for reasons of race, religion, nationality, membership of a particular social group or political opinion, is outside the country of his nationality and is unable or, owing to such fear, is unwilling to avail himself of the protection of that country; or who, not having a nationality and being outside the country of his former habitual residence as a result of such events, is unable or, owing to such fear, is unwilling to return to it.[64]

This definition marked a change from previous measures because it introduced an individualistic approach: the decision to give protection to those requesting it was taken on the basis of each single individual's motivations, meaning refugee status was granted to whoever showed that they had personally suffered, or risked suffering, a specific form of persecution within their own country of origin. In the post-First World War era, as we have seen, protection and relief from the League of Nations were recognised instead on the basis of belonging to a national group (as in the case of the White Russians or the Armenians who escaped genocide) and the granting of the 'Nansen passport' to all the members of a defined community did not coincide with the recognition of their individual right to receive aid.[65]

The Geneva Convention sanctioned that right but tied it to two conditions, one chronological and the other geographical. As specified in article 1, quoted above, men and women could acquire refugee status only if the events leading to their flight had taken place before 1951, or that they could be ascribed to the Second World War or the dynamics that had marked the emergence of the Cold War. In the same article, the possibility was given of placing as a further condition that the events behind the persecution had happened in Europe, in other words allowing the individual governments to exclude those who came from non-European regions from being granted refugee status. Almost all the signatory countries chose this option. The chronological and the geographical limit were put forward in terms essentially the same as in the UNHCR statute, which confirmed the Eurocentric interpretation of the by now historically established recognition of a part of the displaced population as recipients of international protection. There was no mobilisation of any UN agency when, at the end of the 1940s, the separation of India and Pakistan caused the dramatic forced displacement of millions of people.

In the years following its constitution, the UN's more strictly humanitarian commitment on the ground seemed fragmented, delegated to agencies initially thought of as temporary, still heavily in debt – in terms of the activities carried out and the approaches adopted – to the previous experiences of bodies that were formally destined to disappear. The definition of new horizons was squeezed between the inheritance of the post-war rehabilitation and the establishment of the Cold War. The picture changed only with the progression of decolonisation, which imposed new bodies and scenes on international humanitarian action, shifting its operational axis.

Notes

1 Franklin Delano Roosevelt, Letter, 3 November 1944, ldpd_leh_0784_0391, Herbert H. Lehman Papers, Special Correspondence Files, Rare Book and Manuscript Library, Columbia University Library, at http://lehman.cul.columbia.edu/ldpd_leh_0784_0391 (accessed 2 January 2019).

2 See p. 75.

3 Franklin Delano Roosevelt, 'Address of the President of the United States', *United Nations Relief and Rehabilitation Organization. Journal*, 1 (10 November–2 December 1943), p. 1.

4 Elizabeth Borgwardt, *A New Deal for the World: America's Vision for Human Rights* (Cambridge, MA: Belknap Press of Harvard University Press, 2005), pp. 116–121.

5 Jessica Reinisch, 'Relief in the Aftermath of War', *Journal of Contemporary History*, 43:3 (2008), pp. 371–404.

6 Bertrand Taithe, 'The "Making" of the Origins of Humanitarianism?', *Contemporanea: Rivista di storia dell'800 e del '900*, 18:3 (2015), pp. 489–496.

7 Silvia Salvatici, 'Professionals of Humanitarianism: UNRRA Relief Officers in Post-war Europe', in Johannes Paulmann (ed.), *Dilemmas of Humanitarian Aid in the Twentieth Century* (Oxford: Oxford University Press, 2016), pp. 235–262.

8 Jessica Reinisch, 'Internationalism in Relief: The Birth (and Death) of UNRRA', in M. Mazower, J. Reinisch and D. Feldman (eds), 'Post-war Reconstruction in Europe: International Perspectives, 1945–1949', *Past and Present*, 210: suppl. 6 (2011), pp. 258–289; Jessica Reinisch, '"Antie UNRRA" at the Crossroads', in M. Hilton and R. Mitter (eds), 'Transnationalism and Contemporary Global History', *Past and Present*, 218: suppl. 8 (2013), pp. 70–97.

9 Philip Noel-Baker in Julian Huxley et al., *When Hostilities Cease: Papers on Relief and Reconstruction Prepared for the Fabian Society* (London: Victor Gollancz, 1943), p. vi.

10 Dwight D. Eisenhower, Letter, 15 November 1945, ldpd_leh_0266_0001, Herbert H. Lehman Papers, Special Correspondence Files, Rare Book and Manuscript Library, Columbia University Library, at http://lehman.cul.columbia.edu/ldpd_leh_0266_0001 (accessed 2 January 2019).

11 Geoffrey Best, *Humanity in Warfare: The Modern History of the International Law of Armed Conflict* (London: Methuen, 1983), p. 220.

12 François Bugnion, *Le Comité International de la Croix-Rouge et la protection des victimes de la guerre* (Geneva: CICR, 1994), pp. 195–197.

13 Mark Mazower, *Inside Hitler's Greece: The Experience of Occupation, 1941–1944* (New Haven, CT: Yale University Press, 1993), pp. 47–48, 70; Daniel Palmieri and Irène Herrmann, 'Two Crosses for the Same Aim? Swiss and Swedish Charitable Activities in Greece During the Second World War', in Johannes Paulmann (ed.), *Dilemmas of Humanitarian Aid in the Twentieth Century* (Oxford: Oxford University Press, 2016), pp. 171–184.

14 Bugnion, *Le Comité International de la Croix-Rouge*, pp. 229–230.

15 Best, *Humanity in Warfare*, pp. 289–301.

16   David P. Forsythe, *The Humanitarians: The International Committee of the Red Cross* (Cambridge: Cambridge University Press, 2005), pp. 44–50; Jean-Claude Favez, *The Red Cross and the Holocaust* (Cambridge: Cambridge University Press, 1999 [revised and updated edition of *Une Mission impossible? Le Comité International de la Croix-Rouge, les déportations e les camps de concentration nazis*, Lausanne: Éditions Payot, 1988]), pp. 53–81.

17   Sébastien Farré, 'The ICRC and the Inmates of National-Socialist Concentration Camps (1942–1945)', *International Red Cross Review*, 95:888 (2012), pp. 1381–1408.

18   Fabrice Cahen, 'Le Comité International de la Croix-Rouge (CICR) et les visites de camps. Étude d'une controverse', *Revue d'Histoire de la Shoah*, 172 (2001), pp. 7–62.

19   Max Huber, *The Good Samaritan: Reflections on the Gospel and Work in the Red Cross* (London: Victor Gollancz, 1945), p. 66. This pamphlet had originally come out in German in 1943 (Zürich: Schulthess) and in the same year was translated into French (Neuchâtel: La Baconnière).

20   ICRC, 'Commemorating the Liberation of Auschwitz', 27 January 2005, at https://www.icrc.org/eng/resources/documents/statement/68zeb2.htm (accessed November 2018).

21   Maggie Black, *A Cause of Our Times: Oxfam, the First 50 Years* (Oxford: Oxfam and Oxford University Press, 1992), pp. 1–21.

22   Eileen Egan, *Catholic Relief Services: The Beginning Years. For the Life of the World* (New York: CRS, 1988), pp. 1–24.

23   Halik Kochanski, *The Eagle Unbowed: Poland and Poles in the Second World War* (London: Allen Lane, 2012), pp. 237–244.

24   John Ormerod Greenwood, *Quaker Encounters: Friends and Relief* (York: William Sessions, 1975), vol. I, p. 275.

25   Silvia Salvatici, 'Between National and International Mandates: DPs and Refugees in Post-war Italy', *Journal of Contemporary History*, 49:3 (2014), pp. 514–536.

26   Forty British organisations joined the Council of British Societies for Relief Abroad (COBSRA), among them British Red Cross, Friends Relief Service, Friends Ambulance Unit, the Save the Children Fund and the Salvation Army.

27   Forty-eight organisations belonged to it, among them the American Friends, the American Jewish Joint Distribution and the YMCA.

28   Rachel M. McCleary, *Global Compassion: Private Voluntary Organizations and US Foreign Policy Since 1939* (New York: Oxford University Press, 2009), pp. 36–59.

29   Katie Louchheim, 'DP Summer', *Virginia Quarterly Review*, 61:4 (1985), pp. 691–707, at p. 696.

30   Silvia Salvatici, 'Professionals of Humanitarianism'.

31   George Woodbridge, *UNRRA: The History of the United Nations Relief and Rehabilitation Administration* (3 vols) (New York: Columbia University Press, 1950), vol. III, p. 428.

32   *Ibid.*, pp. 411–441.

33   Paul Baerwald, Letter, 10 December 1943, ldpd_leh_0031_0066, Herbert H. Lehman Papers, Special Correspondence Files, Rare Book and Manuscript Library, Columbia University Library, at http://lehman.cul.columbia.edu/ldpd_leh_0031_0066 (accessed 8 January 2019).

34   Woodbridge, *UNRRA*, vol. I, p. 333.

35   For the historiography, see John Lamberton Harper, *America and the Reconstruction of Italy, 1945–1948* (Cambridge: Cambridge University Press, 1986).

36   Woodbridge, *UNRRA*, vol. I, pp. 107–108.

37   See the case of Italy, United Nations Archives (UNA), S-1021-0039-04, UNRRA, Office

of the Historian, Monographs, Country Area Missions and Offices, Italy 19, History of Welfare Division Italian Mission (by Phoebe Bannister).

38   Woodbridge, *UNRRA*, vol. II, p. 470.

39   Silvia Salvatici, 'Sights of Benevolence: UNRRA's Recipients Portrayed', in H. Fehrenbach and D. Rodogno (eds), *Humanitarian Photography: A History* (New York: Cambridge University Press, 2015), pp. 200–222.

40   Silvia Salvatici, '"Fighters without guns": Humanitarianism and Military Action in the Aftermath of the Second World War', *European Review of History: Revue Européenne d'Histoire*, 25:6 (2018), pp. 957–976.

41   Woodbridge, *UNRRA*, vol. II, p. 502.

42   See, among many, Anna Holian, *Between National Socialism and Soviet Communism: Displaced Persons in Postwar Germany* (Ann Arbor, MI: University of Michigan Press, 2011); Daniel G. Cohen, *In War's Wake: Europe's Displaced Persons in Postwar Order* (New York: Oxford University Press, 2012).

43   Chiara Renzo, *'Where Shall I Go?' The Jewish Displaced Persons in Italy (1943–1951)*, thesis submitted to the University of Florence and the University of Siena for the degree of Doctor of Philosophy, 2017.

44   This is the statement of a soldier of the Jewish Brigade, that Hanoch Bartov describes in the autobiographical novel *The Brigade* (New York, 1968), pp. 56, 148, cited in Atina Grossmann, 'Victims, Villains, and Survivors: Gendered Perceptions and Self-Perceptions of Jewish Displaced Persons in Occupied Postwar Germany', *Journal of the History of Sexuality*, 11:1–2 (2002), pp. 291–318, at p. 298.

45   Woodbridge, *UNRRA*, vol. II, p. 77.

46   Francesca M. Wilson, *Advice to Relief Workers: Based on Personal Experiences in the Field* (London: John Murray and Friends Relief Service, 1945), p. 4.

47   On the fear of the spread of diseases and the consequent health policy of the British military government in Germany, see Jessica Reinisch, *The Perils of Peace: The Public Health Crisis in Occupied Germany* (Cambridge: Cambridge University Press, 2013), pp. 164–168.

48   Cited in Matthew Frank, 'The New Morality: Victor Gollancz, "Save Europe Now" and the German Refugee Crisis, 1945–6', *Twentieth Century British History*, 17:2 (2006), pp. 230–256, at p. 238.

49   Matthew Frank, 'Working for the Germans: British Voluntary Societies and the German Refugee Crisis, 1945–1950', *Historical Research*, 82:215 (2009), pp. 157–175.

50   United Nations Archives and Records Management Section, *Oscar Niemeyer and the United Nations Headquarters (1947–1949)*, at https://archives.un.org/content/oscar-niemeyer-and-united-nations-headquarters (accessed November 2018).

51   Mark Mazower, *Governing the World: The History of an Idea, 1815 to Present* (London: Allen Lane, 2012), pp. 218–219; Evan Luard, *A History of the United Nations, Vol. I: The Years of the Western Domination, 1945–1955* (London: Macmillan, 1982), pp. 79–85.

52   Jennifer M. Morris, *The Origins of UNICEF, 1946–1953* (Lanham, MD: Lexington Books, 2015), pp. 31–48.

53   Sara Fieldston, *Raising the World: Child Welfare in the American Century* (Cambridge, MA: Harvard University Press, 2015).

54   Quoted in Burhan B. Ilercil, *UNICEF Programme Assistance to European Countries*, UNICEF History Series, Monograph III (Paris: UNICEF, 1986), p. 3.

55   See the case of Italy, set out by Angela Villani, *Dalla parte dei bambini: Italia e Unicef fra ricostruzione e sviluppo* (Milan: Wolters Kluwer – Cedam, 2016).

56 Silvia Inaudi, 'Assistenza ed educazione alimentare: l'Amministrazione per gli aiuti internazionali, 1947–1965', *Contemporanea: Rivista di storia dell'800 e del '900*, 17:3 (2015), pp. 373–400.

57 Ilercil, *UNICEF Programme Assistance to European Countries*, p. 1.

58 *Ibid.*, p. 5. On the low investment of UNICEF in Africa in the 1950s see Shobana Shankar, 'Blurring Relief and Development: Religious and Secular Politics of International Humanitarian Intervention During Decolonization in Sub-Saharan Africa', in Johannes Paulmann (ed.), *Dilemmas of Humanitarian Aid in the Twentieth Century* (Oxford: Oxford University Press, 2016), pp. 263–288.

59 Rieko Karatani, 'How History Separated Refugee and Migrant Regimes: In Search of Their Institutional Origins', *International Journal of Refugee Law*, 17:3 (2005), pp. 517–541; Kim Salomon, *Refugees in the Cold War: Toward a New International Refugee Regime in the Early Postwar Era* (Lund: Lund University Press, 1991), pp. 239–258.

60 Cohen, *In War's Wake*, pp. 102–125.

61 Louise W. Holborn, *L'organisation internationale pour les réfugiés: agence spécialisée des Nations Unies, 1946–1952* (Paris: Presses Universitaires de France, 1955), p. 364.

62 David Kennedy, *The Dark Sides of Virtue: Reassessing International Humanitarianism* (Princeton, NJ: Princeton University Press, 2004), pp. 199–233; Gil Loescher, *The UNHCR and World Politics: A Perilous Path* (Oxford: Oxford University Press, 2001), pp. 50–81.

63 See pp. 151–152.

64 Convention Relating to the Status of Refugee, article 1A(2).

65 James C. Hathaway, *The Law of Refugee Status* (Toronto: Butterworths, 1991), pp. 2–6.

Part III

From Europe to the Third World

Sir,

We expatriates, working in Biafra, wish to draw attention to the recent intensification of air attacks on civilians here, despite world pressure for peace talks. Over the past week several hundred Biafran civilians have been killed in this way. At Owerri 43 out of 65 dead were children. Deaths in Aba totaled 118.

In an air raid on Umuahia (April 25), of which we were eye-witnesses, 107 bodies were counted in the hospital mortuary, and 130 casualties were admitted, of whom 18 were children; three of the children died, and others will be crippled or maimed for life. At least six of those killed were expectant mothers.[1]

The dry statement of the deaths caused by the bombardments on civilians was sent to *The Times* by a small group of priests who were taking care of the sick and wounded at the hospital in Umuahia, the city where they were present during one of the raids by the Federal Nigerian army against the Biafrans. Although they limited themselves to providing information on what was happening in their immediate area, the Catholic missionaries underlined that civilians had been deliberately struck by the enemy army, whose brutality they reiterated. The English newspaper published their letter in May 1968, when the civil war in Nigeria, better known as the Biafran War, had been in progress for a year, though it had received little consideration by the Western world. Shortly after, though, the tragedy of the Biafrans – killed by Nigerian bombs but above all by hunger – quickly gained the attention of public opinion, placing it at the centre of a vast international mobilisation.

The civil war in Nigeria was 'the first postcolonial conflict to engender a transnational wave of humanitarian concern'.[2] This is also why it is usually identified as a turning point, as the beginning of a new phase in the history of humanitarianism. In this interpretation, the aid sent to the victims of the Nigerian civil war ratified the shift in the humanitarian agencies' range of action, orienting it for good towards the non-European regions that were going through the process of decolonisation and the tensions of the Cold War. In addition, the wide coverage of the 'mass death' in Biafra expressed a new role for the media, which transformed a war largely ignored by the Western world into an event able to 'engender a trans-national wave of humanitarian concern'. Finally, the mobilisation for the conflict that had erupted in western Africa allowed the emergence of the new central role on the international scene of the non-governmental organisations, which played a major part in collecting donations and sending aid to the Biafran population.[3]

The Nigerian civil war was undoubtedly a crucial event that made obvious, fed and accelerated international humanitarianism's transformation. To understand this process, and therefore the reasons that contributed to making 1967–70 a turning point, we need to examine a longer stretch of time, which runs from the early 1950s to the end of the Cold War.

The humanitarian agencies' new global horizon had already developed before the civil war in Nigeria through the development programmes that for almost twenty years had been the main activity for international relief. The aim of these programmes was the social and economic advancement of the 'backward' countries, and went side by side with the promotion of industrialisation and mechanisation of agriculture, healthcare and education and professional training. The settings in which humanitarianism had grown over time became an essen-tial part of the development policies. The humanitarian projects were a vital component in the restatement of the relationships – economic, political, cultural – between North and South after the end of the colonial empires.

During the 1950s the UN had defined its agenda, placing at its centre the development programmes that, in the following decade, also saw the intense involvement of the private agencies. In part these were missionary societies and philanthropic bodies that had lengthy experience of work beyond Europe in sectors like health or education. As well as these there were the organisa-tions started for the post-war relief – mostly in the post-Second World War period – which broadened their areas of expertise, including in development. But above all, the idea of freeing the 'backward' countries from poverty and hunger was the stimulus for setting up new associations that during the 1960s contributed to increasing the number of programmes carried out in the field and of initiatives created to raise awareness in the Western public. The growth of non-governmental organisations (NGOs) – both in quantitative terms and from the point of view of their dimensions – that took place in this period opened up the road to the 'explosion' of NGOs seen during the 1980s.[4]

The campaigns to fight hunger, disease and the 'backwardness' of the Third World were conducted in close connection with the media, which were now part of a complex system within which television had taken on a major role. The circulation of images, articles and reportage in the newspapers, the production of bulletins and specialist information sheets had all been part of humanitarianism in past eras too. Now, though, the use of the media was developed, systematised, integrated within transnational initiatives which aimed to transform into a mass phenomenon the spirit of taking part in the suffering of others, the depth of feeling in the face of the show of misery, and the empathy for the aid recipients.

At the end of the 1960s, in this profoundly altered context, the armed conflicts that shook the fragile and still unstable postcolonial set-up once again brought relief for war victims to the centre of humanitarian action. The conflict immediately following the secession of Biafra from Nigeria (1967–69) was only the first in a series of dramatic events that grabbed the attention of the public and from time to time became a new emergency within which the now complex situation of international relief acted. The secession of Bangladesh and the war between India and Pakistan (1971); the fall of the Pol Pot regime and the Vietnamese occupation of Cambodia (1979); the famine following the dictatorship and internal conflicts in Ethiopia (1984–85): these were the most significant cases through which humanitarianism took on or showed the distinctive features that still distinguish it today.

In the twenty years in which the dramatic events we have just recalled unfolded, the role taken on by the mass media made it easier for donation appeals to be circulated and to get an immediate response on an international scale. The intensity of the appeal from the media was based on the use of dramatic images with very strong emotional impact, such as those of children from Biafra with their bodies deformed by starvation. They were images that stressed the emergency: in the humanitarian narrative of the war, the emphasis placed on the need for immediate relief left little room for the analysis of the highly complex reasons for the conflict. The mobilisation to aid the Biafran people ended up promoting a simplified vision of the Third World, associated with catastrophe and dependence on relief from wealthy, advanced societies. It was a vision that emerged again in the following years until it reached its peak with the initiatives organised by Bob Geldof and other stars from the world of music for Ethiopia when it was hit by famine. The almost two billion people who saw the Live Aid concert in 1985, broadcast across the world, received very little information on the political and social context in which the Ethiopian crisis had exploded. Singers and famous musicians joined together on the stage for a 'humanitarian cause', aimed at conveying a simple message: people in Africa are dying of hunger, and the contribution equivalent to buying a record or ticket for a concert can save the lives of men, women and children.

Not entirely paradoxically, the hyper-simplifications produced by the media and the turning of aid requests into a spectacle corresponded to the complexity of the conflicts in question. These were regional but with profound international implications tied to the changeable dynamics of the Cold War and the inheritance of colonialism. They made clear that humanitarianism had now reached an advanced level of growth, since it could mobilise huge resources, count on a body of professionals that moved from one crisis area to another, and brought together governmental and intergovernmental institutions, associations with long-standing experience and newly formed groups. At the same time, the deployment of relief was heavily conditioned by the dynamics of the wars in progress.

In Nigeria, hunger, but also the request for aid, became genuine instruments of war. The federal Nigerian government fed the Biafrans in order to break their resistance. At the same time, the circulation of images of children reduced to skeletons was a crucial weapon for the authorities in Biafra in building up the international solidarity that was helping to keep the country – militarily very weak and unrecognised by the major powers – alive. 'Starvation broke Biafra and brought Biafra fame and made Biafra last as long as he did';[5] nor did humanitarianism show itself capable of breaking this chain of events. During the war the ICRC attempted to open a safe channel for the circulation of foods and medicines but the negotiations with the warring parties did not prove successful. The airlift organised by a coalition of Christian organisations, without looking for diplomatic solutions, showed the strength the NGOs had acquired but the relief that arrived at the destination far from corresponded to the real needs of the Biafra population and only contributed to slowing down the surrender.

The paradoxes created by the intertwining of relief and warfare emerged with increased clarity ten years later following the Vietnamese invasion of Cambodia. The Phnom Penh government, dependent on that of Hanoi, launched an appeal for aid for the population that had been battered by Pol Pot's bloody dictatorship, by the war against Vietnam and by the victorious army's occupation. But the Cambodian authorities imposed conditions on the organisations willing to meet their appeal (for example relating to the distribution of aid) that implied the violation of the principles of autonomy, neutrality and independence – three principles that humanitarianism recognised as essential. Rejecting the Hanoi government's conditions meant, however, denying relief to millions of civilians laid low by hunger and disease. At the same time, many governmental and nongovernmental organisations rushed to Thailand to aid the Cambodian refugees: their programmes there became innovative laboratories for relief practices for displaced populations. Part of the aid, though, was hijacked by the armed groups that were fighting against the Vietnamese occupation of Cambodia and that controlled most of the camps. So the humanitarian aid ended up feeding the war that was burning itself out on the border between Thailand and Cambodia.

The dynamics were similar some years later in Ethiopia when it was struck by famine and ravaged by internal conflicts. The distribution of international relief ended up underpinning the programme of forced relocation of the population that was wanted by the regime and that increased the number of victims of the famine. The 'crises' that since Biafra had been behind large-scale mobilisations by the international community challenged the idea of a humanitarianism that was neutral and impartial, showing how relief operations could be manipulated and could worsen – rather than lessen – the victims' pain.

Notes

1 T. S. Garrett, et al., 'Civilians bombed. From the Rev. Dr. T. S. Garrett and others', *The Times*, 14 May 1968, p. 11.

2 Lasse Heerten and A. Dirk Moses, 'The Nigeria–Biafra War: Postcolonial Conflict and the Question of Genocide', *Journal of Genocide Research*, 16:2–3 (2014), p. 176.

3 Johannes Paulmann, 'Conjunctures in the History of International Humanitarian Aid During the Twentieth Century', *Humanity: An International Journal of Human Rights, Humanitarianism, and Development*, 4:2 (2013), pp. 215–238.

4 Kevin O'Sullivan, 'A "Global Nervous System": The Rise and Rise of European Humanitarian NGOs (1945–1985)', in M. Frey, S. Kunkel and C. R. Unger (eds), *International Organizations and Development, 1945–1990* (Basingstoke: Palgrave Macmillan, 2014), pp. 197–219. In general, on the increase in the number of NGOs between the 1960s and 1980s see also Thomas Davies, *NGOs: A New History of Transnational Civil Society* (London: Hurst, 2013), pp. 141–154.

5 Chimamanda Ngozi Adichie, *Half of a Yellow Sun* (London: Harper Collins, 2017 [New York, 2006]), p. 237.

6

Fighting poverty and hunger

More than half the people of the world are living in conditions approaching misery. Their food is inadequate. They are victims of disease. Their economic life is primitive and stagnant. Their poverty is a handicap and a threat both to them and to more prosperous areas.

For the first time in history, humanity possesses the knowledge and skill to relieve the suffering of these people.[1]

It was Harry S. Truman who said this at the White House on 20 January 1949 in his inaugural address for his second mandate as president of the United States. As is known, Truman summarised the main aims of his programme in four points: continued support of the UN; continuation of the programmes for world economic recovery; support for the 'freedom-loving nations' against the danger of aggression; finally, beginning 'a bold new program' aimed at making the United States' scientific advances and industrial progress available for 'the improvement and growth of underdeveloped areas'. It was to strengthen this last point that the president of the United States recalled the miserable living conditions of most of the world's population, undernourished and struck by disease, while at the same time underlining the existence – in industrialised societies – of the knowledge and skills needed to aid suffering humanity.

The rhetoric he used echoed tones and arguments from the humanitarian discourse, which had been part of the international political language since the post-First World War era, and cutting to his conclusions Truman underlined that 'Only by helping the least fortunate of its members to help themselves can the human family achieve the decent, satisfying life that is the right of all people'. The motto 'help the people to help themselves' had been promoted by UNRRA and inherited from the philanthropic tradition. Here it was relaunched and re-formulated through the new lexicon of fundamental rights, which in its turn had been legitimised by the Universal Declaration approved the year before by the UN. The fourth point in Truman's inaugural address was destined to gain great success: the following day all the newspapers gave it great prominence. In an article entitled 'Point Four' the magazine *Fortune* stated that the promise of using American know-how to take well-being to the globe's 'backward' areas 'hit the jackpot of the world's political emotions'.[2]

The idea of improving the living conditions of the 'backwards' populations with the superiority of their own resources – material and cultural – was certainly not new in Western countries' political action and thinking. Academic studies – enriched in recent decades by a growing number of contributions[3] – have outlined a long period of development that, according to the most frequent interpretation, had its beginnings in nineteenth-century European colonialism. The colonies' administration was founded on the conviction that Western societies had been granted a 'civilising mission' and that the colonisers had the tasks both of making the conquered territories more productive – principally through infrastructure construction – and of transforming the local population's behaviour and mentality, for example through educational programmes. In Part I we have seen how the intention to 'develop' the peoples of Africa or Asia was also associated with the idea of showing the humanitarian spirit by promoting the improvement of the living conditions of colonised people and thereby relieving their suffering.

In the period between the two World Wars, the development question took shape as such and was placed at the centre of the debate on imperial politics, in the conviction that rationalisation and modernisation would increase the dependent territories' productivity.[4] The reference to development was also an answer from the colonial powers to the criticisms of the 'inhuman' exploitation of the colonies. These criticisms had acquired strength on an international level, as we have seen regarding forced labour and the 'new slaveries'.[5] In order to stabilise their government over the vast imperial regions, the metropolises also invested greater resources in sectors such as education and health.[6] The smallpox vaccine, the struggle against malaria, the measures against infant mortality, the training of paramedic staff were all programmes carried out in the name of progress. But they were also made to happen in the name of sensitivity towards other people's need and out of the commitment to fighting it.

Education and health also continued to be the settings in which the missionary societies, which intended to help the peoples in the colonies by providing the assistance needed to overcome their 'backwardness', worked most intensively. The development policies were then translated into organic, wide-reaching measures during the Second World War when the colonies' human and natural resources became crucial for the warring powers and new tensions crossed the empires. In 1940, for example, the British authorities responded to the growing unrest affecting the colonial workers with the Colonial Development and Welfare Act, putting the territories' productivity and governability at risk.[7] France ratified a similar measure immediately after the end of the war, in 1946.[8] Development was the field where there was an attempt to redefine the relationship between the colonised and the colonisers while the empires were starting to creak.

So what was the innovation brought by the Second World War period and the US initiative? Why has 'point 4' often been presented as the inaugural address of a genuine 'age of development' that began in the second half of the 1940s? The element of change was the shift from the national scale, from colonial policies or regional development, to the transnational scale.[9] The socio-economic advance of the 'backward' peoples – or rather 'underdeveloped', according to a definition that began to spread in those years – became a question of global order, to be dealt with through cooperation between states. At the dawning of the decolonisation process that would take place over the following decades, the subject of develop-ment played a vital role in determining the relationship between the North and South of the world, and at the same time took on a precise ideological meaning in the context of the Cold War.[10] According to one body of opinion centred in the United States, international aid for the progress of the 'primitive and stagnant' peoples could act as an antidote to the spread of communism, which was finding a fertile breeding ground in social discomfort. At the same time, the increase in productivity and the well-being guaranteed by the aid coincided with the triumph of economic liberalism and liberal democracy on an increasingly wide scale.

In this respect, the aims summarised in 'point 4' were similar to those in the Marshall Plan – the programme for the recovery of Europe begun by the US government in 1948 – and both were part of the economic cooperation project that was set up in the Bretton Woods Agreement (1944) and the subsequent setting up of the International Monetary Fund and the World Bank. The ideo-logical meaning acquired by development became a source of genuine conflict between two models of modernisation when, in the latter half of the 1950s, the policies towards the Third World became one of the planks in the Soviet Union's international strategy and the aid war began.[11] Development was one of the fronts of the rivalry between the two superpowers, which identified in the transfer of technology, skills and resources to the 'backward' countries a powerful tool for extending their own economic and social system over the entire globe. Of course, the development programmes were not only the expression of the conflict between the two blocs. We just need to think of the important projects carried out by the Nordic states. Supporters of the UN mission, they invested in the develop-ment projects in the conviction that the improvement of the living conditions in the countries that came into being with decolonisation and still economically 'backwards' was necessary to guarantee world peace and stability.[12]

Naturally, we do not intend to reconstruct here the rather complex history of the development policies started in the latter half of the 1940s and pursued for over twenty years. The aim is instead to focus on the intertwining – anything but simple to untangle – of the development policies and the international humani-tarian programmes. As we will see, the humanitarian organisations pursued the improvement of living conditions for the populations of Asia, Africa and Latin America through projects based on knowledge and technology transfer for public health, nutrition and professional training. These projects took place alongside those for agricultural and industrial mechanisation and became an integral part of them. They were initially promoted in particular by the specialist UN agencies – the WHO, the ILO and UNICEF – but during the 1960s they largely absorbed the work of the NGOs too, as shown by their intense participation in the 'Freedom from Hunger' campaign (1960–65), launched by the Food and Agriculture Organization (FAO). It is the programme to free the world from hunger that provides a useful observation point to understand how the different parties in international humanitarianism interpreted their massive commitment to the development of the Third World. In fact, it seemed to some insiders that the work for advancement of the 'backward' countries distanced the humanitarian societies from their original aims but the discussion on this aspect did not cool 'the new passion for "development"'[13] that was fuelling the international projects planned to help suffering humanity. The commitment to the socio-economic growth of the 'backward' countries was, overall, an important stepping stone in the path of humanitarianism since it provided a significant boost to its global projection, intensified the collaboration between the different parties (the associations, national governments, UN agencies) and encouraged the reformulation in a different framework of the knowledge and experience already gained with post-war relief and 'rehabilitation'.

Before moving on to the reconstruction of the initiatives undertaken to fight poverty and hunger, it is worth recalling that even though the question of development took on great importance, it did not account for the whole of humanitarianism's work in the decades that followed the end of the Second World War. The assistance to the refugee population, which was one of the fields in which humanitarianism had historically developed, kept a significant importance and in this very sector brand new initiatives took shape that influenced the course of the ensuing programmes for international aid.

The 'global turn' of the refugee programmes

We have already recalled that in 1951, the year in which the UNHCR was set up, the question of refugees for the Western governments firstly appeared connected to the growing flow of civilians fleeing the Iron Curtain countries. The urgency of the problem became particularly serious in 1956 with the Red Army's suffocation of Hungary's anti-Soviet revolt. Around 164,000 Hungarians crossed the border to find shelter in Austria, while another 20,000 fled towards Yugoslavia, but the wretched living conditions they found in that country pushed many of them into joining up with their fellow nationals in the Austrian camps. The authorities in Vienna first launched an appeal to their citizens to contribute with donations for the relief of the Hungarian refugees – gathered in around 250 centres – but immediately afterwards they publicly declared that it was impossible for them to deal with the emergency alone.[14] Numerous Western governments intervened on behalf of the men and woman escaping Hungary following the Soviet repression: Canada, the United States, Britain and Switzerland were the countries in which the largest numbers of refugees found a new home.

This was the first major occasion on which the 1951 Geneva Convention was applied and the dynamics of the Cold War significantly influenced the ways in which the individual states interpreted the international agreements. The Convention had introduced an individual approach to the recognition of refugee status,[15] but the importance of nationality now re-emerged surreptitiously, since in the Western countries' eyes, the Hungarian community seeking asylum was the very incarnation of anti-communism.[16] As a consequence, the welcome they received ended up being a tangible proof of democracy: the Western world could demonstrate that it was the champion of freedom by welcoming the opponents of communist tyranny. The humanitarian response to the new refugee crisis that had emerged in the heart of Europe thus strengthened the Western democracies' construction of their identity that was taking place in the framework of the conflict between the two blocs.

The various national governments' asylum programmes were defined starting from these assumptions. The men and women in flight from Hungary were considered victims of political persecution without distinction and the measures for their stay in the welcoming countries were facilitated by the new phase of expansion in the capitalist economies. The United States led by Dwight Eisenhower launched a plan that allowed the entry of around 40,000 Hungarians over a year, thanks also to the introduction, for this specific group of asylum seekers, of a more rapid screening process than the one in force.[17] In Switzerland, the generous reception for the Hungarians in the name of anti-communism signalled a real break with the essential closure shown by the government towards refugees in the post-Second World War era. The 'freedom fighters' from Hungary were admitted *en masse* – in relation to its resident population, Switzerland received the largest number of refugees – and were encouraged to stay through the activation of specific training and job placement programmes.[18]

The measures taken by the governments generally involved the NGOs, and the reception of the Hungarian refugees took on concrete forms through the cooperation between institutions and voluntary agencies. The British authorities considered it necessary to count on the humanitarian associations' skills and resources in order to give assistance to the 17,000 refugees from Hungary and to enable their resettlement in the country. For example, the British Red Cross Society was one of the organisations tasked with setting up the reception centres while the YMCA took part in the creation of educational and recreational activities for the refugees.[19] In Britain, as elsewhere, the voluntary agencies also contributed to the promotion of the campaigns that, from one point of view, were necessary for fundraising and, from another, were needed to raise public awareness in order to encourage the reception of the refugees and stand up against any possible criticism of the governments that had opened their doors.

The Hungarians were usually described as individuals 'naturally' inclined, because of their anti-communist choice, to being integrated in the democratic societies in which they had asked for asylum. The Eisenhower administration and the US voluntary agencies active in the reception and resettlement of the refugees agreed on a media battle aimed at presenting the Hungarians as future citizens of the United States, with all the qualities that marked out 'good Americans'. The newspapers, magazines and television were provided with specifically prepared material and then urged to put out stories of people and families who, having left communist Hungary, had happily begun a new life, showing that they unreservedly shared the values of the country that had received them. The refugees' quick adaptation to the 'American way of life' was demonstrated through stories and images that described the work of the 'new citizens' in factories and offices, their passion for shopping in the big stores, and their love of the cinema and dance music.[20]

With the mass flight of civilians from Hungary after it had been invaded by the Soviet troops the refugee question came to public attention and became a priority for the Western governments. The problem, however, was dealt with exclusively in relation to the specific case – the Hungarian – and therefore within the European theatre. The Eurocentrism of the refugee regime that started in the post-war years and was sanctioned by the Geneva Convention found its confirmation despite the global dimension of the phenomenon of the forced civilian migrations. The two most dramatic cases in terms of quantity concerned the Middle and Far East, and more precisely the Palestinian refugees and the Chinese seeking asylum in Hong Kong.

The 1948 Arab–Israeli war led to territory previously in the British Mandate for Palestine (1922–48) being divided into three distinct areas: the Gaza Strip, controlled by the Egyptians; Transjordan, which was quickly annexed by Jordan; and the state of Israel. Most of the region's population was forced into exile: around 750,000 people found shelter in camps within Lebanon, Syria, Jordan or the Gaza Strip. Some humanitarian organisations had already intervened during the conflict and mounted relief operations for the refugee population, including the Red Cross (both the ICRC and the federation of national societies), the American Friends Service Committee and numerous Protestant churches.[21]

The UN tried to coordinate the NGO work through the institution of the United Nations Relief for Palestinian Refugees (UNRPR), which was not an operational agency but simply an office with the task of rationalising and to an extent financially supporting the operations in all the areas affected by the exiles' arrival.[22] The creation of the UNRPR was, on the one hand, an attempt to fill a gap: the Palestinian refugees did not fall under the mandate of the IRO, which was called upon to resolve the problem of the displaced persons specifically in

Europe.[23] On the other hand, it was the result of the conviction that the problem of the Palestinian refugees would be quickly resolved by negotiating their return in the places of origin. This prediction was soon shown to be mistaken and in May 1950 the United Nations Relief and Works Agency for Palestine Refugees (UNRWA) became operational, an agency set up *ad hoc* by the General Assembly to assist the Palestinian refugees.[24]

When it began its activities, UNRWA made use of the previous NGOs' experience to carry out its own work, for example by taking on many of the Quaker staff who had worked in Gaza.[25] At the same time, the new Agency's institution sanctioned the emergency of the refugees in the Middle East and encouraged the extension of the international humanitarian commitment in the field: for example, in the early 1950s Lutheran World Relief – founded in 1945 to take aid to displaced persons in Europe – was only the first in a series of American associations involved with the Palestinian refugees.[26] Still following the conviction that question of the Palestinian refugees would soon be resolved, UNRWA was planned as a temporary agency but in 1958, ten years after the Arab-Israeli war, half a million people still fell under its mandate.[27]

Equally dramatic was the situation of the civilians who, during the war and following the constitution of the People's Republic of China, had landed in Hong Kong. The demographic impact of that migratory flux was still striking even in 1956: one in three inhabitants of the region – still a British colony – was a refugee. The British administration's position remained ambiguous. It feared the possible transformation of Hong Kong into a safe landing ground for men and women fleeing Maoist China in the years to come, and hoped for the refugees' voluntary repatriation by keeping the reception standards to a minimum. As well as this, the Western countries considered the Chinese refugees to be migrants looking for work because granting them any other status would have meant implicitly stating that the Mao government represented the political power they were persecuted by and this would have had consequences for diplomatic relations with the People's Republic.[28] In November 1957 the UN General Assembly, finally taking action, approved a resolution which recognised 'that the problem [of Chinese refugees in Hong Kong] is such as to be of concern to the international community' and allowed the UNHCR to contribute to their assistance.[29] The UN agency set up for the protection of asylum seekers in Europe[30] could therefore now include among its beneficiaries the Chinese refugees who were crowding the last British possession in the Far East, but only for aid on the spot, without the UNHCR getting involved in their resettlement in other countries.

Hong Kong, like the Middle East, became the destination of those NGOs that considered assistance to refugees an integral part of their humanitarian mission. It was these NGOs that first brought to light the dramatic reality of the forced migrations that affected countries far from Europe, in the wake of the new attention to refugees aroused by the Hungarian case. Although the reception of the Hungarians took place in the name of anti-communism, it contributed to bringing notice to the figure of the refugee, the specifics of refugees' conditions and the type of intervention needed to assist them. The head of communication for the British NGO Christian Aid wrote in the magazine *Onslaught*:

> Here in the British colony of Hong Kong a million Chinese refugees from the Mainland have inundated a territory which can neither support nor accommodate them [...]. They live in their hundreds of thousands in tiny home-made shacks, leaking and insanitary, tier upon tier on the hillside. They live in shelters of cardboard and sacking on the city roof-tops. One act of carelessness with a match or an oil stove and the whole settlement burns like a forest fire.[31]

Reports like this supported by the personal evidence of people involved in humanitarian action, and strengthened the campaign for the proclamation of a World Refugee Year. The campaign principally aimed to project the problem of aid for the refugee population on a global level.

The project for the first World Refugee Year originated in Britain, the country where there was a particularly strong contrast between the reception for the refugees from eastern Europe – '[they] treated us as heroes', declared a Hungarian who arrived in England in 1956[32] – and the lack of commitment to the Chinese in Hong Kong. Among the initiative's leading promoters were two Members of Parliament, Timothy Raison and Christopher Chataway, from the progressive wing of the Conservative Party. Both were not only politicians but also well known journalists: before being elected to parliament Chataway had been a BBC correspondent and Raison had worked for various national newspapers.[33] It is therefore no coincidence that the programme to raise institutions' and citizens' awareness of the refugee problem developed from the beginning on the level of political debate as much as the swaying of public opinion.

Raison and Chataway were among the signatories of a policy statement published in 1958 entitled 'A Plan to Save the Refugees'. This plan was based on two main lines: setting up relief programmes directed in different areas of the globe but coordinated with each other; conducting a fundraising campaign in proportion to the vastness of the problem. These two fronts of action were to be developed over a year officially dedicated to the figure of the refugee. In order to be effective, this project had to go beyond the borders of Britain, to be supported by the broadest possible number of countries and be ratified by the UN.[34]

The campaign to encourage the international community to share the project for the first World Refugee Year was carried forward not only through the media but also through diplomatic means, thanks to the network of political relations activated by Raison and Chataway, which was then rapidly extended and strengthened. In the UN Assembly the greatest difficulties came from the Soviet bloc countries, which, at the setting up of the IRO in 1947, proposed repatriation as the prime solution and opposed the reception policies that involved the settlement of refugees in other countries.[35] In the following years, the flight of civilians from Eastern Europe towards the Western countries added to the reasons for tension between the two blocs. The Western governments received 'as heroes' the 'Iron Curtain refugees', while the Soviet Union accused them of having as their sole interest the acquisition of a labour force for the capitalist system. To get the approval of the Soviet bloc countries, the document presented to the General Assembly cut out the anti-communist references and an amendment was approved in which repatriation was added to the possible solutions to international displacement. The votes in favour were in a large majority and the resolution, passed in December 1958, established that the World Refugee Year would begin in May 1959.[36] As well as promoting interest in the refugee problem, the World Year was intended to obtain financing for *ad hoc* programmes and to put pressure on governments to adopt permanent measures for refugees that would not just be a response to a temporary emergency. This had to happen 'on a purely humanitarian basis':[37] so the UN resolution, from one point of view, was intended to establish the initiative's exclusively humanitarian character – understood as non-political, in contrast to the influence of Cold War dynamics on the refugee question. From another point of view, it was intended to reiterate that seeking asylum was a fundamental right of individuals, as established by the 1951 Geneva Convention.

The UN's deliberation was of course a fundamental step but it had to be followed by the adhesion of individual governments. In some cases this was obtained with some ease: it is what happened, for example, with the Scandinavian countries that approved the project, declaring it in line with their previously demonstrated commitment to international relief. In other cases participation in the World Refugee Year conflicted with questions of internal politics and some governments held an ambiguous position, officially giving their support but reducing to a minimum their commitment to the programme.[38] France provides the best example in this respect. At the end of the 1950s the refugee problem for the French was directly connected to Algerian war of independence, which had led to the forced migration of around 250,000 people to Tunisia and Morocco. Numerous humanitarian organisations – including the League of Red Cross Societies, Oxfam, and the British and American Friends – intervened to provide aid to the Algerians sheltering in tent cities. In addition, relief for the refugees was one of the main activities of the Algerian Red Crescent, which had been set up in the context of the Algerian independence movement. It enjoyed widespread support from the local population and was carrying out a major international awareness-raising campaign to win over world public opinion, as well as concrete aid from the Arab countries.[39] France opposed the recognition of refugee status for the Algerians sheltering in Tunisia and Morocco because this would have meant directly attributing to the French authorities responsibility for the acts of persecution those Algerians were victims of. For those people, the failure to grant refugee status naturally had as a consequence the denial of international protection.[40] In this case, too, the UN took the path of compromise and, through a specific General Assembly resolution, granted the UNHCR the task of assisting the Algerians in Morocco and Tunisia,[41] leaving the recognition of their status unresolved, however. In this context, France's position towards the World Refugee Year was ambiguous: the government officially gave its support but very little was done to develop the activities set out in the programme.[42]

The plan launched for 1959–60 saw the substantial involvement of NGOs, some of which were already distinguished for their assistance given to refugees. In World Refugee Year private agencies (which even though they had a long tradition in the context of international aid had received a major boost during the Second World War and in the period immediately following it) found an important framework in which to strengthen and expand their own activities. Taking part in a programme created under the banner of the UN offered greater opportunities to collaborate with governmental and intergovernmental institutions, to raise their own visibility and to get more recognition of their own fundraising campaigns.[43] Oxfam, for example, increased its staff, multiplied its activities, obtained results beyond every expectation in its fundraising (over £750,000 in twelve months) and was recognised as a charitable organisation on a national level.[44] The World Refugee Year also promoted the coordination of the NGOs on a supranational level and thus significantly boosted their internationalisation.[45]

The initiatives to attract the attention of public opinion and to collect donations were certainly nothing new for private associations but between 1959 and 1960 took on specific characteristics that enhanced and modified elements that had emerged in the past in 'humanitarian communication'. The uses of images, not only photographs, was widespread; technological development now allowed the use of film, through which it was possible to tell genuinely personal and family stories, enabling emotional participation in refugees' suffering. The documentaries, the advertisements, the dramas whose screenplays were inspired by the refugees' experiences were able to reach a wide public thanks to television. Famous personalities – from television, cinema and music – were called on to promote World Refugee Year. Actors, singers and politicians publicly declared their support for the campaign and took part in the various initiatives, which thus became more recognisable, more familiar and more shareable in the eyes of the wider public. The commission set up by the US government to oversee the programme launched by the UN produced a documentary called *A Call from the Stars* in which famous personalities – including Paul Newman and Bing Crosby – 'explain[ed] the refugee problem' and invited viewers to donate something to the commission itself or to one of the associations working in the sector.[46]

Fairs and lotteries were organised to fund aid programmes for the refugees. Prize draws and sales of objects – which made money but also brought individual people closer to the content of the campaign – had been widely used since the times of the anti-slavery movement.[47] In 1959–60 they were used again through formulas that took advantage of the ability of the new consumer goods to attract people. Lotteries could give the luckier people a washing machine, a television or even a car, while in the fairs unusual and exotic objects could be bought.[48] The offer of unusual objects, just like the hope of winning a much-desired prize, increased the pleasure of the purchase, which was in turn joined to that of having done 'a good deed'.

The subject's recurrence in the media, the number and the success of the initiatives organised *ad hoc* and the results of the fundraising together meant it could be stated that in 1959–60 the aim of drawing huge public attention to the refugee question had certainly been achieved. In World Refugee Year four further countries (Greece, New Zealand, Brazil and Portugal) ratified the Geneva Convention, bringing to twenty-seven the number of states that guaranteed the legal protection of refugees. What was missing, though, was a supranational pressure group to keep the commitment of governmental and intergovernmental institutions – and people's interest – on the question of forced population movements. When the twelve months of initiatives developed under the UN's watch finished, the refugees ceased to be on the agenda of humanitarianism. What remained, above all, was the experience of the campaign carried out over that period – the forms of communication that had been tried, the solutions thought up to expand public empathy for the lot of the people receiving the aid, and the network established among the different associations but also the relationship between them and the institutions. All of this joined up, in another iteration, in the international programme 'Freedom from Hunger', launched exactly as World Refugee Year was about to end, with the aim of fighting hunger in Third World countries, through rural development.[49]

In the wake of decolonisation

The decolonisation process played a major part in determining the course of international politics after 1945. The dissolution of the colonial empires and the birth of the new states implied a redefinition of the Eurocentric world order, on which the dynamics of the Cold War had their effect. The development programmes launched from the second half of the 1940s on were placed in this context and we can identify their reasons and purposes in that light. For the ex-colonial powers, the policies for improving the economic conditions of the 'backward' countries were one of the tools through which to reformulate – within the new setting – their relationships with the regions that had once been part of their empires and were now independent states. This reformulation of relationships arose not only out of political and economic needs but also for socio-cultural reasons. The idea of the 'civilising mission' that underpinned colonialism could no longer be put forward in those terms and the West had to change the definition of its own identity.[50] At the same time, development and international aid became key words for the newly constituted countries, which had to deal with the problematic take-off of their national economies and negotiate their relationships with the industrialised powers in the search for a space on the international stage. The development programmes took shape in relation to these new needs, but absorbed and reprocessed past convictions, techniques and aims – particularly in relation to health, education and food – that went back to the long tradition of 'colonial humanitarianism'.[51] The recent experience of the World War was added to that of the long period of colonialism. The relief and rehabilitation programmes that had opened the road to the post-war reconstruction, in Europe especially, were also an important inheritance for the new path of international relief.

From the end of the 1940s on, the improvement in the 'underdeveloped' countries' socio-economic conditions took a major place on the agenda of the intergovernmental organisations, most of all in that of the UN.[52] This orienta-tion was determined initially by the Western countries and primarily the United States. The government in Washington made development one of the key planks of its international policies and considered the international agencies' role crucial in the pursuit of its global politics. Conversely, in most cases the Soviet Union and the countries belonging to the communist bloc entered into agreement between their member states only belatedly, from the end of the 1950s. For all of the previous period, US representatives were able to exercise a great deal of influence on the UN decision-making bodies, including those for humanitarian programmes. This is what happened with the intervention in Korea, through the creation of a specific agency, the United Nations Korean Reconstruction Agency (UNKRA). The UNKRA case provides an important example of how one agency's activities moved on different levels that overlapped and intersected: aid to the populations affected by the war, post-war reconstruction and the socio-economic development of the Republic of Korea, which had come into existence at the end of Japanese colonialism and as a result of the tensions between the United States and the Soviet Union.

The UNKRA, planned as a temporary body, was set up in December 1950, six months after the attack by northern troops on South Korea and the resulting armed response by the UN decided on by the Security Council. The resolution adopted by the General Assembly established that the UNKRA should provide:

Relief and rehabilitation supplies, transport and services to assist the Korean people to relieve the sufferings and to repair the devastation caused by aggression, and to lay the necessary economic foundations for the political unification and independence of the country.[53]

The measure, associating relief and rehabilitation, echoed the approach that had been taken by UNRRA[54] but compared with the resolution establishing the previous agency it stated more explicitly the connection between the relief necessary to respond to the immediate needs of the Korean population and the intention of seeing to the country's economic and political reconstruction. In fact, the UNKRA – which became operational only after the end of the Korean War (1953) – associated the distribution of food relief, the administration of medical treatments and assistance to displaced persons in wider-ranging programmes aimed at generating a profound economic and social transformation in South Korea. The relief actions, from the experience of international humanitarianism, were the essential part of a reconstruction plan that had to lay the foundations for the country's development.[55] The rural areas of Korea received particular attention. The ultimate purpose was to modernise agriculture through the restoration and enhancement of infrastructure, the introduction of new cultivation techniques, mechanisation of work, and the use of chemical fertilisers and new types of crop. In addition, it was crucial to provide countryside workers with training, which was placed within a broader plan for the spread of the knowledge needed for the running of the different production sectors. Emphasis was placed on the training of specialist staff who in the future would supply the national economy with the skills that international experts were then providing.[56]

The process of economic and social transformation followed in South Korea corresponded to a model of liberal development that contrasted with the communist model in the context of a challenge that did not end along the 38th Parallel but took on worldwide dimensions. The general features of the UNKRA intervention plan clearly show how the dynamics of the Cold War imposed a new and more markedly ideological character on the concept of relief as a way of improving the living conditions of other peoples. The political needs and interests in the new international context grafted themselves onto a concept – as we have already seen – whose very roots lay in the history of humanitarianism.

The UNKRA had the responsibility of coordinating the work of the NGOs, most of which were from the United States. Many of these had been present in the field before the war and the setting up of the UNKRA. Indeed, in the second half of the 1940s US governmental agencies had taken enormous advantage – in Korea as in other regions – of collaboration with private associations, which were able to provide experience and skills in the international relief context, and also to supply the necessary qualified staff. NGOs were therefore involved such as Church World Services, Lutheran World Relief and the American Friends Service Committee, in other words, three of the most relevant American private agencies. The Washington policy coincided, not by chance, with the significant increase in the share of the public finances in the overall budget of the individual non-governmental bodies.[57] Their initiatives, therefore, became more closely tied to the government and its priorities. At the same time, the NGOs became very important links between the US government and the countries the relief was intended for. This is how the field of international relief went forward, building up a public–private cooperation that would last over time.[58]

In this respect, the path followed by the organisation CARE (Cooperative American Remittances to Europe), started in 1945 to provide food relief to the European population exhausted by the war, is significant. At the eve of the 1950s, this type of intervention no longer seemed necessary. The NGO, though, could count on an established relationship with the government and, instead of disbanding, it decided to alter its mission in order to concentrate on food aid in non-European countries. The acronym remained the same but in 1953 the name lost all reference to Europe and was changed to Cooperative American Relief Everywhere. South Korea was only one of its many bases – concentrated in Asia – opened by the organisation after the reformulation of its aims.[59] In this phase, then, the presence of NGOs on the world stage already had a relevance, even though it acquired serious importance in the context of development projects only from the beginning of the 1960s.

The areas of intervention in which the UNKRA's work extended were reminiscent of many of the programmes whose purpose had been the socio-economic advancement of 'backward' peoples through the transfer of knowledge and technology. Questions such as food, health protection, professional training, far from being new to humanitarianism, had become recurrent in development interventions and were thought of as preconditions for the success of mechanisation programmes for agriculture and industry. In some cases they became central to the different specialist UN agencies, such as professional training for the ILO and public health for the WHO.

The theme of development was, without doubt, key for the ILO, which had begun in 1919 along with the League of Nations but which had become part of the UN system. Between the second half of the 1940s and the start of the next decade, the ILO gave a boost to the creation of projects on the ground and extended its new operating dimension to a global horizon.[60] Following the geography of the decolonisation process, the ILO opened regional offices in the Middle East and in Asia, as well as in Latin America.[61] The expansion beyond the borders of Europe required greater attention to the agricultural sector but in line with its original mission the ILO still concentrated on the industrial sector, promoting its enhancement through technical assistance and professional training.[62] The latter was the centrepiece of the ILO's activities in 'underdeveloped' areas and is the aspect that most interests us here because it represented an element of continuity with its earlier participation in the 'rehabilitation' programmes launched by international humanitarianism. In the context of the initiatives started up by the League of Nations for holders of the 'Nansen passport' in the years between the two World Wars, the ILO had, for example, organised training courses that were to provide refugees from Russia or Asia Minor with the skills needed to enter the labour market in the industrialised countries.[63]

The programmes launched in the 1950s to bring development to the most 'backward' areas drew on the long experience gained by the ILO and set to work teams of 'training experts' sent by Geneva to the various regions of the world. In countries such as Brazil, Ecuador, Venezuela, Indonesia and Pakistan, international experts led programmes focused on 'training on the job' in which the participants were to 'learn skills and techniques which [did] not exist at home'.[64] The same aim was also pursued through a system of scholarships which enabled local staff to undertake specialist training in the more economically developed countries for a fixed period of time.[65] The use of this solution had already appeared in the years between the two World Wars out of a Rockefeller Foundation initiative and it was later repeated by UNRRA. The Rockefeller Foundation and UNRRA fellowship programmes were principally for the training of healthcare staff and this experience was inherited above all by the WHO.[66]

Unlike the ILO, the WHO was a newly constituted body but its functions and skills were also rooted in the past. Operational since 1948 as a permanent UN agency, the WHO came into being from the merger of three already existing institutions: the Office International d'Hygiène Publique (OIHP), the League of Nations Health Organization and UNRRA's Health Division.[67] The Office International d'Hygiène Publique, based in Paris, was the oldest of the three institutions absorbed by the WHO. Its creation in 1907 had been a significant accomplishment in the process of internationalisation and standardisation in the public health policies developed over the nineteenth century. The Paris Office's task was to coordinate the quarantine of ships and inform individual states, through the publication of a bulletin, about any epidemics and the measures taken against them. Monitoring and information were among the most important tasks of the League of Nations Health Organization too, which had extended the range of its survey though to the Far East as well as investing in epidemiological research and in the training of healthcare staff.[68] In 1948, the WHO inherited all of this along with the bulletin first published by the Paris Office and the initiatives started by UNRRA. UNRRA had also included in its 'relief and rehabilitation' programme some healthcare projects, developed mainly in Europe and concentrated on anti-tuberculosis vaccination and the struggle against malaria.[69]

The WHO received the past experiences and skills, at the same time setting itself new objectives. Firstly, it did not intend to limit itself to suppressing or containing epidemics, as the bodies preceding it had done. Its ultimate goal was much more ambitious since it lay in 'the attainment by all peoples of the highest possible level of health'.[70] To pursue such a magnificent project, the WHO needed, on the one hand, to have an international structure and, on the other, to identify the appropriate operating methods and the practical instruments. Six regional offices, located on different continents, were opened to fulfil the decentralisation set out by its constitution[71] and by the eve of the tenth anniversary of its foundation the WHO claimed a worldwide sphere of action.[72] In the 1950s, however, its operations remained concentrated in certain areas, South-East Asia in particular and the Middle East to a lesser extent, for reasons tied as much to the programmes inherited from the previously existing institutions as to the dynamics of decolonisation. At the same time as the development of its own structure, the WHO identified in technical assistance the cornerstone for guaranteeing humanity 'the highest possible level of health'.

The WHO programmes aimed to spread specific knowledge, techniques and procedures and made the necessary tools available to put them into practice. For example, it was thought that to fight tuberculosis it was necessary to supply the new vaccine then considered effective (the BCG), to give instructions and to provide practical examples to the populations afflicted by this disease on the ways to carry out vaccination campaigns. Standardised practices and notions were the focus of technical assistance, which became the instrument and end of international cooperation in the area of healthcare.[73] On the other hand, this approach – also adopted by other agencies, such as the ILO – seemed convenient for various reasons. Primarily, insisting on the technical and scientific aspect of the programmes allowed distance to be taken from political value that could be attributed to relief. The WHO, but also the other UN agencies, could officially claim a neutral role in the face of the tensions generated by the Cold War. In addition, the idea of removing the deeper cause of the poor state of health of a large part of the world's population was utopian, at least in relation to the human and material resources that the WHO had available.[74] The export of know-how, though, had a decidedly low cost and promised a lot in terms of results. It was considered, in fact, that the transfer of skills, practices and instruments already acquired by the industrialised societies would start more radical exchanges able to reverse the needs of vast regions of the world. For this to happen, it was not enough to reduce the incidence of the most serious diseases that were gripping the 'underdeveloped' regions but to completely eliminate them.

The idea of the eradication of diseases such as smallpox, malaria and yellow fever had already begun to be a part of international relief projects in the years before the war, with the Rockefeller Foundation.[75] Now the conviction was strengthened that eradication itself was a primary aim. The lowering of mortality and improvement in health conditions in the population were in their turn to be two milestones on the road of the social and economic development of the assisted populations. The WHO's newsletter insisted on the connection between disease and poverty and on the idea that a good state of health was one requirement for the ending of people's state of misery.[76] The concept was reiterated of health as the mere absence of disease, which had characterised the humanitarian programmes in the years between the two World Wars. The projects against sleeping sickness in Africa and the world campaign for the eradication of malaria provide two useful examples for analysing the aims the WHO set itself in the 1950s and the ways in which they were pursued.

In various regions of Africa, the fight against sleeping sickness (African trypanosomiasis), caused by a parasite transmitted by the tsetse fly, had been a priority of the health programmes carried out in the colonial period. The colonial administrators had sought to counter the spread of the disease and often used strict measures, which were even coercive: evacuation of the population from the infested zones; frequent inspections of the villages to identify and isolate the sick; long quarantine for suspected cases; obligatory administration of very aggressive medicines. With the end of the colonial empires, the problem landed on the shoulders of the new African states, and this opened the road to intervention by the WHO. For example, in Sudan it began its relationships with the local authorities during the transition period between the British–Egyptian administration and independence, in 1955. Soon after that, the civil war put the local counterpart largely out of the game but the UN agency developed the programme against sleeping sickness in the country's southern regions on the basis of the agreements made.

The elimination of the disease was pursued through the massive use of pentamidine – discovered little more than a decade earlier – which had been shown to be effective if administered in the first phase after contraction of the parasite and used also as a preventive measure. The aim, then, was no longer simply to keep the spread of the disease under control by reducing the exposure of the population to the tsetse fly bite as much as possible. Nonetheless, many of the practices adopted during the colonial period were repeated within the new programme. In the name of the fight against the disease, the WHO exercised pressure on local administrations to obtain measures such as compulsory preventive injections in certain regions, the double administration of pentamidine to the military forces, and the ability to punish those who did not submit to the controls. Additionally, the continuity with the previous policies was represented by the presence of some former British administrators engaged as experts for the new programme. In Sudan but also elsewhere, the experience gained in the medical and healthcare setting in the service of the colonial empires was a useful introduction letter for becoming part of the new UN agency's staff.[77] By the end of the 1950s in south Sudan, as in the other African regions, the number of people affected by sleeping sickness had been drastically reduced. In 1962 the WHO proclaimed the operation's success and declared that the goal of eradication would be achieved within the next twelve months. The intensification of the civil war, though, led first to a rapid decrease in international staff and then to the WHO's withdrawal from the country. With only the local healthcare structures to support the fight against the fly-borne parasite lost its strength and was relaunched only after the end of the civil war (1972) in the face of a new outbreak of the disease.[78]

The challenge the WHO invested in most in its intention to guarantee humanity 'the highest possible level of health' was the one of malaria. The fight against this disease had become urgent during the Second World War when it was combatted by spraying some of the regions where malaria was endemic with DDT. This type of solution was used again in the immediate post-war period – for example by UNRRA in the Italian region of Agro Pontino[79] – and the WHO had raised the practice to an international level with the programmes created in its very first years. In the various countries where it intervened, the WHO made large quantities of DDT available as well as the not particularly sophisticated instruments for using the powerful insecticide, and the technicians to carry out the operations and teach the local staff how to repeat them on their own.[80]

These factors formed the background to the launch in 1955 of the Malaria Eradication Program, which was immediately recognised as the most ambitious public health plan ever put into action on an international level. The means and methods with which the WHO intended to combat malaria remained unchanged from those in the previous period but a leap forward was made in the plan's dimensions and aims. The investment in eradication was planned to extend over three continents – Asia, Africa and Latin America. The ultimate aim was to eliminate a disease that claimed millions of victims every year, and the consequences of which were also evaluated in economic terms. In fact, it was thought that the spread of malaria contributed to reducing the production capacities of the rural areas and was therefore one of the causes of food shortages on a global level.[81] The Malaria Eradication Program extended the scope of activities beyond the mass distribution of DDT, with malariology laboratories being created for the development of research and for the training of specialist local staff. The intention was mainly to provide all the countries involved with the instruments required to implement anti-malaria programmes on their own and, at the same time, to encourage the spread of medical science more generally. In pursuing these aims the WHO made local institutions its points of contact and it collaborated with other organisations – governmental, intergovernmental and non-governmental – active in international humanitarianism.[82] In India, one of the countries where the spread of the disease had been dramatic, the central government and individual states made available the staff needed to carry out all the operations. In 1958 around 90,000 people were employed in the fight against malaria: 'spraymen'; lab technicians; office workers; logistics workers.[83] The organisation of the work was entrusted to the Indian institutions, which therefore played a major part in the practical translation of the methods introduced by the WHO's experts. The financing for the programme to a very large extent came from the International Cooperation Administration (ICA), the US government association for foreign assistance, which in 1961 was renamed the US Agency for International Development (USAID).[84]

The WHO also developed its activities in close cooperation with UNICEF and the Rockefeller Foundation, the influential American philanthropic society with which the League of Nations had cooperated on healthcare matters. UNICEF had already carried out with the WHO the tuberculosis vaccination programmes that had marked its first moves outside Europe. The continued ties between the two organisations were encouraged by the choice of the UN agency for childhood to keep health at the centre of its agenda and to develop an outlook of global action. From this point of view, taking part in the plan to eradicate malaria immediately became a priority, considering that the mortality rate due to this disease was particularly high in children.[85]

The Malaria Eradication Program achieved significant results straight away with the spread of the disease swiftly reducing and the number of deaths it caused doing likewise. Some 45 million fewer cases of malaria were recorded in India in the years following the start of the project. The WHO was thus able to celebrate its success. It seemed that technical assistance in the healthcare environment had been the creator of a net improvement in the living conditions of populations outside of Europe, and in cases like that of the Indian subcontinent it was seen as a triumph of global dimensions. The results of scientific progress were measured in human lives and from this point of view modernisation and humanitarianism became two sides of the same coin.

The conclusion of the Malaria Eradication Program was not due, though, to the achievement of its aim – in other words, the eradication of the disease, which remained endemic in vast regions of the world. The reasons for the closure of the Program were of a different nature, partly tied to the individual national contexts, partly to the changes in the overall international relief scene. In India, for example, the activities for the eradication of malaria slowed down significantly in the mid-1960s when the country was hit by a serious economic and food crisis due both to the wars with China and Pakistan and to the effects of a prolonged drought. Government resources were drastically reduced and healthcare projects were no longer a priority. At the same time, international, and primarily American, financing shrank. By now, the Malaria Eradication Program had used up its power of attraction, and not only because new epidemics had arisen in regions where it was thought the disease had been eliminated once and for all. This undoubtedly caused widespread frustration but above all there was less certainty that the elimination of malaria would in itself be a precursor to the 'backward' countries' social and economic progress.[86] Good public health continued to be considered necessary for development but other questions gained priority, for example family planning, which took an increasingly central role in India as much because of government policies as international relief.[87] Finally, a widespread awareness began to emerge of the damage caused by the massive use of DDT on the environment and human beings. This called into question the very centrepiece of the WHO's project, since the defence of health had been translated into a threat to all living beings.

Various factors coincided with the conclusion of the Malaria Eradication Program, officially formalised in 1969: the clear impossibility of eradicating the disease; the weight of the costs incurred without having shown the operation's effectiveness for development; the spread of the side-effects of using DDT. In the meantime, the topic of the social and economic growth of Third World countries had expanded further among the agencies operating in the international aid field, thanks to the campaign against hunger launched by the UN's Food and Agriculture Organization (FAO).

Freedom from hunger

> When I opened the Campaign, I felt I could best give expression to mounting international concern by quoting one of my favorite poets, John Donne. I used the words 'One man's hunger is every man's hunger – one man's freedom from hunger is neither a free nor a secure freedom until all men are free from hunger'. These words were taken up as a key to the entire campaign.[88]

This was how Binay Ranjan Sen remembered the launch of the Freedom from Hunger Campaign, which took place in 1960. Sen had worked on the ambitious plan to free the world from hunger for a good three years, in other words from the very moment he was elected director general of the FAO. The idea of guaranteeing the entire world population enough food for dignified survival naturally had many points in common with the development programmes started over a decade before, but its origins were distant in time and were intertwined with the long-term path of humanitarianism.

The problem of the availability of food needed to feed the world had already started to emerge at the end of the nineteenth century, within an international debate between agronomists, economists and nutritionists. The last were the first figures of a new science and they introduced criteria and measurement units useful for establishing the quantity and quality of food necessary for each human being. The connection between agriculture, trade and diet therefore became an important political question in the relationship between states. The conviction that only cooperation between the various countries would guarantee an administration of agricultural production able to respond the population's needs had led to the setting up of the International Institute of Agriculture, founded in Rome in 1904, following a congress specially announced by King Vittorio Emanuele III in which the representatives of numerous countries took part. The new body was given the task of processing and distributing information, primarily of a statistical nature, on the success of harvests, price trends and the progress of trade, by then on a global scale. Obtaining this information through an internationally accredited institute was considered necessary to prevent financial speculation and to harmonise the relationship between production, markets and consumption.[89] The aim was twofold: improving the progress of the economy, and bringing relief to the starving population. 'How many blessings such a work would earn', wrote Luigi Luzzatti, economist and future prime minister of Italy, in the hope that the Institute would be the promoter of genuine cooperation between states on agriculture; 'how many tears it would dry, how many economic crimes it would be the means of abolishing!'[90]

The International Institute of Agriculture carried on its work until the Second World War, coordinating with the League of Nations in the years between the two World Wars when the Genevan organisation promoted the most important research on the relationship between the progress in agricultural production and the food standards guaranteed to the population. The League of Nations' studies on nutrition and health carried out in the 1930s – in the light of the consequences of the Great Depression – which explored the connections between surplus and malnutrition, were particularly important. The aim was to point the way out of an apparently paradoxical situation: the overproduction of foodstuffs existed at the same time as the population's growing difficulty in feeding itself. This fact was significant both within individual countries, where the poorest population bands suffered from lack of food, and on a global scale, since malnutrition was even more widespread in the vast territories of the colonies, outside Europe.[91]

The solution proposed by the group of experts who studied the problem and widely debated it in the League of Nations' Assembly envisaged an expansion of agricultural production and a global redistribution of the surplus – rather than a contraction in response to what might have been seen as an oversupply. Economic policies were recommended to national governments that could guarantee each individual an adequate diet since this would protect people's health and relaunch consumption, kicking off a virtuous circle for the economy's recovery. 'A state agricultural policy must form part of a national food policy, the basis of which must be the provision of a diet adequate for health for every member of the community',[92] wrote Sir John Boyd Orr in 1937. Orr was a famous Scottish scientist who had written numerous research papers on the dietary habits of non-European populations[93] for the British Colonial Office and worked closely with the League of Nations. The adequacy of the diet was a crucial point of interconnection in Orr's entire reasoning; food in fact was not just to feed men and women but had also to provide them with vitamins, proteins and carbohydrates in the right amounts. In this regard, the research carried out for the League of Nations reinforced an approach developed by nutritional sciences in the 1930s, when the 'discovery' of vitamins encouraged the identification of the so-called 'protective foods' – such as milk, certain types of fruit and vegetable, fish – as necessary for the growth of children and the good health of adults.

It is also important to remember that in the years between the two World Wars food aid became one of the preferred objectives for humanitarianism, much as it was in relief operations for civilians in certain specific instances, the most important being the famine in the Soviet Union between 1921 and 1923. The programmes carried out in the Soviet Union, by the American Relief Administration in particular, associated the distribution of foodstuffs with the attempt to restart agricultural activities as to re-establish a balance between the country's productive capacity and the population's minimum level of consumption. After the Second World War, when satisfying the fundamental needs of the victims of the conflict had become one of the cornerstones of the humanitarian programmes and the nutritionists' expertise an influential factor in relief planning, UNRRA also emphasised this approach. With UNRRA, the first UN agency, 'relief' was closely connected to 'rehabilitation' and the latter included the supply of seeds, fertilisers and machinery for the recovery of agricultural production, based on the principle that today's relief had to be translated into tomorrow's autonomy.[94]

Both UNRRA and the FAO came into being in 1943, both based in Washington, DC, and it was 1951 before FAO was transferred to Rome. The impetus for setting up the two bodies came from Franklin Delano Roosevelt's project for leading the world towards the conquest of new security and equity and the FAO seemed to answer perfectly to the aim of ensuring 'freedom from want'. The FAO had inherited the functions of the International Institute of Agriculture and to administer its set-up phase a group of experts was called upon who had worked with the League of Nations: John Boyd Orr, elected director general, was the most significant figure among the professionals who had developed their skills and experience in the context of Genevan internationalism. Not only this but their proposals – on the need for decisive state intervention for food policies and the values useful for establishing the basic nutritional requirements – had become operational with war rationing, which could now be an important precedent. Orr thought of the FAO – which became fully functional only in 1946 – as a body tasked with administering world food policies, equipped with full powers to fix the prices of foodstuffs, purchase the production surplus and redistribute it globally. By carrying out these functions the UN agency would ensure the peoples of the different continents not only the necessary quantity and quality of food but also prosperity and peace. Orr's project was in open conflict, though, with Washington's liberal policies and with what was now in the process of being established as the Western position. In addition, the famous British scientist's hypothesis involved full recognition of the organisation's supranational power by its member states, which would delegate the government of international agricultural policies not to their representatives but to a group of experts. The opposition to Orr's programme was unyielding and the director general resigned from the FAO in 1948. The following year he was awarded the Nobel Peace Prize.[95]

For around a decade, the FAO had a fairly backseat role on the scene of international activities and was entrenched behind a rather reductive interpretation of the functions of technical assistance. The election of B. R. Sen as director general in 1956 took place in a changed international context. The Cold War had entered a new phase and the more serious tensions were beginning to loosen, while the countries born out of the decolonisation process found space for international action in the intergovernmental bodies. Their ever greater presence changed the internal dynamics of the UN and made humanitarianism, aid and development central themes in the international political debate.[96] It was therefore no coincidence that Sen was the first director general of a UN agency from the Third World. Behind him he had a doctorate in economic history from Oxford and a rapid career as an official in the Indian administration in the final period of British rule. Between 1943 and 1946 he was the head of food supplies in India, a position created following the dramatic famine that had struck Bengal and led to the death of millions of people. Dealing with the Bengali tragedy of 1942–43 for Sen meant reflecting on the connection between hunger as an emergency, to which it was necessary to respond with an efficient humanitarian action, and hunger as a consequence of the distortions of the global agricultural production system, to which there needed to be a reaction with specific international policies.

When he became head of the FAO, after being Indian ambassador in various locations, Sen counted on his personal experience as an official of a Third World country in order to carry out his important role: 'All my life I had been in the midst of hunger and poverty in all its stark reality', he wrote in his memoirs.[97] At the same time, the new director general intended to relaunch the organisation's founding values, as its beginning 'had opened a new chapter in international solidarity'.[98] The route which John Boyd Orr had started off on – interrupted by the most authoritative member states' resistance – could not just be picked up again; nevertheless, certain constitutive elements of that initial project returned in the programme started with the 'Freedom from Hunger' campaign (1960–65). The first of these was the idea that the FAO should have as its aim the definitive resolution of the problem of hunger and malnutrition in the world. The second was the conviction that this aim could be pursued only through an authentically international approach, which the rigidity and reticence of the nation states had shown themselves to be an obstacle to. The programme which the FAO promoted at the start of the 1960s aimed, then, at the involvement of a large number of actors, which multiplied the action plans and impeded the member states' possible resistance and their slowing the organisation to a halt. Sen and his colleagues built a network that included the other UN agencies (such as UNICEF, the WHO and the ILO), national governments, NGOs and private companies.[99]

The growth of Third World countries' agricultural productivity was the first target this varied grouping of parties was called upon to deal with. The idea of rural development that inspired the Freedom from Hunger campaign repeated many elements of the programmes carried out in the previous decade, such as the training of local staff and the transfer of know-how and technology. In addition, the FAO was filled with technicians and experts who had worked in the service of the colonial administrations right up to their disappearance and who had therefore brought into the organisation methods and principles developed in the imperial context.

Sen tried to place all of this within a different framework, and proposed an approach that insisted on the need to make the countries in which it intervened as independent as possible: the final goal was helping them achieve the level of production necessary to feed most of the population so as to be less exposed to international market fluctuations. The settings of the FAO plan were significantly different from the US government's policy on food aid, which, in 1958, at the will of President Dwight D. Eisenhower, was summed up in the phrase 'Food for Peace'. The programme envisaged the drawing up of bilateral agreements – in other words, between Washington and the individual countries involved – and responded mainly to the need to ensure the sale of US agricultural over-production, of expanding US trade networks and of strengthening the ties between the destination of the foodstuffs and the US foreign policy. The American government could not, however, remain indifferent to the FAO's new horizon of action, which was gaining consensus; at the same time, the UN agency had difficulty pursuing its own aims without also counting on the support of the most powerful of its member states. Furthermore, the FAO was taking an active role in the management of food aid, which, according to Sen, had to be used to overcome moments of crisis, due for example to famines, but had to remain subordinate to the promotion of agricultural development.[100]

The negotiations between Washington and Rome started with Eisenhower and carried on with the presidency of John F. Kennedy, during which development became one of the linchpins of US international policy and therefore acquired greater prominence than in the previous administrations. Kennedy boosted the 'Food for Peace' programme and in 1962 its director, the Democrat senator George McGovern, sealed the agreements between US government and the FAO which led to the birth of a new body, the World Food Programme (WFP). Initially planned to exist for just three years but destined to become one of the UN's permanent agencies, the WFP was a compromise between the two different positions. On the one hand, it envisaged multilateral management of food aid– and not just bilateral, meaning between the United States and the individual countries involved; on the other hand, it dealt above all with using Western countries' agricultural surplus for humanitarian purposes. In fact, the WFP assigned part of its resources to the creation of pilot projects for rural development, but most of all it saw to distributing foodstuffs resulting from over-production in order to respond with the provision of food to immediate emergencies – famines and natural disasters – as well as to the devastating effects of chronic malnutrition in entire populations. The idea that humanitarian action should not merely correspond to the distribution of essential goods, an idea in circulation for some time but forcefully relaunched after the Second World War, was in this way contradicted in order to guarantee the availability of excess products in certain regions of the world.[101]

The projects carried out in the context of the Freedom from Hunger campaign were planned to alter local economies across their full breadth through the introduction of advanced techniques and new agricultural equipment along with the spread of new types of crop. The effectiveness of these measures was bound to lead to a change in the aid recipients' dietary customs. One of the Freedom from Hunger campaign's priorities lay in promoting the cultivation and consumption of 'protective foods':

> The importance of high-protein and other protective foods – stated a UNICEF report, relating to the projects carried out in the context of the FFHC [Freedom from Hunger campaign] – has to be recognized before people will go out of their way to produce them and feed them to their children. Hence nutrition education is an indispensable part of any campaign to combat malnutrition and a necessary adjunct to all the [other] measures. It must include an effort to teach parents the basic principles of child nutrition, a general drive to persuade people to make better use of the protective foods already available to them, and an attack on harmful dietary customs. The attack on harmful customs must often be a subtle one, for these may be firmly entrenched in local tradition.[102]

According to the humanitarian agencies, liberation of the Third World from hunger involved the passing on of a process of modernisation which concerned not only cultivation systems but also dietary customs, which had to conform to the nutritional principles whose universal value Western science reiterated. From this standpoint, the problem did not lie only in undernourishment, understood as a lack of food, but also in malnutrition, understood as the inability to be fed correctly.

The rural development projects carried out in Third World countries represented only one of the three pillars on which the campaign launched by the FAO stood, while the other two were scientific research and public information. So, in one way, the documentation work that the International Institute of Agriculture had done continued and in the early 1960s it produced a series of studies on specific questions – climate and food, malnutrition and disease, daily diet and capacity to work. It also published some surveys that sketched a general picture of the relationship between trends in agricultural production and the inequality in the nutrition levels between the global North and South. In particular, the studies highlighted that in the more developed countries agricultural productivity had grown in comparison with the years before the war, just as the per capita availability of food had, while this growth had been much slower in Latin America, the Middle East and Asia. In Africa there was even a fall in agricultural production capacity and in all the less developed regions the level of food consumption was more constrained. More than this, though, it was further from the standard diet considered necessary to maintain the health of men and women: in South American, African and Asian countries, the highest number of calories came from carbohydrates, while the intake of animal proteins was fairly low. This image had emerged in a study of the state of agriculture published in 1962[103] and was later developed in the *Third World Food Survey* – begun the same year and finished in 1964 – which showed that less than half of the world population was able to feed itself adequately.

Surveys of this sort were designed to form the scientific background to the FAO's policies but their results – simplified and reworked for the general public – were also useful for the information work that was the pillar of the Freedom from Hunger campaign. The aim of this was raising awareness of people in developed countries about the problem of underfeeding and malnutrition. The involvement of public opinion in the identification of hunger as the byword for need, and therefore as the priority intervention for humanitarianism, was certainly nothing new. Now, though, it was becoming the subject of a global appeal which inherited the experience of the World Year of Refugees in terms of its intensity, its forms of communication and the solutions adopted. The publication of bulletins and specific periodicals – for example the magazine *Ceres* – and the production of radio and television programmes were used in the battle against hunger as they had been for the initiatives planned to spread knowledge about the seriousness of the refugees' situation and to get common people to support the aid operations. In this case, too, famous people from the world of politics, culture and entertainment were involved in winning greater visibility for the campaign. For example, the actor Peter Ustinov – famous from successful films such as *Spartacus* and *Topkapi* – was the narrator of the documentary *The Secret Hunger*, which was produced in 1964 to illustrate the reasons for and the aims of the programme against hunger.[104] The advertising message associated with the campaign called on each citizen to contribute and at the same time it strengthened the conviction that Western societies had the complete power to resolve the problem.

The Freedom from Hunger campaign introduced certain new elements, such as education. The most significant activities in this respect were carried out in Britain, where specific guides were distributed for teachers in 6,000 primary and secondary schools, while concepts of and surveys on world hunger became part of the curriculum and exam texts.[105] These initiatives were in line with the conviction that education and pressure on institutions were not an unimportant aspect of humanitarian action since they could lead to a change in government policies,[106] something that was necessary to balance the asymmetries between the First and Third Worlds.

Taken as a whole, the awareness-raising initiatives in industrialised societies were translated into the spread of greater understanding on different levels of agricultural production on the various continents and a mass involvement in the problem of undernourishment as a humanitarian emergency that connected the global North and South. The terms in which this connection was thought of reworked many elements from the past in a new framework. In an ex-colonial country like Britain, the debates on the poor and hungry regions echoed the imperial rhetoric on Europeans' responsibility towards other peoples. In the allocation of the aid to Asia and Africa the old British territorial possessions were favoured: most of the projects were carried out in states like India, Uganda and Ceylon (modern Sri Lanka).[107] On the other hand, the European countries without a colonial past followed the geography of the missions, as in the case of Sweden, which, when it started its first development programmes, chose to begin from Ethiopia, the destination of Swedish missionaries from the last decades of the nineteenth century. This selection criterion was considered natural because it provided continuity to a long-standing relationship between the aid-givers and its recipients, at the same time allowing use to be made of existing contacts and networks. According to one of the most important heads of the Stockholm government's aid programmes it was important that 'hundreds of Swedes [...] knew the country and its development needs'.[108] Counting on prior knowledge, Sweden's projects kept important elements of contact with previous missionary activity, for example the concentration on educational activities and training for women. The continuity between the postcolonial international aid and the colonial philanthropy must be considered though in the light of the changed context. In the 1960s – but also in the previous decade – the humanitarian pro- grammes were one of the instruments through which the relationship between the newly formed countries and the old colonial powers was defined, not only in terms of economics but also culture and identity.[109]

Information and education in Western countries, and concrete action in the 'underdeveloped' regions: these were the three closely connected operational fronts that made up the nucleus of the Freedom from Hunger campaign, drawn up under Sen's management, in which the FAO naturally played an important role in driving forward and managing. Equally important was the active participation of NGOs, crucial players in giving shape and content to the campaign. The humani- tarian agencies had a huge inherited wealth of skills, experience and relations to spend in conducting the battle against hunger. The initiatives to win the atten- tion of public opinion, to encourage fellow citizens to take part and to collect donations were part of how the associations had been built up together from their constitution. Within the various countries participating in the Freedom from Hunger campaign, they had local roots, in that they were supported by their own religious community or by political activism, or because they were tied to philanthropic bodies and local institutions.

Sen identified the NGOs from the beginning as the essential contact points for his campaign and in January 1959 had launched an appeal to them to contribute in stimulating public interest in the problem of hunger.[110] Oxfam devoted its entire annual congress to this subject the following year and 150 delegates, British and foreign, took part. The opening speech, significantly entitled 'The Survival of Mankind', was given by the great historian Arnold Toynbee, and among the other speakers the name of John Boyd Orr stood out. This first high-profile event was followed by so many other appointments that an activist in the organisation later described Oxfam as 'the main vehicle whereby the new crusade on behalf of the poor overseas took root in British hearts and minds'.[111] In reality this 'taking root' was the work of a wide range of actors, not all of whom came from the world of the voluntary agencies. For example, in Britain youth organisations were also very active and contributed to determining the nature and aims of the campaign against hunger. The humanitarian commitment became the vehicle through which a new generation of British citizens attempted to reposition themselves on the global stage after the end of the empire.[112]

Sen's appeal arose from the specific need to develop the campaign against hunger on a number of levels, as interactions between supranational agencies and non-governmental bodies had earlier been shown to be one of the linchpins for humanitarian action. Such interaction had proved their value after the First World War with the League of Nations and after the Second World War with UNRRA. The Freedom from Hunger campaign, though, marked a turning point because the interactions between the FAO and the private agencies were intense, systematic and took on a global dimension. In this way, the Freedom from Hunger campaign encouraged the first emergence of an international NGO community[113] with shared contact points (the United Nations, the Western governments, the newly constituted countries), aims and fields of action.

The mass participation in the global battle against hunger led the NGOs to a widespread presence in the Third World and a fairly consistent commitment to cooperation in development. As we have seen in the case of Korea, first in the field were the US associations, which in the early 1950s were Washington's preferred partners in the implementation of the policies for modernising 'backward' countries. It was only in the 1960s, though, that the social and economic growth of the poor regions fully arrived on the agenda of the international NGOs, which took up most of their energy. In general, the change in field of action was experienced by private associations as a turning point that some thought coincided with getting further from and others with getting closer to the 'authentic' aims of humanitarianism. Within the American NGO Lutheran World Relief, for example, there was a destructive split because some founding members feared that the heavy investment in training and technical assistance projects distanced the organisation from the spirit of Christian charity that had led to its creation. This position was also influenced by the reluctance to see Lutheran World Relief ever more closely bound to the US government, whose aid policies did not necessarily prioritise 'the poorest of the poor', as the teaching of Christ wished. The sceptics remained in the minority though and the promotion of the social and economic growth of the Third World was the setting for the organisation's main intervention in the 1960s.[114]

In the case of Oxfam, the doubts about whether aid for development could be considered humanitarian aid were raised not from within the organisation but by the Charity Commission, set up by the British government, which had the task of monitoring the activities of philanthropic associations. At the end of 1963, just when the Freedom from Hunger campaign had reached its highest point, the Charity Commission officially called into question the legitimacy of the Oxfam programmes that were not planned in order to provide immediate relief to hunger in the world but to allow the poor countries to be able, in the future, to feed their own citizens. Were these programmes a deviation from the organisation's original humanitarian vocation or were they a higher expression of it? The controversy went on for over a year and aroused wide discussion – which took place in Parliament and between experts – about which activities could be defined as 'charitable'. The matter concluded with a revision of the official statement of Oxfam's mission to include the term 'development', which therefore also formally became part of the agenda of international humanitarianism.[115]

Beyond the specific case of Oxfam, 'development' became a watchword in the world of the NGOs, many of which enthusiastically took part in the Freedom from Hunger campaign. Bernard Llewellyn – who represented Oxfam in Asia and was a professional with lengthy experience developed with the Quaker organisations and Save the Children but also with UNRRA – wrote that, with the FAO campaign, 'U.N. agencies, national governments, voluntary societies, town and village committees, and ordinary people from all walks of life were encouraged to feel part of a movement to feed the hungry world'.[116] In the aims and activities within the Freedom from Hunger campaign, the different parties involved identified a leap forward in comparison with the humanitarian programmes of the past. The economic growth of the countries in which the population was suffering from hunger and disease seemed to offer the ideal solution for 'help[ing] the people to help themselves'; in other words, for creating the aspiration to go beyond 'simple' immediate relief and generate instead a profound change that would remove the reasons for the others' condition of need. What is more, they found a place inside the development programmes for all the activities which humanitarianism had used in the past to 'rehabilitate' the recipients of aid: education; professional training; public health work. Self-help was reformulated in a global dimension and in terms of an economic and social modernisation that led the 'backward' populations to self-sufficiency.

The battle against hunger, fought using the development of the 'disadvantaged' countries, kept its central position on the landscape of international humanitarianism until the second half of the 1960s but towards the end of the decade it began to weaken.

One of the reasons for this change can be identified in the end of Sen's mandate at the FAO and in the different orientation the organisation then took: it preferred the approach put forward by the now prevalent 'green revolution'. The FAO went back to interpreting its function as providing technical assistance, and the improvement of agricultural productivity was mainly pursued through the distribution of selected seeds, fertilisers and weedkillers, and large-scale equipment, rather than through a transformation of the rural societies in the Third World that would lead to their self-sufficiency.[117] The battle against hunger had, though, contributed to broadening attention on the subject of development, which remained highly significant as much for the NGOs as for the intergovernmental agencies. In 1970, the UN declared a second Decade of Development (the first had been inaugurated in 1961) and the increasingly central role of Third World countries within the General Assembly significantly influenced the definition of its new aims. Over the decade, however, emergency relief once again imposed itself as a priority for humanitarian operations.

Notes

1   Harry S. Truman, 'Inaugural Address', 20 January 1949, at http://www.trumanlibrary. org/whistlestop/50yr_archive/inagural20jan1949.htm (accessed November 2018).
2   Cited in Nick Cullather, *The Hungry World: America's Cold War Battle Against Poverty in Asia* (Cambridge, MA: Harvard University Press, 2010), p. 75.
3   Frederick Cooper, 'Writing the History of Development', *Journal of Modern European History*, 8:1 (2010), pp. 5–23; Corinna R. Unger, 'Histories of Development and Modernization: Findings, Reflections, Future Research', H-Soz-u-Kult, 9 December 2010, at http:// hsozkult.geschichte.hu-berlin.de/forum/2010-12-001 (accessed November 2018); Marc Frey and Sönke Kunkel, 'Writing the History of Development: A Review of the Recent Literature', *Contemporary European History*, 20:2 (2011), pp. 215–232; Joseph Morgan Hodge, 'Writing the History of Development (Part 1: The First Wave)', *Humanity: An International Journal of Human Rights, Humanitarianism, and Development*, 6:3 (2015), pp. 429–463; Joseph M. Hodge, 'Writing the History of Development (Part 2: Longer, Deeper, Wider)', *Humanity: An International Journal of Human Rights, Humanitarianism, and Development*, 7:1 (2016), pp. 124–174.
4   Frederick Cooper, 'Development, Modernization, and the Social Sciences in the Era of Decolonization: The Examples of British and French Africa' [2004], in M. Jerónimo and A. Costa Pinto (eds), *The Ends of European Colonial Empires: Cases and Comparisons* (Basingstoke: Palgrave Macmillan, 2015), pp. 15–50.
5   See pp. 86–87.
6   Randall Packard, 'Visions of Postwar Health and Development and Their Impact on Public Health Interventions in the Developing World', in F. Cooper and R. Packard (eds), *International Development and the Social Sciences* (Berkeley, CA: University of California Press, 1997), pp. 93–96; Joseph M. Hodge, Gerald Hödl and Martina Kopf (eds), *Developing Africa: Concepts and Practices in Twentieth-Century Colonialism* (Manchester: Manchester University Press, 2014), in particular part III, 'Social development and welfare'.
7   Frederick Cooper, *Decolonization and African Society: The Labor Question in French and British Africa* (Cambridge: Cambridge University Press, 1996), pp. 110–140.
8   This was the Fonds d'Investissement et de Développement Économique et Sociale (FIDES). See Cooper, 'Development, Modernization, and the Social Sciences', pp. 22–23.
9   Sara Lorenzini, *Una strana guerra fredda: Lo sviluppo e le relazioni Nord–Sud* (Bologna: il Mulino, 2017), pp. 41–53.
10 Corinna R. Unger, 'Postwar European Development Aid – Defined by Decolonization, the Cold War, and European Integration?', in S. Macekura and E. Manela (eds), *The Development Century: A Global History* (Cambridge: Cambridge University Press, 2018), pp. 240–260.
11 Lorenzini, *Una strana guerra fredda*.

12 Sunniva Engh, 'The Conscience of the World? Swedish and Norwegian Provision of Development Aid', *Itinerario*, 33:2 (2009), pp. 67–68.

13 Maggie Black, *A Cause for Our Time: Oxfam, the First 50 years* (Oxford: Oxfam and Oxford University Press, 1992), p. 74.

14 Peter Gatrell, *Free World? The Campaign to Save the World's Refugees 1956–1963* (Cambridge: Cambridge University Press, 2011), pp. 50–51.

15 See pp. 136–137.

16 Jessica Reinisch and Matthew Frank, 'Refugees and the Nation State in Europe, 1919–1959', *Journal of Contemporary History*, 49:3 (2014), p. 484.

17 Carl J. Bon Tempo, *Americans at the Gate: The United States and Refugees During the Cold War* (Princeton, NJ: Princeton University Press, 2008), pp. 66–70.

18 Regula Ludi, 'More and Less Deserving Refugees: Shifting Priorities in Swiss Asylum Policy from the Interwar Era to the Hungarian Refugee Crisis of 1956', *Journal of Contemporary History*, 49:3 (2014), pp. 596–598.

19 Tony Kushner and Katharine Knox, *Refugees in an Age of Genocide: Global, National and Local Perspectives During the Twentieth Century* (London: Frank Cass, 1999), pp. 248–252.

20 Bon Tempo, *Americans at the Gate*, pp. 75–81. Later on, the narrative of successful resettlement turned into one of unemployment and frustration; see Stephen R. Porter, *Benevolent Empire: U.S. Power, Humanitarianism, and the World's Dispossessed* (Philadelphia, PA: University of Pennsylvania Press, 2016), pp. 153–180.

21 Catherine Rey-Schyrr, 'Le CICR et l'assistance aux réfugiés arabes palestinens (1948–1950)', *Revue international de la Croix-Rouge*, 83:843 (2001), pp. 739–761; Nancy Gallagher, *Quakers in the Israeli–Palestinian Conflict: The Dilemmas of NGO Humanitarian Activism* (Cairo: American University in Cairo Press, 2007); Daniel G. Cohen, 'Elusive Neutrality: Christian Humanitarianism and the Question of Palestine, 1948–1967', *Humanity: An International Journal of Human Rights, Humanitarianism, and Development*, 5:2 (2014), pp. 184–210.

22 Ilana Feldman, 'Difficult Distinctions: Refugee Law, Humanitarian Practice, and Political Identification in Gaza', *Cultural Anthropology*, 22:1 (2007), pp. 129–169.

23 See pp. 134–135.

24 UNRWA defined Palestine refugees as 'persons whose normal place of residence was Palestine during the period 1 June 1946 to 15 May 1948, and who lost both home and means of livelihood as a result of the 1948 conflict'. See http://www.unrwa.org/who-we-are (accessed November 2018).

25 Ilana Feldman, 'The Quaker Way: Ethical Labor and Humanitarian Relief', *American Ethnologist*, 34:4 (2007), pp. 689–705.

26 John W. Bachman, *Together in Hope: 50 Years of Lutheran World Relief* (New York/ Minneapolis, MN: LWR/Kirk House Publishers, 1995), p. 44.

27 Gatrell, *Free World?*, p. 65.

28 Glen Peterson, 'The Uneven Development of the International Refugee Regime in Postwar Asia: Evidence from China, Hong Kong and Indonesia', *Journal of Refugee Studies*, 25:3 (2012), pp. 331–336.

29 General Assembly Resolutions, 26 November 1957, 1167 (XII), at http://www.unhcr.org/3ae69ee618.html (accessed November 2018).

30 See p. 135.

31 'In Hong Kong: You Live Here', *Onslaught*, written and edited by Hugh Samson, 1959, London, p. 19, cited in Gatrell, *Free World?*, p. 60. Only one issue of the magazine ever appeared.

32 Andy Rumi interviewed by Katharine Knox (Winchester, 1995), quoted in Kushner and Knox, *Refugees in an Age of Genocide*, p. 241.

33 Gatrell, *Free World?*, pp. 79–80.

34 *Ibid.*, pp. 79–84.

35 The Soviet Union, Poland, Yugoslavia, Belarus and the Ukraine had voted against the UN General Assembly's resolution that set up the IRO; see Louise W. Holborn, *L'organisation internationale pour les réfugiés: agence spécialisée des Nations Unies, 1946–1952* (Paris: Presses Universitaires de France, 1955), p. 48.

36 Gatrell, *Free World?*, p. 88.

37 General Assembly Resolutions, 5 December 1958, 1285 (XII), at http://www.unhcr.org/3ae69ef3a.html (accessed November 2018).

38 Gatrell, *Free World?*, pp. 90–91.

39 Jennifer Johnson Onyedum, '"Humanize the Conflict": Algerian Health Care Organizations and Propaganda Campaigns, 1954–1962', *International Journal of Middle East Studies*, 44:4 (2012), pp. 713–731; Young-Sun Hong, 'The Algerian War, Third World Internationalism, and the Cold War Politics of Humanitarian Assistance', in Johannes Paulmann (ed.), *Dilemmas of Humanitarian Aid in the Twentieth Century* (Oxford: Oxford University Press, 2016), pp. 295–96, 298–301.

40 UNHCR, *The State of World's Refugees 2000: Fifty Years of Humanitarian Action* (Oxford: Oxford University Press, 2000), pp. 38–41.

41 General Assembly Resolutions, 5 December 1958, 1286 (XIII), at http://www.unhcr.org/uk/excom/bgares/3ae69ef910/refugees-morocco-tunisia.html (accessed November 2018).

42 Gatrell, *Free World?*, pp. 110–111.

43 Kevin O'Sullivan, 'A "Global Nervous System": The Rise and Rise of European Humanitarian NGOs (1945–1985)', in M. Frey, S. Kunkel and C. R. Unger (eds), *International Organizations and Development, 1945–1990* (Basingstoke: Palgrave Macmillan, 2014), pp. 201–204.

44 Black, *A Cause for Our Time*, pp. 57–62.

45 O'Sullivan, 'A "Global Nervous System"', p. 202.

46 Gatrell, *Free World?*, pp. 155–156.

47 See p. 28.

48 Gatrell, *Free World?*, pp. 158–163.

49 *Ibid.*, pp. 227–232.

50 Unger, 'Postwar European Development Aid'.

51 See p. 28.

52 Amy L. Sayward, *The United Nations in International History* (London: Bloomsbury: 2017), pp. 135–145.

53 General Assembly Resolutions, 1 December 1950, 409 (V), at http://www.un.org/en/ga/search/view_doc.asp?symbol=A/RES/410%28V%29&Lang=E&Area=RESOLUTION (accessed November 2018).

54 See pp. 124–131.

55 David Ekbladh, *The Great American Mission: Modernization and the Construction of an American World Order* (Princeton, NJ: Princeton University Press, 2010), pp. 135–145.

56 *Ibid.*

57 Rachel M. McCleary, *Global Compassion: Private Voluntary Organizations and US Foreign Policy Since 1939* (New York: Oxford University Press, 2009), pp. 80–82.

58 Heike Wieters, 'The World's Hungry: American NGOs and New Private–Public Partnership after WWII', *Contemporanea: Rivista di storia dell'800 e del '900*, 18:3 (2015),

pp. 355–372; Heike Wieters, *The NGO CARE and Food Aid from America, 1945–1980: 'Showered with Kindness'?* (Manchester: Manchester University Press, 2017).

59   Sébastien Farré, 'De l'économie de guerre au secours philanthropique: CARE et les enjeux de l'aide américaine dans l'Europe de l'après-guerre', *Relations internationales*, 2 (2011), pp. 25–41; Heike Wieters, 'Reinventing the Firm: From Post-war Relief to International Humanitarian Agency', *European Review of History: Revue Européenne d'Histoire*, 23:1–2 (2016), pp. 116–135; Wieters, *The NGO CARE*.

60   Daniel R. Maul, *Human Rights, Development and Decolonization: The International Labour Organization, 1940–70* (Basingstoke: Palgrave Macmillan, 2012 [first edition Essen, 2007]), pp. 86–151.

61   'International Labour Organization Since the War', *International Labour Review*, 92:2 (1953), p. 127.

62   Maul, *Human Rights, Development and Decolonization*, pp. 31–33.

63   See pp. 197–198.

64   'International Labour Organization Since the War', p. 127.

65   Véronique Plata-Stenger, 'New Missionaries for Social Development: The ILO Internship Program (1950–1963)', in L. Tournès and G. Scott-Smith (eds), *Global Exchange: Scholarships and Transnational Circulation in the Modern World* (New York: Berghan, 2017), pp. 156–170.

66   Yi-Tang Lin, Thomas David and Davide Rodogno, 'Fellowship Programs for Public Health Development: The Rockefeller Foundation, UNRRA, and WHO (1920s – 1970s)', in L. Tournès and G. Scott-Smith (eds), *Global Exchange: Scholarships and Transnational Circulation in the Modern World* (New York: Berghan, 2017), pp. 140–155.

67   Amy L. S. Staples, *The Birth of Development: How the World Bank, Food and Agriculture Organization, and World Health Organization Changed the World, 1945–1965* (Kent, OH: Kent State University Press, 2006), pp. 123–132.

68   See pp. 86–87.

69   *Report of the Interim Commission to the First World Health Assembly, Part 1: Activities*, Official Records of the World Health Organization, No. 9 (New York, 1948), pp. 20–25.

70   Constitution of the World Health Organization, article 1.

71   *Ibid.*, articles 44–54.

72   WHO, *The First Ten Years of the World Health Organization* (Geneva: WHO, 1958), p. 85. The six regional offices active on 31 December 1957 were in Copenhagen, New Delhi, Alexandria in Egypt, Brazzaville, Manila and Washington, DC.

73   Staples, *The Birth of Development*, pp. 137–160.

74   *Ibid.*

75   Nancy Leys Stepan, *Eradication: Ridding the World of Diseases Forever* (London: Reaktion Books, 2011), pp. 140–183.

76   Davide Rodogno and Thomas David, 'All the World Loves a Picture: The World Health Organization's Visual Politics, 1948–1973', in H. Fehrenbach and D. Rodogno (eds), *Humanitarian Photography: A History* (New York: Cambridge University Press, 2015), pp. 223–248.

77   Jennifer J. Palmer and Pete Kingsley, 'Controlling Sleeping Sickness Amidst Conflict and Calm: Remembering, Forgetting and the Policy of Humanitarian Knowledge in Southern Sudan, 1954–2005', in C. Bennett, M. Foley and H. B. Krebs (eds), *Learning from the Past to Shape the Future: Lessons from the History of Humanitarian Action in Africa*, ODI Humanitarian Policy Group Working Paper, October 2016, pp. 31–48, at https://www.odi.org/sites/odi.org.uk/files/resource-documents/11148.pdf (accessed November 2018).

78 *Ibid.*

79 Frank M. Snowden, 'Latina Province, 1945–50', *Journal of Contemporary History*, 43:3 (2008), pp. 509–526.

80 Staples, *The Birth of Development*.

81 Thomas Zimmer, 'In the Name of World Health and Development: The World Health Organization and Malaria Eradication in India, 1949–1970', in Marc Frey, Sönke Kunkel and Corinna R. Unger (eds), *International Organizations and Development, 1945–1990* (Basingstoke: Palgrave Macmillan, 2014), p. 131.

82 Staples, *The Birth of Development*.

83 Zimmer, 'In the Name of World Health and Development', p. 136.

84 *Ibid.*

85 Maggie Black, *Children First: The Story of UNICEF, Past and Present* (New York: Oxford University Press, 1996), pp. 8–9.

86 Zimmer, 'In the Name of World Health and Development', pp. 138–142.

87 Sunniva Engh, 'Donors' Dilemmas: Scandinavian Aid to the Indian Family Planning Programme, 1970–80', *Social Scientist*, 30:5–6 (2002), pp. 36–61.

88 Binay R. Sen, *Towards a Newer World* (Dublin: Tycooly International Publishing, 1982), p. 139.

89 Mark Mazower, *Governing the World: The History of an Idea, 1815 to Present* (London: Allen Lane, 2012), pp. 103–104.

90 Luigi Luzzatti, 'The International Institute of Agriculture', *North America Review*, 182:594 (1906), p. 656.

91 Paul Weindling, 'The Role of International Organisations in Setting Nutritional Standards in the 1920s and 1930s', in H. Kamminga and A. Cunningham (eds), *The Science and Culture of Nutrition, 1840–1940* (Amsterdam: Rodopi, 1995), pp. 319–332; Nick Cullather, 'The Foreign Policy of the Calorie', *American Historical Review*, 112:2 (2007), pp. 337–364; Cullather, *The Hungry World*, pp. 28–34.

92 John B. Orr, *What Science Stands For* (London: George Allen & Unwin, 1937), p. 13.

93 Joseph Morgan Hodge, *Triumph of the Expert: Agrarian Doctrines of Development and the Legacies of British Colonialism* (Athens, OH: Ohio University Press, 2007), pp. 171–177.

94 See p. 126.

95 Mazower, *Governing the World*, pp. 283–284; Staples, *The Birth of Development*, pp. 84–96.

96 O'Sullivan, 'A "Global Nervous System"', pp. 204–205.

97 Sen, *Towards a Newer World*, p. 137.

98 *Ibid.*

99 Staples, *The Birth of Development*.

100 Antonietta Di Blase and Sergio Marchisio, *L'Organisation des Nations Unies pour l'Alimentation et l'Agriculture (FAO)* (Geneva: Institut Universitaire de Hautes Études Internationales, 1986), pp. 70–74; Staples, *The Birth of Development*.

101 Di Blase and Marchisio, *L'Organisation des Nations Unies*, pp. 73–74; D. John Shaw, *The World's Largest Humanitarian Agency: The Transformation of the UN World Food Programme and of Food Aid* (London: Palgrave Macmillan, 2011), pp. 1–20.

102 *Ibid.*, p. 61.

103 FAO, *The State of Food and Agriculture* (Rome: FAO, 1962), in particular pp. 32–34.

104 The advertising of the programme also included very famous actresses such as Sofia Loren, Shirley Temple and Michèle Morgan; see Matthew James Bunch, *All Roads Lead to Rome: Canada, the Freedom from Hunger Campaign, and the Rise of NGOs, 1960–1980*,

thesis submitted to the University of Waterloo, Ontario, for the degree of Doctor of Philosophy, 2007, pp. 104–106 and 112–116.

105 Black, *A Cause for Our Time*, p. 72.

106 In these years many British NGOs 'realized that if the problems they were tackling were to be dealt with more systematically then political intervention was necessary': Matthew Hilton, James McKay, Nicholas Crowson and Jean-François Mouhot, *The Politics of Expertise: How NGOs Shaped Modern Britain* (Oxford: Oxford University Press, 2013), p. 109.

107 Anna Bocking-Welch, 'Imperial Legacies and Internationalist Discourses: British Involvement in the United Nations Freedom from Hunger Campaign, 1960–70', *Journal of Imperial and Commonwealth History*, 40:5 (2013), pp. 879–896.

108 Sexten Heppling, 'The Very First Years – Memories of an Insider', in Pierre Frühling (ed.), *Swedish Development Aid in Perspective: Policies, Problems and Results Since 1952* (Stockholm: Almqvist and Wicksell, 1986), p. 20, cited in Engh, 'The Conscience of the World?', p. 67.

109 Kevin O'Sullivan, Matthew Hilton and Juliano Fiori, 'Humanitarianisms in Context', *European Review of History*, 23:1–2 (2016), p. 5.

110 Staples, *The Birth of Development*, pp. 106–107.

111 Black, *A Cause for Our Time*, p. 70.

112 Anna Bocking-Welch, 'Youth Against Hunger: Service, Activism and the Mobilisation in 1960s Britain', *European Review of History*, 23:1–2 (2016), pp. 154–170. See also the case of Canada in Tamara Myers, 'Local Action and Global Imagining: Youth, International Development, and the Walkathon Phenomenon in 1960s and 1970s Canada', *Diplomatic History*, 38:2 (2014), pp. 282–293.

113 O'Sullivan, 'A "Global Nervous System"', p. 202.

114 Bachman, *Together in Hope*, pp. 63–64.

115 Black, *A Cause for Our Time*, pp. 85–108.

116 Bernard Llewellyn, *The Poor World* (London: Zenith Books, 1967), p. 102.

117 Di Blase and Marchisio, *L'Organisation des Nations Unies*.

7

Humanitarian emergencies

In the period when most of the international programmes were dedicated to development, war relief certainly did not disappear from humanitarianism's sphere of action, as we have seen in aid operations for the civilians fleeing armed conflicts in the Middle East, Asia and North Africa between the 1940s and 1950s. In this area of intervention, new parties established themselves that identified in humanitarian commitment a tool with which to claim the independence of the colonial territories or to assert the full sovereignty of the newly constituted countries. We have seen this with the Algerian Red Crescent in the years of Algerian war of independence but the case of the Egyptian Red Crescent during the Suez crisis is equally significant.

After the Franco-British attack in late 1956, the Egyptian Red Crescent immediately set itself into action not just with aid operations but also with promoting an international solidarity movement with the Egyptian population. To do this, the organisation counted on its network of relationships within both the Red Crescent and the Red Cross movements. However, the quest for a balance between activation of the transnational relief circuit and a desire to reassert Egyptian national sovereignty – humiliated by the European powers' attack – proved difficult. Collaboration between Western and non-Western members of the Red Crescent and the Red Cross movements had a fragile basis because there was a lack of established procedures and experience. Additionally, there was the weight of the dynamics of the conflict, an event symbolic of the turbulent definition of a postcolonial order. From this point of view, problems emerged especially in the relationship between the British Red Cross and the Egyptian Red Crescent. Both societies interpreted their humanitarian mission in close relation to the political commitments to their own national governments and this placed them in conflict on crucial issues, such as services for prisoners of war.[1]

The decolonisation process also marked what happened in wars in the next decade and assistance to refugees reasserted itself as one of the preferred areas of intervention for international humanitarianism. The region of the Great Lakes of Africa was where the problem revealed itself most seriously and it is no co-incidence that it was in this area that most of the 850,000 refugees recorded in Africa in 1965 were to be found. These people – usually gathered in large camps situated on the borders of the countries they were escaping from – did not have any international protection because the 1951 Geneva Convention stated that refugee status could be granted only to those who found themselves far from their own country 'as a result of events occurring before 1 January 1951' (article 1). Even though they were not considered technically to be asylum seekers, the UNHCR provided displaced persons in Africa with basic assistance when, from time to time, it was given a specific assignment by the General Assembly; the extent of such emergencies grew by such a degree that by the end of the 1960s the organisa-tion was spending in Africa two-thirds of its budget for field operations.[2]

The wars that were devastating the Great Lakes region neither won the atten-tion of the Western media nor became high-profile points on the international community's agenda. They did, however, make clear the discrepancy between the existing system for refugees – drawn up for post-Second World War Europe – and the weight acquired by forced population transfers with the redefinition of the borders imposed by decolonisation. This was why the New York Protocol, signed in 1967, lifted the time limitation introduced by the Geneva Convention[3] and established that the signatories of the new agreement should also give up the geographical limitation[4] whereby asylum seekers had to come from Europe. Anyone, regardless of their origin and the date of the events that had led to their flight, could now ask for the recognition of their refugee status on the grounds of religious, political or racial persecution.

Assistance for the refugee population was also one of the main problems in Vietnam, where humanitarian operations were an integral part of the United States' participation in the conflict. The big US NGOs, which already had a special relationship with the Washington authorities for the post-war reconstruc-tion programmes in Korea, played a major role in carrying out relief work for Vietnamese civilians. The most significant example is Catholic Relief Services (CRS), which, in the second half of the 1950s, administered over 50 per cent of the aid sent to South Vietnam. The most urgent intervention for which CRS was approached concerned the assistance of around a million refugees, many of them Catholic, who crossed the 17th Parallel in 1954 to escape the communist government in North Vietnam. The programmes for the refugee population not only provided assistance at the moment of arrival and transfer to other regions of the country but were positioned as a continuation in part of past interventions for the 'rehabilitation' of the displaced and in part of projects for the development of 'backward' countries. The CRS staff – but also those of other organisations such as CARE and Lutheran World Relief – coordinated the creation of hundreds of new villages, financing the construction of houses, schools, hospitals and orphanages, but also making available the capital and expertise necessary for starting up new businesses, for professional training and the promotion of building social and cultural associations intended for young people, workers and women.[5] The approach was inspired by the projects for community development and the humanitarian agencies reiterated that their commitment was not simply to aid the Vietnamese population but to 'saving a free Vietnam'. In relating to the supporters of the work it was carrying out, CRS stressed how important it was 'for an agency of the Church [to develop] a large program in a country plagued by want and by the presence of a human tide of agony and misery composed of refugees from communism'.[6] The organisation was calling upon American Catholics to share an idea of humanitarianism that did not mean liberating the South Vietnamese people only from the suffering caused by the war but also from the risk of communism, at the same time offering them the tools to build a prosperous and democratic country.

For over a decade, this idea remained dominant but in the second half of the 1970s CRS had to deal with the rapid break-up of that consensus. The humanitarian agencies working in Vietnam, and CRS in particular, became the target of bitter criticism and were accused of having subordinated their own activities to the strategies of the US army and had therefore contributed to armed terror even though their purpose was to relieve the wounds of the war.[7] The criticisms of a 'compliant' humanitarianism naturally reflected the much greater dissent felt towards the Vietnam War which was now broadly spread over the United States. CRS did not withdraw from Vietnam but found itself compelled to radically review the terms of its intervention in the country. On the one hand, it was the government authorities themselves that loosened their collaboration with the big humanitarian societies: between 1967–68 and 1970–71 the financing from USAID for CRS was reduced by 80 per cent, while the distribution of foodstuffs and the administration of the community development programmes passed directly into the hands of the experts in the US peacemaking troops. On the other hand, CRS began to work exclusively on immediate relief and short-term assistance, letting go of that demanding project of transforming Vietnamese society, which was at one with the warlike business of defeating communism in the North.[8]

The events in Vietnam mainly affected the government and the associations of the United States. They did, however, expose the problem of the role and meaning that humanitarianism was coming to take on in the context of those conflicts that marked the reshaping of the global order fostered by the end of colonial empires. It was a problem that, at the end of the 1960s, exploded with the civil war in Nigeria, where the whole international community was involved.

Relief and bearing witness: the Biafran war

'Take his picture', the priest said with an intensity bordering on madness. 'Take his picture and maybe the people outside will believe what is going on here'.[9]

The photo in question was that of an agonised child and appeared in *Life*, in a piece on the Biafran war in July 1968. The report's author, Michael Mok, had noted in his diary (published a year later) the words of Father Daniel O'Connell. The fact that leading Mok through the bodies of the Biafran victims of starvation and enemy raids was a religious man – more precisely, an Irish priest from the Holy Ghost Congregation – was no coincidence. The presence of religious groups in the region was the result of a long history of Protestant and Catholic missionary activity; this was why the population of Biafra, and in particular the Igbo ethnic group (which was the majority), was mostly Christian while the rest of Nigeria was largely Islamic. Between the spring and summer of 1968 the missionaries had a crucial role in drawing the Western world's attention to the Nigerian civil war, and the media were used to mobilise the international community. The photos in *Life* came after several months of intense contact with journalists, of repeatedly sending the press and television information and press releases, such as the letter from Umuahia we quoted at the beginning of Part III. The pressure from the missionaries on the media was accompanied by an official position taken by religious bodies: the World Council of Churches – the body that united the greatest number of Protestant associations – and the Vatican issued a joint press release in which they called on the parties involved to lay down their weapons and on the international political forces to encourage the start of peace negotiations. In June 1968 the World Council of Churches and the Catholic Church declared that they were 'deeply concerned with the needs for relief in necessities of life among suffering peoples', and called 'for cooperation among all international relief agencies in meeting the grave needs, which will continue long after armed hostilities have ceased'.[10] Out of the cooperation between Catholic and Protestant churches to deal with the humanitarian crisis in Biafra some months later came Joint Church Aid.[11]

But what was happening in Biafra? What were the causes of a war with such dramatic consequences for the civilian population? In order to reconstruct the course of events, we must first remember that it was only in 1960 that Nigeria had gained independence from Britain and had become a federal republic. The borders of the new state had followed – as was the case for many other countries that came into being at the end of the empires – those traced by the colonial administration, and within these there were different populations, each with its own ethnicity, religion, and social and economic organisation. Independence was followed by violent tensions which culminated in 1966, after a series of coups d'état, in an open attack on the Igbo people by the ethnic groups most represented in the federal government. There were thousands of dead while around two million refugees hurriedly left the north of the country, where the Igbo were in the minority, to reach the south-east area, where instead they were the largest ethnic group. In May 1967, the regions populated by the Igbo proclaimed their independence from Nigeria and took the name Republic of Biafra. After a few weeks the Nigerian army attacked the new state and the federal authorities imposed an embargo that isolated the Biafran territory, with the aim of reducing the enemy population to starvation.

The Republic of Biafra was recognised by very few governments and even Nigeria's military attack and its strategy of closing the borders did not provoke major reactions. Britain, as the former mother country, had close relations with the Nigerian authorities and after the start of the conflict it continued to support the federal government.[12] The US government followed the British line.[13] France demonstrated its support for the secessionist state only at a later stage, with the aim of weakening Nigeria (partly because of Nigeria's ties with Britain but also because it was a large, potentially threatening country in a region under French influence). Nevertheless, the government in Paris did not go so far as to officially recognise the Republic of Biafra, either immediately after its declaration of independence or later.[14] The first year of the conflict met with a sort of diplomatic silence on the part of the Western world, and received scant public interest.

The situation in Biafra dramatically worsened with the dragging on of the war. A turning point was in May 1968 with the conquest by the federal troops of the city of Port Harcourt, the Biafrans' only remaining access point to the sea. International attention was grabbed by photos like those published in *Life*, by witnesses' shocking accounts, by television reports that showed the bodies of women and children devoured by hunger. It certainly was not the first time the media had shown Western citizens the suffering of other people, expecting to arouse horror, emotional involvement, indignation and pity. But at the end of the 1960s, within a media system in which television was by now the central figure, the power and pervasiveness of the message were amplified. The news and images leapt out of the television news reports onto the front pages of the daily papers and vice versa, and then reached the in-depth weeklies and the popular press. The war in Biafra became an international media event. What emerged was the insistence on the inhumanity of a war that, more than any other, had produced child victims, since it was fought not with arms but hunger. The media catalysed attention on a Third World that the Freedom from Hunger campaign had contributed to making seem closer, and it was in this context that people started talking about a new genocide, which the Biafran population were the victims of and which could be compared to that of the Jews.

The references to the Holocaust were frequent in the war reports of Western journalists and commentators. After the fall of Port Harcourt, for example, expressions were used in the British press such as 'fate could be as dreadful as that of the victims of the Nazi concentration camps', 'worse than Bergen-Belsen'.[15] The same type of comparison was repeated in television programmes. In August 1968, Jaques Siclier, a French television reporter, noted the similarity between what was happening in Biafra and the extermination of the Jews in his narration for a report filmed among the victims of the Nigerians:

No image as terrible as this has ever been filmed since those of the discovery of the concentration camps in Germany in 1945. Children's bodies that are skeletal or deformed by edemas, faces on which you can read the resigned stupefaction, half-naked women stripped of their flesh, who instinctively grasp the poor creatures who can no longer feed.[16]

In the same period the Italian investigative television programme *TV7* included a report with similar images, narrated by Goffredo Parise, a well known writer and journalist. Parise had just returned from his trip to Biafra, where he had seen many refugee camps that 'had brought to mind the death camps of Auschwitz and Buckenwald [sic]'.[17] In the *TV7* report, Parise's commentary was accompanied by the statements of a Biafran government representative who accused the federal authorities of genocide: 'they want to completely exterminate our race', he asserted. 'That is their aim.'[18]

The statements made in the Italian programme were anything but improvised. The Biafran authorities constantly returned to the accusation of genocide and this accusation was the centre of their propaganda message. In the communication to the Western world, the evocation of the extermination of an entire people and the parallels with the Holocaust took on a compelling force, powerfully expressed through the photos that were reminiscent of the Nazi concentration camps.[19] The content and persuasive ability of the account of the war given to the outside world were crucial for the Biafran government, which aimed to involve international public opinion in a way that would overturn the diplomatic lack of engagement. 'There were two wars fought in Nigeria', said a member of Biafra's Propaganda Directorate almost twenty years later, 'the first was the military war, the second was the propaganda war'.[20]

The appeal to empathy launched through the telling, or, rather, the depiction of the suffering of the civilians was able to guarantee the secessionist authorities more rapid and effective results compared with winning over international consent for the country's political agenda. The information circulated by the Biafran government on the war's progress was often self-contradictory and unreliable[21] but the insistence on the image of an entire people forced into starvation was coherent and uninterrupted. To promote it and keep international attention high on the war, the Biafran Propaganda Directorate relied on a public relations firm based in Geneva, the Markpress. This private agency, which could count on solid skills and a vast network of contacts in the media world, issued official press releases, circulated photos, selected and spread information and, above all, facilitated the arrival of journalists in the field.[22] Markpress had a fundamental part in bringing about the delivery to the world over of a 'colossal and at the same time sinister journalistic scoop',[23] based on the reports and images of the agonies of the Biafran civilians. The Republic of Biafra certainly won the propaganda war and quickly seized the attention and sympathy of public opinion. The answers to the appeal for help did not unanimously come from humanitarian agencies.

The rising public attention and the direct and indirect pressure of the Biafran government had little effect on the UN agencies, whose cautiousness ended up being translated into inertia. The UN's mandate excluded intra-state conflicts and the organisation entrenched itself behind this formal limit in order to maintain its distance from a war that not only saw Britain and France taking conflicting positions but also risked encouraging further secessions in the unstable post-colonial situation on the African continent. At the same time, the individual agencies' statutes, if taken literally and given a narrow interpretation, placed restrictions on them that prevented them taking an active role in relief operations. The case of the UNHCR is a good example. The UN agency for refugees was directly called into action by the dramatic population movements that had marked the events in the civil war in Nigeria when the representatives of Biafra specifically asked the general headquarters in Geneva for aid. In its reply the UNHCR excluded any chance of its intervention and referred to the impossibility of going beyond its mandate:

> The statute of the Office empowers [the High Commissioner] to assist in solving problems of refugees at the request of governments of country of asylum. A refugee, in this context, is a person who is outside his country and does not, for various specified reasons, wish to avail himself of the protection of his country of origin. Since 'Biafra' is not recognized as a separate state, the displaced people from other parts of Nigeria into Eastern Nigeria do not fall into the mandate of the Office and, therefore, there is nothing the Office could do for them.[24]

The New York Protocol had removed the chronological and geographical limits imposed by the 1951 Geneva Convention but crossing the borders of the country of origin continued to be a necessary condition for an individual to be recognised as a refugee: a large number of fleeing men and women remained excluded from international assistance, and among these were the Biafrans, caught in the grip of an isolation that forced them into starvation.

Instead, it was NGOs that were the driving force behind the mobilisation for Biafra. During the civil war in Nigeria the NGO community, which had already been among the leading players of the Freedom from Hunger campaign, grew stronger and branched out rapidly. This leap into action was not only by the big agencies (such as Oxfam, Save the Children, CRS, the YMCA), which had by now acquired great credibility in the field of international relief and worked as much with their own countries' institutions as with the intergovernmental bodies. On top of these were smaller societies, religious groups, philanthropic bodies and numerous associations founded to respond to the 'Biafran emergency'. In many Western cities – from Dublin to Frankfurt, from Zurich to London, from Hamburg to New York – starting from spring 1968 new organisations specifically for Biafra came into being. These groups of activists came mainly (but not exclusively) from the student world and had the aim of increasing public awareness and raising funds to send aid to the population of Biafra.[25]

The NGOs recaptured, nurtured and amplified the media's interest in the Nigerian civil war. In some cases they carried out directly the role of information gathering and distribution. An important example of this is Africa Concern, which came into being in Dublin in March 1968 out of a meeting of missionaries, volunteers and other people interested in what was happening in Nigeria. The new organisation installed its telex service to send the Irish media updated reports from western Africa and in this way managed to have a certain influence on the news agenda.[26] Although they had different methods and means, all the NGOs promoted information campaigns and specific initiatives for fundraising for the starving Biafrans. In doing this they presented themselves to Western citizens as the instruments through which each of them could show their solidarity with another people. It was no longer about being benevolent towards subjects who lived in distant parts of the empire but about carrying out an ethical, responsible act for the representatives of the Third World. This was forcing Western societies to rethink their roles in the new world order. The 'people to people' approach, already experimented in the Freedom from Hunger campaign, became central for the humanitarian action of the private agencies,[27] which, in taking on the task of providing information, raising awareness and keeping interest high in the ongoing tragedy, 'effectively became translators of Biafra for the watching public in the West'.[28]

The image focused on by the NGOs to 'translate' Biafra for the West was analogous to the one promoted by the secessionist authorities and carried forward by the media, so it remained concentrated on starvation, on the extreme suffering, on the emergency imposed by the mass deaths of children. Many of those who actively participated in the campaigns for Biafra considered that 'the tragic urgency [...] lay in a single news item to be given and to be seen: around six thousand children die from hunger every day in this country, today, right now: tomorrow, the day after tomorrow there'll be more'.[29] The insistence on the 'tragic urgency', which correlated the possible salvation of those children with the immediate donations of Western citizens, prevailed over the analysis of the complex reasons for the conflict. 'The dominant humanitarian representations depoliticized the civil war'.[30] Meanwhile, Biafra became synonymous with death from hunger and its children's swollen bellies became the symbols of the despair in Africa.[31] The mobilisation to aid the people of Biafra ended up promoting a simplified representation of the Third World, associated with catastrophe, with inescapable misery, with dependence on the aid of rich, advanced societies. It was a representation humanitarianism continued to rely on in the following decades.

The NGOs' campaigns for Biafra had notable success and the fundraising gave results that had never been achieved in the past. In Britain, for example, all the NGOs recorded an increase in income and certain initiatives were particularly successful. The Nigerian War Victims Appeal, launched at the end of 1968 thanks to the coordination of five NGOs (Oxfam, Save the Children, War on Want,

Christian Aid, the British Red Cross), raised £100,000 in less than four weeks.[32] Such positive responses were the result of the power of the message carried by the media but they also expressed the positive public opinion of these private agencies, which seemed more capable of discharging the humanitarian mission than were the international agencies, in their impasse. The civil war in Nigeria made clear the possible sphere of action for the NGOs and what the limits were for the governmental and intergovernmental bodies.[33]

Donations reached an exceptional level but getting the relief to its recipients was very difficult because it was necessary to cross the territory over which the federal Nigerian authorities had control. To open a safe channel through which foodstuffs and medicines could regularly pass it was necessary to define a plan that would be accepted by the representatives both of the Nigerian government and those of the self-proclaimed Republic of Biafra. It was the ICRC – already committed to relief work for the Biafran civilians[34] – that took on the task of managing the negotiations for fine-tuning this plan and putting it into operation. The Genevan organisation seemed the most appropriate body to carry out this task, especially because of those principles of neutrality, impartiality and independence that had been clearly stated a few years earlier in the document approved by the XX International Conference of the Red Cross movement, the culmination of a long internal debate following the events of the Holocaust.[35] However, the strength the Committee could have exercised in the conduct of the negotiations was undermined in the first place by its loss of authority in the new constellation of international organisations that had developed since the Second World War. Forced after 1945 to accept a considerable reduction in budget and staff, the ICRC was no longer – as it had been in the decades following its foundation – the main point of reference for international humanitarianism.[36] In addition, the agreements did not offer any useful tools because the Convention on civilian victims in wartime, ratified in 1949, did not include the victims of intrastate conflicts, who, only ten years after the Biafran conflict – in 1977 – would be protected by humanitarian law.[37] The difficulty in finding any common ground was, then, determined by the strategic, military and political value that mass starvation and relief held for both warring parties.

Caught between the pressures of public opinion and the dead end the talks were in, the ICRC started an airlift that ran from September 1968 until early June the following year when a Red Cross aircraft was hit by the Nigerian army. Faced with the federal government's hostile attitude, the ICRC put an end to the air connection with Biafra and in the second half of 1969 it progressively reduced its activities in the field.[38] At the same time as the ICRC airlift, another had started, run by Joint Church Aid (JCA), the organisation that came out of the cooperation between the Catholic and Protestant Churches. The planes took off from the island of São Tomé, still a Portuguese colony, and went straight to the landing strip at Uli, on Biafran territory. The trips were made at night to escape the notice of the federal authorities, even if this increased the risk of accidents such as the one that happened in December 1968 when a DC-7 loaded with powdered milk crashed and the four crew were killed.[39] The JCA airlift also became emblematic of the NGOs' commitment to fulfilling their humanitarian mission[40] because – unlike those organised by the ICRC – they were never interrupted. According to declarations made by JCA in September 1969 it was transporting at least 100 tons of food every night, which was nonetheless far from meeting the Biafrans' needs.[41]

The diplomatic impasse and the insufficient relief that was getting to Biafra had repercussions among the Red Cross staff. A group of young doctors working for the French Red Cross decided to make a public statement in order to tell the world about the dramatic situation of the Biafran population and launch an appeal for mobilisation to help it. Two of these doctors – Max Récamier and Bernard Kouchner – returned to France and in November 1968 published an article in the paper *Le Monde* entitled 'De retour du Biafra, deux médecins français temoignent'. In this article Récamier and Kouchner gave an account of the work they carried out during the two months they spent in the field. They underlined the limitedness of the humanitarian intervention compared with the tragedy to be dealt with and they explained their effort was to 'bring aid to a people [that of Biafra] that underwent with courage and determination the terrifying devastation of the ongoing war'.[42] This lengthy account, published in the centre pages of the famous French newspaper, implicitly claimed for humanitarianism a role of bearing witness (*témoignage*) against abuse and aggression as well as assisting victims. This was the conscious overturning of the principles of neutrality and confidentiality stated by the ICRC. This overturning was reiterated, in the weeks following the publication of the article in *Le Monde*, by the organisation of public meetings and protest marches asking the Western governments to give political support to the Republic of Biafra and to urgently relaunch the humanitarian aid programmes. The 'Biafran doctors' and their supporters repeated that what was happening in western Africa was genocide, and the comparison with the Holocaust strengthened the call to back the ethical imperative that should have been driving humanitarian action.[43] The very aims of humanitarianism were being put up for discussion: 'Pity is no longer enough; the massacre must be stopped', wrote *Le Figaro* in January 1969, reporting the statement of one of the activists in the mobilisation for Biafra.[44]

In January 1970 the Republic of Biafra was defeated by the federal army and its territory was re-annexed by Nigeria: the victory won in the 'propaganda war' had only put off the secessionists' failure in the 'military war'. A wave of violence by the victors followed the conclusion of the war but the embargo came to an end and foodstuffs began to circulate again in the region. In the meantime, the 'Biafran doctors' had set up the Groupe d'Intervention Medical et Chirurgical d'Urgence and had taken part in some other international relief operations. In 1971, along with the editors of the specialist magazine *Tonus*, inside which an important debate had started on the ethical values of the medical profession, the 'Biafrans' founded the NGO Médecins Sans Frontières (MSF), which soon became one of the most prominent players in international aid.[45]

The association between the Nigerian civil war and the birth of MSF has been emphasised in the memories of the organisation's leading members and in some studies. Indeed, there has been an insistence on presenting the crisis in Biafra as the founding event behind MSF,[46] and at the same time the setting up of MSF has been pointed out as the main reason the crisis in Biafra was a breaking point in the history of humanitarianism. On the basis of this conviction, the Nigerian civil war was talked about as a 'new Solferino', destined to alter the course of international relief and to start the 'modern humanitarian movement'.[47] The value of the foundation of MSF and the emergency in Biafra as a watershed in many respects repeated the rhetoric of the 'new start' we have seen at work in the history of humanitarianism. Naturally, the birth of MSF had an undeniable importance and its rapid establishment deeply influenced the concept and practice of international relief. It is worthwhile, though, analysing all this in the political and cultural context of the 1960s and 1970s, looking at the deeper reasons that led to MSF being set up and reconnecting this event with the transformations that marked the world of international relief as a whole in the same period.

The 'Biafran doctors' came from the far left and the student movement. This political background was the root of their commitment to the Third World and their idea of solidarity, which marked a deviation from the insistence – typical of humanitarian rhetoric – on the tie of empathy between every human worth being considered such and their fellow beings in a state of suffering. Solidarity was understood, rather, as a form of militancy, as conscious dedication to a cause as opposed to mere compassion. This different interpretation of humanitarian action, termed *sans-frontiérisme*,[48] laid claim to the political value of humanitarian action by reconnecting it to a twofold moral duty: caring for suffering humanity, and bearing direct witness to the abuses perpetrated against it. In other words, humanitarian aid could not be split from the recognition of individuals' universal and inalienable rights. Xavier Emmanuelli, one of the founders of MSF, would later express this conviction with these words:

> Someone who performs a humanitarian action does so with a generous impulse, enthusiastically and skilfully, and this action is greater than the man because he does it in the name of a transcendent concept of man. Each man in the midst of a humanitarian action is at the same time himself and the symbol of all humanity.[49]

The central role given to the recognition of basic rights by MSF on the one hand recalled an inherited ideal that went back to the tradition of the French Revolution and to the idea of the Republic of France as parent and protector of the rights of man.[50] On the other hand, it reconnected to that international movement for human rights that was widely developing in the 1970s and gaining broad visibility.[51] We only need to think of the success of Amnesty International, the association started in 1961 to protect political prisoners, which in little over a decade had multiplied the number of its offices and become the champion *par excellence* of basic rights, to the extent that it received the Nobel Prize for Peace in 1977. MSF, which did not intend to be absorbed into the associations for the defence of human rights, nonetheless considered it essential to speak out regarding their violation. In the 1978 the *Bulletin Médecins sans Frontières* stated:

> There is of course no question of taking the place of organizations of the protection of individuals, such as Amnesty International or the Human Rights League, that have turned this into profession, and passing one's time denouncing all the violations encountered here and there, but it is probably more detestable still to sanction, by our silent presence, errors or, worse, heinous acts.[52]

The choice of not remaining 'silent' also gave a specific meaning to the systematic use of the media by MSF, in other words the quest for the 'media uproar' (*tapage mediatique*), in Bernard Kouchner's famous definition.[53] The close relationship with the communication media certainly followed in the tracks of a long habit of humanitarian assistance, for which its supporters' 'awareness raising' was crucial, but at the same time it was expressing a new demand: adding value to 'bearing witness' to the perpetration of a crime through conquering the widest public possible.

It was not simply the decision of certain doctors working in Biafra that led to the birth of MSF. The organisation's origins were more complex and the innovative elements introduced by the organisation into the field of humanitarianism were fully defined in the years following the Nigerian civil war. At any rate, this war marked a fundamental step in the historic path of the private agencies working in relief. In fact, they had a central role in the operations and a visibility they had rarely enjoyed in the past and they established themselves in relation to the new conflicts destined to break out shortly afterwards.

Problems at international borders

The war in Biafra makes it clear that, from the end of the 1960s, humanitarianism was called on to take on a different field of action, decided by conflicts across the postcolonial world. Far-reaching events of huge importance – in terms of the loss of life, enforced movements of populations, degree of overall devastation – were taking place and their images entered the homes of people in Western countries in their newspapers and on their televisions. The tensions went back to complex international dynamics on which the legacy of colonialism and the developments in the Cold War, with its regional implications, had their influence. The world of private associations was more immediately reactive to the new picture that was being defined but the UN agencies – after their substantial inaction during the

Biafran crisis – also redefined their functions and extended their spectrum of actions. The crisis in West Pakistan was in this sense a crucial event.

Since its constitution as an independent state – following the partition of the Indian sub-continent in 1947 – Pakistan had been divided into two regions, positioned respectively on the north-west and north-east borders of India, and the western region had always dominated national politics. For over twenty years the country was governed by a military dictatorship, until free elections were held in December 1970. The popular consultation awarded the absolute majority of seats to the Awami League, the most widely spread party in eastern Pakistan, where it took almost all its votes. The negotiations between the election winners, the army and the bigger political forces in western Pakistan did not go well, the inauguration of the national assembly was postponed and the country returned to military government. In spring 1971 violent protests broke out in the eastern region, which declared itself an independent state, the People's Republic of Bangladesh. The Pakistani army then launched a massive operation against the secessionists. The general repression was so violent that it caused tens of thousands of deaths and a flight of civilians so vast as to be comparable to that of over twenty years earlier following the separation of India and Pakistan.[54] The international context and the set-up of the humanitarian system had profoundly changed, though, and this time major relief programmes were launched.

The fleeing Bengalis, in absolute majority over the Hindus, crossed the border with India, where, by May 1971, more than four million refugees had arrived, becoming almost ten million by the end of the year. The Indian authorities – and the country's UN representative in particular – asked for the international community's intervention to deal with what was becoming an alarming health crisis, since there was a rapid spread of cholera within the refugee population. The response to the Indian government's request for aid took on meanings that went beyond the humanitarian dimension. In fact, the refugee question reopened the tensions between Pakistan and India, since the latter feared the mass expulsion of Hindus was one of the instruments with which the Pakistanis intended to proceed with the armed reconquest of authority over eastern Bengal. The conflict between the two countries on the Asian subcontinent brought into play the dynamics of Cold War alliances: Pakistan enjoyed the support of the United States but also of China, while under Indira Gandhi's leadership India swung between getting closer to the Soviet Union and aspiring to 'non-alignment'.[55]

The international mobilisation to assist the Bengali refugees developed in this complicated setting and on the wave of attention paid to the question by the Western media.[56] It was the UNHCR that took on relief coordination. This was the most important mission of the UN agency for refugees since its inception (1951) and marked a turning point in the organisation's development as it formalised its involvement in the Third World and broadened its range of action. The UNHCR had the task of coordinating the relief programmes both of the other UN agencies – in particular the WHO, the WFP and UNICEF – and of the NGOs; above all, it had to act as the interface between all these bodies and the Indian government. In fact, it was the latter which dealt with the overall management of the crisis on its territory and which directly carried out a large part of the work of distributing foodstuffs and medicines, to some extent counting on the Indian Red Cross. Most of the international organisations' work was done in New Delhi, while the administration of the numerous, and overcrowded, refugee camps in western Bengal remained under the tight control of Indian government officials.[57]

It was not altogether a paradox that the war between India and Pakistan marked the end of the emergency represented by the Bengali refugees. In fact, in December 1971, the feared conflict broke out between those two countries. A few months before India had signed a twenty-year agreement with the Soviet Union that envisaged mutual support in the case of belligerence. Although the dynamics of the alliances caused fear of expansion, and even the use of nuclear weapons, the war ended in a few weeks with the defeat of Pakistan – and the independence of Bangladesh. Immediately afterwards, operations to repatriate the refugees started, managed by the UNHCR. This was something strongly wished for by the Indian government, which had always considered those escaping eastern Bengal as temporary refugees for whom the only practical solution was return to their country of origin. At the end of February 1972 over nine million men and women had already returned to Bangladesh and while it is true that, at the time of their departure, each of them had received foodstuffs for their journey and basic rations for two weeks, what was waiting them was an impoverished country that offered those returning very little chance of looking after themselves.

The problem of mediation between national and international authorities on the subject of relief for the refugee population, and more generally carrying out the relief, came to light even more dramatically some years later with the 'Cambodian crisis'. In 1979 the war with Vietnam marked for Cambodia the end of the bloody dictatorship of the Khmer Rouge led by Pol Pot but the country was invaded by enemy forces and the government which was set up was in reality a Hanoi puppet regime. To escape the advance of the Vietnamese and their control of a large part of the territory, tens of thousands of Cambodians had fled to Thailand, where they found refugee camps set up near the border. The emergency then was twofold: on the one hand, there were the refugee camps, which fell under the responsibility of the Thai government but were actually controlled by anti-Vietnamese guerrilla forces – primarily the Khmer Rouge – and which formed a reservoir of resources and fighters; on the other hand, there was the Cambodian population, exhausted by the ferocity of the Pol Pot dictatorship, by the war against Vietnam and, finally, by the occupation of the victorious army.

The Phnom Penh authorities themselves – seeking aid but also international legitimisation – launched an appeal for aid at the beginning of July 1979. In a letter addressed to the various UN agencies, the foreign minister, Hun Sen, recalled the suffering of the Cambodian people in the years of the Pol Pot dictatorship and added:

> On the other hand, after the country's recent liberation hundreds of thousands of people are still searching for their disappeared families; those who have returned to their villages often find themselves in an unstable situation: with houses destroyed, without tools or animals in the face of uncultivated fields. So the crops are late and wide areas right for cultivation have not been planted. We have to add to all of this that the remains of the old regime's army, as it was fleeing, furiously sacked and destroyed barns and crops in order to force part of the population to follow them. The consequence of all this is that famine threatens two million of our fellow citizens. [...]
>
> Since the consequences are too hard and the needs are pressing, I have the honour, in the name of the People's Revolutionary Council, of making this request to you for urgent aid in the form of foodstuffs and other food products to thwart the famine [...].[58]

The appeal was answered by UNICEF and the ICRC, which had in the previous months fruitlessly asked the Cambodian authorities for authorisation to relieve the population's needs within the country. The Cambodian Foreign Ministry, however, placed conditions on the organisations that were ready to intervene: they had to delegate the aid distribution to local bodies, they must not give any aid in the refugee camps on Thai land and they must not pass on food or medicine intended for Cambodia over the border with Thailand.

Humanitarianism was wrapped up in the dynamics of war that were tearing apart a country from the inside but had complicated international implications, determined by the Cold War. Accepting the requirement not to take any assistance to the Cambodian refugees in the Thai camps would have meant renouncing the principle of impartiality, which was considered one of the linchpins of humanitarian action. And at the same time it would have meant supporting a government that was a puppet of the Vietnamese government. The decision to help the refugees had repercussions that went far beyond relieving the suffering of the camp inhabitants, since some of the food and medicines ended up in the hands of the anti-Vietnamese guerrillas, who included the Khmer Rouge – the supporters of the dictatorship that between 1975 and 1979 had led to the deaths of around two million Cambodians. Despite the very serious responsibilities that weighed upon them, many people looked on the Khmer Rouge with a certain favour, since it was at the centre of the armed resistance to the forces occupying Cambodia. On the one hand, this prolonged the state of war, whose effects on the population were dramatic, but, on the other hand, it was useful as a way of countering the consolidation of Vietnamese power in the region. From this point of view, the United States, China and all the South East Asian states that were hostile to Vietnam were placed together. This included Thailand itself, which had an ambiguous attitude towards the refugees because, on the one hand, it wanted to get rid of them but, on the other, it saw the tie between the camps and the anti-Vietnamese guerrillas in a good light. The humanitarian dilemma developed – materially and symbolically – across a border, that between Thailand and Cambodia, which at the same time separated and strongly bound the slaughterers and the victims of the immediate past, who were now both the possible beneficiaries of international aid.[59]

Humanitarian agencies were forced to deal with the Cambodian dilemma and, in certain cases, they took different paths. UNICEF and the ICRC welcomed Phnom Penh's request for aid but at the same time they started negotiations to define the conditions for their intervention. The delegation of aid distribution to the local authorities could be negotiated but the two organisations considered any waiver of the principle of impartiality unacceptable and so they were resolute in rejecting the requirement not to give assistance to the Cambodian refugees in Thailand. The final agreement reflected this position and was signed in September 1979 in a climate of increased tension due to the General Assembly resolution according to which the Cambodian government in exile, which the Khmer Rouge was part of, represented the country at the United Nations.[60]

In the meantime, the NGO world had also mobilised through the setting up of a consortium of around forty European humanitarian agencies,[61] which was started by an initiative from Oxfam or, more precisely, by its representative, James C. Howard. As a technical expert in the emergencies office, Howard had visited Cambodia in July 1979 and the seriousness of the situation struck him profoundly, regardless of his long experience in the world of humanitarian relief. He was a Quaker who had been in central India with the Friends' Service Council to manage a development project and then had worked for Oxfam in Bihar during the famine and in western Bengal with the arrival of the refugees from Bangladesh. After his return to London, Howard had first tried to contribute to raising public awareness about the Cambodian disaster, for which his work with the journalist John Pilger was crucial. Pilger was famous for his reports from Cambodia published in the *Daily Mirror,* and thanks to the preferential treatment he received from the Vietnamese government he made the television documentary *Year Zero: The Silent Death of Cambodia,* broadcast by the BBC in October 1979. The images and words of *Year Zero* – which showed piles of rubble, barren fields and mutilated bodies, and which reported direct witness statements and pleas for help from the Cambodians – had an enormous impact on British viewers. The documentary and the awareness-raising campaign made by Oxfam insisted on the urgency of aid, which would prevent the deaths of more than two million people in a few months.[62]

The conviction that intervening was urgent pushed Howard to consider aid programmes an absolute priority, in the face of which any resistance to the conditions imposed by the Cambodian government made no sense. The consortium of NGOs led by Oxfam made separate agreements with Phnom Penh and accepted the condition of not intervening in the refugee camps in Thailand, thus deciding (albeit implicitly) to defer the principle of impartiality. This resolution was justified, on the one hand, by the seriousness of the emergency and, on the other, by the realisation that the international community could not declare itself innocent in the face of the 'silent death' of Cambodia. In fact, previously it had been totally uninterested in the crimes perpetrated by Pol Pot and now it was leaving the politics of aid to be shaped by Cold War dynamics, more exactly the hostility of the Western bloc and its allies towards communist Vietnam. Marking a contrast to the slowness of the diplomatic roads – taken by UNICEF and the ICRC – the immediacy of the action in the name of an authentic humanitarian spirit gave Oxfam a leadership role in the context of non-governmental interventions in Cambodia. This role contributed significantly to increasing its operational abilities and its national and international standing.[63] In May 1980, when the aid operations were going ahead at full pace, the journalist Caroline Moorehead – already well known for her interest in humanitarianism and fundamental rights – wrote in *The Times* that, thanks to Pilger's denunciations and Howard's confirmations of them, the Cambodian crisis had 'acquired the status of disaster', and that following the Oxfam-led intervention the country 'may be off the danger list by Christmas'.[64] Moorehead was underlining Pilger's and Howard's individual merits but the whole operation of the Oxfam-led consortium was above all a further expression of, and an advance on, the growing central role of Western NGOs in the international aid scene.[65]

According to the agreements, aid distribution was to take place in a collaboration between the Cambodian authorities and the NGOs in the consortium, which, in reality, had by and large lost control over the operations inside the country. From this point of view the approach adopted by all the humanitarian agencies present in the area was substantially similar and was fraught with consequences, firstly for the conditions of the food, equipment and medicines sent to Cambodia. The inefficiency of the local organisations hampered their rapid use, corruption reduced the quantity of foodstuff distributed to the population needing it and, above all, the allocation of aid favoured the military forces at the expense of civilians. Humanitarianism ended up feeding one of the parties in the internal conflict that was still tormenting Cambodia. This was not all: the Cambodian authorities were hampering the monitoring work by 'external bodies' and so none of the humanitarian agencies ever knew how serious the needs were and how they were distributed over the territory.[66]

The improper use of aid and more generally what seemed a manipulation of aid by the Phnom Penh government, supported by Hanoi, were for some international humanitarianism agents so deplorable as not to be allowed to pass in silence. This was the position of MSF, which decided to raise the question publicly, in line with its members' wish to be 'actors who bear witness – or witnesses who act'.[67] MSF was completing an internal restructuring and redefinition of its aims that had started in the years immediately before, when an important part of the staff in the field had advocated strengthening the organisation from the points of view of efficiency and professionalism, in order to achieve 'a perfect machine, a solid structure, equipped with the means, the right materials and the right emergency logic'.[68] Those who were against this change – most of all Bernard Kouchner – thought that the greater efficiency would be paid for with over-bureaucratisation and with giving up the strategies of improvisation, in other words, the distortion of the organisation's original characteristics.

The tensions between the two different visions of the future of MSF had exploded in November 1978, when Kouchner, as representative of MSF, joined up to the 'Un Bateau pour le Vietnam' initiative, which involved the use of a salvage boat to aid people fleeing Vietnam after the victory of communism. Since 1975, the number of Vietnamese refugees had gradually been increasing. Some traversed the borders with Thailand, Cambodia, Laos and China but many more of the men, women and children who were escaping from the communist regime took the sea route on large boats. The so-called 'boat people' who managed to survive the terrible journey had soon settled the numerous, overcrowded refugee camps that were spread over the region and administered partly by the UNHCR and partly by local governments.[69] By 1978 around 68,000 people had left Vietnam, many of Chinese origin. The countries where they landed had not signed up to the 1951 Geneva Convention and none of them granted indefinite leave to remain, while some did not even offer temporary asylum. Singapore refused to let refugees disembark if they were not due to receive, within ninety days, a resettlement guarantee from another country. Until 1979 – the year in which an international agreement was reached for the settlement of the Vietnamese refugees in other countries – Malaysia and Thailand frequently sent back from their respective coasts boats loaded with escapees.[70]

The 'Un Bateau pour le Vietnam' initiative had started in this context but was also to push the government in Paris to accept a greater number of refugees from Vietnam. The initiative had been launched by intellectuals and leading figures in French society and had had a very strong media impact. Its fame spread so far beyond national borders that it prompted similar initiatives in other countries.[71] Kouchner had been criticised by many members of MSF for having signed up to it, and attaching greater importance to visibility over a more thought-through evaluation of the effectiveness of the project and its implications. At the MSF's general assembly in spring 1979, the advocates of 'a perfect machine, a solid structure' had won majority agreement; Kouchner and his supporters had left MSF to set up a new association, Médecins du Monde.[72]

At the beginning of this new stage, MSF had to deal with the problem of Cambodia. The organisation's new leadership underlined the urgency of an intervention that would save millions of people from hunger and disease but at the same time rejected the conditions imposed by the authorities in Phnom Penh and claimed back complete autonomy in distributing the aid. This autonomy alone would have prevented a totalitarian regime such as Cambodia's from transforming aid into an instrument of oppression.[73] To make the Cambodian government's responsibilities clear, MSF staged a protest. The initiative took the name of 'Marche pour la Survie du Cambodge' and was created in collaboration with other associations, like Action Internationale contre la Faim – recently set up on the initiative of a group of French journalists and intellectuals – and the International Rescue Committee, an American NGO founded during the Second World War. On 8 February 1980 a large group of intellectuals, politicians and show-business personalities – including Elie Wiesel, the Soviet dissident Alexander Ginzburg, Joan Baez and Liv Ullmann – marched on the border between Thailand and Cambodia to symbolically breach the barrier that was stopping aid getting to Cambodians. The demonstration was a great success from the point of view of its international impact, with many countries' television news featuring interviews with the most famous participants and the images of the group, sitting in front of the military controlled border singing 'We Shall Overcome'. La Marche pour la Survie du Cambodge marked an important moment for the 'right to speak out' advocated by MSF but it triggered a lively debate within the organisation. Some of its members harshly criticised both the instrumental use of celebrities and the unilateral denunciation of a pro-Vietnam government, which could be interpreted as the crushing of the organisation on the Western bloc's positions.[74]

Apart from the questions raised by the internal disputes, the protest organised by the French doctors certainly cast the spotlight on only one side of the border and none on what was happening on the other side, in Thai territory, where MSF was at work. The refugee camp situation was extremely complex. The arrival of men and women fleeing Cambodia had started in the years of the Pol Pot dictatorship, when around 34,000 Cambodians had managed to reach Thailand, even though the local authorities barely tolerated the mass influx of forced migrants. The Bangkok government had not signed the 1951 Geneva Convention so did not recognise refugee status and prohibited refugees from moving towards the interior of the country. The number of camps close to the border had grown with the Vietnamese invasion of Cambodia and the downfall of the Khmer Rouge.[75] Thanks to a specific agreement with Thailand, the UNHCR had set up and was administering some centres while all the others were managed by the local authorities and controlled by the army. The treatment received by the refugees was decidedly better where the UN agency was directly in charge. It was important for the UNHCR to give an account of its own operations to international public, which was paying close attention to what was going on in such a crucial area for global political balance.

Khao-I-Dang, which was the biggest centre managed by the UNHCR and came to house more than 100,000 people, was open to visitors and journalists and was defined by the press as 'the most elaborately serviced refugee camp in the world'.[76] The activities within the structure – thanks to US, Australian, Japanese and European funding – included education, health and mental health, policing and peace programmes.[77] This variety of services was guarded by the presence of several dozen NGOs, which provided further evidence of the private agencies' expansion in the international setting and their by now close collaboration with the intergovernmental agencies such as the UNHCR. There was another reason why Khao-I-Dang came to represent a sort of 'promised land' to such an extent that refugees corrupted security guards to let them enter clandestinely and the fear of being discovered then made them victims of intimidation and blackmail.[78] Staying in this camp meant you could nourish the hope, however remote, that you would be resettled in another country, such as the United States, Australia or France.[79]

For all those who did not have the chance to enter resettlement programmes, life dragged on without any certainty, since the refugees' fates depended on Cambodia's internal situation and also on the armed conflict that had developed between the Vietnamese army and the forces of the mixed Cambodian resistance. The refugee population was subjected to a huge variety of pressures, violence and oppression. The Vietnamese armed forces would cross the border and attack the camps, since they were largely controlled by the Khmer Rouge or other guerrilla groups. In their turn, these groups exercised their power despotically: they imposed a tax regime that was used to finance armed resistance; they used any means possible to recruit new combatants; and they managed a substantial part of the relief, in whatever way they liked. Finally, the Thai army had a major role in the surveillance of the camps and it had no scruples about abusing its position.[80] All of this affected the tangible consequences of the relief the humanitarian agencies were bringing to the scene.

UNICEF and the ICRC organised a joint mission that supplied food, medicines and other basic necessities for most of the refugee centres; the relief also arrived from the World Food Programme and from some of the biggest US organisations, such as Catholic Relief Services and CARE. The delivery and distribution practices for what the agencies brought to the Thai border varied according to the context: rations were often handed over directly to the camp leaders but in other cases they first went through the Thai military. It was undoubtedly the case, though, that a significant amount of rice, oil and blankets did not get to the refugee families but was diverted to the clandestine military bases or else was sold on the black market and the earnings went to supplying the armed resistance against the Vietnamese forces and the Phnom Penh government.[81] For example, based on a monitoring operation carried out in 1980 in the Nong Samet camp – one of the largest (those in charge said it housed around 200,000 people) – about 64 per cent of the rice to be distributed never reached the refugees' barracks and they showed clear signs of chronic malnutrition.[82]

The 'vanished' rations that the inhabitants of Nong Samet – controlled by the Khmer People's National Liberation Force, one of the biggest non-communist groups in the anti-Vietnamese resistance – should have enjoyed bore the symbols of the Red Cross and UNICEF but in the early years of their intervention the two organisations showed they were unaware of what was happening, there or elsewhere. Some seriously worrying signs came to light in the ICRC's internal reports in early 1980. In January, for example, one of the operatives sent to Thailand underlined that 'the distribution criteria [of the organization] are not respected', recalled that there were 'incessant efforts to make [refugee] people understand that food is not for the Khmer Rouge army' and insisted that there should soon be 'more severe measures'.[83] The allegations of misconduct intensified steadily and at the end of the year the ICRC withdrew from the food programme for Cambodian refugees and from the joint UNICEF mission. UNICEF – even though it had shared the information about the illicit use of supplies and the attempts to take counter-measures with the Genevan organisation – continued the distribution of rations in the camps on the Thai–Cambodian border for a further year.[84]

In 1982, after UNICEF's withdrawal, the coordination of aid in the whole border zone was taken on by the United Nations Border Relief Operation (UNBRO), a temporary *ad hoc* agency. The appearance of the new body did not alter the situation (either for the refugee population or in terms of the control exerted in the camps by the different armed groups). However, the 'hijacking' of supplies intended for the refugees was not necessarily incompatible with the political interests of some of the donor countries – such as the United States, Japan and France – which at least tolerated the development of armed Cambodian resistance, as it was anti-Vietnamese. This meant, though, maintaining good relations with the Thai government and shutting an eye to the abuses harming the refugee population.[85]

Some change occurred only later – between 1984 and 1985 – following the very strong Vietnamese army offensive against the guerrillas that took place along the border between Thailand and Cambodia. Many camps were completely destroyed; UNBRO organised the transfer of their inhabitants and managed, in the construction of new centres, to at least partly separate civilians and combatants. The tie between the camps and the armed groups was certainly not severed but in some cases UNBRO was able to guarantee greater security to the refugees and to start new programmes and services for them.[86] A typical example is Site 2, a large-scale camp (it eventually housed about 200,000 people) that, like Khao-I-Dang, hosted the work of many NGOs and an extraordinary variety of projects that attempted to define and deal with the specific needs of the Cambodian refugees, going beyond distribution of food and basic medical care. In this respect, research into and work on mental health were particularly significant. In part they were the continuation of the trend to identify 'typical' pathologies in the displaced population, such as apathy.[87] This trend had already emerged in the past in the setting of relief programmes for camp inhabitants. At the same time, the specific nature of the case of the Cambodian refugees was established through initiatives that focused on the trauma they had undergone as victims of Pol Pot's genocidal violence.[88]

The camps started to be emptied in 1989 with the withdrawal of Vietnamese armed forces, even though the last of the camps, including Khao-I-Dang and Site 2, were dismantled only four years later. In May 1993, elections were held in Cambodia under the auspices of the UN. Humanitarianism underwent a crucial turning point in Thailand, inside the refugee population stuck on the border with Cambodia, between the end of the 1970s and the start of the 1990s – for various and in certain respects contradictory reasons. On the one hand, the inter-twined dynamics of relief and postcolonial conflict conditioned by the Cold War proved inextricable and had apparently paradoxical effects on the outcomes of the humanitarian programmes. Food and medicines partly kept the refugees alive and partly went to feed the Cambodian resistance, but thereby contributed to extending the armed conflict with the Vietnamese army, for whom the camps became strategic targets. On the other hand, some large structures, administered by the UN with the participation of many NGOs, became genuine laboratories for highly complex refugee aid practices, defined through the dialogue between relief workers from different countries and aimed at building up a fund of knowledge to be used in later programmes. Through its experience with the Cambodian refugees, humanitarianism gained strength and new tools but at the same time demonstrated its limits and was compelled to face new dilemmas.

'Do they know it's Christmas?'

> We are going to have trouble here in Ethiopia in the coming year because of crop failure, food shortage, movement of people and all the usual elements that are part of life in Ethiopia. [...]
>
> Our problem is to prepare ourselves for a disaster which we may not be able to do anything about. [...]
>
> I should also like to ask you or anyone else in an influential position to encourage donors – especially governments – to supply ICSM [instant corn soya mix] and high protein biscuits and oil, all of which are extremely useful and can be stock-piled.[89]

These are the words Libby Grimshaw used at the end of 1983 to express her worries for the future, in a letter to her contact at the Save the Children headquarters in London. She was in Korem, in the Tigray region, in northern Ethiopia, running a food programme. During the spring of the same year she had been kidnapped along with other representatives of humanitarian organisations by the Tigray's People Liberation Front, the armed movement fighting the central military government for the region's independence. Libby Grimshaw and the others were kept hostage for six weeks. After their release Save the Children withdrew from the country and would resume its work there only months later. Back to work on the food programme, Grimshaw anxiously observed the situation deteriorating in one of the regions hit by some of the worst droughts and tried to alert the heads of the organisation in Europe. At the same time, she hoped her understanding of the situation was wrong and concluded her letter saying: 'Perhaps I am being over-pessimistic about the coming year....'.

Unfortunately, Libby Grimshaw's predictions were not overly pessimistic. Over the course of the next two years the famine she had seen begin caused the death of at least 400,000 people in northern Ethiopia. In terms of human lives, this was an even more dramatic disaster than the famine which had hit the country ten years earlier, which had significantly contributed to the downfall of Emperor Haile Selassie in 1974.[90] During that previous period of extreme crisis, humanitarian organisations – such as Save the Children – had come to Ethiopia, and stayed even when a Marxist military regime, supported by the Soviet Union, seized power. Even though the new government declared that famine had been defeated once and for all, food continued to be scarce and the risk of a new crisis was a constant one, which tragically became reality in 1983. The famine, which hit the northern regions hardest, was said to be caused by the droughts, which had certainly played a role in the poor harvests and therefore the scarcity of food. However, the death by starvation of hundreds of thousands was not solely caused by the climate. In fact, the causes were to be found in the effects of the war economy imposed by the regime.

The dictatorship relied on a very large army, which took resources for agriculture (which had not undergone a process of automation) and at the same time absorbed great quantities of food. Ethiopian soldiers were on the border with Somalia because in 1977 the Somalian army had crossed the south-east border to take the Ogaden region. However, the Ethiopian military forces were mostly deployed, over vast areas of the national territory, against internal rebel armed groups; these conflicts had rendered infertile about 40 per cent of the land fit for cultivation, causing the protracted failures of harvests. Furthermore, the endemic fighting between the army and the 'internal enemies' had interrupted roads and commerce, damaging the market and isolating the areas that did not produce enough to satisfy the needs of the population. The obstruction of commerce – along with the bombing of villages, the forced population displacement, the decimation of cattle and the poisoning of waters – had been one of the strategies used by Menghistu Haile Mariam's central government to fight the pro-independence forces of Eritrea and Tigray in a particularly violent war that took place between 1978 and 1984.[91]

The drought had therefore worsened an already dramatic situation caused by the violent internal conflicts and particularly the way in which they were being fought. The gravity of the situation and its possible deterioration had led the Ethiopian government to request in early 1984 international aid through its Relief and Rehabilitation Commission, the organisation established to respond to the consequences of the famine of 1973–74. Since then, it had maintained relations with foreign humanitarian organisations. However, the request, made through diplomatic channels, was not successful, for various reasons. On the one hand, Western governments were not willing to intervene in a pro-Soviet country. On the other hand, the members of the Commission took an ambiguous stand: they lobbied to receive aid from the international community but at the same time they avoided advertising the famine inside and outside the country. The worries expressed by the Relief and Rehabilitation Commission followed the alarm raised by some European diplomats and by the representatives of humanitarian organis-ations active in the territory, like Libby Grimshaw of Save the Children.[92] All this, however, was mostly ignored in the Western world, both on an institutional level and in the media: until the autumn of 1984, the international media paid very little attention to the famine. This situation was completely reversed when, at the end of October 1984, the BBC broadcast a report from Ethiopia by Michael Buerk and Mohammed Amin.

The 'media discovery' of the mass starvation of the Ethiopian population happened thanks to the random convergence of a number of factors. The Kenyan photo-reporter Mohammed Amin had obtained permission to enter a centre for undernourished people in the city of Korem, in the north of the country. There he filmed very powerful footage of masses of men, women and children reduced to skeletons, desperately waiting for food, standing in the sun, or crumpled on the ground. The British journalist Michael Buerk recorded an extremely effective commentary for the film footage: while in the background you could hear the constant lamentations of people and the agonising crying of babies, Buerk said the Ethiopian famine was a disaster of biblical proportions, reminding viewers that every twenty minutes one of the hungry and sick children they were watching on television was dying. A BBC editor recognised the importance of the story and gave the two journalists more time to develop the piece, which had a prominent spot on the evening news. The absence of noticeable news from other non-European countries also supported his decision.[93]

The seven-minute item about Korem made by Buerk and Amin left a great impression on the British public and launched a news story that gained global attention extremely quickly. The media space dedicated to the famine in the Horn of Africa multiplied and the BBC report was subsequently shown on 425 television channels all over the world and was seen by 470 million viewers.[94] The exceptional visibility of the issue made the 'Ethiopia crisis' rise to the top of the agenda of humanitarianism. Government and intergovernmental agencies dedicated special funds and emergency programmes to it. Associations imme-diately launched new campaigns to collect donations, which contributed not only to the organisation of emergency aid but also to increasing the interest in the problem of the Ethiopian famine. Most importantly, the media space dedicated to it originated a specific form of mobilisation, which had incredible resonance, remained in the collective memories of Western societies for decades and introduced new elements in the history of humanitarianism: the music and concerts of Bob Geldof and Band Aid.

In his autobiography — published in 1986 and drawing on the great popularity he gained very quickly — Bob Geldof gave credit to Buerk and Amin's journalistic effort for his own mobilisation for the victims of the famine shown on the BBC. In fact, it was after seeing their report that Geldof, musician and member of a well known rock band in Britain, decided to do fundraising through the production of a record.[95] In collaboration with Ultravox member Midge Ure, he wrote the song 'Do they know it's Christmas?', which was then recorded by a group of prominent artists under the name Band Aid. The record had the fastest success in the history of singles and sold over three million copies, for a total of over £8 million. Shortly after the release of the single 'Do they know it's Christmas?' Geldof organised a concert. It wasn't an entirely new idea: in 1971 George Harrison and the Indian musician Ravi Shankar had called a number of artists to perform in support of the Bangladeshi population. Geldof's initiative, however, was even more impressive than Harrison's and Shankar's. He organised two concerts, which took place at the same time in two locations – London and Philadelphia – and involved many renowned artists, including Phil Collins, Tina Turner and Bob Dylan. The event, called Live Aid, was attended by 172,000 people but was followed on radio and television by 1.5 billion people from all over the world, as the sixteen hours of live music were broadcast in 150 countries. The revenue of Live Aid, entirely donated to the victims of famine in Ethiopia, was over £110 million.[96]

The success of Geldof's initiatives undoubtedly increased the availability of food for the famine victims but it also had consequences on the collective perception of the Ethiopian crisis. The lyrics to the song 'Do they know it's Christmas?' exhorted everyone not to forget that outside the windows lit up during the Christmas holidays there was 'a world of dread and fear / where the only water flowing is the bitter sting of tears'. During the performances at Wembley stadium and in Philadelphia, videos of the malnourished Ethiopian population were projected that included some particularly shocking scenes. The communication around the events focused on the sense of urgency and on the seriousness of the situation; there was, though, little in the way of explanation. The mobilisation of musicians took to extremes the oversimplification of facts already carried out by newspapers and television, which described the famine as a consequence of a natural disaster without reporting sufficiently on the specific political and socio-economic context of Ethiopia. Even Buerk and Amin's report mentioned the country's situation only towards the end, explaining in less than one minute that the civil war made the distribution of aid in the northern regions difficult. Live Aid rendered the context even more abstract. The song 'Do they know it's Christmas?' talked only about 'Africa' ('and there won't be snow in Africa this Christmastime'), with no specific reference to Ethiopia: the 'world of dread and fear' was the African continent in general. The simplification was confirmed by the initiative's logo, in which the colour black distinguished Africa from all other continents. The extremely vague geographic indication helped to circulate the call for contributions from the wider public by making their destination more familiar. At the same time, however, 'the Dark Continent' was becoming the place *par excellence* of unproductiveness, deprivation and hunger associated with the Third World, the other side of the coin of the wealthy, modern and compassionate society proving itself to be able to 'throw [its] arms around the world at Christmastime', according to the lyrics of the Band Aid song.

Geldof's solution to the problem of fundraising to 'feed the world' (this was the call that ended the Band Aid song) was not an absolute novelty in humanitarian campaigns.[97] Anti-slavery associations had commercialised sugar bowls, badges and bracelets carrying the symbols of the anti-slavery struggle,[98] and in much more recent years campaigns to support refugees and international development programmes had included lotteries, shows and charity sales.[99] Selling a record, a ticket or merchandise related to these musical performances was a new way of exploiting commercial music for humanitarian purposes; the success of the strategy, though, still lay in the combination of the pleasure of buying and the satisfaction derived from doing a good deed. What changed were the scale and the significance of the marketing operation – the key to this 'circumstantial humani-tarianism' came unexpectedly to life in response to an emergency deemed worse than others. Band Aid and Live Aid aimed for big sales, relying on the consumer-ism of the 1980s,[100] on mass consumption of music and on the incredible fame of the musicians involved. Another strong point of the campaign was its simplicity: all there was to do was buy a record, go to a concert or watch it on TV, sing a song and increase its popularity.[101]

The massive simplification of the display of compassion towards humanity was facilitated by the fact that the call for support was not issued by organisations with a history and an established political, religious or cultural vision but by show-biz celebrities, with whom the public easily identified. These figures were not only associating themselves with various organisations as they had in the past: they were the direct promoters of mass mobilisation in support of a 'noble cause' through encouraging the public to 'consume' their musical product. Their message was that the moral duty of compassion coincided with the act of buying and donating, and everything seemed immediate and easy: people were starving and so it was necessary to fundraise to buy food and medicines to send to those who had none, and many lives would be saved. The fundraising was organised in a very effective way but saving the people proved much harder.

From the end of 1984, international mobilisation was widespread and intense even outside Geldof's initiatives. 'Naturally there was a time-lag of some months between a commitment and the arrival of shipments in Ethiopian ports [...], but by June 1985 a total of 801.000 tonnes [of supplies] had arrived'.[102] The UN opened an office in Addis Ababa to coordinate the work of different agencies – including

UNICEF, the WFP and the FAO – that were going to implement the aid programmes in the country. Kurt Jansson, who had led the UNICEF and Red Cross mission in Cambodia, was appointed head of the UN coordination mission. The choice recognised the role taken on by 'emergency experts' in managing 'humanitarian crises', regardless of the context in which they happened. NGOs also played a key role in organising aid programmes in Ethiopia. Some had already worked locally while many others became active following the growing international attention given to the famine. It is significant that in 1985 more than sixty 'foreign' organisations were present in Addis Ababa.[103] NGOs had by then established themselves as part of the international aid system. The financial contribution of numerous foreign governments finalised the substantial arrival of food and medicines in Ethiopia: over thirty-six countries designed intervention programmes in aid of the starving population. The most significant of these programmes was the US one.

The United States had suspended all its development programmes in Ethiopia in 1979, a few years after the establishment of the military dictatorship, and had left the country soon after. In 1984, however, taking part in a humanitarian operation that was receiving so much media attention was an important opportunity for the Reagan administration. The president of the United States was reaching the end of his first mandate and after years of extreme tension with the Soviet Union he intended to begin a phase of more collaborative relations. Through a generous aid programme for Ethiopia, Ronald Reagan could show the world – and his electorate – America's moral high ground and its power on a field other than the arms race. The White House therefore decided to give to Ethiopia 'the largest ever emergency relief effort' launched by the United States[104] – 800,000 tonnes of food and economic support for several different projects for a total of $60 million – despite the doubts voiced by some members of Congress and in some areas of government. There were doubts about aiding a country supported by the Soviet Union as well as the fact that in terms of *Realpolitik* the famine could have had positive effects, such as destabilising Menghistu's government to the point of its fall, as had happened a decade earlier with Haile Selassie.[105] Despite these concerns, Ethiopia, although aligned to the communist bloc, received aid and the apparent contradiction was justified with the phrase 'A hungry child knows no politics'. The slogan was attributed to the Christian organisation Bread for the World[106] but its message was not new in the history of humanitarianism.[107]

The broadcast of Buerk's and Amin's documentary allowed international mobilisation to grow exponentially but there were two serious problems slowing down, or even preventing, the distribution of food and medicines to the starving population. One was the civil war: the conflict between rebel forces and the Ethiopian army was unfolding precisely in the regions worst hit by the famine, in the north of the country, which were therefore inaccessibile. The other was that the regime intended to limit the foreign organisations' room for manoeuvre as far as possible, prioritising instead the government's plan to relocate one and half million people from the northern to the southern regions of the country. The programme had been launched in 1984 and the Ethiopian authorities had presented it as the main national strategy to tackle the consequences of famine, since, according to the Relief and Rehabilitation Commission, 'the Northern provinces of Tigrai and Wello [were] uninhabitable wasteland'[108] and thus their inhabitants were to be moved. The forced relocation of the local population was not only a response to the famine – it was a key point of government policy. It had already been used as a strategy to redistribute land to loyal soldiers or to deprive the regime's opponents of the support of their local communities by uprooting the latter. In combination with 'villagisation' – the construction of villages from scratch while dismantling the old ones – relocation was a social engineering programme that should have built the foundations for the development and the modernisation of the country. By supporting the Ethiopian government's own relief plan, therefore, international aid ran the risk of reinforcing the Menghistu's regime's repressive policies.[109]

The government was not the only point of contact for humanitarian organisations, however: they could also distribute aid through the 'rebel' armed forces. This enabled the northern regions to be reached much more easily. However, it showed the will to support Eritrea's and Tigray's struggle for independence. On the other hand, collaborating with the government allowed them to take a neutral stance. In 1981, an ecumenical NGOs consortium had been formed by Lutheran World Relief, Swedish Church Relief, the British Christian Aid and the Danish DanChurchAid.[110] The consortium was based in Sudan, on the border with Eritrea, so the aid they sent indirectly supported the armed struggle for independence. The rebel military forces had organised groups dedicated to helping civilians. The food made available by international aid allowed them to organise shelters to feed the population, some of which were just across the border in Sudan. This location guaranteed safety and basic healthcare but at the same time it forced exhausted, starving people to travel extensively.[111]

The programme that developed on the border between Sudan and Ethiopia remained marginal in the wider context of the relief efforts. The majority of humanitarian organisations, in fact, chose to rely on the authority of Addis Ababa. The Relief and Rehabilitation Commission channelled, directly or indirectly, the majority of the resources from abroad. It managed about one-third of the food resources while the rest was managed by NGOs, which had to work through local staff and to sign specific agreements with the Commission itself.[112]

The main problem with distributing resources through the government was reaching the northern regions, which were utterly brought to their knees by the famine but which were also largely controlled by rebel forces. At the end of 1984, it was estimated that government representatives had access to less than half of the famine victims and a few months later the *Times* correspondent from

Addis Ababa wrote that, according to the UN, 'food given by the international community [was] not reaching the two million people estimated to be affected by famine in the Northern areas'.[113]

The first attempts to reach a shared solution did not succeed but in March 1985 the United States – which was the country making the largest donations – managed to reach an agreement with the central government and launched the Food for the North Initiative. This programme aimed to build food shelters in northern Ethiopia, both in Tigray and in Eritrea. It was funded by the US government, which put two NGOs in charge of its implementation: World Vision and CRS. CRS delegated operations to the Ethiopian Catholic Secretariat, the representative organisation of Catholic churches in the country. This organisation was then in charge of feeding about 350,000 people in shelters across the territory.[114] The Food for the North Initiative seemed to offer an initial solution to the problem, stressed by several parties, of supplying aid to the regions caught between the armed rebels and the national army. However, it also helped in some way to implement the forced relocation programme. In Tigray, the food centres, set up thanks to the aid, became a hub that set thousands of starving families on the move, and every centre thus became a step on a forced journey from north to south. For example, the farming families who went to the two shelters in western Tigray did not receive extra rations and were not allowed to go back to their homes, but they were held there and then redirected to the southern regions. The government's plan for the 'redistribution' of the population thereby found support in the Food for the North Initiative as well as more widely in the deployment of international aid.[115] This enforced travelling also caused many more deaths of exhausted and often ill men, women and children. Furthermore, the relocation of farming families worsened agricultural production instead of revitalising it.[116]

Doubts about the role aid was playing in facilitating Menghistu's resettlement programme were widespread among the organisations active in Ethiopia. MSF was the organisation to take a stand and bring the issue to the attention of the international general public in an effort to put pressure on the UN, on the governments funding the aid and on the other NGOs.[117] In April 1985, following the decision by Ethiopian authorities to disperse the population of one shelter without recognising that a cholera epidemic had broken out there, the MSF's general assembly decided to protest against the abuses of the military regime, even if this meant running the risk of being expelled from the country. The following October, Rony Brauman, president of MSF, used a speech on humanitarian aid to explain how it was impossible to open a shelter for children in an area where the local government intended to relocate all the inhabitants. He concluded his speech by saying 'if the situation doesn't change, we will be forced to leave'.[118] A few moths later, tensions peaked when, during a press conference upon his return from Addis Ababa, Brauman stated that 'an extraordinary movement of solidarity is being turned against the people who are supposed to be helped [...] the aid is being used not to save, but to oppress them'.[119] Following this, the Ethiopian authorities removed MSF from the country.

The decision to speak up against the exploitation of aid by the dictatorship caused the distribution of aid to victims to come to a halt, which is why Kurt Jansson, head of the UN office in Addis Ababa, later called MSF's decision 'immature'.[120] The other organisations did not jeopardise their relations with the Ethiopian authorities and remained operative in the country at least until 1986, when the worst phase of the crisis seemed resolved and the new harvest nurtured hopes that the famine had been defeated. The problem, however, presented itself again the following year, even though it was basically ignored by the international public. Ethiopia received media attention again only in 1991, when Menghistu was overthrown by armed forces and Eritrea became an independent state.

The intervention in Ethiopia following the famine in 1984–85 highlighted issues that went beyond the specific context of the country. The accusations made by MSF against the government and its consequent expulsion from the country showed the Gordian knot which could bring the humanitarian organisations to paralysis. Expressing a critical opinion on the use of humanitarian aid by a dictatorship meant abandoning action but in order to remain active it was necessary to remain silent in the face of abuse. In both cases, the fundamental principles of humanitarianism were contradicted. The 'French doctors' wished to highlight this precise dilemma and their speaking up in Ethiopia was not only a testament to the abuse suffered by victims but was also aimed at starting a conversation on the potential negative effects that the organisation's activities, and international aid in general, could have. Reflecting twenty years later on what had happened in Ethiopia, Rony Brauman said that the mobilisation against the famine in the Horn of Africa was the moment when it became apparent that 'aid can turn against the very people it is intended for, and the actors of humanitarianism can be integrated in a system of oppression'.[121] In the mid-1980s, MSF had already stated that acknowledging these contradictions was a moral duty not only of those directly involved in humanitarian aid but of all citizens who supported international aid initiatives. The issue was shortly about to explode with the end of the Cold War, when the deployment of international aid became linked with new conflicts, undertaken in the name of the fundamental rights of oppressed peoples and defined as 'humanitarian'.

Notes

1 Esther Moeller, 'The Suez Crisis of 1956 as a Moment of Transnational Humanitarian Engagement', *European Review of History: Revue Européenne d'Histoire*, 23:1–2 (2016), pp. 136–153.

2 UNHCR, *The State of World's Refugees 2000: Fifty Years of Humanitarian Action* (Oxford: Oxford University Press, 2000), pp. 47–52.

3   See p. 136.

4   The Protocol gave those states that had already ratified the 1951 Convention the right to retain the geographically restricted definition.

5   Christopher J. Kauffman, 'Politics, Programs, and Protests: Catholic Relief Services in Vietnam, 1954–1975', *Catholic Historical Review*, 41:2 (2005), pp. 223–250; Bruce Nichols, *The Uneasy Alliance: Religion, Refugee Work, and US Foreign Policy* (New York: Oxford University Press, 1988), pp. 100–107.

6   'CRS in the Far East: Annual Reports 1943–1993', Baltimore, MD, Catholic Relief Services – United States Catholic Conference Archive Research Center, 1993, p. 21, cited in Scott Flipse, 'The Latest Casualty of War: Catholic Relief Services, Humanitarianism, and the War in Vietnam, 1967–68', *Peace and Change*, 27:2 (2002), p. 245.

7   *Ibid.*

8   *Ibid.*; Kauffman, 'Politics, Programs, and Protests'.

9   Michael Mok, *Biafra Journal* (New York: Time-Life Books, 1969), p. 21, cited in Ken Waters, 'Influencing the Message: The Role of Catholic Missionaries in Media coverage of the Nigerian Civil War', *Catholic Historical Review*, 90:4 (2004), p. 707.

10 Cited in Ndubisi Obiaga, *The Politics of Humanitarian Organizations Interventions* (Dallas, TX: University Press of America, 2004), p. 85.

11 Arua Oko Omaka, 'Humanitarian Action: The Joint Church Aid and Health Care Intervention in the Nigeria–Biafra War, 1967–1970', *Canadian Journal of History/Annales canadiennes d'histoire*, 49:1 (2014), p. 430. Joint Church Aid (JCA) was to have a role in international aid to Biafra, as discussed here on pp. 189–190.

12 Obiaga, *The Politics of Humanitarian Organizations Interventions*, pp. 17–19.

13 Joseph E. Thompson, *American Policy and African Famine: The Nigeria–Biafra War 1966–1970* (New York: Greenwood Press, 1990).

14 Jean-Pierre Bat, *Le syndrome de Foccart: La politique française en Afrique, de 1959 à nos jours* (Paris: Gallimard, 2012), pp. 295–303.

15 Karen E. Smith, 'The UK and Genocide in Biafra', *Journal of Genocide Research*, 16:2–3 (2014), p. 251.

16 Cited in Yves Lavoinne, 'Médecins en guerre: du témoignage au "tapage médiatique" (1968–1970)', *Le Temps des Médias*, 4 (2005), p. 117.

17 Goffredo Parise, *Biafra* (Milan: Feltrinelli, 1968), p. 63.

18 'La strage nel Biafra', *La Stampa*, 10 August 1968, p. 6.

19 Lasse Heerten, '"A" as in Auschwitz, "B" as in Biafra: The Nigerian Civil War, Visual Narratives of Genocide, and the Fragmented Universalization of the Holocaust', in Heide Fehrenbach and Davide Rodogno (eds), *Humanitarian Photography: A History* (New York: Cambridge University Press, 2015), p. 252; Lasse Heerten, *The Biafran War and Postcolonial Humanitarianism: Spectacles of Suffering* (Cambridge: Cambridge University Press, 2017), pp. 175–204.

20 Statement made by Paddy Davies, Biafran Propaganda Directorate, in the documentary *Biafra: Fighting a War Without Guns*, directed by Michael Stewart for BBC1 in 1995.

21 Françoise Ugochukwo, 'The Nigerian Civil War and Its Media: Groping for Clues', *Media, War and Conflict*, 3:2 (2010), pp. 182–201.

22 Roy Doron, 'Marketing Genocide: Biafran Propaganda Strategies During the Nigerian Civil War 1967–1970', *Journal of Genocide Research*, 16:2–3 (2014), p. 251.

23 Parise, *Biafra*, p. 9.

24 Notes of a confidential UNHCR meeting with Mr Udo Affia, Commissioner for Health of breakaway Eastern Nigeria, 'Biafra,' of 9 November 1967, cited in Nathaniel H. Goez,

'Humanitarian Issues in the Biafra Conflict', Working Paper No. 36, April 2011, at http://www.unhcr.org/3af66b8b4.html (accessed November 2018).

25 Konrad J. Kuhn, '"The credibility of our humanitarian effort is at risk": Tensions Between Solidarity and Humanitarian Aid in the Late 1960s', in Johannes Paulmann (ed.), *Dilemmas of Humanitarian Aid in the Twentieth Century* (Oxford: Oxford University Press, 2016), pp. 314–321; Brian McNeil '"And starvation is the grim reaper": The American Committee to Keep Biafra Alive and Genocide Question During the Nigerian Civil War, 1968–1970', *Journal of Genocide Research*, 16:2–3 (2014), pp. 317–336.

26 Kevin O'Sullivan, 'Humanitarian Encounters: Biafra, NGOs and Imaginings of the Third World in Britain and Ireland, 1967–70', *Journal of Genocide Research*, 16:2–3 (2014), p. 304. On British NGOs and on their media work during the 1960s see Matthew Hilton, James McKay, Nicholas Crowson and Jean-François Mouhot, *The Politics of Expertise: How NGOs Shaped Modern Britain* (Oxford: Oxford University Press, 2013), pp. 146–187.

27 O'Sullivan, 'Humanitarian Encounters', pp. 299–315.

28 Kevin O'Sullivan, 'Biafra's Legacy: NGO Humanitarianism and the Nigerian Civil War', in Christina Bennett, Matthew Foley and Hanna B. Krebs (eds), *Learning from the Past to Shape the Future: Lessons from the History of Humanitarian Action in Africa*, ODI Humanitarian Policy Group Working Paper, October 2016, at https://www.odi.org/sites/odi.org.uk/files/resource-documents/11148.pdf (accessed November 2018).

29 Parise, *Biafra*, p. 59.

30 O'Sullivan, 'Humanitarian Encounters'.

31 Lasse Heerten, 'The Dystopia of Postcolonial Catastrophe: Self-Determination, the Biafran War of Secession, and the 1970s Human Rights Movement', in J. Eckel and S. Moyn (eds), *The Breakthrough: Human Rights in the 1970s* (Philadelphia, PA: University of Pennsylvania Press, 2014), pp. 29–30; Heerten, *The Biafran War and Postcolonial Humanitarianism*, pp. 140–174.

32 Heerten, *The Biafran War*, p. 302.

33 O'Sullivan, 'A "Global Nervous System": The Rise and Rise of European Humanitarian NGOs (1945–1985)', in M. Frey, S. Kunkel and C. R. Unger (eds), *International Organizations and Development, 1945–1990* (Basingstoke: Palgrave Macmillan, 2014), pp. 210–211.

34 Marie-Luce Desgrandchamps, 'Revenir sur le mythe fondateur de Médecins sans frontières: Les relations entre médecins français et le CICR pendant la guerre du Biafra (1967–1970)', *Relations internationales*, 146 (2011), p. 98.

35 See pp. 121–122.

36 David P. Forsythe, *The Humanitarians: The International Committee of the Red Cross* (Cambridge: Cambridge University Press, 2005), pp. 63–68; Marie-Luce Desgrandchamps, '"Organiser à l'avance imprévisible": la guerre Nigéria-Biafra et son impact sur le CICR', *Revue Internationale de la Croix Rouge*, 94:4 (2012), pp. 221–246.

37 In 1977 a second protocol was added to the Geneva Convention of 12 August 1949 relating to the protection of the victims of non-international armed conflicts. On the 1949 Convention see pp. 120–121.

38 Marie-Luce Desgrandchamps, '"Organiser à l'avance imprévisible"', pp. 224–225.

39 Our correspondent – Geneva, 'Four Men Killed in Biafra Relief Flight Crash', *The Times*, 9 December 1968, p. 5.

40 O'Sullivan, 'Biafra's Legacy', p. 6.

41 Our correspondent, 'Biafra's Pessimism Over Food Airlift', *The Times*, 9 September 1969, p. 6.

42 Bernard Kouchner and Max Récamier, 'De retour du Biafra, deux médecins français témoignent', *Le Monde*, 27 November 1968, p. 15.

43 Eleonor Davey, *Idealism Beyond Borders: The French Revolutionary Left and the Rise of Humanitarianism, 1954–1988* (Cambridge: Cambridge University Press, 2015), pp. 40–43.

44 Cited in Lavoinne, 'Médecins en guerre', p. 120.

45 Anne Vallaeys, *Médecins sans Frontières: la biographie* (Paris: Fayard, 2004), pp. 107–126.

46 Davey, *Idealism Beyond Borders*, pp. 19–22.

47 Jean-Christophe Rufin, *Le piège: Quand l'aide humanitaire remplace la guerre* (Paris: Lattès, 1986), p. 61; Pierre Micheletti, *Humanitaire, s'adapter ou renoncer* (Paris: Marabout, 2008), p. 29.

48 Davey, *Idealism Beyond Borders*, pp. 19–49.

49 Xavier Emmanuelli, *Au vent du monde* (Paris: Flammarion, 1990), cited in Pierre-Edouard Deldique and Catherine Ninin, *Globe doctors: 20 ans d'aventure humanitaire* (Paris: Belfond, 1991), p. 33.

50 Bertrand Taithe, 'Reinventing (French) Universalism: Religion, Humanitarianism and the "French Doctors"', *Modern and Contemporary France*, 12:2 (2004), pp. 147–158.

51 Samuel Moyn, *The Last Utopia. Human Rights in History* (Cambridge, MA: Harvard University Press, 2010); Jan Eckel, 'The Rebirth of Politics from the Spirit of Morality: Explaining the Human Rights Revolution of the 1970s', in Jan Eckel and Samuel Moyn (eds), *The Breakthrough: Human Rights in the 1970s* (Philadelphia, PA: University of Pennsylvania Press, 2014), pp. 226–260.

52 P. Pradier, 'A propos d'une réunion à Bordeaux', *Bulletin Médecins sans Frontières*, 7 (April 1978), cited in Michal Givoni, 'Humanitarian Governance and Ethical Cultivation: Médecins Sans Frontières and the Advent of the Expert-Witness', *Millennium*, 40:1 (2011), p. 56.

53 Lavoinne, 'Médecins en guerre'.

54 The question of the number of victims of the repression and the war is very controversial; according to Sarmila Bose at least 50,000–100,000 people died, and every figure above this is uncertain. Sarmila Bose, *Dead Reckoning: Memories of the 1971 Bangladesh War*, (London: Hurst, 2011), p. 181.

55 On the history of East Pakistan in an international context, see Srinath Raghavan, *1971: A Global History of the Creation of Bangladesh* (Cambridge, MA: Harvard University Press, 2013).

56 Florian Hannig, 'Humanitarianism and Politics: Operation Omega's Border-Breaching Missions During the East Pakistan Crisis of 1971', in Johannes Paulmann (ed.), *Dilemmas of Humanitarian Aid in the Twentieth Century* (Oxford: Oxford University Press, 2016), pp. 329–344; see also Florian Hannig, 'The 1971 East Pakistan Crisis and the Origins of the UN's Engagement with Humanitarian Aid', in Simon Jackson and Alanna O'Malley (eds), *The Institution of International Order: From the League of Nations to the United Nations* (New York: Routledge, 2018).

57 UNHCR, *The State of World's Refugees 2000*, pp. 59–74.

58 The document (originally in French) is fully reported in William Shawcross, *The Quality of Mercy: Cambodia, Holocaust and Modern Conscience* (London: Andre Deutsch, 1984), pp. 437–438.

59 *Ibid.*; see also Peter Walker and Daniel Maxwell, *Shaping the Humanitarian World* (London: Routledge, 2009), pp. 49–51.

60 Forsythe, *The Humanitarians*, pp. 78–81.

61 According to Brian Walker (director general of Oxfam 1974–83), the core group of the

consortium was a coalition with representatives from the League of Red Cross and Red Crescent Societies and other major voluntary agencies, including Oxfam, Catholic Relief Services and the Lutheran World Federation; B. Walker, 'NGOs Break the Cold War Impasse in Cambodia', in L. Minear and H. Smith (eds), *Humanitarian Diplomacy: Practitioners and Their Craft* (Tokyo: United Nations University Press, 2007), p. 137.

62 Maggie Black, *A Cause for Our Time: Oxfam, the First 50 years* (Oxford: Oxfam and Oxford University Press, 1992), pp. 218–221.

63 *Ibid.*; see also Walker and Maxwell, *Shaping the Humanitarian World*, pp. 50–51.

64 Caroline Moorehead, 'How Disaster Gets the Intensive Care Treatment', *The Times*, 17 May 1980, p. 14.

65 Kevin O'Sullivan, 'A "Global Nervous System"', pp. 210–211.

66 Shawcross, *Quality of Mercy*, pp. 253–281. According to Fabrice Weissman, 'there wasn't actually a famine [in Cambodia] – not because the government distributed the aid that reached them, but because there was not widespread food shortage'. Fabrice Weissman, 'Silence Heals … From the Cold War to the War on Terror, MSF Speaks Out: A Brief History', in C. Magone, M. Neuman and F. Weissman (eds), *Humanitarian Negotiations Revealed: The MSF Experience* (London: Hurst & Company, 2011), p. 180.

67 Rony Brauman, *Penser dans l'urgence: Parcours critique d'un humanitaire. Entretiens avec Catherine Portevin* (Paris: Éditions du Seuil, 2006), p. 94.

68 These terms were used by Claude Malhuret, who was elected president of MSF in 1978 and remained in office for eight years; cited in Vallaeys, *Médecins sans Frontières*, p. 246.

69 Peter Gatrell, *The Making of the Modern Refugee* (Oxford: Oxford University Press, 2013), pp. 208–210.

70 UNHCR, *The State of World's Refugees 2000*, pp. 81–91.

71 See in particular the story of the German rescue ship *Cap Anamur*: Patrick Merziger, 'The "Radical Humanism" of "Cap Anamur" / "German Emergency Doctors" in the 1980s: A Turning Point for the Idea, Practice and Policy of Humanitarian Aid', *European Review of History: Revue européenne d'histoire*, 23:1–2 (2016), pp. 171–192; Michael Vössig, 'Competition over Aid? The German Red Cross, the Committee Cap Anamur, and the Rescue of Boat People in South-East Asia, 1979–1982', in Johannes Paulman (ed.), *Dilemmas of Humanitarian Aid in the Twentieth Century* (Oxford: Oxford University Press, 2016), pp. 345–370.

72 Weissman, 'Silence Heals…', p. 178; Davey, *Idealism Beyond Borders*, pp. 195–200.

73 Weissman, 'Silence Heals…', pp. 180–181.

74 Davey, *Idealism Beyond Borders*, pp. 203–207.

75 Gatrell, *The Making of the Modern Refugee*, pp. 214–215.

76 UNHCR, *The State of World's Refugees 2000*, p. 93.

77 Bertrand Taithe, 'The Cradle of the New Humanitarian System? International Work and European Volunteers at the Cambodian Border Camps, 1979–1993', *Contemporary European History*, 25:2 (2016), pp. 335–358.

78 UNHCR, *The State of World's Refugees 2000*, p. 95.

79 On the resettlement in the United States see Aihwa Ong, *Buddha Is Hiding: Refugees, Citizenship, the New America* (Berkeley, CA: University of California Press, 2003); Sucheng Chan, *Survivors: Cambodian Refugees in the United States* (Urbana, IL: University of Illinois Press, 2004).

80 Gatrell, *The Making of the Modern Refugee*, pp. 214–215.

81 Fiona Terry, *Condemned to Repeat? The Paradox of Humanitarian Action* (Ithaca, NY: Cornell University Press, 2002), pp. 128–134.

82　Linda Mason and Roger Brown, *Rice, Rivalry, and Politics: Managing Cambodian Relief* (Notre Dame, IN: University of Notre Dame Press, 1983), p. 69.

83　*Ibid.*, p. 140.

84　Shawcross, *The Quality of Mercy*, pp. 328–354.

85　Gatrell, *The Making of the Modern Refugee*, p. 214.

86　Courtland Robinson, 'Refugee-Warriors at the Thai–Cambodian Border', *Refugee Survey Quarterly*, 19:1 (2000), pp. 23–37.

87　Eduard Bakis, 'D.P. Apathy', in H. Murphy and B. Megget (eds), *Flight and Resettlement* (Lucerne: UNESCO, 1955), pp. 80–91.

88　Taithe, 'The Cradle of the New Humanitarian System?'

89　Cited in Peter Gill, *A Year in the Death of Africa: Politics, Bureaucracy and the Famine* (London: Paladin Grafton Books, 1986), p. 27.

90　Alex de Waal, *Famine Crimes: Politics and the Disaster Relief Industry in Africa* (Oxford: James Currey, 1997), pp. 106–108.

91　Human Rights Watch, *Evil Days: 30 Years of War and Famine in Ethiopia* (New York: Human Rights Watch, 1991), pp. 131–144; de Waal, *Famine Crimes*, pp. 112–121.

92　Edward Kissi, 'Beneath International Famine Relief in Ethiopia: The United States, Ethiopia, and the Debate over Relief Aid, Development Assistance, and Human Rights', *African Studies Review*, 48:2 (2005), pp. 111–132.

93　Suzanne Franks, *Reporting Disasters: Famine, Aid, Politics and the Media* (London: Hurst & Company, 2013), pp. 11–40.

94　*Ibid.*, pp. 43–46.

95　Bob Geldof with Paul Vallely, *Is That It?* (London: Sidgwick & Jackson, 1986).

96　Keith Tester, *Humanitarianism and Modern Culture* (University Park, PA: Pennsylvania State University Press, 2010), pp. 1–34; Andrew Jones, 'Band Aid Revisited: Humanitarianism, Consumption and Philanthropy in the 1980s', *Contemporary British History*, 31:2 (2017), pp. 189–209.

97　Jones, 'Band Aid Revisited'.

98　See p. 28.

99　See p. 156.

100　Jones, 'Band Aid Revisited'; Ilan Kapoor, *Celebrity Humanitarianism: The Ideology of Global Charity* (Oxon: Routledge, 2013), pp. 12–46.

101　Tester, *Humanitarianism and Modern Culture*.

102　Kurt Jansson, 'The Emergency Relief Operation', in K. Jansson, M. Harris and A. Penrose, *The Ethiopian Famine* (London: Zed Books, 1990 [1st edition 1987]), p. 45.

103　*Ibid.*, pp. 22–23.

104　USAID, *Final Disaster Report: Ethiopia Draught/Famine. Fiscal Year 1985–1986*, (Addis Ababa: USAID, May 1987), p. iii.

105　Kissi, 'Beneath International Famine Relief in Ethiopia'.

106　*Ibid.*, p. 123.

107　See in particular pp. 88–93.

108　Relief and Rehabilitation Committee, *The Challenges of Drought: Ethiopia's Decade of Struggle in Relief and Rehabilitation* (Addis Ababa, 1985), p. 180, cited in Human Rights Watch, *Evil Days*, p. 211.

109　Alula Pankhurst, *Resettlement and Famine in Ethiopia: The Villagers' Experience* (Manchester: Manchester University Press, 1992); Jason W. Clay, 'Ethiopian Famine and the Relief Agencies', in B. Nichols and G. Loescher (eds), *The Moral Nation: Humanitarianism and US Foreign Policy Today* (Notre Dame, IN: University of Notre Dame Press, 1999), pp. 233–277.

110 Two British organisations, Oxfam and War on Want, also took part in the relief operations across the Ethiopia–Sudan border; see Tony Waux, 'Humanitarian Involvement in Wars of Liberation in Africa in the 1980s: An Oxfam Perspective', in C. Bennett, M. Foley and H. B. Krebs (eds), *Learning from the Past to Shape the Future: Lessons from the History of Humanitarian Action in Africa*, ODI Humanitarian Policy Group Working Paper, October 2016, pp. 61–69, at https://www.odi.org/sites/odi.org.uk/files/resource-documents/11148.pdf (accessed November 2018).

111 Ondine Barrow, 'International Responses to Famine in Ethiopia, 1983–1985', in O. Barrow and M. Jennings (eds), *The Charitable Impulse: NGOs and Development in East and Northeast Africa* (Oxford: James Currey, 2001), pp. 63–80; Gayle Smith, 'Ethiopia and the Politics of Famine Relief', *MERIP Middle East Report*, 145 (1987), pp. 31–37.

112 Jansson, 'The Emergency Relief Operation', p. 23.

113 Paul Vallely, 'Armed Food Convoys Promised for Rebel Areas', *The Times*, 2 February 1985, p. 5.

114 USAID, *Final Disaster Report*, p. 9; Smith, 'Ethiopia and the Politics of Famine Relief', p. 36.

115 Smith, 'Ethiopia and the Politics of Famine Relief'.

116 Human Rights Watch, *Evil Days*, pp. 223–225.

117 Weissman, 'Silence Heals…', p. 182.

118 Cited in Vallaeys, *Médecins sans Frontières*, p. 532.

119 Rony Brauman in Pierre Haski, 'Pendant ce temps en Ethiopie', *Libération*, 15 July 1985, cited in Davey, *Idealism Beyond Borders*, p. 230.

120 Jansson, 'The Emergency Relief Operation', p. 25.

121 Brauman, *Penser dans l'urgence*, p. 131.

Epilogue: a 'new humanitarianism'?

In late 1986, when most of the humanitarian organisations left Ethiopia because the food crisis seemed to have been overcome, the spotlights on the Horn of Africa were switched off. Ethiopia received media attention again only in 1991, when Eritrea became an independent state and Menghistu was overthrown by armed forces. These events were the consequence of the country's internal but also external dynamics. Indeed, in the space of a few years the international picture had profoundly altered. In 1990, after the revolutionary wave that had overturned the eastern European regimes and led to the collapse of the Berlin Wall, the Soviet Union broke off sending any sort of aid to Ethiopia. When the anti-Menghistu troops, brought together in the Ethiopian People's Revolutionary Democratic Front, marched on Addis Ababa the Soviet Union did not intervene.

The end of the Cold War not only modified the political context in which the famine had developed – the famine that had led to the largest ever mobilisation in the history of humanitarianism – but it also so deeply influenced the structure of international aid as a whole that historians have generally followed the interpretation put forward by political scientists and international relations scholars that its end was an epoch-defining event.[1]

I myself have considered it to be so and in this volume I have wanted to reconstruct the events and processes that preceded it. In the concluding pages of my work, however, I would like to take into consideration certain elements that are now seen as forming part of the news from the start of the 1990s. My intention is not so much to show how radical the change was that took place after the end of the Cold War but to reiterate the usefulness of a long-term view, as it may offer important keys to interpreting and then understanding present times.

Many observers think that the emergence of a 'new humanitarianism' is primarily due to the arrival, after 1989, of the so-called humanitarian interventions. In the Introduction to this volume, which opened with the war in Kosovo, we recalled the main effects of this type of military initiative. The literature on international aid has underlined, on the one hand, that one part of the humanitarian world (from the UN agencies to some NGOs) supported the 'inter-ventionism' of the Western governments; on the other hand, it has highlighted that the relief organisations as a whole increased their volume of work and gained greater visibility in the context of the first Gulf War (1990–91) and the post-war context.[2] This happened also because of the military forces which offered the humanitarians the necessary protection and built up a collaborative relation-ship with them.[3] In other words, over the last quarter of a century the various central players in the assistance of war victims have acquired growing weight but this has coincided with the progressive strengthening of the intertwining of humanitarianism with warfare.[4] Some studies, however, do not see these trans-formations only as a consequence of humanitarian interventions, and consider that it was more generally the different nature of the conflicts following the end of the opposition between the two blocs that altered the constituent natures of the regime for international aid: the emergence of a 'new humanitarianism' was therefore closely connected to that of the 'new wars'.[5]

In this interpretation, the elements that characterised the 'new wars' also shaped the new forms of relief. The flare-ups of ethnic and intercommunal conflicts, the resort to violence by state and non-state actors, the emergence of a decentralised war economy, largely based on illicit trafficking and predatory practices: all of this generated the 'complex emergencies' that represented a new type of challenge for the humanitarian world.[6] Characterised by 'extensive violence and loss of life; massive displacements of people; widespread damage to societies and economies', the complex emergencies require 'large scale, multi-faceted humanitarian assistance'.[7] The identification of this need contributed to the significant growth in financial resources intended for international relief[8] – between 1990 and 2006 it increased almost fivefold.[9] The increase in financing for 'humanitarian crises' caused by armed conflicts went at the same pace as the establishment of what some observers have defined the 'tyranny of emergency', in other words the tendency to consider relief 'an immediate protective reflex' at the expense of 'a sober quest for long term solutions'.[10]

One of the main consequences of the 'tyranny of emergency' is the fact that since the early 1990s until today the public and private donors have increasingly favoured humanitarian programmes strictly conceived as such, usually put into action in war situations,[11] rather than development projects.[12] Since the streams of international money intended for relief have remained the same overall,[13] donors' preference for relief has been translated into an acceleration of the competition for resources that has made clearer 'the separation or, if you wish, the unrealized symbiosis between emergency relief assistance and sustainable development'.[14] The solution to pursue this symbiosis, which still seems a long way from being achieved, has been identified in recourse to 'the middle ground of rehabilita-tion'.[15] Exactly because it is considered 'the middle ground' between mere relief and long-term projects, rehabilitation has remained a difficult-to-define solution.

This was true, in fact, when the term first entered the institutional vocabulary of humanitarianism, in the post-Second World War period. Rehabilitation should go beyond relief (tents, food, medicines) and offer its recipients economic and social assistance without getting itself confused with reconstruction programmes. Nevertheless, the instability in the post-war contexts, the fluctuations in financing (caused at times by new crises) and the difficulties of adapting international schemes to local situations have reduced the potential for and value acknowledged for the 'rehabilitation assistance aimed at effecting a transition from fierce crisis to a viable future'.[16] Observers particularly highlighted that the 'new humanitarianism', despite having been able to count on growing resources, 'did not go far enough in addressing the long-term problem of ethnic cleansing or genocide' and has very modestly limited its own operations to immediate relief.[17]

The increase in the financial resources available for international aid, the demands imposed by the complex emergencies, the intertwining of aid and military actions – all of this also affected the various actors in the humanitarian world, who increased in number, modified their internal organisation and redefined their aims. Within the UN, humanitarian affairs took on growing significance not only because the historically established agencies in this sector (UNHCR, UNICEF, WFP) increased their volume of work but also because other agencies extended their field of action by including relief, for example the UN Educational, Scientific and Cultural Organization (UNESCO).[18] The multiplication of the programmes and the intention of responding to simultaneous emergencies with 'large scale, multifaceted humanitarian assistance' created the need for a coordination and control body and therefore in 1991 the Department of Humanitarian Affairs was set up, which was reformed into the Office for the Coordination of Humanitarian Affairs (OCHA) in 1998. The OCHA extended its coordination efforts beyond the UN system, to include the NGOs,[19] which have been of growing importance within a global relief system that has become very complex.

Most of the literature says that the central role of the NGOs was the most relevant news item to be established after the end of the Cold War: NGOs were more numerous, had grown in size and were equipped with greater expertise; they soon became one of the pivots on which the system for international relief hinged. Some believe that 'in the 1990s, NGOs effectively broke the ICRC's and the UN's monopoly on humanitarian action'.[20] It is difficult to substantiate this statement with concrete data primarily because the NGOs are an extremely heterogeneous group, not just in terms of their size but also in terms of their aims, internal structures and intervention methodologies.[21] In addition, assessing and classifying them according to their specific areas of expertise is complicated because they extended and intertwined their intervention plans: apart from relief, they included peacekeeping, the environment, the defence of basic rights and so on. The remarks on the private agencies' new relevance are to a large extent based on the analysis of their financial resources. It has been calculated that in 2001 the biggest NGOs administered between 45 and 55 per cent of all global humanitarian assistance.[22] The vast resources managed by these NGOs did not come only from voluntary donations but also from finances received for the implementation of specific projects from the UN agencies, the regional intergovernmental organisations such as the European Civil Protection and Humanitarian Aid Operations (ECHO) and national governments.[23] In the by now complex global network through which international relief moves, the NGOs as a whole have reached the point where they 'form the backbone of the delivery mechanism'[24] and are in the front line of work in the field.

Finally, according to much of the literature, the chief promoters of humanitarian action are now largely nation states; this marks a major change characterising the period following the Cold War, although there are undoubtedly also substantial elements of continuity. On the one hand, the international response to complex emergencies has seen the involvement of an increasingly larger number of states, not just from the West. In certain regional crises, for example in the Middle East and Afghanistan, donors such as China, Saudi Arabia and India have played a leading role. At the same time, most of the resources feeding the relief system have continued to come from Western countries: a genuine oligopoly has been established, of which the United States and the European Union form a primary part.[25] The widening to the non-Western context and the overall growth of the financial commitment of nation states to relief programmes may be considered the litmus test of the by now stable position acquired by humanitarian questions in the international relations system.[26] But they also reflect the long-lasting asymmetries of a humanitarian regime that has been shaped historically in close symbiosis with the power relations created by the Western countries with the rest of the world.

From my reading of the studies in 'new humanitarianism', briefly referred to here, I have the impression they intertwine a new thread in a warp that has largely stayed the same. The links between humanitarianism and warfare, the controversial relationship between relief and rehabilitation, the co-construction of humanitarian action (of its ends, its programmes and its operating methods) through the interaction of the various actors (the intergovernmental organisations, the nation states and the NGOs), the role played by relief in international relations and in the determination of the relationship between the global North and South: these elements have marked out the entire path of humanitarianism, just as we have reconstructed it over the long term. The changes following the end of the Cold War have altered their direction, intensity and set-up; humanitarianism has not become something different compared with the past – it has simply taken on a different appearance, which turns out to be more easily understood in the light of the previous path. Naturally, I do not mean that everything has remained unaltered – a claim of the sort would deny the very existence of history. Mine is above all an exhortation to not forget the potential of a long-term view, which 'enables us to see that the tensions and challenges the humanitarian enterprise faces today have been present from the start: they are not new phenomena, and approaching them as if they were makes our understanding of them incomplete, narrows the scope of analysis and limits the chances of progress'.[27]

Notes

1 Johannes Paulmann, 'Conjunctures in the History of International Humanitarian Aid During the Twentieth Century', *Humanity: An International Journal of Human Rights, Humanitarianism, and Development*, 4:2 (2013).

2 Peter Walker and Daniel Maxwell, *Shaping the Humanitarian World* (London: Routledge, 2009), pp. 60–78.

3 Mark R. Duffield, 'Risk-Management and the Fortified Aid Compound: Every-Day Life in Post-interventionary Society', *Journal of Intervention and Statebuilding*, 4:4 (2010), pp. 453–474.

4 Nils Gilman, 'Preface: Militarism and Humanitarianism', *Humanity: An International Journal of Human Rights, Humanitarianism, and Development*, 3:2 (2012), pp. 173–178.

5 Peter J. Hoffman and Thomas G. Weiss, *Humanitarianism, War and Politics: Solferino to Syria and Beyond* (London: Rowman & Littlefield, 2018).

6 David Keen, *Complex Emergencies* (Cambridge: Polity Press, 2008).

7 Office for the Coordination of Humanitarian Affairs (OCHA), *OCHA Orientation Handbook on Complex Emergencies* (OCHA, August 1999), p. 4, at https://reliefweb.int/sites/reliefweb.int/files/resources/OCHA%C2%A0ORIENTATION%20HANDBOOK.pdf (accessed November 2018).

8 James D. Fearon, 'The Rise of Emergency Relief Aid', in M. Barnett and Th. G. Weiss (eds), *Humanitarianism in Question: Politics, Power, Ethics* (Ithaca, NY: Cornell University Press, 2008), pp. 49–72.

9 Ian Smillie and Larry Minear, *Charity of Nations: Humanitarian Action in a Calculating World* (Bloomfield, CT: Kumarian Press, 2004), pp. 8–10, 195.

10 Jérôme Bindé, 'Toward an Ethic of the Future', in Arjun Appadurai (ed.), *Globalization* (Durham, NC: Duke University Press, 2001), p. 91.

11 According to Randel and German, aid allocated to natural disasters accounts for a small share of humanitarian assistance; Judith Randel and Tony German, 'Trends in Financing of Humanitarian Assistance', in J. Macrae (ed.), *The New Humanitarianism: A Review of Trends in Global Action* (London: Overseas Development Institute, 2002), pp. 19–28.

12 'In 1989 relief accounted for less than 5% of ODA [official development assistance]. By 1999 this had doubled, to 10.1% and stood at 10.5% in 2000'; Joanna Macrae, 'Analysis and Synthesis', in Joanna Macrae (ed.), *The New Humanitarianism: A Review of Trends in Global Action* (London: Overseas Development Institute, 2002), p. 11.

13 *Ibid.*

14 Jonathan Moore, 'The Humanitarian–Development Gap', *International Review of the Red Cross*, 81:833 (1999), p. 103.

15 *Ibid.*

16 *Ibid.*, p. 107.

17 Hoffman and Weiss, *Humanitarianism, War and Politics*.

18 M. Barnett and Th. G. Weiss (eds), *Humanitarianism in Question: Politics, Power, Ethics* (Ithaca, NY: Cornell University Press, 2008), p. 32.

19   Walker and Maxwell, *Shaping the Humanitarian World*, p. 99.

20   Hoffman and Weiss, *Humanitarianism, War and Politics*.

21   *Ibid.*, p. 121.

22   Barnett and Weiss, *Humanitarianism in Question*, p. 31.

23   Development Initiatives, *Global Humanitarian Assistance 2003* (London: Overseas Development Institute, 2003).

24   Walker and Maxwell, *Shaping the Humanitarian World*, p. 131.

25   Barnett and Weiss, *Humanitarianism in Question*, p. 33.

26   Adam Roberts, 'The Role of Humanitarian Issues in International Politics in the 1990s', *International Review of the Red Cross*, 81:833 (1999), pp. 24–35.

27   Humanitarian Policy Group, *Time To Let Go: Remaking Humanitarian Action for the Modern Era* (London: Overseas Development Institute, 2016), p. 23.

Bibliography

Abbé Pierre and Bernard Kouchner, *Dieu et les hommes: Dialogues et propos recueillis par Michel-Antoine Burnier* (Paris: Robert Laffont, 1993).

Abruzzo, Margaret, *Polemical Pain: Slavery, Cruelty, and the Rise of Humanitarianism* (Baltimore, MD: Johns Hopkins University Press, 2011).

Adichie, Chimamanda Ngozi, *Half of a Yellow Sun* (London: Harper Collins, 2017 [New York, 2006]).

American Red Cross Council, *Statement of Henry P. Davison, Chairman, on Behalf of the American Red Cross Council* (Washington, DC: American Red Cross, 1919).

Amrith, Sunil, *Decolonizing International Health: India and Southeast Asia, 1930–65* (London: Palgrave Macmillan, 2006).

Anderson, Dorothy, *The Balkan Volunteers* (London: Hutchinson, 1968).

Bachman, John W., *Together in Hope: 50 Years of Lutheran World Relief* (New York/Minneapolis, MN: LWR/Kirk House Publishers, 1995).

Baerwald, Paul, Letter, 10 December 1943, ldpd_leh_0031_0066, Herbert H. Lehman Papers, Special Correspondence Files, Rare Book and Manuscript Library, Columbia University Library, at http://lehman.cul.columbia.edu/ldpd_leh_0031_0066 (accessed 8 January 2019).

Bakis, Eduard, 'D.P. Apathy', in Murphy and Megget (eds), *Flight and Resettlement*.

Balakian, Peter, *Black Dog of Fate: A Memoir* (New York: Basic Books, 2009 [1st edition 1997]).

Balińska, Marta Aleksandra, 'Assistance and Not Mere Relief: The Epidemic Commission of the League of Nations, 1920–1923', in Weindling (ed.), *International Health Organizations*.

Balińska, Marta Aleksandra, *Une vie pour l'humanitaire: Ludwik Rajchman, 1881–1965* (Paris: La Découverte, 1995).

Barnett, Michael, *Empire of Humanity: A History of Humanitarianism* (Ithaca, NY: Cornell University Press, 2011).

Barnett, Michael, and Thomas G. Weiss (eds), *Humanitarianism in Question: Politics, Power, Ethics* (Ithaca, NY: Cornell University Press, 2008).

Barrow, Ondine, 'International Responses to Famine in Ethiopia, 1983–1985', in Barrow and Jennings (eds), *The Charitable Impulse*.

Barrow, Ondine, and Michael Jennings (eds), *The Charitable Impulse: NGOs and Development in East and Northeast Africa* (Oxford: James Currey, 2001).

Bartoloni, Stefania, *Italiane alla Guerra: L'assistenza ai feriti 1915–1918* (Venice: Marsilio, 2003).

Barton, Clara, *The Red Cross of the Geneva Convention: What It Is* (Washington, DC: Rufus H. Darby, Steam Power Book and Job Printer, 1878).

Barton, James L., *Story of the Near East Relief (1915–1930)* (New York: Macmillan, 1930).

Bass, Gary J., *Freedom's Battle: The Origins of Humanitarian Intervention* (New York: Alfred A. Knopf, 2008).

Bat, Jean-Pierre, *Le syndrome de Foccart: La politique française en Afrique, de 1959 à nos jours* (Paris: Gallimard, 2012).

Baughan, Emily, '"Every Citizen of Empire Implored to Save the Children!" Empire, Internationalism and the Save the Children Fund in Inter-war Britain', *Historical Research*, 86:231 (2013).

Baughan, Emily, *Saving the Children: British Humanitarianism in Europe and Africa, 1914–1945*, thesis submitted to the University of Bristol for the degree of Doctor of Philosophy, 2014.

Baughan, Emily, and Juliano Fiori, 'Save the Children, the Humanitarian Project and the Politics of Solidarity: Reviving Dorothy Buxton's Vision', *Disasters*, 39:2 (2015).

Becker, Annette, *Oubliés de la Grande Guerre: Humanitaire et culture de guerre 1914–1918. Populations occupées, déportés civils, prisonniers de guerre* (Paris: Éditions Noêsis, 1998).

Bender, Thomas (ed.), *The Antislavery Debate: Capitalism and Abolitionism as a Problem in Historical Interpretation* (Berkeley, CA: University of California Press, 1992).

Bennett, Christina, Matthew Foley and Hanna B. Krebs (eds), *Learning from the Past to Shape the Future: Lessons from the History of Humanitarian Action in Africa*, ODI Humanitarian Policy Group Working Paper, October 2016, at https://www.odi.org/sites/odi.org.uk/files/resource-documents/11148.pdf (accessed November 2018).

Benthall, Jonathan, 'Relief', in Akira Iriye and Pierre-Yves Saunier (eds), *The Palgrave Dictionary of Transnational History* (New York: Palgrave Macmillan, 2009).

Bergland, Betty Ann, 'Settler Colonists, "Christian Citizenship" and the Women's Missionary Federation at the Bethany Indian Mission in Wittenberg, Wisconsin, 1884–1934', in B. Reeves-Ellington, K. K. Sklar and C. A. Shemo (eds), *Competing Kingdoms: Women, Mission, Nation, and the American Protestant Empire, 1812–1960* (Durham, NC: Duke University Press, 2010).

Best, Geoffrey, *Humanity in Warfare: The Modern History of the International Law of Armed Conflict* (London: Methuen, 1983).

Bettati, Mario, *Le devoir d'ingérence* (Paris: Denoël, 1987).

Bettati, Mario, *Le droit d'ingérence: mutation de l'ordre international* (Paris: Éditions Odile Jacob, 1996).

Bindé, Jérôme, 'Toward an Ethic of the Future', in A. Appadurai (ed.), *Globalization* (Durham, NC: Duke University Press, 2001).

Black, Maggie, *A Cause for Our Time: Oxfam, the First 50 years* (Oxford: Oxfam and Oxford University Press, 1992).

Black, Maggie, *Children First: The Story of UNICEF, Past and Present* (New York: Oxford University Press, 1996).

Blackburn, Robin, *The American Crucible: Slavery, Emancipation and Human Rights* (London: Verso, 2011).

Blackburn, Robin, *The Overthrow of Colonial Slavery 1776–1848* (London: Verso, 1988).

Blackett, Richard J. M., *Building an Antislavery Wall: Black Americans in the Atlantic Abolitionist Movement 1830–1860* (Baton Rouge, LA: Louisiana State University Press, 1983).

Bocking-Welch, Anna, 'Imperial Legacies and Internationalist Discourses: British Involvement in the United Nations Freedom from Hunger Campaign, 1960–70', *Journal of Imperial and Commonwealth History*, 40:5 (2013).

Bocking-Welch, Anna, 'Youth Against Hunger: Service, Activism and the Mobilisation in 1960s Britain', *European Review of History*, 23:1–2 (2016).

Boissier, Pierre, 'Henry Dunant', *International Review of the Red Cross*, 14:161 (1974).

Bon Tempo, Carl J., *Americans at the Gate: The United States and Refugees During the Cold War* (Princeton, NJ: Princeton University Press, 2008).

Borgwardt, Elizabeth, *A New Deal for the World: America's Vision for Human Rights* (Cambridge, MA: Belknap Press of Harvard University Press, 2005).

Bose, Sarmila, *Dead Reckoning: Memories of the 1971 Bangladesh War* (London: Hurst, 2011).

Brauman, Rony, *Penser dans l'urgence: Parcours critique d'un humanitaire. Entretiens avec Catherine Portevin* (Paris: Éditions du Seuil, 2006).

Brönte, Charlotte, *Jane Eyre* (Oxford: Oxford University Press, 1993 [first edition 1847]).

Brown, Christopher Leslie, *Moral Capital: Foundations of British Abolitionism* (Chapel Hill, NC: University of North Carolina Press, 2006).

Bugnion, François, *Le Comité International de la Croix-Rouge et la protection des victimes de la guerre* (Geneva: CICR, 1994).

Bunch, Matthew James, *All Roads Lead to Rome: Canada, the Freedom from Hunger Campaign, and the Rise of NGOs, 1960–1980*, thesis submitted to the University of Waterloo, Ontario, for the degree of Doctor of Philosophy, 2007.

Buxton, Dorothy F., and Edward Fuller, *The White Flame: The Story of the Save the Children Fund* (London: Longmans, Green and Co., 1931).

Cabanes, Bruno, *The Great War and the Origins of Humanitarianism (1914–1918)* (New York: Oxford University Press, 2014).

Cahen, Fabrice, 'Le Comité International de la Croix-Rouge (CICR) et les Visites de Camps. Étude d'une Controverse', *Revue d'Histoire de la Shoah*, 172 (2001).

Chan, Sucheng, *Survivors: Cambodian Refugees in the United States* (Urbana, IL: University of Illinois Press, 2004).

Chaplin, Joyce E., 'Slavery and the Principle of Humanity: A Modern Idea in the Early Lower South', *Journal of Social History*, 24:2 (1990).

Clark, Bruce, *Twice a Stranger: How Mass Expulsion Forged Modern Greece and Turkey* (Cambridge, MA: Harvard University Press, 2006).

Clay, Jason W., 'Ethiopian Famine and the Relief Agencies', in Nichols and Loescher (eds), *The Moral Nation*.

Cleall, Esme, *Missionary Discourses of Difference: Negotiating Otherness in the British Empire, 1840–1900* (London: Palgrave Macmillan, 2012).

Cohen, Daniel G., 'Elusive Neutrality: Christian Humanitarianism and the Question of Palestine, 1948–1967', *Humanity: An International Journal of Human Rights, Humanitarianism, and Development*, 5:2 (2014).

Cohen, Daniel G., *In War's Wake: Europe's Displaced Persons in Postwar Order* (New York: Oxford University Press, 2012).

Conklin, Alice L., *A Mission to Civilize: The Republican Idea of Empire in France and West Africa, 1895–1930* (Stanford, CA: Stanford University Press, 1997).

Conklin, Alice L., 'Colonialism and Human Rights, a Contradiction in Terms? The Case of France and West Africa, 1895–1914', *American Historical Review*, 103:2 (1998).

Cook, Edward Tyas, *The Life of Florence Nightingale* (London: Macmillan, 1913).

Cooper, Frederick, *Decolonization and African Society: The Labor Question in French and British Africa* (Cambridge: Cambridge University Press, 1996).

Cooper, Frederick, 'Development, Modernization, and the Social Sciences in the Era of Decolonization: The Examples of British and French Africa' [2004], in M. Jerónimo and

A. Costa Pinto (eds), *The Ends of European Colonial Empires: Cases and Comparisons* (Basingstoke: Palgrave Macmillan, 2015).

Cooper, Frederick, 'Writing the History of Development', *Journal of Modern European History*, 8:1 (2010).

Coudreau, Marin, 'Le Comité International de Secours à la Russie, l'action Nansen e le Bolcheviks (1921–1924)', *Relations Internationales*, 151 (2012/13).

Coursier, Henri, *La Croix-Rouge Internationale* (Paris: Press Universitaires de France, 1959).

Cullather, Nick, 'The Foreign Policy of the Calorie', *American Historical Review*, 112:2 (2007).

Cullather, Nick, *The Hungry World: America's Cold War Battle Against Poverty in Asia* (Cambridge, MA: Harvard University Press, 2010).

Curti, Merle E., *American Philanthropy Abroad: A History* (New Brunswick: Rutgers University Press, 1963).

Daughton, James P., 'Behind the Imperial Curtain: International Humanitarian Efforts and the Critique of French Colonialism in the Interwar Years', *French Historical Studies*, 34:3 (2011).

Daughton, James P., 'ILO Expertise and Colonial Violence in Interwar Years', in Sandrine Kott and Joëlle Droux (eds), *Globalizing Social Rights: The International Labour Organization and Beyond* (Basingstoke: Palgrave Macmillan, 2013).

Davey, Eleonor, *Idealism Beyond Borders: The French Revolutionary Left and the Rise of Humanitarianism, 1954–1988* (Cambridge: Cambridge University Press, 2015).

David, Huw T., 'Transnational Advocacy in the Eighteenth Century: Transatlantic Activism and the Antislavery Movement', *Global Networks: A Journal of Transnational Affairs*, 7:3 (2007).

Davies, Thomas, *NGOs: A New History of Transnational Civil Society* (London: Hurst, 2013).

Davis, Adam J., and Bertrand Taithe, 'From the Purse and the Heart: Exploring Charity, Humanitarianism, and Human Rights in France', *French Historical Studies*, 34:3 (2011).

Davis, David Brion, *The Problem of Slavery in Western Culture* (Ithaca, NY: Cornell University Press, 1966).

de Waal, Alex, *Famine Crimes: Politics and the Disaster Relief Industry in Africa* (Oxford: James Currey, 1997).

Deirdre, David, *Rule Britannia: Women, Empire and Victorian Writing* (Ithaca, NY: Cornell University Press, 1995).

Deldique, Pierre-Edouard, and Catherine Ninin, *Globe doctors: 20 ans d'aventure humanitaire* (Paris: Belfond, 1991).

Desgrandchamps, Marie-Luce, *L'humanitaire en guerre civile. La crise du Biafra (1967–1970)* (Rennes: PUR, 2018).

Desgrandchamps, Marie-Luce, '"Organiser à l'avance imprévisible": la guerre Nigéria-Biafra et son impact sur le CICR', *Revue Internationale de la Croix Rouge*, 94:4 (2012).

Desgrandchamps, Marie-Luce, 'Revenir sur le mythe fondateur de Médecins sans frontières: Les relations entre médecins français et le CICR pendant la guerre du Biafra (1967–1970)', *Relations internationales*, 146 (2011).

Development Initiatives, *Global Humanitarian Assistance 2003* (London: Overseas Development Institute, 2003).

Di Blase, Antonietta, and Sergio Marchisio, *L'Organisation des Nations Unies pour l'Alimentation et l'Agriculture (FAO)* (Geneva: Institut Universitaire de Hautes Études Internationales, 1986).

Doron, Roy, 'Marketing Genocide: Biafran Propaganda Strategies During the Nigerian Civil War 1967–1970', *Journal of Genocide Research*, 16:2–3 (2014).

Dos Passos, John, *1919* (New York: Library of America, 1932).

Drescher, Seymour, *Abolition: A History of Slavery and Antislavery* (Cambridge: Cambridge University Press, 2009).

Drescher, Seymour, 'British Way, French Way: Opinion Building and Revolution in the Second French Slave Emancipation', *American Historical Review*, 96:3 (1991).

Drescher, Seymour, *Capitalism and Antislavery: British Mobilization in Comparative Perspective* (London: Macmillan, 1986).

Droux, Joëlle, 'Life During Wartime: The Save the Children International Union and the Dilemmas of Warfare Relief, 1919–1947', in Paulmann (ed.), *Dilemmas of Humanitarian Aid*.

Droux, Joëlle, 'L'internationalisation de la protection de l'enfance: acteurs, concurrences et projets transnationaux (1900–1925)', *Critique internationale*, 3 (2011).

Dubin, Martin David, 'The League of Nations Health Organisation', in Weindling (ed.), *International Health Organisations*.

Duffield, Mark R., 'Risk-Management and the Fortified Aid Compound: Every-Day Life in Post-interventionary Society', *Journal of Intervention and Statebuilding*, 4:4 (2010).

Duffy, John, *The Sanitarians: A History of American Public Health* (Urbana, IL: University of Illinois Press, 1990).

Dulles, Foster Rhea, *The American Red Cross: A History* (New York: Harper & Brothers, 1950).

Dunant, Henry, *A Memory of Solferino* (Geneva: ICRC, 2013 [reprint of the 1939 edition by the American Red Cross]).

Dynes, Russell R., 'The Lisbon Earthquake of 1755: The First Modern Disaster', in Th. E. D. Braun and J. B. Radner (eds), *The Lisbon Earthquake of 1755: Representations and Reactions* (Oxford: Voltaire Foundation Publications, 2005).

Eckel, Jan, 'The International League for the Rights of Man, Amnesty International, and the Changing Fate of Human Rights:. Activism from the 1940s through the 1970s', *Humanity: An International Journal of Human Rights, Humanitarianism, and Development*, 4:2 (2013).

Eckel, Jan, 'The Rebirth of Politics from the Spirit of Morality: Explaining the Human Rights Revolution of the 1970s', in Eckel and Moyn (eds), *The Breakthrough*.

Eckel, Jan, and Samuel Moyn (eds), *The Breakthrough: Human Rights in the 1970s* (Philadelphia, PA: University of Pennsylvania Press, 2014).

Eden, Emily, *Up the Country: Letters from India* (London: Virago, 1983).

Egan, Eileen, *Catholic Relief Services: The Beginning Years. For the Life of the World* (New York: CRS, 1988).

Eisenhower, Dwight D., Letter, 15 November 1945, ldpd_leh_0266_0001, Herbert H. Lehman Papers, Special Correspondence Files, Rare Book and Manuscript Library, Columbia University Library, at http://lehman.cul.columbia.edu/ldpd_leh_0266_0001 (accessed 2 January 2019).

Ekbladh, David, *The Great American Mission: Modernization and the Construction of an American World Order* (Princeton, NJ: Princeton University Press, 2010).

Engh, Sunniva, 'Donors' Dilemmas: Scandinavian Aid to the Indian Family Planning Programme, 1970–80', *Social Scientist*, 30:5–6 (2002).

Engh, Sunniva, 'The Conscience of the World? Swedish and Norwegian Provision of Development Aid', *Itinerario*, 33:2 (2009).

FAO, *The State of Food and Agriculture* (Rome: FAO, 1962).

Farré, Sébastien, 'De l'économie de guerre au secours philanthropique: CARE et les enjeux de l'aide américaine dans l'Europe de l'après-guerre', *Relations internationales*, 2 (2011).

Farré, Sébastien, 'The ICRC and the Inmates of National-Socialist Concentration Camps (1942–1945)', *International Red Cross Review*, 95:888 (2012).

Fassin, Didier, *Humanitarian Reason: A Moral History of the Present* (Berkeley, CA: University of California Press, 2012).

Fassin, Didier, and Mariella Pandolfi (eds), *Contemporary States of Emergency: The Politics of Military and Humanitarian Interventions* (New York: Zone Books, 2010).

Favez, Jean-Claude, *The Red Cross and the Holocaust* (Cambridge: Cambridge University Press, 1999 [revised and updated edition of *Une Mission impossible? Le Comité International de la Croix-Rouge, les déportations e les camps de concentration nazis*, Lausanne: Éditions Payot, 1988]).

Fearon, James D., 'The Rise of Emergency Relief Aid', in Barnett and Weiss (eds), *Humanitarianism in Question*.

Fehrenbach, Heide, and Davide Rodogno (eds), *Humanitarian Photography: A History* (New York: Cambridge University Press, 2015).

Feldman, Ilana, 'Difficult Distinctions: Refugee Law, Humanitarian Practice, and Political Identification in Gaza', *Cultural Anthropology*, 22:1 (2007).

Feldman, Ilana, 'The Quaker Way: Ethical Labor and Humanitarian Relief', *American Ethnologist*, 34:4 (2007).

Feldman, Ilana, and Miriam Ticktin (eds), *In the Name of Humanity: The Government of Threat and Care* (Durham, NC: Duke University Press, 2010).

Fieldston, Sara, *Raising the World: Child Welfare in the American Century* (Cambridge, MA: Harvard University Press, 2015).

Fiering, Norman S., 'Irresistible Compassion: An Aspect of Eighteenth-Century Sympathy and Humanitarianism', *Journal of the History of Ideas*, 37:2 (1976).

Flipse, Scott, 'The Latest Casualty of War: Catholic Relief Services, Humanitarianism, and the War in Vietnam, 1967–68', *Peace and Change*, 27:2 (2002).

Forsythe, David P., *The Humanitarians: The International Committee of the Red Cross* (Cambridge: Cambridge University Press, 2005).

Fox, Fiona, 'New Humanitarianism: Does It Provide a Moral Banner for the 21st Century?', *Disasters*, 25:4 (2001).

Fox, George, *Gospel family-order, being a short discourse concerning the ordering of families, both of whites, blacks, and Indians / by G.F. (1676)* (London?, s.n., 1676).

Frank, Matthew, 'The New Morality: Victor Gollancz, "Save Europe Now" and the German Refugee Crisis, 1945–6', *Twentieth Century British History*, 17:2 (2006).

Frank, Matthew, 'Working for the Germans: British Voluntary Societies and the German Refugee Crisis, 1945–1950', *Historical Research*, 82:215 (2009).

Franks, Suzanne, *Reporting Disasters Famine, Aid, Politics and the Media* (London: Hurst & Company, 2013).

Frey, Marc, and Sönke Kunkel, 'Writing the History of Development: A Review of the Recent Literature', *Contemporary European History*, 20:2 (2011).

Frey, Marc, Sönke Kunkel and Corinna R. Unger (eds), *International Organizations and Development, 1945–1990* (Basingstoke: Palgrave Macmillan, 2014).

Frost, Mark R., 'Humanitarianism and the Overseas Aid Craze in Britain's Colonial Straits Settlements, 1879–1920', *Past and Present*, 236:1 (2017).

Fuller, Pierre, 'North China Famine Revisited: Unsung Native Relief in the Warlord Era, 1920–1921', *Modern Asian Studies*, 47:3 (2013).

Furlanetto, Valentina, *L'industria della carità: Da storie e testimonianze inedite il volto nascosto della beneficenza* (Milan: Chiarelettere, 2013).

Gallagher, Nancy, *Quakers in the Israeli–Palestinian Conflict: The Dilemmas of NGO Humanitarian Activism* (Cairo: American University in Cairo Press, 2007).

Garrett, T. S., et al., 'Civilians bombed. From the Rev. Dr. T. S. Garrett and others', *The Times*, 14 May 1968, p. 11.

Gatrell, Peter, *Free World? The Campaign to Save the World's Refugees 1956–1963* (Cambridge: Cambridge University Press, 2011).

Gatrell, Peter, *The Making of the Modern Refugee* (Oxford: Oxford University Press, 2013).

Geldof, Bob, with Paul Vallely, *Is That It?* (London: Sidgwick & Jackson, 1986).

Giesberg, Judith Ann, *Civil War Sisterhood: The US Sanitary Commission and Women's Politics in Transition* (Boston, MA: Northeastern University Press, 2000).

Gilbert, Helen, and Chris Tiffin (eds), *Burden or Benefit? Imperial Benevolence and Its Legacies* (Bloomington, IN: Indiana University Press, 2008).

Gill, Peter, *A Year in the Death of Africa: Politics, Bureaucracy and the Famine* (London: Paladin Grafton Books, 1986).

Gill, Rebecca, *Calculating Compassion: Humanity and Relief in War, Britain 1870–1914* (Manchester: Manchester University Press, 2013).

Gill, Rebecca, '"The Rational Administration of Compassion": The Origins of British Relief in War', *Le Mouvement Social*, 227:2 (2009).

Gilman, Nils, 'Preface: Militarism and Humanitarianism', *Humanity: An International Journal of Human Rights, Humanitarianism, and Development*, 3:2 (2012).

Givoni, Michal, 'Humanitarian Governance and Ethical Cultivation: Médecins Sans Frontières and the Advent of the Expert-Witness', *Millennium*, 40:1 (2011).

Goez, Nathaniel H., 'Humanitarian Issues in the Biafra Conflict', Working Paper No. 36, April 2011, at http://www.unhcr.org/3af66b8b4.html (accessed November 2018).

Gorman, Daniel, *The Emergence of International Society in the 1920s* (Cambridge: Cambridge University Press, 2012).

Granick, Jaclyn, 'Waging Relief: The Politics and Logistics of American Jewish War Relief in Europe and the Near East (1914–1918)', *First World War Studies*, 5:1 (2014).

Grant, Kevin, *A Civilised Savagery: Britain and the New Slaveries in Africa* (New York: Routledge, 2005).

Grant, Kevin, 'Trust and Self-determination: Anglo-American Ethics of Empire and International Government', in Mark Bevir and Frank Trentmann (eds), *Critiques of Capital in Modern Britain and America: Transatlantic Exchanges 1800 to the Present Day* (London: Palgrave, 2002).

Greenwood, John Ormerod, *Friends and Relief* (York: William Sessions, 1975).

Greenwood, John Ormerod, *Quaker Encounters: Friends and Relief* (York: William Sessions, 1975).

Grimshaw, Patricia, and Peter Sherlock, 'Women and Cultural Exchanges', in N. Etherington (ed.), *Missions and Empire* (Oxford: Oxford University Press, 2005).

Grossmann, Atina, 'Victims, Villains, and Survivors: Gendered Perceptions and Self-Perceptions of Jewish Displaced Persons in Occupied Postwar Germany', *Journal of the History of Sexuality*, 11:1–2 (2002).

Haggis, Jane, 'White Women and Colonialism: Towards a Non-recuperative History', in C. Midgley (ed.), *Gender and Imperialism* (Manchester: Manchester University Press, 2003).

Haines, Anna J., *Health Work in Soviet Russia* (New York: Vanguard Press, 1928).

Hall, Catherine, *Civilizing Subjects: Metropole and Colony in the Imagination 1830–1867* (Chicago, IL: University of Chicago Press, 2002).

Hall, Catherine, *Macaulay and Son: Architects of Imperial Britain* (New Haven, CT: Yale University Press, 2012).

Halttunen, Karen, 'Humanitarianism and the Pornography of Pain in Anglo-American Culture', *American Historical Review*, 100:2 (1995).

Hannig, Florian, 'Humanitarianism and Politics: Operation Omega's Border-Breaching Missions During the East Pakistan Crisis of 1971', in Paulmann (ed.), *Dilemmas of Humanitarian Aid*.

Hannig, Florian, 'The 1971 East Pakistan Crisis and the Origins of the UN's Engagement with Humanitarian Aid', in Jackson and O'Malley (eds), *The Institution of International Order*.

Harper, John Lamberton, *America and the Reconstruction of Italy, 1945–1948* (Cambridge: Cambridge University Press, 1986).

Haskell, Thomas, 'Capitalism and the Origins of the Humanitarian Sensibility', *American Historical Review*, 90:2–3 (1985).

Hathaway, James C., *The Law of Refugee Status* (Toronto: Butterworths, 1991).

Heerten, Lasse, '"A" as in Auschwitz, "B" as in Biafra: The Nigerian Civil War, Visual Narratives of Genocide, and the Fragmented Universalization of the Holocaust', in Fehrenbach and Rodogno (eds), *Humanitarian Photography*.

Heerten, Lasse, *The Biafran War and Postcolonial Humanitarianism: Spectacles of Suffering* (Cambridge: Cambridge University Press, 2017).

Heerten, Lasse, 'The Dystopia of Postcolonial Catastrophe: Self-Determination, the Biafran War of Secession, and the 1970s Human Rights Movement', in Eckel and Moyn (eds), *The Breakthrough*.

Heerten, Lasse, and A. Dirk Moses, 'The Nigeria–Biafra War: Postcolonial Conflict and the Question of Genocide', *Journal of Genocide Research*, 16:2–3 (2014).

Hemingway, Ernest, *A Farewell to Arms* (New York: Charles Scribner's Sons, 1929).

Hill, Patricia R., *The World Their Household: The American Woman's Foreign Mission Movement and Cultural Transformation, 1870–1920* (Ann Arbor, MI: University of Michigan Press, 1985).

Hilton, Matthew, Emily Baughan, Eleanor Davey, Bronwen Everill, Kevin O'Sullivan and Theila Sasson, 'History and Humanitarianism: A Conversation', *Past and Present*, 241:1 (2018), e1–e38, at https://academic.oup.com/past/article/241/1/e1/5108353 (accessed November 2018).

Hilton, Matthew, James McKay James, Nicholas Crowson and Jean-François Mouhot, *The Politics of Expertise: How NGOs Shaped Modern Britain* (Oxford: Oxford University Press, 2013).

Hodge, Joseph Morgan, *Triumph of the Expert: Agrarian Doctrines of Development and the Legacies of British Colonialism* (Athens, OH: Ohio University Press, 2007).

Hodge, Joseph Morgan, 'Writing the History of Development (Part 1: The First Wave)', *Humanity: An International Journal of Human Rights, Humanitarianism, and Development*, 6:3 (2015).

Hodge, Joseph Morgan, 'Writing the History of Development (Part 2: Longer, Deeper, Wider)', *Humanity: An International Journal of Human Rights, Humanitarianism, and Development*, 7:1 (2016).

Hodge, Joseph M., Gerald Hödl and Martina Kopf (eds), *Developing Africa: Concepts and Practices in Twentieth-Century Colonialism* (Manchester: Manchester University Press, 2014).

Hoffman, Peter J., and Thomas G. Weiss, *Humanitarianism, War and Politics: Solferino to Syria and Beyond* (London: Rowman & Littlefield, 2018).

Hoffmann, Stefan-Ludwig, 'Human Rights and History', *Past and Present*, 232:1 (2016).

Holborn, Louise W., *L'organisation internationale pour les réfugiés: agence spécialisée des Nations Unies, 1946–1952* (Paris: Presses Universitaires de France, 1955).

Holian, Anna, *Between National Socialism and Soviet Communism: Displaced Persons in Postwar Germany* (Ann Arbor, MI: University of Michigan Press, 2011).

Hong, Young-Sun, 'The Algerian War, Third World Internationalism, and the Cold War Politics of Humanitarian Assistance', in Paulmann, *Dilemmas of Humanitarian Aid*.

Huber, Max, *The Good Samaritan: Reflections on the Gospel and Work in the Red Cross* (London: Victor Gollancz, 1945).

Human Rights Watch, *Evil Days: 30 Years of War and Famine in Ethiopia* (New York: Human Rights Watch, 1991).

Humanitarian Policy Group, *Time To Let Go: Remaking Humanitarian Action for the Modern Era* (London: Overseas Development Institute, 2016).

Hunt, Lynn, *Inventing Human Rights: A History* (New York: W. W. Norton, 2007).

Hunt, Lynn, 'The Long and the Short of the History of Human Rights', *Past and Present*, 233:1 (2016).

Hutchinson, John F., *Champions of Charity: War and the Rise of the Red Cross* (Boulder, CO: Westview Press, 1996).

Hutchinson, John F., '"Custodian of the sacred fire": The ICRC and the Postwar Reorganisation of the Red Cross', in Weindling (ed.), *International Health Organisations*.

Hutchinson, John F., 'Disasters and the International Order: Earthquakes, Humanitarians, and the Ciraolo Project', *International History Review*, 1 (2000).

Huxley, Julian, et al., *When Hostilities Cease: Papers on Relief and Reconstruction Prepared for the Fabian Society* (London: Victor Gollancz, 1943).

ICRC, 'Commemorating the Liberation of Auschwitz', 27 January 2005, at https://www.icrc. org/eng/resources/documents/statement/68zeb2.htm (accessed November 2018).

Ilercil, Burhan B., *UNICEF Programme Assistance to European Countries*, UNICEF History Series, Monograph III (Paris: UNICEF, 1986).

Inaudi, Silvia, 'Assistenza ed educazione alimentare: l'Amministrazione per gli aiuti internazionali, 1947–1965', *Contemporanea: Rivista di storia dell'800 e del '900*, 17:3 (2015).

International Commission on Intervention and State Sovereignty, *The Responsibility to Protect: Report of the International Commission on Intervention and State Sovereignty* (Ottawa: International Development Research Centre, 2001).

'International Labour Organization Since the War', *International Labour Review*, 92:2 (1953).

Irwin, Julia F., *Making the World Safe: The American Red Cross and a Nation's Humanitarian Awakening* (New York: Oxford University Press, 2013).

Irwin, Julia F., 'Nation Building and Rebuilding: The American Red Cross in Italy During the Great War', *Journal of the Gilded Age and Progressive Era*, 8:3 (2009).

Jackson, Simon, and Alanna O'Malley (eds), *The Institution of International Order: From the League of Nations to the United Nations* (New York: Routledge, 2018).

Jansson, Kurt, 'The Emergency Relief Operation', in K. Jansson, M. Harris and A. Penrose, *The Ethiopian Famine* (London: Zed Books, 1990 [1st edition 1987]).

Jebb, Eglantyne, *Cambridge: A Brief Study in Social Questions* (Cambridge: Macmillan & Bowes, 1906).

Jennings, Lawrence C., *French Anti-Slavery: The Movement for the Abolition of Slavery in France, 1802–1848* (Cambridge: Cambridge University Press, 2000).

Jones, Andrew, 'Band Aid Revisited: Humanitarianism, Consumption and Philanthropy in the 1980s', *Contemporary British History*, 31:2 (2017).

Jones, Marian Moser, *The American Red Cross from Clara Barton to the New Deal* (Baltimore, MD: Johns Hopkins University Press, 2013).

Kaplan, Cora, 'Imagining Empire: History, Fantasy and Literature', in C. Hall and Sonya O. Rose (eds), *At Home with the Empire: Metropolitan Culture and the Imperial World* (Cambridge: Cambridge University Press, 2006).

Kapoor, Ilan, *Celebrity Humanitarianism: The Ideology of Global Charity* (Oxon: Routledge, 2013).

Karatani, Rieko, 'How History Separated Refugee and Migrant Regimes: In Search of Their Institutional Origins', *International Journal of Refugee Law*, 17:3 (2005).

Käser, Frank, 'A Civilized Nation: Japan and the Red Cross, 1877–1900', *European Review of History: Revue européenne d'histoire*, 23:1–2 (2016).

Kauffman, Christopher J., 'Politics, Programs, and Protests: Catholic Relief Services in Vietnam, 1954–1975', *Catholic Historical Review*, 41:2 (2005).

Keen, David, *Complex Emergencies* (Cambridge: Polity Press, 2008).

Kennedy, David, *The Dark Sides of Virtue: Reassessing International Humanitarianism* (Princeton, NJ: Princeton University Press, 2004).

Kévonian, Dzovinar, 'L'organisation non gouvernementale. Nouvel acteur du champ humanitaire. Le Zemgor et la Société des Nations dans les années 1920', *Cahiers du monde russe*, 46:4 (2005).

Kévonian, Dzovinar, *Réfugiés et diplomatie humanitaire: Les acteurs européens et la scène proche-orientale pendant l'entre-deux-guerres* (Paris: Publications de la Sorbonne, 2004).

Kissi, Edward, 'Beneath International Famine Relief in Ethiopia: The United States, Ethiopia, and the Debate over Relief Aid, Development Assistance, and Human Rights', *African Studies Review*, 48:2 (2005).

Klose, Fabian (ed.), *The Emergence of Humanitarian Intervention: Ideas and Practice from Nineteenth Century to the Present* (Cambridge: Cambridge University Press, 2015).

Klose, Fabian, and Mirjam Thulin (eds), *Humanity: A History of European Concepts in Practice from the Sixteenth Century to the Present* (Göttingen: Vandenhoeck & Ruprecht, 2016).

Kochanski, Halik, *The Eagle Unbowed: Poland and Poles in the Second World War* (London: Allen Lane, 2012).

Kouchner, Bernard, and Mario Bettati, *Le devoir d'ingérence* (Paris: Denoël, 1987).

Kouchner, Bernard, and Max Récamier, 'De retour du Biafra, deux médecins français témoignent', *Le Monde*, 27 November 1968.

Kuhn, Konrad J., '"The credibility of our humanitarian effort is at risk": Tensions Between Solidarity and Humanitarian Aid in the Late 1960s', in Paulmann (ed.), *Dilemmas of Humanitarian Aid*.

Kushner, Tony, and Katharine Knox, *Refugees in an Age of Genocide: Global, National and Local Perspectives During the Twentieth Century* (London: Frank Cass, 1999).

'La strage nel Biafra', *La Stampa*, 10 August 1968, p. 6.

Laqua, Daniel, 'The Tensions of Internationalism: Transnational Anti-Slavery in the 1880s and 1890s', *International History Review*, 33:4 (2011).

Laqueur, Thomas, 'Bodies, Details and the Humanitarian Narrative', in Lynn Hunt (ed.), *The New Cultural History* (Berkeley, CA: University of California Press, 1989).

Laqueur, Thomas, 'Mourning, Pity and the Work of Narrative in the Making of Humanity', in R. Ashby Wilson and R. D. Brown (eds), *Humanitarianism and Suffering: The Mobilization of Empathy* (Cambridge: Cambridge University Press, 2009).

Lavoinne, Yves, 'Médecins en guerre: du témoignage au "tapage médiatique" (1968–1970)', *Le Temps des Médias*, 4 (2005).

Lester, Alan, 'Thomas Fowell Buxton and the Networks of British Humanitarianism', in Gilbert and Tiffin (eds), *Burden or Benefit?*

Lester, Alan, and David Lambert, 'Geographies of Colonial Philanthropy', *Progress in Human Geography*, 28:3 (2004).

Lester, Alan, and Fae Dussart, *Colonization and the Origins of Humanitarian Governance: Protecting Aborigines Across the Nineteenth-Century British Empire* (Cambridge: Cambridge University Press, 2014).

Lin, Yi-Tang, Thomas David and Davide Rodogno, 'Fellowship Programs for Public Health Development: The Rockefeller Foundation, UNRRA, and WHO (1920s–1970s)', in Tournès and Scott-Smith (eds), *Global Exchange*.

Little, Branden, 'An Explosion of New Endeavours: Global Humanitarian Responses to Industrialized Warfare in the First World War Era', *First World War Studies*, 5:1 (2014).

Llewellyn, Bernard, *The Poor World* (London: Zenith Books, 1967).

Loescher, Gil, *The UNHCR and World Politics: A Perilous Path* (Oxford: Oxford University Press, 2001).

Lorenzini, Sara, *Una strana guerra fredda: Lo sviluppo e le relazioni Nord–Sud* (Bologna: il Mulino, 2017).

Losh, James, and William Knibb, *Speeches of James Losh, Esq., and the Rev. William Knibb, on the Immediate Abolition of British Colonial Slavery* (Newcastle: J. Blackwell & Co., 1833).

Louchheim, Katie, 'DP Summer', *Virginia Quarterly Review*, 61:4 (1985).

Lowe, Vaughan, and Antonios Tzanakopoulos, 'Humanitarian intervention', in *Max Planck Encyclopedia of Public International Law* (2011), at http://opil.ouplaw.com/search?sfam= &q=humanitarian+intervention&prd=EPIL&searchBtn=Search (accessed 5 December 2018).

Luard, Evan, *A History of the United Nations, Vol. I: The Years of the Western Domination, 1945–1955* (London: Macmillan, 1982).

Ludi, Regula, 'More and Less Deserving Refugees: Shifting Priorities in Swiss Asylum Policy from the Interwar Era to the Hungarian Refugee Crisis of 1956', *Journal of Contemporary History*, 49:3 (2014).

Luzzatti, Luigi, 'The International Institute of Agriculture', *North America Review*, 182:594 (1906).

Macrae, Joanna, 'Analysis and Synthesis', in Macrae (ed.), *The New Humanitarianism*.

Macrae, Joanna (ed.), *The New Humanitarianism: A Review of Trends in Global Action* (London: Overseas Development Institute, 2002).

Mahood, Linda, 'Eglantyne Jebb: Remembering, Representing and Writing a Rebel Daughter', *Women's History Review*, 17:1 (2008).

Mahood, Linda, *Feminism and Voluntary Action: Eglantyne Jebb and Save the Children, 1876–1928* (London: Palgrave Macmillan, 2009).

Mahood, Linda, and Vic Satzewich, 'The Save the Children Fund and the Russian Famine of 1921–23: Claims and Counter-Claims about Feeding "Bolshevik" Children', *Journal of Historical Sociology*, 22:1 (2009).

Makita, Yoshiya, 'The Alchemy of Humanitarianism: The First World War, the Japanese Red Cross and the Creation of an International Public Health Order', *First World War Studies*, 5:1 (2014).

Manderson, Lenore, 'Wireless Wars in the Eastern Arena: Epidemiological Surveillance, Disease Prevention and the Work of the Eastern Bureau of the League of Nations Health Organisation, 1925–1942', in Weindling (ed.), *International Health Organisations*.

Marshall, Dominique, 'Humanitarian Sympathy for Children in Times of War and the History of Children's Rights, 1919–1959', in J. A. Marten (ed.), *Children and War: A Historical Anthology* (New York: New York University Press, 2002).

Mason, Linda, and Roger Brown, *Rice, Rivalry, and Politics: Managing Cambodian Relief* (Notre Dame, IN: University of Notre Dame Press, 1983).

Maul, Daniel R., 'American Quakers, the Emergence of International Humanitarianism, and the Foundation of the American Friends Service Committee, 1890–1920', in Paulmann (ed.), *Dilemmas of Humanitarian Aid*.

Maul, Daniel R., *Human Rights, Development and Decolonization: The International Labour Organization, 1940–70* (Basingstoke: Palgrave Macmillan, 2012 [first edition Essen, 2007]).

Mazlish, Bruce, *The Idea of Humanity in a Global Era* (New York: Palgrave Macmillan, 2009).

Mazower, Mark, *Governing the World: The History of an Idea, 1815 to Present* (London: Allen Lane, 2012).

Mazower, Mark, *Inside Hitler's Greece: The Experience of Occupation, 1941–1944* (New Haven, CT: Yale University Press, 1993).

Mazower, Mark, *Salonica, City of Ghosts: Christians, Muslims and Jews 1430–1950* (London: Harper Perennial, 2005).

McCleary, Rachel M., *Global Compassion: Private Voluntary Organizations and US Foreign Policy Since 1939* (New York: Oxford University Press, 2009).

McDaniel, W. Caleb, 'Abolitionism', in A. Iriye and Pierre-Yves Saunier (eds), *The Palgrave Dictionary of Transnational History* (London: Palgrave Macmillan, 2009).

McNeil, Brian, '"And starvation is the grim reaper": The American Committee to Keep Biafra Alive and Genocide Question During the Nigerian Civil War, 1968–1970', *Journal of Genocide Research*, 16:2–3 (2014).

Merziger, Patrick, 'The "Radical Humanism" of "Cap Anamur"/"German Emergency Doctors" in the 1980s: A Turning Point for the Idea, Practice and Policy of Humanitarian Aid', *European Review of History: Revue européenne d'histoire*, 23:1–2 (2016).

Metzger, Barbara, 'Towards an International Human Rights Regime During the Inter-War Years: The League of Nations' Combat of Traffic in Women and Children', in K. Grant, Ph. Levine and F. Trentmann (eds), *Beyond Sovereignty. Britain, Empire and Transnationalism, c. 1880–1950* (Basingstoke: Palgrave Macmillan, 2007).

Micheletti, Pierre, *Humanitaire, s'adapter ou renoncer* (Paris: Marabout, 2008).

Midgley, Clare, 'Slave Sugar Boycotts, Female Activism and the Domestic Base of British Anti-slavery Culture', *Slavery and Abolition: A Journal of Slave and Post-Slave Studies*, 17:3 (1996).

Midgley, Clare, *Women Against Slavery: The British Campaigns 1780–1870* (London: Routledge, 1992).

Miers, Suzanne, *Britain and the Ending of the Slave Trade* (London: Longman, 1975).

Miers, Suzanne, 'Humanitarianism at Berlin: Myth or Reality?', in S. Förster, W. J. Mommsen and R. Robinson (eds), *Bismarck, Europe and Africa: The Berlin Conference 1884–1885 and the Onset of Partition* (Oxford: Oxford University Press, 1988).

Minear, Larry, and Hazel Smith (eds), *Humanitarian Diplomacy: Practitioners and Their Craft* (Tokyo: United Nations University Press, 2007).

Moeller, Esther, 'The Suez Crisis of 1956 as a Moment of Transnational Humanitarian Engagement', *European Review of History: Revue Européenne d'Histoire*, 23:1–2 (2016).

Moore, Jonathan, 'The Humanitarian–Development Gap', *International Review of the Red Cross*, 81:833 (1999).

Moorehead, Caroline, 'How Disaster Gets the Intensive Care Treatment', *The Times*, 17 May 1980.

Moriz, Amanda B., *The Empire of Humanity: The American Revolution and the Origins of Humanitarianism* (New York: Oxford University Press, 2016).

Morris, Jennifer M., *The Origins of UNICEF, 1946–1953* (Lanham, MD: Lexington Books, 2015).

Moyn, Samuel, 'The End of Human Rights History', *Past and Present*, 233:1 (2016).

Moyn, Samuel, *The Last Utopia: Human Rights in History* (Cambridge, MA: Harvard University Press, 2010).

Moynier, Gustave, *La Croix-Rouge, son passé et son avenir* (Paris: Sandoz & Thuillier, 1882).

Moynier, Gustave, and Appia Luis, *La guerre et la charité: traité théorétique et pratique de philanthropie appliquées aux armées en campagne* (Geneva: Cherbuliez, 1867).

Mulley, Clare, *The Woman Who Saved the Children: A Biography of Eglantyne Jebb Founder of Save the Children* (Oxford: Oneworld Publications, 2009).

Murphy, Henry, and Brian Megget (eds), *Flight and Resettlement* (Lucerne: UNESCO, 1955).

Myers, Tamara, 'Local Action and Global Imagining: Youth, International Development, and the Walkathon Phenomenon in 1960s and 1970s Canada', *Diplomatic History*, 38:2 (2014).

Nash, George H., *The Life of Herbert Hoover, Vol. II: The Humanitarian 1914–1917* (New York: W. W. Norton, 1988).

National Society for Aid, *Report of the Operations of the British National Society for Aid to the Sick and Wounded in War During the Franco-Prussian War 1870–1871* (London: Harrison & Sons, 1871).

Nichols, Bruce, *The Uneasy Alliance: Religion, Refugee Work, and US Foreign Policy* (New York: Oxford University Press, 1988).

Nichols, Bruce, and Gil Loescher (eds), *The Moral Nation: Humanitarianism and US Foreign Policy Today* (Notre Dame, IN: University of Notre Dame Press, 1999)

Obiaga, Ndubisi, *The Politics of Humanitarian Organizations Interventions* (Dallas, TX: University Press of America, 2004).

Office for the Coordination of Humanitarian Affairs (OCHA), *OCHA Orientation Handbook on Complex Emergencies* (OCHA, August 1999), at https://reliefweb.int/sites/reliefweb.int/files/resources/OCHA%C2%A0ORIENTATION%20HANDBOOK.pdf (accessed November 2018).

Omaka, Arua Oko, 'Humanitarian Action: The Joint Church Aid and Health Care Intervention in the Nigeria–Biafra War, 1967–1970', *Canadian Journal of History/Annales canadiennes d'histoire*, 49:1 (2014).

Ong, Aihwa, *Buddha Is Hiding: Refugees, Citizenship, the New America* (Berkeley, CA: University of California Press, 2003).

Onyedum, Jennifer Johnson, '"Humanize the Conflict": Algerian Health Care Organizations and Propaganda Campaigns, 1954–1962', *International Journal of Middle East Studies*, 44:4 (2012).

Orr, John B., *What Science Stands For* (London: George Allen & Unwin, 1937).

O'Sullivan, Kevin, 'A "Global Nervous System": The Rise and Rise of European Humanitarian NGOs (1945–1985)', in Frey, Kunkel and Unger (eds), *International Organizations and Development*.

O'Sullivan, Kevin, 'Biafra's Legacy: NGO Humanitarianism and the Nigerian Civil War', in Bennett, Foley and Krebs (eds), *Learning from the Past to Shape the Future*.

O'Sullivan, Kevin, 'Humanitarian Encounters: Biafra, NGOs and Imaginings of the Third World in Britain and Ireland, 1967–70', *Journal of Genocide Research*, 16:2–3 (2014).

O'Sullivan, Kevin, Hilton Matthew and Fiori Juliano, 'Humanitarianisms in Context', *European Review of History*, 23:1–2 (2016).

Our correspondent, 'Biafra's Pessimism Over Food Airlift', *The Times*, 9 September 1969.

Our correspondent – Geneva, 'Four Men Killed in Biafra Relief Flight Crash', *The Times*, 9 December 1968.

Özbeck, Nadir, 'Defining the Public Sphere During the Late Ottoman Empire: War, Mass Mobilization and the Young Turk Regime (1908–1918)', *Middle Eastern Studies*, 43:5 (2007).

Packard, Randall, 'Visions of Postwar Health and Development and Their Impact on Public Health Interventions in the Developing World', in F. Cooper and R. Packard (eds), *International Development and the Social Sciences* (Berkeley, CA: University of California Press, 1997).

Palmer, Jennifer J., and Pete Kingsley, 'Controlling Sleeping Sickness Amidst Conflict and Calm: Remembering, Forgetting and the Policy of Humanitarian Knowledge in Southern Sudan, 1954–2005', in Bennett, Foley and Krebs (eds), *Learning from the Past to Shape the Future*.

Palmieri, Daniel, and Irène Herrmann, 'Two Crosses for the Same Aim? Swiss and Swedish Charitable Activities in Greece During the Second World War', in Paulmann (ed.), *Dilemmas of Humanitarian Aid*.

Pankhurst, Alula, *Resettlement and Famine in Ethiopia: The Villagers' Experience* (Manchester: Manchester University Press, 1992).

Parise, Goffredo, *Biafra* (Milan: Feltrinelli, 1968).

Patenaude, Bertrand M., *The Big Show in Bololand: The American Relief Expedition to Soviet Russia in the Famine of 1921* (Stanford, CA: Stanford University Press, 2015).

Paulmann, Johannes, 'Conjunctures in the History of International Humanitarian Aid During the Twentieth Century', *Humanity: An International Journal of Human Rights, Humanitarianism, and Development*, 4:2 (2013).

Paulmann, Johannes (ed.), *Dilemmas of Humanitarian Aid in the Twentieth Century* (Oxford: Oxford University Press, 2016).

Paulmann, Johannes, 'The Dilemmas of Humanitarian Aid: Historical Perspectives', in Paulmann, *Dilemmas of Humanitarian Aid*.

Pedersen, Susan, 'Back to the League of Nations', *American Historical Review*, 112:4 (2007).

Pedersen, Susan, *The Guardians: The League of Nations and the Crisis of Empire* (Oxford: Oxford University Press, 2015).

Peterson, Glen, 'The Uneven Development of the International Refugee Regime in Postwar Asia: Evidence from China, Hong Kong and Indonesia', *Journal of Refugee Studies*, 25:3 (2012).

Pétré-Grenouilleau, Olivier, *Les traites négrières: Essai d'histoire globale* (Paris: Éditions Gallimard, 2004).

Piana, Francesca, 'L'humanitaire d'après-guerre: prisonniers de guerre et réfugiés russes dans la politique du Comité international de la Croix-Rouge et de la Société des Nations', *Relations Internationales*, 151 (2012/13).

Piller, Elisabeth, 'German Child Distress, US Humanitarian Aid and Revisionist Politics, 1918–24', *Journal of Contemporary History*, 51:3 (2016).

Plata-Stenger, Véronique, 'New Missionaries for Social Development: The ILO Internship Program (1950–1963)', in Tournès and Scott-Smith (eds), *Global Exchange*.

Poirier, Jean-Paul, *Le tremblement de terre de Lisbonne: 1755* (Paris: Odile Jacob, 2005).

Porter, Andrew, *Religion Versus Empire? British Protestant Missionaries and Overseas Expansion, 1700–1914* (Manchester: Manchester University Press, 2004).

Porter, Andrew, 'Trusteeship, Anti-slavery, and Humanitarianism', in A. Porter (ed.), *The Oxford History of British Empire, Vol. III: The Nineteenth Century* (New York: Oxford University Press, 2001).

Porter, Stephen R., *Benevolent Empire: U.S. Power, Humanitarianism, and the World's Dispossessed* (Philadelphia, PA: University of Pennsylvania Press, 2016).

Quarenghi, Nina, *Solferino e San Martino tra realtà e memoria* (Verona: Cierre, 1999).

Raghavan, Srinath, *1971: A Global History of the Creation of Bangladesh* (Cambridge, MA: Harvard University Press, 2013).

Randel, Judith, and Tony German, 'Trends in Financing of Humanitarian Assistance', in Macrae (ed.), *The New Humanitarianism*.

Reeves, Caroline, 'Developing the Humanitarian Image in Late Nineteenth- and Early Twentieth-Century China', in Fehrenbach and Rodogno (eds), *Humanitarian Photography*.

Reeves, Caroline, 'Red Cross, Blue Express: Chinese Local Relief in an Age of Humanitarian Imperialism, Shandong 1923', in Paulman (ed.), *Dilemmas of Humanitarian Aid*.

Reinisch, Jessica, '"Auntie UNRRA" at the Crossroads', in M. Hilton and R. Mitter (eds), 'Transnationalism and Contemporary Global History', *Past and Present*, 218: suppl. 8 (2013).

Reinisch, Jessica, 'Internationalism in Relief: The Birth (and Death) of UNRRA', in M. Mazower, J. Reinisch and D. Feldman (eds), 'Post-war Reconstruction in Europe: International Perspectives, 1945–1949', *Past and Present*, 210: suppl. 6 (2011).

Reinisch, Jessica, 'Relief in the Aftermath of War', *Journal of Contemporary History*, 43:3 (2008).

Reinisch, Jessica, *The Perils of Peace: The Public Health Crisis in Occupied Germany* (Cambridge: Cambridge University Press, 2013).

Reinisch, Jessica, and Matthew Frank, 'Refugees and the Nation State in Europe, 1919–1959', *Journal of Contemporary History*, 49:3 (2014).

Renzo, Chiara, *'Where Shall I Go?' The Jewish Displaced Persons in Italy (1943–1951)*, thesis submitted to the University of Florence and the University of Siena for the degree of Doctor of Philosophy, 2017.

Report of the Interim Commission to the First World Health Assembly, Part 1: Activities, Official Records of the World Health Organization, No. 9 (New York, 1948).

Rey-Schyrr, Catherine, 'Le CICR et l'assistance aux réfugiés arabes palestinens (1948–1950)', *Revue international de la Croix-Rouge*, 83:843 (2001).

Ribi Forclaz, Amalia, *Humanitarian Imperialism: The Politics of Anti-Slavery Activism, 1880–1940* (Oxford: Oxford University Press, 2015).

Ricoeur, Paul, 'Remarques d'un philosophe', in Institut d'Histoire du Temps Present, *Ecrire l'histoire du temps présent: En hommage à François Bédarida* (Paris: CNRS Editions, 1992).

Rieff, David, *A Bed for the Night: Humanitarianism in Crisis* (New York: Simon & Shuster, 2002).

Roberts, Adam, 'The Role of Humanitarian Issues in International Politics in the 1990s', *International Review of the Red Cross*, 81:833 (1999).

Roberts, M. J. D., *Making English Morals: Voluntary Association and Moral Reform in England, 1787–1886* (Cambridge: Cambridge University Press, 2004).

Roberts, Siân, *Place, Life Histories and the Politics of Relief: Episodes in the Life of Francesca Wilson, Humanitarian Educator Activist*, thesis submitted to the University of Birmingham for the degree of Doctor of Philosophy, 2010.

Robertson, Stacey M., 'Marketing Social Justice: Lessons from Our Abolitionist Predecessors', *Moving the Social: Journal of Social History and the History of Social Movements*, 57 (2017).

Robinson, Courtland, 'Refugee-Warriors at the Thai–Cambodian Border', *Refugee Survey Quarterly*, 19:1 (2000).

Rodogno, Davide, *Against Massacre: Humanitarian Interventions in the Ottoman Empire, 1815–1914* (Princeton, NJ: Princeton University Press, 2011).

Rodogno, Davide, 'Non-state Actors' Humanitarian Operations in the Aftermath of the First World War: The Case of the Near East Relief', in Klose (ed.), *The Emergence of Humanitarian Intervention*.

Rodogno, Davide, and David Thomas, 'All the World Loves a Picture: The World Health Organization's Visual Politics, 1948–1973', in Fehrenbach and Rodogno (eds), *Humanitarian Photography*.

Roosevelt, Franklin Delano, 'Address of the President of the United States', *United Nations Relief and Rehabilitation Organization. Journal*, 1 (10 November–2 December 1943).

Roosevelt, Franklin Delano, Letter, 3 November 1944, ldpd_leh_0784_0391, Herbert H. Lehman Papers, Special Correspondence Files, Rare Book and Manuscript Library, Columbia University Library, at http://lehman.cul.columbia.edu/ldpd_leh_0784_0391 (accessed 2 January 2019).

Rosenberg, Emily, 'Missions to the World: Philanthropy Abroad', in L. J. Friedman and M. D. McGarvie (eds), *Charity, Philanthropy, and Civility in American History* (Cambridge: Cambridge University Press, 2003).

Rufin, Jean-Christophe, *Le piège: Quand l'aide humanitaire remplace la guerre* (Paris: Lattès, 1986).

Rupp, Leila J., *Worlds of Women: The Making of an International Women's Movement* (Princeton, NJ: Princeton University Press, 1997).

Salomon, Kim, *Refugees in the Cold War: Toward a New International Refugee Regime in the Early Postwar Era* (Lund: Lund University Press, 1991).

Salvatici, Silvia, 'Between National and International Mandates: DPs and Refugees in Post-war Italy', *Journal of Contemporary History*, 49:3 (2014).

Salvatici, Silvia, '"Fighters without guns": Humanitarianism and Military Action in the Aftermath of the Second World War', *European Review of History: Revue Européenne d'Histoire*, 25:6 (2018).

Salvatici, Silvia, 'Professionals of Humanitarianism: UNRRA Relief Officers in Post-war Europe', in Paulmann (ed.), *Dilemmas of Humanitarian Aid*.

Salvatici, Silvia, 'Sights of Benevolence: UNRRA's Recipients Portrayed', in Fehrenbech and Rodogno (eds), *Humanitarian Photography*.

Sasson, Tehila, 'From Empire to Humanity: The Russian Famine and the Imperial Origins of International Humanitarianism', *Journal of British Studies*, 55:3 (2016).

Sayward, Amy L., *The United Nations in International History* (London: Bloomsbury, 2017).

Schloms, Michael, 'Le dilemme inévitable de l'action humanitaire', *Cultures et Conflits*, 60 (2005).

Schulz, Matthias, 'Dilemmas of "Geneva" Humanitarian Internationalism: The International Committee of Red Cross and the Red Cross Movement, 1863–1918', in Paulmann (ed.), *Dilemmas of Humanitarian Aid*.

Sen, Binay R., *Towards a Newer World* (Dublin: Tycooly International Publishing, 1982).

Shankar, Shobana, 'Blurring Relief and Development: Religious and Secular Politics of International Humanitarian Intervention During Decolonization in Sub-Saharan Africa', in Paulmann (ed.), *Dilemmas of Humanitarian Aid*.

Sharma, Sanjay, *Famine, Philanthropy and the Colonial State: North India in the Early Nineteenth Century* (New York: Oxford University Press, 2001).

Shaw, D. John, *The World's Largest Humanitarian Agency: The Transformation of the UN World Food Programme and of Food Aid* (London: Palgrave Macmillan, 2011).

Shawcross, William, *The Quality of Mercy: Cambodia, Holocaust and Modern Conscience* (London: Andre Deutsch, 1984).

Sheffer, Talia, 'Taming the Tropics: Charlotte Yonge Takes on Melanesia', *Victorian Studies*, 47:2 (2005).

Shemmassian, Vahram L., 'The League of Nations and the Reclamation of Armenian Genocide Survivors', in R. G. Hovannisian (ed.), *Looking Backward, Moving Forward: Confronting the Armenian Genocide* (New Brunswick: Transaction, 2003).

Simms, Brendan, and Trim, D. J. B. (eds), *Humanitarian Intervention: A History* (Cambridge: Cambridge University Press, 2011).

Simpson, John Hope, *The Refugee Problem: Report of a Survey* (London: Oxford University Press, 1939).

Sjöberg, Tommie, *The Powers and the Persecuted: The Refugee Problem and the Intergovernmental Committee on Refugees (IGCR), 1938–1947* (Lund: Lund University Press, 1991).

Sklar, Kathryn Kish, and James Brewer Stewart (eds), *Women's Rights and Transatlantic Anti-slavery in the Era of Emancipation* (New Haven, CT: Yale University Press, 2007).

Skran, Claudena M., 'Profile of the First Two High Commissioners', *Journal of Refugee Studies*, 1:3–4 (1988).

Skran, Claudena M., *Refugees in Inter-war Europe: The Emergence of a Regime* (Oxford: Oxford University Press, 1995).

Smillie, Ian, and Larry Minear, *Charity of Nations: Humanitarian Action in a Calculating World* (Bloomfield, CT: Kumarian Press, 2004).

Smith, Gayle, 'Ethiopia and the Politics of Famine Relief', *MERIP Middle East Report*, 145 (1987).

Smith, Karen E., 'The UK and Genocide in Biafra', *Journal of Genocide Research*, 16:2–3 (2014).

Snowden, Frank M., 'Latina Province, 1945–50', *Journal of Contemporary History*, 43:3 (2008).

Society for the Promotion of Female Education in the East, *History of the Society for the Promotion of Female Education in the East* (London: Edward Suter, 1847).

Staderini, Chiara, *La Croce Rossa Italiana fra dimensione associativa e riconoscimento istituzionale* (Florence: Noccioli Editore, 1995).

Staples, Amy L. S., *The Birth of Development: How the World Bank, Food and Agriculture Organization, and World Health Organization Changed the World, 1945–1965* (Kent, OH: Kent State University Press, 2006).

Steiner, Zara, *The Lights That Failed: European International History, 1919–1933* (Oxford: Oxford University Press, 2005);

Steinert, Johannes-Dieter, 'Food and the Food Crisis in Post-War Germany, 1945–1948: British Policy and the Role of British NGOs', in F. Just and F. Trentmann (eds), *Food and Conflict in Europe in the Age of the Two World Wars* (Basingstoke: Palgrave Macmillan, 2006).

Stepan, Nancy Leys, *Eradication: Ridding the World of Diseases Forever* (London: Reaktion Books, 2011).

Steuer, Kenneth, *Pursuit of an 'Unparalleled Opportunity': The American YMCA and Prisoner-of-War Diplomacy Among the Central Power Nations During World War I, 1914–1923*, Gutenberg-e Series (New York: Columbia University Press, 2009).

Stillé, Charles J., *History of the Sanitary Commission Being the General Report of Its Work During the War of the Rebellion* (Philadelphia, PA: J. B. Lippincott, 1866).

Stoessinger, John G., *The Refugee and the World Community* (Minneapolis, MN: University of Minneapolis Press, 1956).

Stornig, Katharina, 'Between Christian Solidarity and Human Solidarity: Humanity and the

Mobilisation of Aid for Distant Children in Catholic Europe in the Long Nineteenth Century', in Klose and Thulin (eds), *Humanity*.

Sussman, Charlotte, *Consuming Anxieties: Consumer Protest, Gender and British Slavery, 1713–1833* (Stanford, CA: Stanford University Press, 2000)

Taft, William H., and Frederick Morgan Harris, *Service with Fighting Men: An Account of the Work of the American Young Men's Christian Association in the World War* (New York: Association Press, 1922).

Taithe, Bertrand, *Defeated Flesh: Welfare, Warfare and the Makings of Modern France* (Manchester: Manchester University Press, 1999).

Taithe, Bertrand, 'Reinventing (French) Universalism: Religion, Humanitarianism and the "French Doctors"', *Modern and Contemporary France*, 12:2 (2004).

Taithe, Bertrand, 'The Cradle of the New Humanitarian System? International Work and European Volunteers at the Cambodian Border Camps, 1979–1993', *Contemporary European History*, 25:2 (2016).

Taithe, Bertrand, 'The "Making" of the Origins of Humanitarianism?', *Contemporanea: Rivista di storia dell'800 e del '900*, 18:3 (2015).

Taithe, Bertrand, 'The Red Cross Flag in the Franco-Prussian War: Civilians, Humanitarians, and War in the "Modern" Age', in R. Cooter et al. (eds), *War, Medicine and Modernity* (Stroud: Sutton, 1998).

Terry, Fiona, *Condemned to Repeat? The Paradox of Humanitarian Action* (Ithaca, NY: Cornell University Press, 2002).

Tester, Keith, *Humanitarianism and Modern Culture* (University Park, PA: Pennsylvania State University Press, 2010).

Thompson, Joseph E., *American Policy and African Famine: The Nigeria–Biafra War 1966–1970* (New York: Greenwood Press, 1990).

Tournès, Ludovic, 'La philanthropie américaine, la société des nations et la coproduction d'un ordre international (1919–1946)', *Relations Internationales*, 151 (2012/13).

Tournès, Ludovic, and Gilles Scott-Smith (eds), *Global Exchange: Scholarships and Transnational Circulation in the Modern World* (New York: Berghan, 2017).

Tournier, Maurice, 'Humanitaire est-il apolitique de naissance?', *Mots: Les languages du politique*, 65 (2001).

Towers, Bridget, 'Red Cross Organisational Politics 1922: Relations of Dominance and the Influence of the United States', in Weindling (ed.), *International Health Organisations*.

Truman, Harry S., 'Inaugural Address', 20 January 1949, at http://www.trumanlibrary.org/whistlestop/50yr_archive/inagural20jan1949.htm (accessed November 2018).

Tyrrel, Ian, *Reforming the World: The Creation of America's Moral Empire* (Princeton, NJ: Princeton University Press, 2010).

Ugochukwo, Françoise, 'The Nigerian Civil War and Its Media: Groping for Clues', *Media, War and Conflict*, 3:2 (2010).

Unger, Corinna R., 'Histories of Development and Modernization: Findings, Reflections, Future Research', H-Soz-u-Kult, 9 December 2010, at http://hsozkult.geschichte.hu-berlin.de/forum/2010-12-001 (accessed November 2018).

Unger, Corinna R., *International Development: A Postwar History* (London: Bloomsbury, 2018).

Unger, Corinna R., 'Postwar European Development Aid: Defined by Decolonization, the Cold War, and European Integration?', in S. Macekura and E. Manela (eds), *The Development Century: A Global History* (Cambridge: Cambridge University Press, 2018).

UNHCR, *The State of World's Refugees 2000: Fifty Years of Humanitarian Action* (Oxford: Oxford University Press, 2000).

USAID, *Final Disaster Report: Ethiopia Draught/Famine. Fiscal Year 1985–1986*, (Addis Ababa: USAID, May 1987).

Vallaeys, Anne, *Médecins sans Frontières: la biographie* (Paris: Fayard, 2004).

Vallely, Paul, 'Armed Food Convoys Promised for Rebel Areas', *The Times*, 2 February 1985.

Vellacot, Jo, 'A Place for Feminism and Transnationalism in Feminist Theory: The Early Work of the Women's International League for Peace and Freedom', *Women's History Review*, 2:1 (1993).

Vernon, James, *Hunger: A Modern History* (Cambridge, MA: Harvard University Press, 2007).

Villani, Angela, *Dalla parte dei bambini: Italia e Unicef fra ricostruzione e sviluppo* (Milan: Wolters Kluwer – Cedam, 2016).

Voltaire, *Poem on the Lisbon Disaster; or an Examination of the Axiom, 'All is Well'*, in *Toleration and Other Essays*, translation and introduction by Joseph McCabe (New York: G. P. Putnam's Sons, 1912).

Vössig, Michael, 'Competition Over Aid? The German Red Cross, the Committee Cap Anamur, and the Rescue of Boat People in South-East Asia, 1979–1982', in Paulman (ed.), *Dilemmas of Humanitarian Aid*.

Walker, Brian 'NGOs Break the Cold War Impasse in Cambodia', in Minear and Smith (eds), *Humanitarian Diplomacy*.

Walker, Peter, and Daniel Maxwell, *Shaping the Humanitarian World* (London: Routledge, 2009).

Walpole, Horace, *Memoirs of the Reign of King George the Second* (London: Henry Colburn, 1846).

Watenpaugh, Keith David, *Bread from Stones: The Middle East and the Making of Modern Humanitarianism* (Oakland, CA: University of California Press, 2015).

Watenpaugh, Keith David, 'League of Nations' Rescue of Armenian Genocide Survivors and the Making of Modern Humanitarianism, 1920–27', *American Historical Review*, 115:5 (2010).

Waters, Ken, 'Influencing the Message: The Role of Catholic Missionaries in Media Coverage of the Nigerian Civil War', *Catholic Historical Review*, 90:4 (2004).

Watson, Robert Spence, *The Villages Around Metz* (Newcastle upon Tyne: J. M. Carr, 1870).

Waux, Tony, 'Humanitarian Involvement in Wars of Liberation in Africa in the 1980s: An Oxfam Perspective', in Bennett, Foley and Krebs (eds), *Learning from the Past to Shape the Future*.

Weindling, Paul (ed.), *International Health Organisations and Movements, 1918–1939* (Cambridge: Cambridge University Press, 1995).

Weindling, Paul, 'The Role of International Organisations in Setting Nutritional Standards in the 1920s and 1930s', in H. Kamminga and A. Cunningham (eds), *The Science and Culture of Nutrition, 1840–1940* (Amsterdam: Rodopi, 1995).

Weissman, Fabrice, 'Silence Heals … From the Cold War to the War on Terror, MSF Speaks Out: A Brief History', in C. Magone, M. Neuman and F. Weissman (eds), *Humanitarian Negotiations Revealed: The MSF Experience* (London: Hurst & Company, 2011).

Westerman, Thomas D., 'Touring Occupied Belgium: American Humanitarians at "Work" and "Leisure" (1914–1917)', *First World War Studies*, 5:1 (2014).

WHO, *The First Ten Years of the World Health Organization* (Geneva: WHO, 1958).

Wieters, Heike, 'Reinventing the Firm: From Post-war Relief to International Humanitarian Agency', *European Review of History: Revue Européenne d'Histoire*, 23:1–2 (2016).

Wieters, Heike, *The NGO CARE and Food Aid from America, 1945–1980: 'Showered with Kindness'?* (Manchester: Manchester University Press, 2017).

Wieters, Heike, 'The World's Hungry: American NGOs and New Private–Public Partnership After WWII', *Contemporanea: Rivista di storia dell'800 e del '900*, 18:3 (2015).

Wilson, Ann Marie, 'In the Name of God, Civilization, and Humanity: The United States and the Armenian Massacres of the 1890s', *Le Mouvement Social*, 2 (2009).

Wilson, Francesca M., *Advice to Relief Workers: Based on Personal Experiences in the Field* (London: John Murray and Friends Relief Service, 1945).

Wilson, Francesca M., *In the Margins of Chaos: Recollections of Relief Work in and Between Three Wars* (London: John Murray, 1944).

Wilson, Richard Ashby, and Richard D. Brown, *Humanitarianism and Suffering: The Mobilization of Empathy* (Cambridge: Cambridge University Press, 2009).

Woodbridge, George, *UNRRA: The History of the United Nations Relief and Rehabilitation Administration* (3 vols) (New York: Columbia University Press, 1950).

Zimmer, Thomas, 'In the Name of World Health and Development: The World Health Organization and Malaria Eradication in India, 1949–1970', in Frey, Kunkel and Unger (eds), *International Organizations and Development*.

Index

Abolition Society *see* Society for Effecting
    the Abolition of the Slave Trade
abolitionism (anti-slavery movement)
    and the recognition of human suffering
       21, 22–25
    forms of mobilisation 21, 25–28, 44
    global networks 21, 28–32, 43, 86
Ador, Gustave 84, 94
Africa Concern 188
Algerian War of Independence 154
American Civil War 60, 70
American Friends' Service Committee
    (AFSC) 74–75
American Jewish Joint Distribution
    Committee ('Joint') 75, 116, 123, 125,
    130
American Red Cross (ARC) *see* Red Cross
    Society, American
American Relief Administration (ARA)
    80–82, 106–111, 115, 118, 126
Amin, Mohammed 204–205, 207
Amnesty International 192
anti-slavery movement *see* abolitionism
Anti-Slavery Society 26, 27, 30
Appia, Louis 54, 57, 70
Arab–Israeli War (1948) 151
Ayrton Gould, Barbara 88

Baerwald, Paul 125
Baez, Joan 199
Balkan Wars 94
Band Aid 205–206, 208
Baptist Missionary Society 29
Barnett, Michael x, 5–6
Barton, Clara 70–71
Barton, James L. 102–103

Berlin African Conference 31
Bettati, Mario 1
Biafran War *see* Nigerian Civil War
Bismarck, Otto von 31
Boldrini, Laura 4–5
Brauman, Rony 209, 210
Bretton Woods Agreement 148
British and Foreign Anti-Slavery Society 30
British Colonial Office 166
Brontë, Charlotte 35–36, 43
Brown, William Wells 29
Brussels Anti-Slavery Conference 31
Buerk, Michael 204–205, 207
Buxton, Charles Roden 90
Buxton, Dorothy Frances 90
Buxton, Thomas Fowell 39

Cambodian–Vietnamese War 194
Catholic Relief Services (CRS) 122–123,
    182–183, 187, 209
Charity Organisation Society (COS) 90
Chataway, Christopher 153
children
    aid for 45–46, 83, 89, 91–92, 104–105,
       108–109, 125, 130, 133–134
    Declaration of the Rights of the Child
       92–93
    trafficking of 85, 88, 105
Chilinguirian, Hagop 101
Chilinguirian, Nafina Hagop 101
Chirac, Jacques 4
Christian Aid 153, 189, 208
Church Missionary Society 29
Collins, Phil 205
colonial administrations and relief 17, 36–42,
    147–148, 162, 166

Commission of Inquiry for the Protection
    of Women and Children in the Near
    East 104
Commission for Relief in Belgium 106
Condorcet, Marie-Jean-Antoine-Nicolas
    Caritat, Marquis of 23–24, 25
consumption
    as a solidarity act 28, 155–156, 206
    boycott of slavery goods 27–28
Cooperative American Remittances to
    Europe (later, Cooperative American
    Relief Everywhere) (CARE) 159, 182,
    200
Coursier, Henri 53, 54
Crimean War 53, 53–56
Crosby, Bing 155

DanChurchAid 208
Davison, Henry 83–84
Debray, Régis 3–4
development
    and colonialism 147
    and humanitarian programmes 148–149,
    156–164, 168–175, 182–183
dichlorodiphenyltrichloroethane (DDT)
    125, 162–164
displaced persons (after Second World War)
    127–130, 134–135
Dodge, Cleveland H. 102
Donne, John 165
Dos Passos, John 73
Douglass, Frederick 29
Dufour, Guillaume-Henri, 57
Dumbarton Oaks Conference 119
Dunant, Henry 53–54, 56–59, 61, 64, 68, 70,
    76, 117
Dylan, Bob 205

Eden, Emily 38
Eden, George 38
education 17, 43–44, 76, 92, 129, 130, 142, 147,
    150, 157, 171–172, 174, 200
Eisenhower, Dwight D. 119, 150, 151, 169
Emmanuelli, Xavier 203
Eritrean War of Independence 203–204,
    207–208
Evian Conference 100

famine
    in Cambodia 195–196
    in China 102
    in Ethiopia 203–210

in India 38–39
    in Russia 105–111
Fassin, Didier 4, 5
Fight the Famine Council (FFC) 90–91
First World War
    and the League of Nations 85–88
    and the Red Cross movement 72–74
    in the Middle East 101–104
    NGOs in the field 74–76
Food and Agriculture Organization (FAO)
    149, 165, 167–174, 207
Food for the North Initiative 209
food programme(s) 83, 103, 106–111,
    125–126, 133, 158, 169, 189–190, 195, 200,
    207–209
Forchhammer, Henni 105
Fox, Fiona 5
Fox, George 20, 22
Franco-Prussian War 61–66
Friends' Ambulance Units (FAU) 74
Friends' War Victims Relief Committee
    (FWVRC) 65, 74
Fry, Augusta 66
Fry, Elizabeth 66

Garnett, Henry Highland 29
Geldof, Bob 205–206, 143
Geneva Convention for the Amelioration
    of the Condition of the Wounded in
    Armies in the Field 59–60, 68, 69, 70,
    71, 72, 76
Geneva Convention on the Status of
    Refugees 135, 136, 150, 151, 154, 156, 182,
    187, 198, 199
Ginzburg, Alexander 199
Gollancz, Victor 131
Gorky, Maxim 105–106, 107, 108
Grawitz, Ernst 121
Greco-Turkish War 97, 99
Grégoire, Abbot 25
Grey, George 40
Grimshaw, Libby 202, 203, 204

Haile Selassie, Emperor of Ethiopia 203,
    207
Haines, Anna J. 110
healthcare 17, 41–42, 44, 73, 81, 85–86, 92, 93,
    126, 129–131, 142, 147, 157, 160–164, 166,
    170, 200, 208
Hemingway, Ernest 73
Hispano-American War 71
Hitler, Adolf 100, 120, 121, 123

Hollande, François 3
Holy Childhood Association 45
Hoover, Herbert 81, 106–110, 118
Howard, James C. 196, 197
human rights
  and humanitarianism 8–10, 191–192
  Universal Declaration of Human Rights
    135
humanitarian interventions 2–3, 5, 10, 11 n.
  3, 217, 218
Hussein, Saddam 10

India–Pakistan War 194
International Children Emergency Fund
  (ICEF) 133–134
International Committee of Red Cross
  (ICRC) 19, 49–50, 53–54, 61, 63, 65,
  67–68, 70, 72, 74, 76, 84–85, 92, 94, 98,
  111, 107, 117, 120–122, 144, 151, 189–190,
  195–197, 200–201, 219
International Labour Organization (ILO)
  87, 97–98, 134, 149, 159–161, 168
International Monetary Fund 148
International Refugee Organization (IRO)
  134–135, 151, 153

Jansson, Kurt 207, 210
Jebb, Eglantyne 89–93, 108
Jeppe, Karen 104, 105
'Joint' *see* American Jewish Joint
  Distribution Committee
Joint Church Aid (JCA) 189–190

Kingsley, Zephaniah 25
Knibb, William 28, 29
Koch, Robert 41
Korean War 157–158
Kosovo War 1–2
Kouchner, Bernard 1, 2, 4, 190, 192, 198

Le Corbusier, 132
League of Nations 50–52, 81–100, 104–105,
  118–119, 122, 128–129, 132–134, 136,
  159–160, 163, 166–167, 173
League of Red Cross and Red Crescent
  Societies 111 n. 8, 214 n. 61
League of Red Cross Societies 104, 107,
  111 n. 8
Lehman, Herbert H., 116, 117, 119, 124, 125
Leopold II, King of Belgium 31
Lepsius, Johannes 104
Live Aid 143, 205–206

Llewellyn, Bernard 174
London Missionary Society 29
Longfellow, Henry Wadsworth 56
Loren, Sophia 179 n. 104
Louchheim, Katie 124
Loyd-Lindsay, Robert 61
Lutheran World Relief 152, 158, 173, 182, 208
Luzzatti, Luigi 165

Malaria Eradication Program 163–165
Marshall Plan (European Recovery
  Program) 127, 148
Maunoir, Théodore 57
McDonald, James G. 100
McGovern, George Stanley 169
Médecins du Monde 198
Médecins Sans Frontières (MSF) 1, 9,
  191–192, 197–199, 209–210
media and humanitarian campaigns 26, 30,
  55, 89, 110–111, 131, 142–143, 151, 155, 171,
  184–186, 190, 196, 199, 204–205
Menghistu Haile Mariam 203, 207, 208, 209,
  210, 217
Mirabeau, Honoré Gabriel Riqueti, Count
  of 25
missionary humanitarianism 17, 35–36,
  42–46, 103–104, 142, 147, 172, 184, 188
Mitterand, François 3, 4
Mok, Michael 184
Montesquieu, Charles-Louis de Secondat,
  Baron of La Brède and of 23
Moorehead, Caroline 197
Morgan, Michèle 179 n. 104
Morgenthau, Henry 102
Moynier, Gustave 54, 56–57, 58, 59, 61, 62, 67,
  70, 76
Murray, Gilbert 131

Nansen, Fridtjof 94–98, 108, 129
Nansen passport 95–97, 99, 101, 136, 159
Napoleon I 30
Napoleon III 56
New Deal 52, 116, 117, 124, 127
Newman, Paul 155
Niemeyer, Oscar 132
Nigerian Civil War (Biafran War) 141–142,
  144, 183–192
Nightingale, Florence 53, 54–56, 60
Nobel Peace Prize 120, 167
Noel-Baker, Philip 118
North Atlantic Treaty Organization
  (NATO) 1–3, 10

O'Connel, Daniel 184
Office for the Coordination of
    Humanitarian Affairs (OCHA) 219
Orr, John Boyd 166, 167, 168, 172
Oxfam (Oxford Famine Relief Committee)
    122, 131, 154, 155, 172, 173–174, 187, 188,
    196–197
Oxford Famine Relief Committee *see*
    Oxfam

Pasteur, Louis 41
Pilger, John 196, 197
Pol Pot 8, 143, 144, 194, 195, 197, 199
professional training 76, 97, 103, 105, 130, 134,
    142, 149, 159, 174, 183

Raison, Timothy 153
Rajchman, Ludwik 86
Reagan, Ronald 207
Récamier, Max 190
Red Crescent Society
    Algerian 154, 181
    Egyptian 181
    Ottoman 68, 11 n. 8
Red Cross Society
    American 70–71, 73–76, 83–84, 93–94,
        99
    British 60, 63–64, 66, 69, 150, 181, 189
    Bulgaria 69
    French 60, 190
    Indian 194
    Italian 67–68, 73
    Japanese 73–74
    Montenegrin 69
    Prussian 63–64, 66
    Serb 69
refugee(s)
    Algerians 154
    and the Evian Conference 100
    and the League of Nations 81, 85, 93–100,
        136
    Cambodian in Thailand 194–202
    Chinese in Hong Kong 152
    First World War 73, 80
    from East Pakistan 193–194
    from eastern Europe 149–151, 154
    in the Middle East after First World War
        101, 103–105
    in the region of Great Lakes (Africa)
        181–182
    Nigerian Civil War 184, 186–187
    Palestinian 151–152

Second World War 80, 123, 127, 127–130,
    134–135
    Vietnamese 183, 198
Responsibility to Protect (R2P) 2
Reynolds, Richenda 66
Rieff, David 3
Rockefeller Foundation 88, 132, 160, 161, 163
Roosevelt, Franklin Delano 100, 116, 117, 118,
    124, 127, 167
Roume, Ernest 41–42
Russell, Earl 131
Russo-Turkish War 68–69

San Francisco Conference 119
sans-frontiérisme 191
Sarkozy, Nicolas 3, 4
Save the Children Fund (SCF) 50, 80,
    89, 91–92, 99, 108, 122, 174, 187, 188,
    202–204
Save the Children International Union
    (SCIU) 92
Second World War
    and the ICRC 120–122
    formation of new NGOs 122–124
    population displacement 127–132
Sen, Binay Ranjan 165, 167–169, 172, 173, 174
Sen, Hun 194
Sharp, Granville 22, 25
Shaw, George Bernard 108
Siclier, Jacques 185
Sieyès, Emmanuel Joseph 48
Simpson, John Hope 99, 100
Smith, Adam 23
Società Antischiavista d'Italia 30
Société Antiesclavagiste de Belgique 30
Société Antiesclavagiste de France 30
Société des Amis des Noirs 25, 30
Société Française pour l'Abolition de
    l'Esclavage 30
Society for Effecting the Abolition of the
    Slave Trade (Abolition Society) 25,
    26, 42
Solferino, battle of 49, 53–54
Spanish Civil War
Suez crisis 181
survivor(s)
    of Armenian genocide 96, 101–103
    of Holocaust 128, 130
Swedish Church Relief 208

technical assistance 86, 159, 161, 164, 167–168,
    173, 174

Temple, Shirley 179 n. 104
Toynbee, Arnold 172
Traynham, Floyd 111
Truman, Harry S. 146
Turner, Tina 205

Ullmann, Liv 199
United Nations Border Relief Operation
    (UMBRO) 201
United Nations Educational, Scientific and
    Cultural Organization (UNESCO)
    219
United Nations High Commissioner for
    Refugees (UNHCR) 4–5, 134–136,
    149, 152, 155, 182, 187, 193–194, 198–200,
    219
United Nations International Children's
    Emergency Fund, later United Nations
    Children's Fund (UNICEF) 105, 134,
    255, 163, 168, 170, 194–201, 207, 219
United Nations Korean Reconstruction
    Agency (UNKRA) 157–159
United Nations Relief and Rehabilitation
    Administration (UNRRA) ix, 52, 93,
    116–119, 124–134, 146, 157, 160, 163, 167,
    173–174
United Nations Relief and Works Agency for
    Palestine Refugees (UNRWA) 135, 152
Ure, Midge 205
US Agency for International Development
    (USAID) 163, 183
Ustinov, Peter 171

Vietnam War 182–183
Vittorio Emanuele II, King of Italy 67
Vittorio Emanuele III, King of Italy 165
Voltaire 15

Walpole, Horace 15
War on Want 188
War Relief Control Board 124
Watson, Robert Spence 65, 66
Wiesel, Elie 199
Wilberforce, William 25, 26, 39
Wilson, Francesca Mary 80–83, 108, 109,
    123, 130
Wilson, Thomas Woodrow 73, 74, 75, 84, 85,
    106, 117
Women's International League for Peace and
    Freedom (WILPF) 90, 91
Woodbridge, George 126
World Bank 148
World Council of Churches
World Food Programme (WFP) 169, 194,
    200, 207, 219
World Health Organization (WHO) 9, 149,
    159–164, 168, 194
World Refugee Year 153–156
World Vision 209
World War I see First World War
World War II see Second World War

Yonge, Charlotte 43
Young Men's Christian Association
    (YMCA) 56, 75–76, 99, 123, 130, 150, 187